Balancing Power without Weapons

Why do states block some foreign direct investment on national security grounds even when it originates from within their own security community? Government intervention into foreign takeovers of domestic companies is on the rise, and many observers find it surprising that states engage in such behavior not only against their strategic and military competitors, but also against their closest allies. Ashley Thomas Lenihan argues that such puzzling behavior can be explained by recognizing that states use intervention into cross-border mergers and acquisitions as a tool of statecraft to internally balance the economic and military power of other states through non-military means. This book tests this theory using quantitative and qualitative analysis of transactions in the United States, Russia, China, and fifteen European Union states. It deepens our understanding of why states intervene in foreign takeovers, the relationship between interdependence and conflict, the limits of globalization, and how states are balancing power in new ways.

ASHLEY THOMAS LENIHAN is a fellow at the Centre for International Studies at the London School of Economics and Political Science, and a term member of the Council on Foreign Relations. Her research focuses on the relationship between state power and foreign direct investment from an international relations perspective.

Balancing Power without Weapons

State Intervention into Cross-Border Mergers and Acquisitions

Ashley Thomas Lenihan
London School of Economics and Political Science

CAMBRIDGE
UNIVERSITY PRESS

CAMBRIDGE
UNIVERSITY PRESS

University Printing House, Cambridge CB2 8BS, United Kingdom

One Liberty Plaza, 20th Floor, New York, NY 10006, USA

477 Williamstown Road, Port Melbourne, VIC 3207, Australia

314–321, 3rd Floor, Plot 3, Splendor Forum, Jasola District Centre, New Delhi - 110025, India

79 Anson Road, #06-04/06, Singapore 079906

Cambridge University Press is part of the University of Cambridge.

It furthers the University's mission by disseminating knowledge in the pursuit of education, learning, and research at the highest international levels of excellence.

www.cambridge.org

Information on this title: www.cambridge.org/9781107181861
DOI: 10.1017/9781316855430

When citing this work, please include a reference to the DOI 10.1017/9781316855430

First published 2018

Printed in the United Kingdom by Clays, St Ives plc

A catalogue record for this publication is available from the British Library.

ISBN 978-1-107-18186-1 Hardback

This book is dedicated to my family – especially my mother Judy, father Harry, husband Bob, and son Bo – whose love, help, and support made this possible. It is dedicated to my mentors and colleagues who read countless drafts and held me to the highest standard, with special thanks to George. And finally, it is dedicated in loving memory to my aunt Jan, who inspired me every day to be curious about the world around us.

Contents

Figures

Preface

Since Bretton Woods, Western leaders have worked to establish an international order founded on economic liberalism and free trade. Yet, in recent years, the very same states that helped to found the liberal economic order have been acting in a way that seems to contradict it – by implementing (or encouraging) the creation of domestic barriers to cross-border mergers and acquisitions (M&A) in industries they deem vital to national security.

Even more puzzling is the fact that states are engaging in such behavior not only against their strategic and military competitors, but against their closest allies as well. Traditional interest group and domestic politics explanations cannot account for this behavior, because states are often intervening against the parochial interests of companies and other domestic groups on behalf of national interest and security.

This book argues that such government intervention into foreign takeovers constitutes a form of non-military internal balancing, which allows states to secure and enhance their relative power for long-term gain, without destroying the greater meta-relationship between the states involved in the transaction. It is hypothesized that such behavior is motivated by the desire to increase the relative power and prestige of the state through non-military means in response to either economic nationalism or pressing geostrategic concerns. The exact form that intervention takes, and the motivations behind it, are determined to vary with both the relationship of the countries involved and the exact nature of the threat posed by the transaction in question.

The book employs a rigorous multi-method approach to test the theory presented within. First, the hypotheses are tested qualitatively, using the case study method to examine ten critical cases. They are then tested quantitatively using categorical data analysis (CDA). Four multinomial logit models (MNLMs) are used to examine a large-n population of cross-border merger and acquisitions cases that occurred over a six-year period in an identified set of national security-related sectors. These tests are found to support the theory of non-military internal balancing presented in this work, and to provide a solution to the puzzle.

Acknowledgments

I would like to thank those mentors and colleagues who were kind enough to provide their guidance and to critique this work in one of its many iterations, including George Shambaugh, Charlie Kupchan, Chris Joyner, Kate McNamara, and Linda Hantrais, as well as Tony Arend, Kirsten Ainley, and Leslie Vinjamuri for their encouragement along the way. I would also like to thank my editor John Haslam at Cambridge University Press for his support from proposal to finished product, as well as the Centre for International Studies at the London School of Economics and Political Science for their support.

Abbreviations

ABCANZ	American, British, Canadian, Australian and New Zealand Multilateral Master Information Exchange Treaty
ADM	Archer Daniel Midland
AIG	American International Group
AMF	Autorité des Marchés Financiers (France)
AML	Anti-Monopoly Law
APEC	Asia-Pacific Economic Cooperation
BEIS	UK Department for Business, Energy, and Industrial Strategy
BERR	UK Department for Business Enterprise and Regulatory Reform
BIS	UK Department for Business, Innovation, and Skills
BP	British Petroleum
CDA	categorical data analysis
CFIUS	Committee on Foreign Investments in the United States
CMA	UK Competition and Markets Authority
CPII	Columbia Program on International Investment
CSI	Container Security Initiative
CVCF	China Venture Capital Fund
DHS	US Department of Homeland Security
DOD	US Department of Defense
DOJ	US Department of Justice
DPA	1950 Defense Production Act (US)
DPW	Dubai Ports World
DSS	US DOD Defense Security Service
EEA	European Economic Area
EIU	Economist Intelligence Unit
ESRC	US–China Economic & Security Review Commission
EU	European Union
FAS	Federal Antimonopoly Service (Russia)

FBI	US Federal Bureau of Investigation
FDI	foreign direct investment
FIE	Foreign Invested Enterprise (China)
FINSA	2007 Foreign Investment and National Security Act (US)
FIRB	Foreign Investment Review Board (Australia)
FOCI	Foreign Ownership, Control or Influence
FTA	1973 Fair Trading Act (UK)
FTC	US Federal Trade Commission
FTZ	free trade zone
IEA	International Energy Agency
IEEPA	1977 International Emergency Economic Powers Act (US)
IFDI	inward foreign direct investment
ISC	UK Parliament's Intelligence and Security Committee
ISS	Inchcape Shipping Services
JV	joint venture
M&A	cross-border mergers and acquisitions
MAP	Ministry of the Russian Federation on Antimonopoly Policy and Support to Entrepreneurship (Russia)
MDA	MacDonald Detweiller
MOFCOM	Ministry of Commerce (China)
NATO	North Atlantic Treaty Organization
NDRC	National Development and Reform Commission (China)
NIC	US National Intelligence Council
NISP	National Industrial Security Program (US)
NOC	national oil company
NSA	National Security Agency (US)
OECD	Organisation for Economic Co-operation and Development
OPEC	Organization of the Petroleum Exporting Countries
PA	Proxy Agreement
P&O	Peninsular & Oriental Steam Navigation Company
PDVSA	Petróleos de Venezuela
PGAP	Pew Global Attitudes Project
SAIC	State Administration of Industry and Commerce (China)
SASAC	State Asset Supervision and Administration Commission (China)
SCA	Security Control Agreement
SEC	US Securities and Exchange Commission

SOE	state-owned enterprise
SSA	Special Security Agreement
SWF	sovereign wealth fund
TCIC	Tangshan Caofeidian Investment Corporation
TWEA	1917 Trading with the Enemy Act (US)
UDI	United Defense Industries
UNCTAD	United Nations Commission on Trade and Development
VTA	Voting Trust Agreement
VTB	Vneshtorgbank
VW	Volkswagen
WPO	World Public Opinion
WTO	World Trade Organization

Introduction

Each morning before sunrise an army of traders arrive at their desks, switch on their screens, and start fielding calls. On most days, the flow of trades that pass through their hands represents the normal activity of an ever-deepening, globally interdependent financial market. These traders coordinate a complicated international marketplace, where orders usually come from institutional investors motivated solely by the maximization of profit.

Yet, some days are different, and on those occasions this army of civilians may receive calls motivated not by profit, but by a different calculus entirely: a calculus based on a long-term understanding of the power of states, and of how that power is achieved, managed, and balanced over time. When that happens, these traders in front of their Bloomberg terminals seem more like frontline soldiers manning the radars, as a battle for national power – where the economy of the nation is understood to be paramount to its future fortunes – is played out through them.

Such battles on the open market do happen. One only need talk to the traders who witnessed the dawn raid on Rio Tinto's stock in 2008 to understand this. At that time, the Australian mining company BHP Billiton was planning to acquire Rio Tinto, a miner and producer of iron ore, aluminum, copper, and other metals that was listed on both the Sydney and the London stock exchanges. China, already the largest importer of iron ore, showed concern that the combination of Rio and BHP would lead to a near monopoly over the seaborne iron ore imports vital to its growing and industrializing economy, potentially exposing it to price manipulation and/or future reductions in supply.[1] A combined Rio and BHP would have accounted for around 40% of the iron ore exported globally, and the bulk of both companies' seaborne iron ore traveled from their mines in Australia to China and East Asia. Just one other company, Brazil's Vale, held an additional 30% of the market share at the time. Thus, while China was not the only country showing concern over the potential anti-competitive implications of the tie-up,[2] it was likely to be the most directly affected buyer of seaborne iron ore.

Chinese regulators could review the deal, but because Chinese assets were not being acquired as part of the transaction, a ruling by these regulators would be difficult to enforce without cooperation from the companies involved.

And so, in the early hours of February 1, 2008, the Chinese government-owned Aluminum Corporation of China (Chinalco), in conjunction with the US aluminum company Alcoa, began purchasing stock of Rio Tinto on the open market in a widely acknowledged effort to block its planned takeover by BHP Billiton. Together, they took an overall stake in Rio Tinto of 9% for $14 billion, paying a premium of 21% over Rio's stock price, and making a potential takeover by BHP more difficult (Bream 2008; Bream & Smith 2008). No formal statement or diplomatic action was necessary – China accomplished its goal through a quick, targeted financial transaction on the open market. The dawn raid not only halted BHP's attempt to fully acquire Rio, it also signaled China's willingness to protect its interests by preventing the acquisition of one company by another company on the global stage.

The market is in many ways the next frontier of strategic interaction for states. When national security is involved, strategic interactions involving cross-border mergers and acquisitions (M&A) can have deep parallels to more traditional inter-state balance-of-power dynamics, yet they are rarely discussed within the context of international relations theory. This book uncovers these parallels and the insights they provide. It examines when, how, and why states intervene in the cross-border M&A of companies to balance against other states in the international system.

International Finance and International Security

For decades, the M&A of companies across national borders has acted as a key driver of globalization. This fundamental role within globalization remains the same, despite a natural rise and fall in the number of deals that occur during economic booms and contractions. The general trend among nations has been toward "investment liberalization" (UNCTAD 2016b, 90), and, in many sectors of the economy, from service to consumer goods, cross-border M&A activity now occurs with few impediments beyond those that domestic M&A deals normally face. In other sectors, long identified by states as vital to their national security – such as aerospace and defense, energy, basic resources, and high technology – acquisitions by foreign companies may face greater scrutiny. This is because *all states maintain the sovereign right to veto attempts by foreign entities to acquire domestically based companies (in these or any other sector of the economy), when they believe the transaction in question poses a risk to national security.*

While the resort to formal vetoes of the foreign takeovers of companies is relatively rare,[3] the employment of other means to block or prevent such transactions is not. Indeed, the threat (and use) of domestic barriers to block foreign acquisitions on national security grounds is an increasingly typical phenomenon with which global economic actors must contend.[4] There have been numerous examples in recent years of such barriers being implemented or encouraged at the state level. These have ranged from government actions taken to block or modify specific transactions, to the introduction or fine-tuning of wider legal and regulatory measures designed to generally improve the state's ability to address the national security issues raised by some cross-border M&A – though it should be noted that the latter move toward greater regulation has often been spurred by the state's actions in relation to specific transactions and the national debate surrounding these actions.

Some of the most well-known examples of government intervention into cross-border M&A on national security grounds include when the US House of Representatives passed legislation instrumental in getting the China National Offshore Oil Corporation's subsidiary CNOOC to withdraw its bid for the American-based Unocal Corporation in 2005, and when it passed legislation forcing Dubai Ports World (DPW) to divest the US ports involved in its acquisition of the Peninsular & Oriental Steam Navigation Company (P&O) in 2006. In both cases, Congress cited concerns over the deals' security implications. Other well-known examples include the 2005 French government decree specifying eleven different *strategic sectors* it considers vital to national security, making M&A in those industries subject to prior authorization by its Ministry of the Economy. This was largely in response to an unwanted attempt by the American company Pepsi to take over Danone, a French national champion (see Chapter 3). France widened the scope of its list of strategic sectors again in 2014, in order to ensure government approval would be needed before General Electric, another American company, could acquire Alstom, a French conglomerate involved in industries from high-speed trains to nuclear power (see Carnegy et al. 2014; Shumpeter 2014). France even created a sovereign wealth fund (SWF) in 2008, the Fond Stratégique d'Investissement, to help protect its strategic companies from foreign acquisition. Similarly, the Italian government issued a decree in 2011 protecting Italian companies in strategic sectors from foreign acquisition, and also created a state investment fund (the Fondo Strategico Italiano, subsequently renamed CDP Equity) to bolster Italian companies in eight designated strategic sectors and to decrease their sense of the term. In a world where nuclear power has lessened the rewards of territorial conquest and made great power hot wars less likely, many advanced industrial and industrializing states have less reason to fear that their territorial sovereignty will be jeopardized (Mandelbaum 1998/99; Mueller 1988). At the same time, the expansion of economic globalization has increased the reasons for states to be concerned that their economic sovereignty will remain intact. As a result, states are now as concerned with the economic component of power as they are with its military component, and will seek to balance both appropriately.

This type of non-military internal balancing will take different forms or guises when it is motivated by different factors. Non-military internal balancing through intervention into cross-border M&A may, for example, be *unbounded* in nature, meaning that the state takes direct action intended to *block* a specific transaction. Alternatively, such balancing may be *bounded*, meaning that the state takes direct action to instead *mitigate* the negative effects of the deal, while still allowing it to occur in modified form.

The puzzle can then be solved if the use of such domestic barriers to block or mitigate foreign takeovers on national security grounds is understood to be primarily motivated by either pressing geostrategic concerns or economic nationalism.[9] In the latter instance, such behavior is evidence of a desire for enhanced national economic power and prestige vis-à-vis other states, friend and foe alike. In the former case, this behavior constitutes a more severe form of non-military internal balancing, which allows states to secure and enhance their relative power for long-term gain, without destroying the greater meta-relationship between the two states in the short run. The exact form that intervention takes, and the motivations behind it, will vary with the nature of the relationship between the countries involved and the exact nature of the threat posed by the transaction in question.

The geostrategic dimensions may also extend beyond industries that are traditionally associated with national security. For example, states may use the terms *national security* and *strategic sector* in this context in ways that go beyond the realms, and industries, neorealists and neoliberals might traditionally consider vital to hard power. The French, for instance, originally included the gaming sector on their list of strategic industries, because of its potential connection to money laundering (Buck et al. 2006b), and in the 2010s various groups within the US and China called for the recognition of certain elements of the agricultural sector as essential to critical infrastructure and national security due to concerns over bio- and food security. It may also sometimes seem that states use the types of barriers discussed here selectively, and in a manner that can appear both opaque and inconsistent. Yet, once it is determined why states are willing to engage in such ostensibly protectionist strategies in the most unlikely cases (i.e., within security communities founded on economic integration), one should be better able to predict what companies and sectors they will seek to protect, and when.

Intervention in Empirical Context

The US Example

History is marked by periods of increased government intervention into foreign takeovers on the grounds of national security, and the US provides an excellent example of this phenomenon. Times of heightened security awareness combined with surges in protectionist sentiment – most notably surrounding World War I, World War II, the 1970s, the 1980s, and the post-9/11 period – have corresponded to the implementation of formal government measures to ensure that cross-border M&A does not jeopardize US national security (Graham & Marchick 2006; Kang 1997). The 1917 Trading with the Enemy Act (TWEA) was implemented in response to concerns over German attempts during World War I to conduct espionage and other war-related activities through the takeover of US companies, giving the President new controls and power over US subsidiaries of foreign-owned companies (Graham & Marchick 2006). In 1975, the Committee on Foreign Investments in the United States (CFIUS) was established by Executive Order 11858 in response to mounting concern over a rise in foreign investment from states within the Organization of the Petroleum Exporting Countries (OPEC), which was feared to be politically motivated in the aftermath of OPEC's 1973–74 oil embargo (see Jackson 2010, 2011b; Kang 1997, 302, 311). Executive Order 11858 gave the new interagency committee, chaired by the Secretary of the Treasury, the "responsibility within the Executive Branch for monitoring the impact of foreign investment in the US, . . . coordinating the implementation of US policy on such investment," and "review[ing] investments in the US which . . . might have major implications for US national interests."[10]

Fears over high levels of Japanese investment in the 1980s, combined with concern over the potential Japanese acquisition of sensitive US high-technology companies, eventually led to the 1988 Exon-Florio amendment to Section 721 of the Defense Production Act (DPA) of 1950 (Jackson 2010).[11] This provision provides the US President with the authority and specific jurisdiction to prohibit foreign takeovers deemed to threaten national security when existing laws beyond the

International Emergency Economic Powers Act (IEEPA) cannot provide for its adequate protection. That same year, Executive Order 12661 amended Executive Order 11858 to delegate the President's authority to investigate and review such foreign takeovers to CFIUS. By 1992, the Byrd Amendment to the DPA further stipulated that CFIUS be mandated to investigate proposed takeovers in which the acquirer was "controlled by or acting on behalf of a foreign government."[12]

Since the 2000s, the US has seen a new surge in both intervention and related legislation, and intense media coverage and political debate has surrounded the proposed foreign takeovers of a number of US companies. This surge arguably began when, on June 22, 2005, the majority government-owned China National Offshore Oil Corporation's subsidiary CNOOC announced its bid to acquire the California-based Unocal Corporation. Extensive national and congressional debate over the sale of one of the largest US oil and gas companies eventually resulted in legislation that left CNOOC with extensive delays and facing the likelihood of further opposition to the deal, effectively giving it little choice but to withdraw its bid.[13] On November 29, 2005, the UAE-based DPW launched its bid for P&O, a British ports operator. Few concerns were raised in Britain, which has close ties with Dubai, and few were expected from the US, an ally of the UAE in the Global War on Terror. Yet the deal, which involved the transfer of five US container ports from P&O to DPW, eventually raised a furor that resulted in a surprising "70% of all Americans . . . opposed" to the transaction (Frum 2006). Faced with the possibility of the deal being blocked, P&O offered to divest the ports in question, and eventually sold them to the American International Group (AIG), allowing them to remain under US control (Wright & Kirchgaessner 2006).

Around that time, the Department of Defense (DOD) also raised concerns over the proposed purchase of the US high-tech network security firm Sourcefire by the Israeli company Check Point Software Technologies (Martin 2006). Check Point subsequently withdrew its bid while it was being reviewed by CFIUS, only "a week before a federal . . . report which insiders say would have blocked the merger on the grounds of national-security interests" (Lemos 2006). In 2006, CFIUS also undertook a retroactive review of a 2005 takeover involving the purchase of a US voting machines firm, Sequoia Voting Systems, by a Venezuelan software company, Smartmatic, due to fears that the company might have ties to the Venezuelan government of Hugo Chávez (Golden 2006). By November 2007, Smartmatic had announced it had sold Sequoia to its American management, in order to avoid having to undergo a full investigation by CFIUS (O'Shaughnessy 2007; Smartmatic 2007).

This surge in concern over such takeovers eventually led to the passage of the Foreign Investment and National Security Act of 2007 (FINSA), which aimed to clarify the foreign acquisition review process in the US and strengthen its protection of national security. Following FINSA, a number of other deals were blocked or mitigated on national security grounds, though only three resulted in a formal presidential veto. For example, in December 2009, the Chinese company Northwest Non-ferrous withdrew its bid for a majority stake in the US mining company FirstGold after CFIUS informed both parties it would recommend the President block the deal, which raised "serious, specific, and consequential national security issues," including the proximity of FirstGold properties "to the Fallon Naval Air Base and related facilities" (Legal Memorandum 2009; Reuters 2009). The US government was also reportedly concerned that the deal would give China access to the particularly dense metal tungsten, which is used in making missiles (Kirchgaessner 2010). The Chinese company Tangshan Caofeidian Investment Corporation (TCIC) withdrew its planned majority stake in the US solar power and telecommunications company Emcore in June 2010, "in the face of national security-based objections" raised by CFIUS, which may have been related to Emcore's position as "a leading developer and manufacturer of fiber-optic systems and components for commercial and military use" (Keeler 2010). The takeover of the US company Sprint by Japan's Softbank was allowed in 2013, but was mitigated (i.e., modified) by CFIUS on national security grounds, as Sprint provides telecommunications services to the US government. Concern was expressed that Softbank might, in the future, use the Chinese firm Huawei – branded the previous year by Congress' Permanent Select Intelligence Committee as "a threat to US national security" – as a supplier of network components; a concern which arose in part because Clearwire, a company Sprint itself was in the process of buying, already used equipment supplied by Huawei (Kirchgaessner & Taylor 2013; US Congress House 2012). Modifications to the deal therefore included giving the US government veto power over the combined entity's future suppliers of network equipment (Taylor 2013).[14] It should be noted that CFIUS also successfully mitigated or blocked the foreign takeovers of a number of foreign-headquartered companies on national security grounds.[15]

In addition, since FINSA, the US has conducted several retroactive reviews of investments that were not voluntarily filed with CFIUS prior to their completion. In February 2011, CFIUS effectively forced Huawei to divest the computing technology assets it acquired from 3Leaf Systems in May 2010 (see Jackson 2016a; Raice & Dowell 2011). In June

2013, Procon Mining and Tunneling, which is affiliated with the Chinese state-owned enterprise (SOE) Sinomach, announced it would divest its investment in Canada's Lincoln Mining following a CFIUS review that allegedly raised national security concerns over "the proximity of Lincoln's properties to US military bases" (Pickard et al. 2013). In 2013, CFIUS also ordered the divestment of the Indian company Polaris' majority stake in the US firm Identrust, which provided cybersecurity services to banks and the US government (Matheny 2013). Each of these companies voluntarily complied with CFIUS' recommendations before it became necessary to force a presidential decision on them. This was not the case, however, when one company's refusal to comply with a CFIUS divestment order resulted in the second formal presidential veto of a foreign investment in US history, and the first veto to be made in twenty-two years. On September 28, 2012, Barack Obama issued a Presidential Order for Ralls, a company owned by two Chinese nationals, to divest its four wind farm sites – located in close proximity to restricted air space in Oregon used for testing drones – to an approved purchaser on the grounds of the national security concerns raised by the deal (see Crooks 2012; Obama 2012).[16]

In December 2016, President Obama also formally vetoed the acquisition of the US business of a German semiconductor company, Aixtron, by an ultimately Chinese-owned fund, Grand Chip Investment, on national security grounds (see Obama 2016). According to a press statement by the US Treasury Department, Grand Chip's owners had financing from a company owned by the China IC Industry Investment Fund, which is a "Chinese government-supported . . . fund established to promote the development of China's integrated circuit industry" (US DOT 2016b). The same press release disclosed that the national security concern flagged in the deal "relates, among other things, to the military applications of the overall body of knowledge and experience of Aixtron" in the area of semiconductors (US DOT 2016b). Notably, Germany had already pulled its initial approval of Grand Chip's purchase of Aixtron in October 2016, and was re-reviewing the deal at the time of the US veto because of the security risk it was believed to pose (see Chazan & Wagstyl 2016).

Less than a year later, President Donald Trump formally vetoed the acquisition of the US company Lattice Semiconductor by Canyon Bridge, an acquisition company whose primary investor was the China Venture Capital Fund (CVCF). The deal had been announced in early November 2016, and it quickly emerged that CVCF was ultimately owned and funded by a Chinese SOE (China Reform Holdings) linked to China's State Council and intended to "invest in strategic emerging industries related to national security" (Baker, Qing, & Zhu 2016). By early December 2016, just days after President Obama vetoed the Aixtron deal in the same industry, twenty-two US congressmen wrote to the Chair of CFIUS arguing that the acquisition of Lattice Semiconductor should be blocked on national security grounds, including the potential threat it posed to the "US military supply chain" (Roumeliotis 2016). After three separate filings with CFIUS, President Trump vetoed the deal in September 2017 over national security concerns that both the President and CFIUS believed "cannot be resolved through mitigation," including the integrity of the "semiconductor supply chain . . . and the use of Lattice products by the US government," as well as "the potential transfer of intellectual property to the foreign acquirer [and] the Chinese government's role in supporting" the deal (US DOT 2017; see also Trump 2017).

Intervention Worldwide

This phenomenon is not limited to the United States. Government interventions into M&A activities that result in effectively blocking or changing deals between multinational corporations are not uncommon.[17] While states have long reserved the sovereign right to intervene in foreign takeovers on national security grounds, and a number of states already had mechanisms for screening such investments, the surge of intervention that began in the 2000s was accompanied by a related wave of national legislation updating these mechanisms, or setting up formal regulatory procedures to replace processes that may have been less transparent or more ad hoc in nature (see UNCTAD 2016b, 93–100).

The spate of government intervention into cross-border M&A activity within the EU raised concern that there had been a rise in economic nationalism in the region; a concern that remains strong in the wake of the Euro crisis and the UK's decision to leave the EU.[18] As already discussed, much of this interventionism has surprisingly also been aimed at foreign takeovers originating from within the EU's own security communities. The Spanish government, for example, blocked the attempted takeover of the Spanish energy company Endesa by the German company E.ON in 2006, in defiance of the European Commission, resulting in three separate rulings by the Commission and a ruling by the European Court of Justice in 2008.[19] The initial efforts of a number of European governments to block the takeover of the French steel company Arcelor by the Dutch-based steel company Mittal in 2006, on the perceived basis that it was run by an individual of Indian origin (even though he was a British resident), further serves to highlight the capability of governments to see even military allies as economic foes. The rumored acquisition of the UK's BAE Systems by the Dutch-registered EADS in 2012, which would have required approval from their UK and their French and German government shareholders respectively, as well as from the US authorities, collapsed after little more than a month of discussions over the inability to find common ground on a variety of security and other concerns.

Hungary passed a law in 2007 designed to protect those companies it believes are strategically important from foreign takeover. Intended to defend the Hungarian oil and gas company MOL from a takeover bid by Austria's OMV, it came to be known as the "Lex MOL." The law had to be modified in 2008 after the European Commission informed the Hungarian government that some of its provisions went beyond European law (see FT 2009; Platts 2008). In 2015, Poland adopted the Act on the Control of Certain Investments, creating a mechanism for screening foreign investments of more than 20% in companies in strategic sectors like energy, telecommunications, and defense, which gave the Polish Minister of the State Treasury the ability to block such investments on the grounds of "security and public governance" (Krupa 2015; UNCTAD 2016b, 93).

The German government added a mechanism for screening foreign investment stakes of over 25% hailing from non-EU and European Free Trade Association states for national security risks in 2004, initially in specific industries around weapons and cryptography, though the scope was broadened to include enterprises involved in tanks and tracked vehicle engines in 2005 (US DOS 2014b, 3). By 2009, after widespread public debate over the effect of foreign SWF investments in the country, the national security review process was expanded "to apply to a German company of any size or sector in cases where a threat to national security or public order is perceived" (US DOS 2014b, 3). Despite the wording of its regulatory regime, however, the German government has also shown concern over investments hailing from within the EU itself. Citing national security concerns over the sensitive technology involved, it decided in 2008 that it was better to buy back its national printing press, the Bundesdruckerei, rather than see it auctioned to foreign bidders such as France's Sagem or the Netherlands' Gemalto, when it seemed that no German company would try to win the auction.[20]

Similarly, tensions arose between Italy and France in 2011, when a series of large Italian companies (including Bulgari and Parmalat) were taken over by French ones and Italy's Finance Minister Giulio Tremonti sought to stem the tide by trying to prevent Edison, an Italian power company, from being taken over by the French group EDF.[21] In 2012,

Italy established a formal mechanism for screening foreign takeovers of companies engaging in strategic activities (Wehrlé & Pohl 2016, 58). Under this mechanism, investments in the transport, energy, and communications industries are assessed for their threat to the wider concept of *national interest*, and such reviews are only applied to foreign investors hailing from outside the EU and European Economic Area (EEA). However, investments in companies engaged in defense and national security are assessed on the basis of their threat to the "essential interests of the state" (i.e., national security), and that review applies to *all* foreign investors, including those from within the EU (Wehrlé & Pohl 2016, 58). The Italian government did later allow the takeover of the Italian aerospace manufacturing company Piaggio Aero by the UAE's Mubadala Development Co., as well as the takeover of the Italian aerospace technology firm Avio SpA by the US' General Electric in 2013, "but subjected both transactions to strict conditions, such as compliance with requirements imposed by the Government on the security of supply, information and technology transfer" (UNCTAD 2016b, 97). Interestingly, Finland replaced its previous screening mechanism with a dual review system similar to Italy's in 2014, and it now looks at all foreign investors – including those from the EU – when assessing cross-border M&A in the defense sector (Wehrlé & Pohl 2016, 52–3).

Other governments actively seeking to block hostile foreign takeovers on national security grounds include Australia, Canada, China, Japan, and Russia, to name but a few.[22] In China, reports were already emerging in 2006 that "acquisitions of Chinese enterprises by foreign companies are increasingly being challenged amidst a growing mood of 'economic patriotism'" (Yan 2006). The Chinese government, for example, blocked the Australian bank Macquarie's bid for its biggest phone company, PCCW, and "stalled" the American-based Carlyle Group's bid for Xugong, the country's biggest maker of construction equipment (Bloomberg 2006; Yan 2006). It is also widely held that economic nationalism played a role in the Chinese government's 2008 refusal to allow Coca Cola to buy the Huiyuan Juice company, an attitude many analysts believe remains prevalent in China (see e.g., Browne & Dean 2010; Harmsen 2009). Additionally, China adopted a number of new laws and regulations in 2007/08, 2011, 2015, and 2016, updating and formalizing some of its mechanisms for screening foreign takeovers (see Chapter 5). Together, these rules prohibit foreign investment in particular industries, and set up a "mandatory national security review system for foreign acquisitions of target military... enterprises" and for businesses in a number of strategic sectors related to national security, such as energy and infrastructure (Wehrlé & Pohl 2016, 50).

Russia also updated its foreign takeover laws in 2008, identifying forty-two strategic industries where investment may be reviewed for national security risks, approval is required for acquisitions of stakes larger than 25%, and majority stakes require a special permit from a review committee led by the Russian Prime Minister.[23] As discussed further in Chapter 5, the scope of this national security review was widened in 2014 to include activities related to infrastructure and transport. In 2013, Russia blocked the proposed takeover of Petrovax Pharm, one of its vaccine producers, by the US company Abbot Laboratories on national security grounds (UNCTADb 2016, 96, 99).

In Japan, Article 27 of the 1949 Foreign Exchange and Foreign Trade Act gives the Minister of Finance the power to prohibit foreign investment when it is determined that "national security is impaired, the maintenance of public order is disturbed, or the protection of public safety is hindered."[24] Though Japanese FDI laws are generally relaxing, concerns have emerged within that country that foreign acquisitions by "developing countries could [threaten] Japan's strategic interests," causing its Trade Ministry in 2006, for example, to encourage Japanese "steelmakers to adopt poison pills to protect themselves from foreign takeovers" (Economist 2006a). In 2007, the regulatory regime was amended to widen the number of sectors in which investors must notify the Minister of Finance in advance of a transaction, in order to "prevent the proliferation of weapons of mass destruction and damage to . . . defence production and technology infrastructure" (UNCTAD 2016b, 96). Notably, Japan blocked the UK's TCI fund from increasing its minority stake in the Japanese electricity company J-Power on national security grounds, as it felt the group might be able to "affect the planning, operation and maintenance of key facilities such as power transmission lines and implementation of Japan's nuclear power generation" (Terada 2008).

Australia and Canada have also strengthened their foreign investment laws, following periods of national debate over the desirability of foreign investment. Yet, while both countries undertake *national security reviews* of proposed foreign acquisitions, these are carried out alongside (or as part of) larger *net benefit* and *national interest tests* that include broader considerations like the effect of a specified transaction on competition, the economy as a whole, and national culture or community.

Under the 1985 Investment Canada Act, for example, Canada may review sizeable foreign investments on the basis of their "net benefit" to society, which in both theory and practice can be used to block transactions that raise national security concerns. The first time Canada blocked a foreign takeover on net benefit grounds *was* over security concerns, when in 2008 it refused to allow the US company Alliant Techsystems to acquire the Canadian company MacDonald Detweiller (MDA), which held sensitive satellite technology as part of its Radarsat program (Lexology 2016; Simon 2008, 2009). Canada adopted a formal mechanism to review the national security implications of foreign investments a year later. By March 2016, it reported that these national security reviews led it to block three foreign acquisitions, retroactively order two divestments by foreign investors, and mitigate two deals (ISED 2016, 10). In one case, an investment was also "abandoned" by the acquirer before it could be blocked (ISED 2016, 10). Deals blocked on national security grounds include the attempted purchase of Manitoba Telecom Services' Allstream division by the Egyptian company Accelero Capital Holdings in 2013, because Allstream ran "a national fibre optic network that provides critical telecommunications services to businesses and governments, including the Government of Canada" (Moore 2013). An investment by the Chinese SOE Beida Jade Bird, which would have installed a facility for manufacturing fire alarms in close proximity to the Canadian Space Agency, was also blocked for security reasons (Lexology 2016). In November 2010, however, Canada famously blocked BHP Billiton's bid for PotashCorp on the grounds that it would not be of "net benefit" to Canada, *without* citing national security concerns (see Simon et al. 2010).

Australia's Foreign Acquisitions and Takeovers Act of 1975 establishes a screening process for foreign purchases over certain thresholds and under certain conditions. The Foreign Investment Review Board (FIRB) makes these assessments, and the Treasurer of Australia then has the power to block foreign acquisitions that are not found to be in the national interest, including deals that pose a risk to national security.[25] The Act was amended in 2015 to, among other things, lower some thresholds for review and give the FIRB and Treasurer new powers.[26] Yet, while Australia has formally blocked deals only a handful of times, it has not always been clear about whether the "national interest" being contravened involves national security or not. For instance, the Treasurer blocked a 2001 bid by the European-based Royal Dutch Shell to become a majority owner in the Australian oil company Woodside on the basis that it would be "contrary to the national interest" to allow Woodside to relinquish its control over the joint-venture project it had with Shell to develop Australia's North West Shelf natural gas resource (Australian Treasurer 2001). In April 2011, Australia rejected an attempt by Singapore's stock exchange, SGX, to acquire the Australian Securities Exchange, ASX, arguing the deal was not in the "national interest" given the "critically important" nature of the business to Australia's economy (Smith 2011). In 2013, Australia also rejected the proposed purchase of the Australian agribusiness Graincorp by the American company Archer Daniel Midland (ADM), both because of its importance to Australia's economy (it held 85% of the market) and because "allowing it to proceed could risk undermining public support for the foreign investment regime and ongoing foreign investment more generally" (Australian Treasurer 2013). The Australian government did, however, explicitly cite national security concerns in 2015 when it blocked the purchase of the Kidman & Company land portfolio from *all* foreign bidders, which were rumored to include both Canadian and Chinese investors, because Kidman is "one of the largest private land owner[s]" in Australia, and 50% of one of its cattle stations (Anna Creek) "is located in the Woomera Prohibited Area," used for weapons testing (Australian Treasurer 2015; Thomas & Lilly 2016).[27]

Placing the Theory behind Intervention in Context

A Global Perspective and Parsimonious Theory

Though all of this serves to illustrate that strategic intervention into cross-border M&A is not confined to a particular geography, scholarly explanations of these events are mostly limited in context to government intervention by the US.[28] Such inquiries provide a depth of valuable insight into how the US operates vis-à-vis foreign takeovers. They also provide invaluable comparisons to the antagonism surrounding takeovers of American companies by the Japanese in the 1980s and early 1990s (Graham & Marchick 2006; Kang 1997). These inquiries do not, however, test their assumptions across different states, or seek to create a generalizable theory that can explain when and why states intervene in M&A activity on national security grounds. While I do not disagree that states evaluate all foreign takeovers on a case-by-case basis according to their own internal national security criteria, there do seem to be some general tendencies among states concerning when and why they engage in this behavior. These may in turn be used to create parsimonious theory. Moreover, by not adopting a more global scope of inquiry, many theorists fail to examine some of the truly puzzling aspects of state behavior regarding foreign takeovers that are discussed in the following chapters. With that in mind, this book will seek to build on and draw from the work of these scholars, the public policy world, financial research, interviews, and empirical data to create a generalizable and probabilistic theory of when and why the governments of advanced industrial and industrializing societies intervene in foreign takeovers on national security grounds.

Foreign Direct Investment: Why Focus on Foreign Takeovers Alone?

Though states interact strategically over other forms of FDI, this book focuses specifically on cross-border M&A in order to fully understand its unique dynamics and implications for how states balance power in the economic sphere. As defined by Graham and Krugman, FDI involves the "ownership of assets in one country by residents of another for purposes of controlling the use of those assets" (Graham & Krugman 1995, 8). FDI primarily consists of cross-border M&A and new greenfield investment, but may also include financial restructuring and the extension of capital for the purpose of expanding existing business operations (OECD 2008, 203).[29] In technical terms, cross-border M&A entails "the partial or full takeover or the merging of capital assets and liabilities of existing enterprises in a country by [enterprises] from other countries," and greenfield investment refers to the "establishment of new production facilities such as offices, buildings, plants, and factories, as well as the movement of intangible capital (mainly in services)" (Gilpin 2001, 278; OECD 2008, 87; UNCTAD 2006, 1, 15). More simply put, cross-border M&A involves the purchase or sale of existing assets or equity, while greenfield investment establishes new assets.

These alternative modes of market entry often have different implications and raise different concerns for the countries involved. For the state and society in which the target company of a cross-border merger or acquisition is located, there is a great deal of uncertainty that attends the transaction process. Existing operations may face "expansion . . . or reduction" (UNCTAD 2006, 15), jobs may be lost, domestic workers may be replaced with foreign nationals, cutting-edge technology may go to another country that is viewed as a competitor, or control over domestic resources might be lost. On the other hand, greenfield investment "directly adds to production capacity" and "contributes to capital formation and employment generation in the host country" (UNCTAD 2006, 15). Foreign takeovers might also lead to the same good fortune, but it remains difficult for the host country to forecast such outcomes in advance, and, as will be shown, this can contribute to greater uncertainty surrounding M&A and a resulting focus on relative advantages as states interact within the international financial environment.

Cross-border M&A and greenfield foreign investments are thus often governed by (and subject to) different legal and regulatory frameworks in the target state, because of the varying implications for the economies receiving them. In other words, companies face different rules governing market entry, depending on the type of FDI they pursue. In the US, for example, the CFIUS process described earlier does not apply to greenfield investments, which traditionally have not been viewed as posing the same type of national security risk as the takeover of an existing entity. Often, the regulatory regimes covering foreign takeovers of companies, which provide for formal government reviews of the effect of a particular transaction on competition and national security, are specific to that particular type of FDI, and foreign investment restrictions on national security grounds "do not generally [apply] to new establishments" (Jackson 2013, 6). Where countries do not have separate regimes for screening different types of FDI, they may still have different thresholds for triggering reviews of these different modes of investment.[30] Moreover, most interventions into FDI discussed here have been focused on cross-border M&A, while instances of concern over greenfield FDI on national security grounds have been less widespread. This inquiry thus focuses specifically on cross-border M&A, rather than all forms of FDI including greenfield investments, in order to maintain the best possible comparison across countries of the type of behavior under investigation; though the latter would be an interesting area for further study.

Cross-Border M&A, Economic Interdependence, and Globalization

Any theory examining the relationship between the state, foreign takeovers, and the balance of power must also recognize the role that cross-border M&A plays within the global economy and the international system as a whole. As discussed in the next chapter, when an individual cross-border merger or acquisition is completed successfully, it can create certain economic dependencies between the states involved in the transaction. Some states will seek to take advantage of these dependencies, triggering the balance of power dynamics examined in this book. At the same time, however, cross-border M&A activity as a whole is part of the broader process of the deepening of economic interdependence among states within the international system, and of "the growing *integration* of economies and societies around the world" referred to as "globalization" (World Bank 2009, emphasis added).[31] There is thus an integral connection between foreign takeovers, economic interdependence, and globalization.

The role of foreign takeovers as a driver of economic globalization has also grown over time. Cross-border M&A has not only increased globally in volume and value, but it also now accounts for a much larger portion of total inward FDI than it did at the beginning of the twentieth century. In the US, for instance, most inward FDI was made up of greenfield investments before World War I, after which the composition of inward FDI gradually "shifted away from greenfield investments and toward mergers and acquisitions" (Graham & Marchick 2006, xvi). By the late 1980s, "foreign takeovers of extant US firms" accounted for most of the FDI coming into the US (Graham & Krugman 1995, 20).

Yet, while globalization is not a new phenomenon (Dombrowski 2005), it is also not linear in its progression. Economic interdependence only recently reached the levels it obtained prior to World War I,[32] and scholars caution that the history of the last century implies that the continued progress of globalization is far from inevitable.[33] Nye, for example, notes that after

> two world wars, the great social diseases of totalitarian fascism and communism, the end of European empires, the end of Europe as the arbiter of world power . . . economic globalization was reversed and did not again reach its 1914 levels until the 1970s. Conceivably, it could happen again. (Nye 2002, 3)

A look at the global picture since the 1990s illustrates the swings that can occur in cross-border M&A activity alone, and the deep impact of the global economic crisis on this activity only serves to illustrate the fragility of the globalization process. Data from the United Nations Commission on Trade and Development's (UNCTAD) 2016 World Investment Report shows an unprecedented surge in foreign takeovers in the late 1990s, culminating in the year 2000 with 10,517 cross-border M&A globally, together valued at almost $960 billion. The post-9/11 period saw a relative drop in activity, and then a rather steady climb to a new high of 12,044 cross-border deals worldwide in 2007, valued at almost $1,033 billion. Cross-border M&A activity then began to slow significantly in 2008 with the onset of the financial crisis, and it has been slow to reach full recovery, with the value of deals in 2015 being just 70% of that in 2007, or almost $311 billion less globally (see Figures 1 and 2).[34]

Of course, a number of possible factors could negatively impact cross-border M&A and the other drivers of globalization, in addition to war and systemic economic crises. Reports by the US National Intelligence Council (NIC) argue that a significant deceleration in globalization could be part of a possible future scenario in which the world's great powers tended toward fragmentation in response to increased levels of threat abroad (NIC 2010, 14), and that a global pandemic, terrorism, or a "popular backlash against globalization" could slow it down or even reverse it (NIC 2004, 30). One NIC report suggests that such a backlash could result from a "white collar rejection of outsourcing in . . . wealthy countries" or a "resistance in poor countries whose people saw themselves as victims of globalization" (NIC 2004, 30).

Figure 1 Number of cross-border M&A deals (by economy of seller)

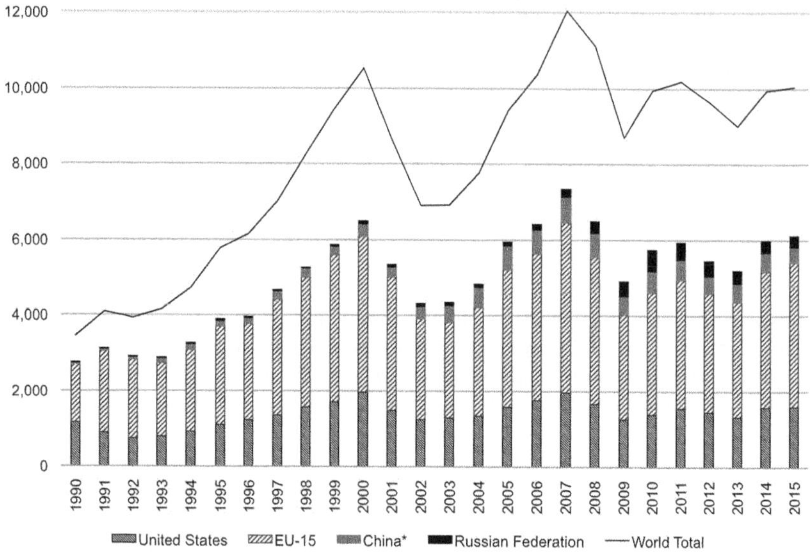

Data Source: UNCTAD World Investment Report 2016, Annex Table 11
Note: China includes data for both mainland China and Hong Kong.*

The misuse or abuse of state intervention into foreign takeovers could also have a potentially negative impact on cross-border M&A activity. Repeated politicization of foreign takeovers based on contrived or spurious national security concerns combined with rising economic nationalism in one or more powerful countries could even contribute to a backlash against globalization more generally (see e.g., Kekic & Sauvant 2006). This caution may take on a greater sense of urgency, given the deep contraction in international commerce that occurred as a result of the Great Recession that began in 2008, and the rise in populist and economic nationalist sentiment in a number of advanced industrial states marked by political events in 2016.[35] For example, Britain's "Vote Leave" campaign during the referendum on EU membership and Donald Trump's campaign for the US presidency both successfully employed anti-globalization rhetoric as part of their platforms, promising a return to domestic control over their respective national economies. Such developments make less surprising the earlier forecast in the NIC's Global Trends 2030 report, which listed as its "most plausible worst-case scenario" a future world in which "the US and Europe turn inward and globalization stalls" (NIC 2012, ii, 135).

Figure 2 Value of cross-border M&A deals (by economy of seller in millions of dollars)

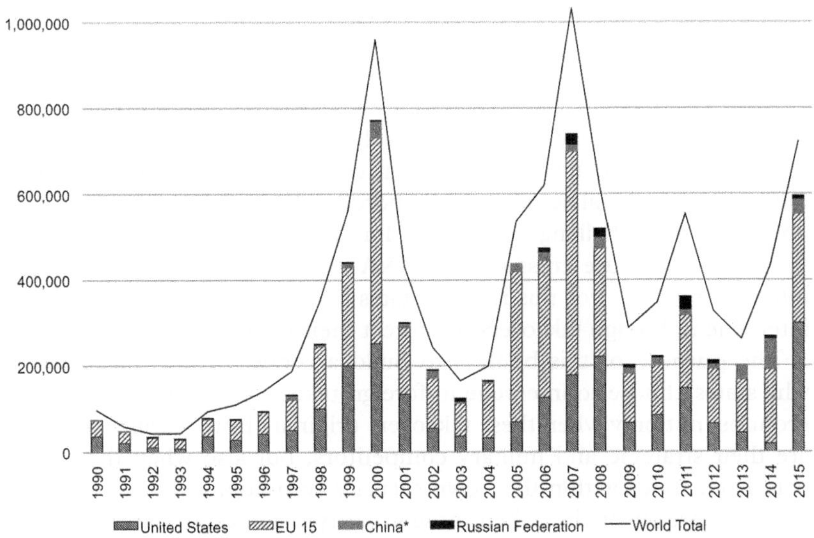

Data Source: UNCTAD World Investment Report 2016, Annex Table 9
Note: China includes data for both mainland China and Hong Kong.*

Thus, even though economic interdependence has now returned to pre-World War I levels and cross-border M&A appears to be expanding as a key driver of globalization, there is no assurance that economic interdependence and the deeper process of economic integration will continue to be forward-moving. The forward progress of economic globalization requires the presence of a benign hegemonic military power that both desires a liberal economic order and is able to ensure economic integration is possible by signaling its willingness to protect that order (see e.g., Gilpin 1981).[36] Europe's position as the dominant military power ensured the survival of the economically interdependent system it favored before World War I, and the US has played a similar role in the post-World War II era (see e.g., Gilpin 1981; Ikenberry 2001).[37] Thus, if the US (or other great powers) were to repeatedly *misuse* intervention into foreign takeovers on national security grounds – not as an act of balancing but as part of a wider domestic backlash against economic globalization – it could be taken as a signal of unwillingness to foster economic liberalization, which in turn could lead to a deeper, if unintended, impact on globalization.[38] The theory and cases examined in this book therefore highlight the difference between the use of intervention into foreign takeovers for the purpose of strategic balancing and intervention that might be considered an instance of "overbalancing" or miscalculation.

The Significance

Foreign takeovers play an important role in the globalization process, as states embrace the absolute gains that can be realized through the free movement of capital across national borders. But, as the global economy opens up, new challenges also arise for states – including the fact that some states will use cross-border M&A to take advantage of economic interdependence. For this reason, states maintain the right to, and will, intervene in foreign takeovers to protect their national security.

The purpose of this book is to build a robust theory that explains why states choose to intervene in foreign takeovers on national security grounds, not only when these takeovers originate from within states that are their strategic and military competitors, but also when they originate from states within their own security communities. Such behavior is even more surprising when those security communities are based not only on exceptionally close and long-standing alliances, but also on a commitment to economic liberalization, like the EU or the transatlantic community.

The following chapters outline how states use such intervention as a tool of non-military internal balancing, allowing them to balance the power of other states within the international system without disrupting their broader existing relationships with those states. Foreign takeovers can pose long-term risks and challenges to economic and military power that must be addressed, even within security communities. But states do not intervene in every foreign takeover that poses a possible risk; they must choose which battles to fight. So the answer to the puzzle lies in the fact that with this specific tool of balancing, states can use different levels of intervention appropriate to the threat and context, and that states are more likely to intervene in transactions originating from within their own security communities when there is a combination of both high levels of economic nationalism in the receiving state and some underlying geopolitical tensions or concerns between the two states involved, despite their overall close relationship.

Understanding this behavior is important. First and foremost, it is important because it is about much more than ostensible protectionism, even when economic nationalism may play a secondary role in some interventions. Interventions in foreign takeovers on national security grounds are primarily about power, the balance of power, and the evolution of inter-state competition in the economic sphere. The theory of non-military internal balancing presented here explains why states might feel threatened by foreign takeovers, and how they might respond to preserve their positions of relative power in this context. Policymakers and private actors alike need to recognize this behavior for what it is if they are to avoid costly miscalculations in the future.

Second, while such acts of balancing through intervention into foreign takeovers will, by and large, not affect broader patterns of investment, excessive acts of "overbalancing," or the repeated misuse or abuse of this tool, could have a negative economic impact on not only the state, but the system as a whole. As already discussed, government-led barriers to cross-border M&A (especially those originating in the US) may pose a challenge to the future of global economic integration if misused or misunderstood. This could be especially true if governments seek to engage in reciprocal overbalancing behavior, using national security arguments to prevent foreign takeovers in even the most benign of sectors. Indeed, if we look at France and Italy's recent efforts to protect national champions in their food industries, or the blurring of the line between national security and the more nebulous concept of "national interest" in some countries, there is some evidence that overbalancing may already be occurring.

This matters because a reversal, or even slowing, of globalization could have a significant and negative economic impact on the global community. Krugman's work indicates that the gains from FDI are manifold, allowing countries to enhance their "comparative advantage" and create "increasing returns to scale," while leading to "increased competition" and often resulting in "valuable spillovers to the domestic economy" in the form of new technology and more highly skilled workers (Graham & Krugman 1995, 57–9). A backlash scenario against globalization of the type discussed earlier could not only lead to the loss of these benefits, but also pose a "huge opportunity cost in terms of forgone FDI," which the Economist Intelligence Unit (EIU) and the Columbia Program on International Investment (CPII) have placed at "$270bn in FDI inflows per year" globally (Kekic & Sauvant 2006, 14). Given the potential long-term costs of repeated miscalculation, a theory that explains the logic behind legitimate state intervention into foreign takeovers to balance power, and the dynamics surrounding it, may help provide public policymakers with the tools necessary to make better decisions regarding specific foreign takeovers in the future.

Finally, explaining state intervention into foreign takeovers in the most unlikely of cases, within common security and liberal economic communities, may also help deepen our understanding of the theoretical relationship between economic interdependence and levels of conflict within the international system. Liberal theorists tend to view this relationship as positive, expecting lower levels of international conflict as states become increasingly interdependent, the gains from free trade become widespread, and the incentives for conflict are reduced. These observations are one of the very reasons it is so puzzling that barriers to cross-border M&A are being erected between the closest of military and economic allies. Complex interdependence theorists Keohane and Nye (2001) caution that while the tendency toward conflict will largely depend on the form that interdependence takes, we should generally expect less *military* conflict among states tied by extremely high levels of economic interdependence. Consequently, they also note that "conflict will take new forms, and may even increase" as interdependence deepens (Keohane & Nye 2001, 7) – an insight which may help to explain the puzzle, if the barriers to M&A discussed in this book are considered to be a form of conflict.

Why states are willing to engage in a form of conflict that might itself impede the progress of globalization and economic liberalization that brings not only gains from trade, but also a high level of stability to the system (by decreasing the likelihood of *military* competition) must still be explained, however. Structural realism suggests that conflict, especially economic conflict, may increase with interdependence (Waltz 1993). But this explanation is both underspecified and vague, providing little or no clarification of what form such conflict will take, and how those forms might vary according to the different relationships between the states in question. It will be the purpose of this book to fill this theoretical gap, and to test the new theory proposed here.

This book will proceed as follows. Chapter 1 provides an in-depth explanation of the theory of non-military internal balancing, and the different ways states can use intervention into foreign takeovers as a tool of this form of balancing. It also outlines the specific hypotheses underlying this argument, which are tested both quantitatively and qualitatively throughout the rest of the book. Chapter 2 explains the statistical methods used to test these hypotheses over a population of cross-border M&A cases, and provides a discussion of the results. Chapter 3 examines four critical cases of unbounded intervention, in which different states sought to block a foreign takeover in order to maintain their positions of relative power within the international system. Chapter 4 covers a fifth critical case of unbounded intervention, the DPW/P&O deal, which I argue is an outlier case that provides an excellent example of overbalancing. Chapter 5 investigates two cases of bounded intervention, where states mitigated a cross-border M&A transaction to maintain their power.

Chapter 6 considers two cases of "non-intervention" and one of "internal" (or indirect) intervention, where the state involved encouraged a domestic white knight to acquire a vulnerable national champion in order to obviate the need for direct intervention in an unwanted foreign takeover. Finally, the Conclusion discusses the theoretical and practical implications of my findings, and provides a deeper examination of their significance for theory and practice.

NOTES

1 For a longer discussion of these concerns, see e.g., Bream et al. 2008; Freed 2008. Chinese government concern over the issue of seaborne iron ore supply was not surprising given that China accounts for most of the world's demand and global supplies were tight at the time. In 2008 alone, Chinese demand for seaborne iron ore increased by over 40%, reaching 68% of the world total by 2009 (UNCTAD 2010b). By 2010, China was the world's largest producer of crude steel (47% of total global production), but domestic supply of iron ore for this process had not been able to meet demand for some time (UNCTAD 2010a). China accounted for 88% of the increase in global imports of seaborne iron ore in 2014, as domestic production slowed (UNCTAD 2016a). Even as global supplies increase and China's economy seeks to rebalance, China remains "the world's largest producer and consumer of steel" (Hume 2016).

2 The steel industry itself voiced concern over the combination of Rio and BHP through the World Steel Association, then called the International Iron and Steel Institute (IISI). The IISI's Secretary General publicly stated that "any further consolidation between the big three [Rio, BHP, and Vale] would create a virtual monopoly in the business" (WSA 2007). He went on to say that "the steel industry [will] strongly oppose the potential merger of BHP Billiton and Rio Tinto, [and] it is vital that the competition authorities in the EU, USA, China, Australia and Japan also recognize the threat that this merger poses" (WSA 2007). Moreover, he argued that the "merger is not in the public interest and should not be allowed to proceed" (WSA 2007). Not surprisingly, BHP and Rio's later attempt to form a joint venture (JV) of their mining assets in Australia met with the full force of the competition regulators who had been expected to review the merger. BHP and Rio abandoned the JV in October 2010, when they learned it "would not be approved in its current form by the European Commission, Australian Competition and Consumer Commission, Japan Fair Trade Commission, Korea Fair Trade Commission or the German Federal Cartel Office" (E-Mining Jrn. 2010). Notably, the Chinese government decided to investigate the global seaborne iron ore market in 2010, over broad concerns that the "big three" suppliers were "monopolising supplies" (Chikwanha 2010).

3 For a discussion of the rarity of formal vetoes, see e.g., Wehrlé & Pohl 2016, 41.

4 For a discussion of the surge in intervention into cross-border M&A on national security grounds, see e.g., UNCTAD 2006, 222–7, 2016b, 94–100.

5 Germany eventually had to modify the VW Law, but Lower Saxony was able to retain a 20% share, allowing it to block certain voting decisions, and the government encouraged significant cross-shareholding with Porsche SE to prevent an unwanted foreign takeover (see e.g., Barker 2011; Bodini 2013; Harrison 2005).

6 See the European Takeover Directive (European Parliament 2004) and the Consolidated Versions of the Treaty on European Union and the Treaty on the Functioning of the European Union (2016/C 202/01), in particular Chapter 4, Articles 63 (ex Article 56 TEC) and 65 (ex Article 58 TEC) in the latter.

7 A *target company* is one that is the subject of an attempted merger or acquisition. A *white knight* is "a potential acquirer . . . sought out by a target company's management to take over the company to avoid a hostile takeover" (Investor Words 2007). A *hostile takeover* is one that "goes against the wishes of the target company's management and board of directors" (Investor Words 2007).

8 As one observer recently commented, "the blocking of mergers remains one of the few areas left for national authorities to play an interventionist role in a world where markets are increasingly global" (Ahearn 2006, 4).

9 This book adopts Helleiner and Pickel's understanding of economic nationalism as a "set of policies that results from a shared national identity and therefore bears its characteristics" and their idea that "because national purposes vary . . . so must economic nationalisms" (Helleiner & Pickel 2005, 26).

10 For the text of Executive Order 11858 (May 7, 1975), see 40 FR 20263, 3 CFR, 1971–1975.

11 For the text of the Exon-Florio Amendment, see Title V, Subtitle A, Part II, §5021 of the Omnibus Trade and Competitiveness Act of 1988 (PL 100–418, also known as HR 4848).

12 For the full text of the Byrd Amendment, see §837(a) of the National Defense Authorization Act for Fiscal Year 1993 (PL 102–484).

13 For a discussion of the impact that US government opposition and actions had on CNOOC's decision to withdraw its bid for Unocal, see Asia Times 2005; Graham & Marchick 2006; White 2005.

14 Both parties also agreed to appoint a US government-approved security director to Sprint's board, and to remove Huawei-supplied equipment from the Clearwire network if that deal went through (Taylor 2013).

15 For instance, CFIUS reportedly blocked the proposed takeover of Lumileds Holding – a producer and developer of LEDs, and a division of the Dutch company Philips – by the Hong Kong-registered private equity fund Go Scale Capital in 2016 over "unspecified concerns" (Brown & Robinson 2016). In another example, the Chinese company CNOOC's bid for the Canadian oil company Nexen (which had US-based assets) was reportedly mitigated by CFIUS in 2013, which approved the deal on the condition "that CNOOC have no operational control of Nexen's assets that are close to US military installations" as a consequence of the transaction (Carlson et al. 2014, 472–3).

16 Notably, Ralls proceeded to sue President Obama and the US government in 2013 over the CFIUS order, not challenging "whether its deal posed a national security threat" (Chon 2014), but challenging it "under the Administrative Procedure Act and the Due Process Clause of the Fifth Amendment to the United States Constitution" (see *Ralls Corp.* v. *CFIUS*, 926 F.Supp.2d, US District Court, DC 2013; *Ralls Corp.* v. *CFIUS*, 987 F.Supp.2d, US District Court, DC 2013). While the initial case was dismissed, the US Court of Appeals for the District of Columbia Circuit "held that Ralls Corporation was deprived of its property without due process and was entitled to notice of the decision, an accounting of the unclassified information upon which CFIUS had based its recommendation to the President, and an opportunity to rebut the information" (ABASAL 2015, 213; for the full judgment, see *Ralls Corp.* v. *CFIUS*, 758 F.3d 296, US Court of Appeals, DC Circuit 2014). The result is unlikely to affect future CFIUS rulings on national security grounds, as the presidential power to veto investments on national security grounds is not itself subject to judicial review, and that was not challenged in this case – though it may open up the possibility of other companies filing due process claims to gain access to the unclassified information surrounding the dismissal of their investment (see e.g., ABASAL 2015, 214; Chon 2014).

17 For example, the OECD reports that "of the 40 countries that participate in the OECD notification procedures for investment policies" only "13 report that they do not depart from national treatment on security grounds," while the rest "have sectoral policies that restrict foreign investment in a very narrow range of activities" in this area (OECD 2008, 4).

18 For deeper discussion of these concerns, see e.g., Ahearn 2006; Betts 2011; Castle 2011; Euractiv 2006, 2009; Parker & Smyth 2006.

19 For an overview of the outcome of E.ON's bid for Endesa see e.g., EU Commission 2012; Mulligan & Dinmore 2009. The Spanish government denied the validity of a European Commission ruling that tried to prevent its intervention in a deal between the German energy giant E.ON and the Spanish utility Endesa (Bilefsky 2006; Buck 2006). Spain supported a "Spanish solution" to the foreign takeover, first backing the Spanish company Gas Natural to merge with Endesa, and later supporting a "power-sharing" agreement by which Italy's Enel and Spain's Acciona would make a joint bid for Endesa, with Acciona taking a larger share of "management influence" (Betts 2009; Mulligan 2009).

20 The German government decided to renationalize the Bundesdruckerei in 2008, after the country's then Interior Minister, Wolfgang Schäuble, voiced concern "that the company's technology or the personal data it possessed could pass to the wrong owner," and that these "concerns intensified again when France's Sagem and Oberthur Technologies, Gemalto of the Netherlands and 3M of the US began expressing an interest in acquiring the business" (Benoit 2008). The German government purchase was finalized in 2009 (Bundesdruckerei 2009).

21 For a discussion of Italy's efforts to block these takeovers by French companies, and the resulting tensions between the two countries, see e.g.,

Dinmore et al. 2011; Sanderson et al. 2011. While Tremonti was able to squash the initial bid in March 2011, EDF did eventually take control of 80% of Edison in December, through a mollifying agreement that "balanced" the takeover by having "Edison's Italian shareholders acquir[e] a stake in one of its subsidiaries for €600m, effectively separating it from its parent company" (Thompson 2011).

22 For additional countries and recent examples, see e.g., UNCTAD 2016b; Wehrlé & Pohl 2016.

23 For further details, see Russian Federal Law No. 57-FZ, Procedures for Foreign Investments in the Business Entities of Strategic Importance for Russian National Defense and State Security, April 29, 2008.

24 For a translation of Japan's 1949 Foreign Exchange and Foreign Trade Act, see www.steptoe.com/assets/attachments/4066.pdf.

25 FIRB Guidance states that "national interest considerations can include: national security, competition, other Australian Government policies (including tax), impact on the economy and the community, and the investor's character" (Australian Government 2016a, 1).

26 Under the 2015 Act, for example, Australia can now impose legally enforceable obligations on foreign companies whose acquisitions are deemed, retroactively, not to be in the national interest (Australian Government 2016b, 2).

27 In his announcement blocking the Kidman deal, the Australian Treasurer (2015) stated that "the WPA weapons testing range makes a unique and sensitive contribution to Australia's national defence and it is not unusual for governments to restrict access to sensitive areas on national security grounds."

28 These include Graham & Marchick 2006; Kang 1997; Larson & Marchick 2006; Moran 1990, 1993; Tyson 1992. For exceptions to this focus on the US, see e.g., US GAO 1996; Wehrlé & Pohl 2016.

29 Financial restructuring and the extension of capital for the purpose of expanding existing business operations are, however, beyond the scope of this investigation, as they involve different dynamics, concerns, and regulations.

30 Australia, for example, has both monetary and ownership thresholds over which it will review many different forms of FDI, including greenfield FDI, to determine its "net interest" to the nation. These thresholds vary by sector and by investor: for instance, if the investor is a SOE, the threshold will be lower, and if the investor comes from a country with a free trade agreement with Australia, their threshold for review may be higher. Australia waives the review of greenfield investments, for example, for the US as part of the Australia–US Free Trade Agreement (AUFTA) (US DOS 2014a, 2). For more details, see the website of Australia's Foreign Investment Review Board, https://firb.gov.au.

31 Waltz notes that the important distinction between economic globalization and economic interdependence is that the former implies economic "integration," and that "the difference between an interdependent and an integrated world is a qualitative one and not a mere matter of proportionately

more trade and a greater and more rapid flow of capital" (Waltz 1999, 697).

32 In 2001, Gilpin asserted that "the world is not as well integrated [today] at it was in a number of respects prior to World War I... Trade, investment, and financial flows were actually greater in the late 1800s, at least relative to the size of national economies and the international economy, than they are today" (Gilpin 2001, 364). In 1999, Waltz claimed that the "interdependence of states... has increased, but only to about the 1910 level if measured by trade or capital flows as a percentage of GDP; lower if measured by the mobility of labor, and lower still if measured by the mutual military dependence of states" (Waltz 1999, 693).

33 For further scholarly discussion of why globalization's forward progress is not inevitable, see e.g., Dombrowski 2005, 235; Lentner 2004, 19, 49; NIC 2004, 30; Nye 2002, 3; Waltz 1999.

34 These data are sourced and calculated from the Annex Tables of the UNCTAD 2016 World Investment Report. For more detail, see http://unctad.org/.

35 For a good discussion of the rise of populism in the US and Europe and its connection to globalization and other economic factors, as well as political events in 2016 including the election of Donald Trump to the US presidency and Brexit, see e.g., Kazin 2016; Mudde 2016; Nye 2017; Zakaria 2016.

36 Gilpin argues that, in their respective hegemonic roles, the US and UK both successfully "created and enforced the rules of a liberal international economic order," largely because of the power that allowed them to "[impose] their will on lesser states and partially because other states have benefited from and accepted their leadership" (Gilpin 1981, 144–5). Such benefits include a "secure status quo, free trade, *foreign investment*, and a well functioning international monetary system" (Gilpin 1981, 144–5, emphasis added).

37 According to Gilpin's Hegemonic Stability Theory, as the hegemon loses ground to rising challengers who are no longer happy with the current order, the stability of that order founded by the hegemon will be jeopardized, and hegemonic war will become possible. If the hegemon loses to its challenger in such a war, a new order will be created (Gilpin 1981, 9–15). Gilpin stresses that while this does not mean that "the decline of hegemony will lead inevitably to the collapse of a liberal world economy... the dominant liberal power's decline does... greatly weaken the prospects for the survival of a liberal trading system" (Gilpin 1986, 311). Lentner follows this logic when he claims that "should the United States falter or should its allies lose confidence, then circumstances might undergo a substantial change. In short... globalization does not constitute an inexorable juggernaut leading the world onward" (Lentner 2004, 19). Ikenberry, however, raises the possibility that the current liberal economic order might outlive the end of US hegemony, because of the highly "constitutionalized" nature of this order (Ikenberry 2001, 23–9). Nye also provides a thoughtful examination of the challenges to the liberal economic order posed by "populist reactions to globalization" in the US, among other factors, and the effect this might have on the US' leadership of that order going forward (Nye 2017, 14–16).

38 Dombrowski, for example, has argued that increased efforts by the US to expand "its security perimeter" to include the "transportation hubs that facilitate international commerce" after the September 11th terrorist attacks could actually serve to "limit, contain, and perhaps even reverse economic globalization," at least "when combined with new... restrictions on the movements of people and ideas across national borders" (Dombrowski 2005, 235).

1 A Theory of Non-Military Internal Balancing

Introduction

Why do states intervene in the foreign takeover process even within the context of security communities based on economic liberalization and integration? In this chapter, I resolve this puzzle by recognizing that state intervention into cross-border M&A can be understood as a tool of statecraft. I develop a model that explains when, how, and why states use intervention into foreign takeovers strategically to balance the power of other states.

This chapter has five components. In the first section, I examine the link between *national security and foreign takeovers*, providing a necessary backdrop to understanding how and why intervention into cross-border M&A acts as a tool of statecraft. This part of the chapter outlines how states approach national security in relation to foreign takeovers, the legal and regulatory systems they use for restricting such investment on these grounds, and the common types of national security risks states associate with cross-border M&A. The second section examines the relationship between *economic interdependence and power*, and why the distribution of economic power within the international system matters to states. It looks at the theory behind the potential for increased economic competition among interdependent states, how some states act strategically to exploit economic interdependence to their advantage, and why states might seek to balance rising economic and military powers in the economic sphere. In the third part of the chapter, I provide a detailed outline of my *theory of non-military internal balancing* and how it relates to intervention into foreign takeovers. I also propose a probabilistic theory of when and why states are most likely to use intervention into cross-border M&A as such a tool of statecraft, and examine the different *forms* that such intervention may take in practice. This allows me to offer a solution to the puzzle of why this particular tool of non-military internal balancing is used within security communities. The fourth section then details the hypotheses that underpin my theory, and provides a detailed

& Pohl 2016, 20–1).[3] Despite this ambiguity, some common themes, concerns, and perceived risks are identifiable (Jackson 2013; US GAO 2008; Wehrlé & Pohl 2016).

National Security Risks and Cross-Border M&A

The US, once again, provides a useful starting point for understanding the nature of the national security concerns that can be raised by foreign takeovers. Despite the classified and confidential nature of individual FDI reviews, the US scrutiny system for vetting foreign takeovers (the Committee on Foreign Investments in the United States, CFIUS) is arguably among the most transparent and institutionalized in the world, and has been written about the most from theoretical, legal, and informational perspectives. And while the US does not define national security for the purposes of foreign investment screening, it does provide an "illustrative," though not exhaustive, list of the types of "national security factors" the President and CFIUS might take into consideration when assessing whether or not a particular foreign merger or acquisition "poses national security risks" (73 FR 74569). These risks factors are outlined in Section 721(f) of the Defense Production Act of 1950 (DPA) as amended by the Foreign Investment and National Security Act of 2007 (FINSA), codified at 50 U.S.C. App. 2170.[4] They include the potential national security effects of a specified transaction on:

- domestic production needed for projected national defense requirements,
- the capability and capacity of domestic industries to meet national defense requirements, . . .
- the control of domestic industries and commercial activity by foreign citizens as it affects the capability and capacity of the United States to meet the requirements of national security, . . .
- sales of military goods, equipment, or technology to any country . . . that supports terrorism; [is] . . . of concern regarding missile proliferation[, nuclear proliferation, or] . . . the proliferation of chemical and biological weapons; [or] . . . is identified by the Secretary of Defense as posing a potential regional military threat . . .
- United States international technological leadership in areas affecting United States national security; . . .
- critical infrastructure, including major energy assets; . . .
- critical technologies; . . .
- the long-term projection of United States requirements for sources of energy and other critical resources and material; and
- such other factors as the President or the Committee may determine to be appropriate, generally or in connection with a specific review or investigation. (50 U.S.C. App. 2170(f))

This list also includes an assessment of whether or not the transaction is "foreign government-controlled" (50 U.S.C. App. 2170(f)), in the sense that it could lead to "the control of a U.S. business by a foreign government or by an entity controlled by or acting on behalf of a foreign government" (73 FR 74569). If so, or where otherwise appropriate, an assessment is also made of additional risk factors surrounding the country from which the investment ultimately originates, namely: (A) whether or not it adheres "to nonproliferation control regimes"; (B) "its record on cooperating in counter-terrorism efforts"; and (C) whether the transaction could possibly lead to the "transshipment or diversion of technologies with military applications" away from the US, requiring an examination of that country's "national export control laws and regulations" (50 U.S.C. App. 2170(f)).

Even as an arguably benign liberal hegemon, the US recognizes the need to maintain its global technological (and thus military) advantage by pursuing economic policies that foster the health of the defense industrial base, prevent its control by foreign governments, and ensure technology shared with its closest allies is not exported to unfriendly regimes. Undergirding this strategy are the institutions that allow the US government to mitigate or block those foreign mergers or acquisitions it believes to be threatening to national security.[5] As the dangers emanating from such deals are numerous, and the risk factors just enumerated can encompass a wide array of specific activities by a foreign investor, it is worth also highlighting those national security threats that Graham and Marchick (2006) have identified as being the ones CFIUS frequently considers when assessing a potential foreign takeover in the US. These include a number of specific actions foreign investors might possibly take:

> shutting down or sabotaging a critical facility in the United States; impeding a US law enforcement or national security investigation; accessing sensitive data . . . ; limiting US government access to information for surveillance or law enforcement purposes; denying critical technology or key products to the US government or industry; moving critical technology or key products offshore that are important for national defense, intelligence operations, or homeland security; unlawfully transferring technology abroad that is subject to US export control laws; undermining US technological leadership in a sector with important defense, intelligence, or homeland security applications; compromising the security of government and private sector networks in the US; facilitating state or economic espionage through acquisition of a US company; and aiding the military or intelligence capabilities of a foreign country with interests adverse to those of the United States.[6] (Graham & Marchick 2006, 54)

Though both their list and the list provided in the amended DPA focus specifically on US security, they illustrate the types of national security risks that would be of valid concern to almost any country.

Most of these concerns emanate from a state's fear that another state will seek to gain influence over one of its corporations in order to enhance its position and power within the international system. As Graham and Marchick (2006, 54) point out, such predatory behavior may include a foreign government using its influence to encourage one of its domestic companies to acquire a foreign company for the purpose of engaging in espionage.[7] Even worse, a state might endeavor to acquire a vital component of another country's defense industrial base, which it could then destroy, hijack, or generally use to its advantage. The Chinese government, for instance, has a reputation for trying to buy foreign companies in order to acquire military technology through espionage (Graham & Marchick 2006, 112–13; Interview 2007). Not surprisingly, this behavior has affected the reception of Chinese takeover bids within the US (Graham & Marchick 2006, 112–13; Interview 2007).[8] Indeed, the only four foreign acquisitions to be *formally* vetoed by a US President (since the Exon-Florio legislation that originally enabled a president to do so)[9] involved Chinese investors. The first was a Chinese government-owned company (CATIC) that sought to take over a US aerospace components manufacturer (MAMCO) in 1990.[10] The second was when, in 2012, the US President ordered a company owned by Chinese nationals (Ralls) to divest four wind farm site assets located in close proximity to restricted military air space (see Obama 2012). The third was when the President vetoed the acquisition of the US business of a German semiconductor company (Aixtron) by a Chinese-owned investment fund (Grand Chip) over concerns that Aixtron possessed sensitive technology with military applications and that Grand Chip's bid involved financing supported by the Chinese government (US DOT 2016b). The fourth was when the President vetoed the acquisition of the US-based Lattice Semiconductor by a company (Canyon Bridge) ultimately owned and funded by a Chinese SOE directly linked to China's State Council over a series of national security concerns relating to the Chinese government's involvement in the deal, as well as the technology involved, its use by the US government, and concerns over its continued supply (Baker, Qing, & Zhu 2016; US DOT 2017).

Another common concern among many countries is that a state, through entities it either owns or influences, may endeavor to acquire foreign companies in order to increase its control over a valuable resource. Such control could enhance that state's position within the international system by increasing its influence over the behavior of those states that need the resource in question, and which fear an intentional disruption of its supply. The behavior of the Russian government in recent years, which suggests an effort to increase its control over the oil and natural gas industries within Europe in order to augment its influence in the region, illustrates this point well.[11]

These are but a few examples of the national security concerns states might have in the context of foreign takeovers. One of the reasons the US list is so useful and instructive for understanding the common concerns states may have is that it is rare for states to provide such a rich and detailed set of examples.[12] Other countries, when they bother to do so at all, tend to offer more limited examples, but they *do* often exhibit similar concerns, even though these might be worded differently or use different terminology. The 2016 OECD report, however, offers some examples of factors raised by other countries that are not explicitly covered in the US list. For instance, while the US highlights an investing country's relationship with terrorism as a potential risk, other countries – like France, Italy, Lithuania, and New Zealand – also look at the risk from "investments by persons linked to organised crime, . . . or other criminal activities" (Wehrlé & Pohl 2016, 21). Italy considers "investments from foreign countries that do not respect democracy and the rule of law or have held conducts at risk towards the international community" to pose a security risk (Wehrlé & Pohl 2016, 21). Perhaps more controversially, some countries – like Australia, China, Japan, and New Zealand – highlight concerns regarding "the impact of the investment on the economy" as being among their national security considerations (Wehrlé & Pohl 2016, 21).

The scope of national security as it relates to FDI will thus vary in accordance with the different threats individual states perceive to their survival and autonomy within the international system. For example, not all governments (or theorists) will necessarily feel comfortable with the inclusion of a foreign investment's impact on the host economy within the remit of national security considerations. However, if a country defines this particular concern publicly as being within the scope of its national security, and then cites a specific foreign investment as being a *national security* concern for this reason (rather than a *national interest* concern, which might be more closely identified with the language of traditional economic protectionism), than it will be accepted as a national security concern for the purposes of this book. Defining the exact scope and parameters of "acceptable" or "valid" national security concerns is beyond the book's remit, and should be the subject of a separate inquiry. It is also true that, in rare instances, state officials might use the term "national security" instrumentally (or even inappropriately) in the context of FDI, in order to achieve goals other than balancing. I have therefore assessed the national security grounds cited for intervention (if specified)[13] in the cases examined in this book, and have attempted to judge, fairly and without prejudice (insofar as this is feasible), whether the risk cited is in line with a given country's historical approach to national security.

Economic Interdependence and Power

Overall, the types of common national security concerns discussed in the previous section have one clear thing in common. They imply that the state on the receiving end of a particular cross-border merger or acquisition (the target state) believes that the state of the acquirer (the sending state) could be placed at an advantage in terms of military or economic power as a result of that proposed deal, and thus that the transaction could be detrimental to them, the target state. Whether or not the sending state actually intends (or is believed to intend) harm will thus have a great effect on how the government of the target state responds to the proposed transaction.

Clearly, some states *do* seek to take advantage of the interdependent relationships that arise from globalization, in order to increase their economic and military capabilities relative to others. This notion is well documented (Gilpin 1981, 1987, 2001; Hirschman 1945; Moran 1993; Shambaugh 1999; Tyson 1992; Waltz 1993, 1999). And though most theorists of economic interdependence deal with the dependencies that result from foreign trade, rather than FDI, it is a reasonable assumption that these dynamics may be applied to the latter.[14] According to these theorists, states will have different levels of "sensitivity" and "vulnerability" as a result of a mutually dependent relationship, where sensitivity implies that a state *A* can suffer the negative effects of the actions of another state *B* "before policies are altered to try to change the situation," and vulnerability implies that state *A* can be negatively affected by the actions of state *B* "even after policies have been altered" (Keohane & Nye 1989, 13).[15] Hirschman's systematic examination of such phenomena demonstrates not only that "international trade might work to the exclusive or disproportionate benefit of one or a few of the trading nations," but also that states may abuse their position in an asymmetrical trading relationship (Hirschman 1945, 11). He makes the important point that enhancing a state's economic power does "not necessarily lead to an increase in relative power," or "a change in the balance of economic power in favor of any particular country," *unless* states pursue policies that enhance the dependencies of other states on that relationship (Hirschman 1945, 9).[16] As some countries do pursue such policies, states consequently remain concerned with the relative distribution of the gains from trade, even though liberal theorists since Adam Smith have demonstrated the absolute gains to all involved (Hirschman 1945, 5–6; Keohane & Nye 1989, 10; Waltz 1979, 140–3).

States are thus highly likely to focus on the relative distribution of economic power within the international system.[17] This is especially true in an environment where the likelihood of a major power hot war is low (Mandelbaum 1998/99; Waltz 1993) and hard power within the system must be increasingly gained through non-military means.[18] States will therefore seek to increase their economic power, which not only benefits their own domestic economy, but also provides absolute gains to their trading partners, and hopefully increases their ability to influence others by enhancing either their position of dominance or the dependence of other states on their economic policies.[19] As a result, "economic competition" will in all probability "become more intense" (Waltz 1993, 59).

A state will thus feel insecure as another state gains economic power relative to it and will seek to *balance* that rising economic power. Similarly, one state may seek to balance another if the latter attempts to make the former dependent upon it in some way through FDI. When international relations theorists refer to the US backlash against Japanese investment in the 1980s, there is an assumption that this is what occurred. Waltz claims that once Japan recovered from World War II, the US "objected more and more strenuously" to its "protectionist policies" as its economy developed into that of a rising power with a "strategy of 'creating advantages rather than accepting the status quo'" (Waltz 1979, 7–8). In 1991, Borrus and Zysman suggested that Japan and Europe were both pursuing policies to protect their technological industrial bases from foreign acquisition as part of internal balancing strategies meant to create an eventual advantage over the US (Borrus & Zysman 1991, 25, 27). The following year, Tyson strenuously argued for FDI policies that would protect American interests from such Japanese tactics (see Tyson 1992). Graham and Marchick then made a similar argument about the current US backlash against Chinese and Middle Eastern investment in 2006. They asserted that if "the US in the past has sought to protect itself from FDI originating in Germany and Japan," then "today, similar sentiments are harbored toward Middle Eastern countries for their supposed links to terrorist activities, but more importantly towards China, which, as a vast and growing economy, could one day challenge the US in economic might" (Graham & Marchick 2006, 94). Such an attitude, in order to preserve (and sometimes further) technological and industrial advantages that are vital to their military power, or to the resources necessary for their continued existence. Similarly, states have also used intervention to protect national champions deemed vital to their economic power and position. It will be demonstrated in the chapters that follow that most examples of government intervention into foreign takeovers on national security grounds, and in the sectors commonly associated with national security examined in this book, are acts that seek to maintain or maximize the economic and/or military power of the state in response to a threat or challenge to that power posed by the takeover. In other words, the form, intent, and purpose of such interventions are clearly consistent with those of internal balancing, as it is traditionally understood.[23]

The scope of Waltz's definition of internal balancing is indeed wide enough to encompass such government action. For, though many scholars have come to simplify the definition of the term to refer only to the mobilization or enhancement of arms and other military capabilities,[24] the economic element should not be forgotten, especially as it is often integral to the success of the defense industrial base that oils the machine of war. In an effort to further specify the role of economic policy in balancing, Brawley argues that there are clearly separable economic and military components of both internal and external balancing (in Paul et al. 2004).[25] Though his discussion of the economic component of internal balancing revolves primarily around basic trade and financial aid strategies, there is no reason why it might not include strategies for dealing with FDI in sensitive industries or companies of the type examined here. Borrus and Zysman, for example, have claimed that Waltzian internal balancing can be synonymous with "positive industrial adjustment" of the type used by states to gain a competitive economic and military advantage in terms of technology, which they mention can – beyond the trade and industrial policies usually discussed in that context – involve policy that either prevents foreign acquisitions in some sectors or places "local content requirements" on other forms of FDI (Borrus & Zysman 1991). There is thus some precedent for the argument that the behavior examined in this book can act as a type of internal balancing.

Furthermore, I argue that state intervention into foreign takeovers acts – more particularly – as a form of *non-military* internal balancing. Here, the strategy still involves strengthening military and/or economic capabilities, but also has two important non-military elements. First, the tool is clearly one of policy and action that occurs within the context of the economic realm. Second, non-military internal balancing involves *actions that seek to enhance a state's relative power position vis-à-vis another state, or states, without severing the greater meta-relationship at stake between those states*. The goal is still to balance a challenge or threat to power through non-military and internal means, but, unlike Brawley's concept of the economic component of internal balancing, *non-military internal balancing* is classified by this additional *objective* of state behavior, as well as by the *type of conduct* used to achieve those objectives.

It is also important here to clearly differentiate *non-military internal balancing* from *soft balancing*, as some important distinctions exist between these two concepts (see Figure 3). First and foremost, non-military internal balancing is a strategy that may be employed by both hegemonic *and* weaker powers, whereas soft balancing is usually defined as a policy tool that is only used *against* a hegemon (see Pape 2005; Paul 2005; Walt 2005). This is because much of the literature on soft balancing arose out of a desire to explain why states in the post-Cold War period had not formed a countervailing military coalition against US hegemonic power in the way many international relations theorists expected, as well as to categorize the non-military and non-traditional efforts of many states to constrain (or restrain) US unilateralism in the wake of 9/11.[26] These theorists believed "it was a mistake" for structural realists "to expect 'hard balancing' to check the power of the international system's strongest state" after the end of the Cold War because in a unipolar system, "countervailing power dynamics [would] first emerge more subtly in the form of 'soft balancing'" (Brooks & Wolforth 2005). Nye, however, has made a compelling case that while the world might be unipolar in the military realm (and this itself may be changing, with the rise of Russian and Chinese forces in recent years), it is clearly multipolar in the economic one (Nye 2002, 39). If one accepts this, then traditional methods of internal balancing are even more likely to occur in the economic realm than soft balancing theorists currently recognize, and, more importantly, a military hegemon may engage in the same type of non-military internal balancing behaviors as weaker states. This is clearly the case now, as the US seeks to preserve its relative power position through non-military internal balancing against rising powers, just as Italy or Russia might use similar techniques to enhance its own position.

Second, most definitions of soft balancing are based on the policy *tools* states employ, rather than on the policy *objectives* they seek (as with Brawley's concept of the "economic component" of internal balancing). Paul, for example, defines soft balancing as "tacit balancing short of formal alliances . . . often based on a limited arms buildup, ad hoc cooperative exercises, or collaboration in regional or international institutions" (in Paul et al. 2004, 3). This explains why theorists like Pape (2005) argue that such strategies could eventually lead to hard balancing in the future.

takeover and (2) the level of economic nationalism in the target company's home state, controlling for (3) the economic competition concerns raised by the potential takeover and (4) the presence of interest groups that oppose the acquisition of the target company and have access to power in the home state of that company.

The use of case studies allows for a detailed exploration of the various nuances and different dimensions of these variables. Toward this end, the following definitions were used in the investigation of the case studies, though narrower ones were necessary for the purposes of the statistical investigation of this hypothesis, as discussed in Chapter 2.

The presence of *geopolitical competition* between states will be determined qualitatively on the basis of three factors. The first will be the degree to which the *character of the political relationship* between the countries involved in the transaction is positive or negative. In other words, are the two countries formal military allies? If so, are they members of the same security community? Does the potential for strategic competition exist between those countries? Even if states *A* and *B*[31] are allies, is there a prevailing perception within state *A* that state *B* is a threat? The second factor is the degree of *resource dependency* between states *A* and *B*. In other words, what is the general level of state *A*'s dependence on trade to obtain basic resources such as oil, natural gas, and water? Furthermore (to the extent that information is available), what is the specific level of state *A*'s dependence on state *B* for these resources? The third factor is the differential in *relative power* between the two states involved in the transaction. Is the host state of the acquiring company a major power? Is the host state of the target company a major power? Is state *B* rising in relative economic power to state *A*? Is it increasing in military power?

The presence of economic nationalism in state *A* will be determined on the basis of three factors. The first will be the level of national pride that the populace of state *A* professes to have. The second will be the level of anti-globalization sentiment within the populace of state *A*. The third will be the level of domestic support for companies that are considered "national champions." In other words, is the target company often referred to in public parlance as a "national champion"? Does state *A* demonstrate support for national champions in other cases?

The remaining variables represent two possible alternative explanations of government intervention for which this study will need to control. The first is that the specific form of economic protectionism being examined here may be explained by the presence of interest groups pressing for governmental intervention. The case studies will, therefore, seek to identify the presence of individual pressure groups that were involved in the process, and determine their effectiveness in changing the policy of the government in question vis-à-vis the potential takeover.

I expect to find, however, that while interest groups may raise the awareness of state *A* regarding national security issues raised by state *B*'s involvement, or company *Z*'s behavior, this is unlikely to be the *cause* of intervention. In other words, *states will tend to formally intervene (either to block or alter a deal) only when national security issues are actually present, because of the reputational concerns involved.* If we look to the US, for example, it seems that while there is occasionally evidence of a pressure group raising the government's awareness of a deal, once that awareness is raised, pressure groups are largely kept out of the process.[32] As governmental decisions in this area seem to fly in the face of interest group pressure as often as they agree, the results of the hypothesis testing are expected to show little or no correlation to this variable.

The second alternative explanation for government intervention is that the merger or acquisition was blocked on the basis of competition concerns raised by either the host state of the target company, the host state of the acquiring company, or a relevant regional economic authority, such as the EU Commission. Each case will be examined to see if the relevant state (or regional) authority raised competition concerns. This variable is included in the case studies as a control variable, because of the possibility that government review of a given deal might be precluded by a decision that the takeover should be blocked on competition grounds.

It should be noted that other alternative independent variables were considered during the formative stages of the theory presented here. These ranged from additional domestic politics variables, such as the role of *electoral politics* and *racism* in government interventions, to the presence of *competing bidders* and some of the potential *ownership structures* of the acquirer involved in individual transactions. As my aim is to create as parsimonious a theory as possible on a complex subject, I ultimately decided not to include these variables, which in preliminary testing and research proved insignificant across the body of cases and whose inclusion, even as controls, did not appear to improve the explanatory power of the case studies or the fit of the statistical model. (For further discussion of these variables, and why they were not included in the final hypotheses tested, see Appendix A.)

If the sole purpose of this inquiry were to predict the likelihood of intervention in any one particular case, it would be necessary to formulate my argument differently. For instance, Grundman and Roncka have created a comprehensive "risk assessment matrix" to help determine the chances of a US government intervention into a given cross-border merger and acquisition (Grundman & Roncka 2006, 8). They suggest twenty possible variables that might affect a company's chance for survival of the government review process. To name but a few, these include general economic and political variables such as: whether or not the deal is "beneficial to current US customers"; the "viability of current US ownership"; the "amount of media coverage"; and the "lobbying strength of competing bidders" (Grundman & Roncka 2006, 8). Others are focused on how the deal affects the health of the defense industrial base, including: the benefit to the US in terms of the "net technology transfer"; the "requirement for interoperability with the US"; whether or not the "target firm's business" is "commercial" or "defense" related; and whether the target's "level of classification" is "unclassified" or one of "special access" (Grundman & Roncka 2006, 8). Additional variables focus on the national security concerns germane to this inquiry, namely: whether or not the "partner country is [a] US ally"; the degree of "foreign ownership," or "foreign government ownership" or "influence"; whether or not the host state of the acquiring company (or the company itself) has "ties to 'unfriendly' entities"; and the degree to which the "political climate" is "hostile" to the deal (Grundman & Roncka 2006, 8). Clearly, checking off every item on this extensive list of factors is vital for companies engaging in the US review process.

The goal of this book, however, is to offer a theory that is both parsimonious and generalizable, rather than one that is deeply US (or case) specific. Thus, while it is necessary to draw on the work of analysts like Grundman and Roncka, it is also important to ascertain whether or not some of the specific variables they examine might fit into broader categories, or drop out all together. It must be stressed again that the purpose here is to delineate *probabilistic tendencies toward state intervention across countries, cases, and time.* I recognize that states, and the bureaucrats within those states who deal with these issues on a daily basis, approach each foreign takeover as an individual case, and may not even be cognizant of the overarching tendencies in their behavior. I also recognize that many different actors – from bureaucrats and parliamentarians to heads of government – ultimately contribute to a state's final position or stance regarding intervention, and thus all relevant government actors are examined in each case studied in this book.[33] Yet, what is ultimately being investigated here is how the environment in which states must act, on the whole, structures the action of those states in each case, given the presence of the variables outlined in my hypothesis.

The Solution to the Puzzle

Such a probabilistic theory of intervention alone cannot explain the puzzle of why states utilize domestic barriers to foreign takeovers of companies in national security industries, even within security communities founded on economic liberalism and integration.

One way to solve the puzzle is to argue that not all forms of non-military internal balancing through government intervention into M&A on national security grounds can be considered equal. Rather, as in all forms of balancing and power competition, there are variations on the theme that can achieve the same desired effect. State *A* may thus be able to ensure the protection of its national security, and even preserve its long-term power objectives relative to state *B*, by simply altering or mitigating the effects of an M&A deal in some way. This is a more likely option among close allies, especially where some degree of integration of the defense industrial base is preferable, because it widens the scope of competition and enhances opportunities for the development of new technologies, while likely lowering prices. Thus, while governments *will* intervene in cross-border takeovers by allies, that intervention may be more likely to lead to a "changed" deal that protects national security, rather than a "blocked" deal.

Most instances in which deals are blocked will result from geostrategic concerns that arise between countries that are either not allied, or between whom there have arisen issues of trust despite the existence of an alliance relationship. It must be noted that there are examples of even the closest of military allies finding that companies within their state (which they may or may not be connected to) are having their proposed takeovers "effectively" or formally blocked. I argue that this can occur when the host state of the acquiring company, or the acquiring company itself, is viewed as significantly threatening. Some flexibility is required in determining what poses a significant enough threat to lead to a breakdown in trust between two countries; it could range from fears of espionage to a negative perception of the other state arising from actions in the realm of national security, despite the existence of a formal military alliance between those states. As one source within the legal community has pointed out: "there are allies, and there are allies" (Interview 2007). Which "friends" are the most trusted, and in what areas they are trusted, soon becomes quite clear to those looking at government intervention into cross-border M&A.

Forms of M&A Intervention as Non-Military Internal Balancing

I argue that government intervention into cross-border M&A can be considered to take three possible forms, which are classified here as *unbounded, bounded,* and *internal* intervention (Figure 4). Each of these forms is defined in this section, as are the conditions that may allow

Figure 4 Types of M&A intervention as a tool of non-military internal balancing

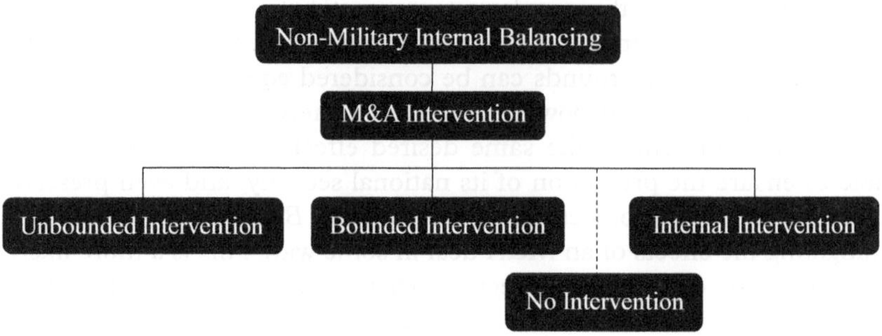

a deal to proceed with little or no intervention. However, in most of the sectors considered by states to be integral to national security, it is extremely rare for a deal not to face some level of mitigation or alteration before it is allowed to go through.

Unbounded Interventions

Unbounded interventions are those in which the intended result of government intervention is the formal, or effective, block of a cross-border merger or acquisition as a consequence of stated concerns regarding national security. A "formal block" occurs when the government, or one of its representative agencies, announces that a deal has been vetoed on national security grounds. An "effective block" occurs when the acquiring company withdraws or rescinds its proposed bid for the target company as a result of one or more of the following actions:

1. The government (and/or its agencies) voices such significant concerns or reservations regarding the deal before the formal review process begins that the acquiring company feels compelled to withdraw its bid in the face of "overwhelming opposition" that would be costly to overcome.
2. The part of the deal involving the target state or a third-party state involved in the transaction has, for all intents and purposes, been vetoed through either a forced divestiture of the facilities/subsidiaries in its country or through some other similar means.
3. A lengthy review process is undertaken, from which the company does not believe its bid will emerge successfully, either because
   a. The review process has extended in time to a point where it is proving too costly for the company to proceed,[34] or because
   b. The government has indicated to the company that it is unlikely to emerge from the process successfully.

Anonymous sources confirm that in the US, for example, CFIUS and/or its member organizations will indicate to a company whether or not it is likely to emerge successfully from a CFIUS review or investigation. This is one of the reasons why the number of withdrawals during the review/investigation process is exponentially higher than the number of vetoes.[35] It is possible that an effective block might not initially succeed in stopping the parties involved in a transaction from trying to conclude a particular deal. However, a state can still *formally* veto a deal if an effective block fails. If the companies involved fail to notify the relevant national authorities before a transaction is completed, many countries also maintain the right to review the takeover after completion, and to unwind it (in whole or in part) if it is deemed to pose a threat to national security.

"Unbounded" opposition is usually motivated by geopolitical concerns, and involves companies that state *A* is concerned with protecting on national security grounds. In the US, these will often be the most highly politicized cases, as interest groups may be able to prey more effectively on post-9/11 sensitivities to national security. It is important to note again, however, that while interest groups might raise the alarm about a deal, they will rarely affect its outcome. It is also possible that some of these cases will simultaneously raise *competition* concerns in other government agencies – agencies that might seek to veto the deal on those grounds instead. It is therefore important to control for such alternative explanations of intervention as the hypothesis is being tested.

Bounded Interventions

Bounded interventions are considered to be those that result in deals that the government has been able to alter in its favor through some means or another. Though the effect of interest groups and competition concerns will be controlled for, it is usually expected that "bounded" balancing will most often be motivated either purely by the national security concerns raised by the geopolitical competition context of the case and/or by economic nationalism surrounding companies in the sectors associated by the state with national security. It is also expected that in the latter case, states may closely identify "national security" with "economic security."

In the US, for instance, mitigation may take a couple of different broad forms. Graham and Marchick, for example, note that "if the DOD believes that the risks [to national security] it identifies can be managed, it may also negotiate mitigation measures with the transaction party," which "generally fall into four categories (in ascending order of restrictiveness)" (Graham & Marchick 2006, 71). These are "board resolution," "limited facility clearance," a "Special Security Agreement (SSA)"[36] or "Security Control Agreement (SCA),"[37] and a "voting trust agreement" or a "proxy trust agreement"[38] (Graham & Marchick 2006, 71–2).

One recent CFIUS decision, concerning the Alcatel/Lucent deal (examined in Chapter 5), also made it clear that *new* forms of mitigation may be emerging. In the review of that takeover, the US included an "evergreen" clause as part of the security agreement between itself and the companies involved, which basically means that the US government retains the right to force a reversal of the deal at any point in the future if it discovers that Alcatel has not lived up to its promises regarding measures to safeguard US national security.[39] Members of the legal community have indicated their belief that such a clause has never been used before in a US security agreement regarding a cross-border acquisition (Interview 2007). It should also be noted that forced divestitures, while not common in the US, do occur there and in other countries as a form of mitigation. (For further discussion of the different types of mitigation used in the US and abroad, see Chapter 5).

Though there are many different forms that mitigation may take, and these forms vary by country, the US forms of mitigation will be used as the standard, as they are the most highly institutionalized and the most is known about them. Similar phenomena will be looked for in the other countries in order to determine whether or not a deal has been altered. That being said, the actual existence of most of these forms of mitigation in an individual case is meant to be confidential, and their content is usually classified. Thus, we will only know of the existence of these forms of mitigation if they have been made public through a press release issued by one of the companies in question, or if news of their existence has been leaked to the press or other open-source intelligence outlets. This will obviously skew any statistical results away from the correlation that this study seeks to find between mitigation and the variables proposed here. This is an acceptable reality, however, as it means that we can largely assume that any correlation found is likely to be much stronger than the statistical results indicate.

One of the reasons why we are more likely to see bounded intervention among the allies of the Western security communities (meaning the transatlantic partnership and the EU) is because the process for the review of cross-border M&A is more highly institutionalized among the Western advanced industrial states. Indeed, it is most highly institutionalized in the US, which is why the US is where we should expect to see the lowest level of interest group influence on outcomes of the review process. The process is less institutionalized within Europe, but

Figure 5 Non-military internal balancing through M&A intervention

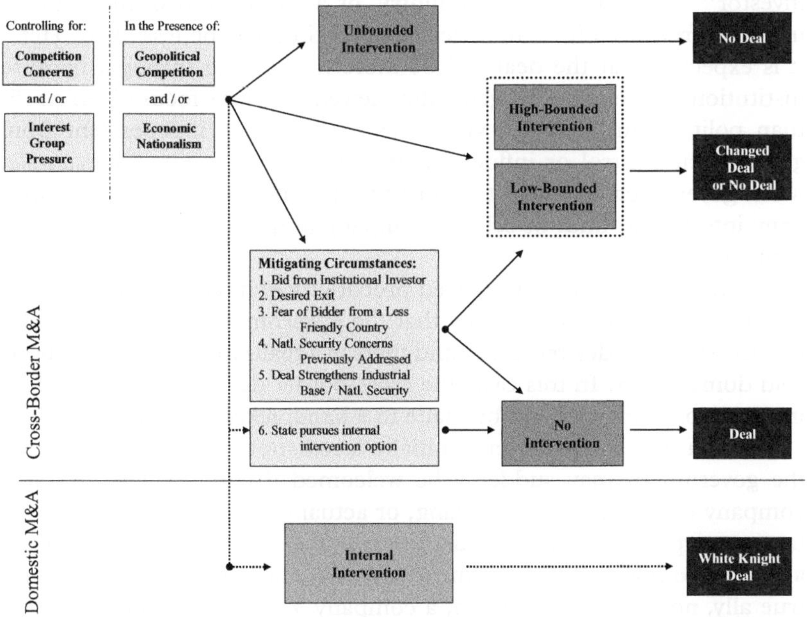

Note: This diagram illustrates the intervention options a state might pursue when it believes a specified cross-border M&A transaction could pose a risk to national security.

still much more advanced than it is in, say, Russia or China, where there is very little transparency about the review process. Higher levels of institutionalization allow allies to find alternative solutions to national security concerns, beyond simply prohibiting a deal or evidencing such overwhelming opposition that the proposed acquirer voluntarily withdraws from the process. Beyond the more closed natures of their markets and the risks they pose for investors, such differences in institutionalization may also contribute to the extremely low levels of cross-border deals in Russia and China for the sectors discussed in this book.

Non-Intervention

The following circumstances allow a proposed deal, that would normally be mitigated, to go through without any visible intervention (Figure 5). (Again, it must be noted that some of those deals that seem to go through without intervention may have actually been mitigated in some way by the host state of the target company, but, due to the classified nature of that mitigation, it may not be possible to tell.)

First, if the bid for the target company comes from an institutional investor[40] based in a foreign country, or a consortium of institutional investors from multiple countries, intervention may be less likely. Here, it is expected that the deal will be more likely to go through, because institutional investors are generally viewed as more focused on profit than politics, and are also viewed as being largely independent from government control or influence. Exceptions may occur: for example, when governments fear that an institutional investor will run the company into the ground, or sell the company in question to an unfriendly country.

Second, there may be a reduced probability of intervention if the deal in question involves a company that the government wishes to be sold, i.e., the sale is a "desired exit," and there is a realization that it cannot be sold domestically. In this case, the cross-border deal is less likely to face intervention if the sale can be made to a handpicked friendly country.

Third, a deal that may have initially faced strenuous opposition from the government may suddenly be welcomed if another, less-desirable company is rumored to be making, or actually announces, a bid for the target company. In other words, imagine that state *A* initially opposes a bid for company *X* by a company *Z* from state *B* (which is neither a true ally, nor an enemy). Then, a company *Y*, influenced or controlled directly by state *C* (with whom state *A* is on a less friendly footing), is known to be contemplating a bid for *X*. The fear of the bidder from state *C* may very well cause state *A* to withdraw its opposition to the initial bid by state *B* (see, e.g., the Arcelor/Mittal deal in Chapter 6).

Fourth, a deal may face little or no opposition if the national security concerns that would normally be raised have been previously addressed in some way. An example of this in the US would be if the company in question had already negotiated a special security agreement for the type of deal at hand, and the government did not feel that it needed to negotiate a new one. (As discussed in Chapter 6, BAE Systems serves as an excellent example of a company that has benefited from already having a comprehensive security agreement with the US government.)

Fifth, a deal may face little or no intervention if it is considered to be advantageous to the defense industrial base in some way, or is perceived to be advantageous to national security.[41] The deal might, for example, increase the competition among companies in the production of a good vital to national security (such as semiconductors), or provide the state in question with access to a resource that it desperately needs.

Finally, (un)bounded intervention into a particular proposed foreign takeover may prove unnecessary if the option of internal intervention is pursued, obviating the need for such direct intervention. This concept is explained in the following section, and again more fully in Chapter 6.

Internal Intervention

Internal intervention is an alternative for governments seeking to protect a specific company from a foreign takeover. It usually occurs when a company considered by the government to be vital to national security (and possibly to be a national champion) is deemed to be a vulnerable takeover target by the market. Rather than waiting for a bid that may potentially come from an unfriendly source, the government in question *proactively* seeks a domestic alternative. This may mean that the government actively encourages another domestic company to take over (or merge with) the vulnerable company, or that it encourages domestic investors, companies, or government-backed entities to purchase a large stake in the company in order to promote a high level of cross-shareholding that makes a foreign takeover more difficult.

Methodology

Three hypotheses emerge from this theory. The primary hypothesis tested here is that government use of domestic barriers to foreign takeovers of companies on national security grounds depends on (1) the geostrategic implications/concerns raised by the potential takeover and (2) the level of economic nationalism in the target company's home state, controlling for (3) the economic competition concerns raised by the potential takeover and (4) the presence of interest groups with access to power in the home state of the target company that oppose the foreign acquisition of that company (Figure 6).

The second hypothesis follows from this, namely: that the outcome of a proposed cross-border merger or acquisition will be strongly affected by the type of intervention employed by state *A* (Figure 7). In other words, it is expected that unbounded interventions will typically lead to a "no deal" outcome, i.e., where the proposed takeover is blocked or thwarted. Bounded intervention will be expected to result in a deal that

Figure 6 Hypothesis #1

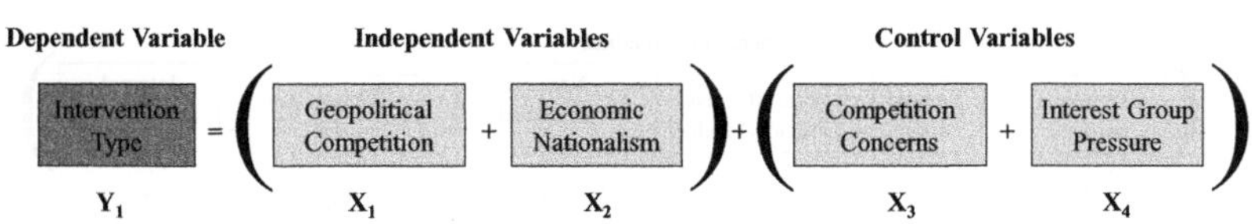

Figure 7 Hypothesis #2

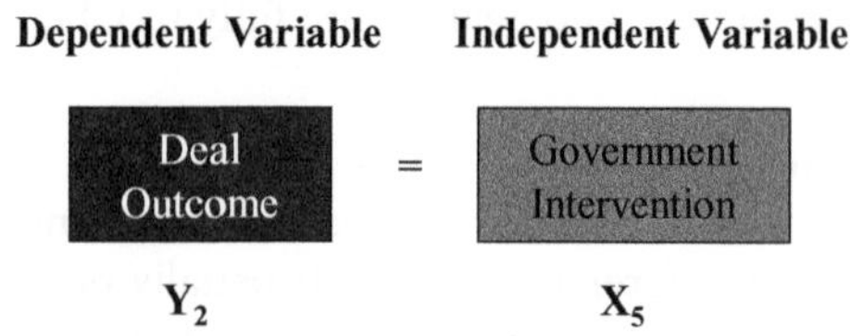

is changed or altered to the target state's advantage, and occasionally to lead to a "no deal" outcome. No intervention on the part of the target state's government, on the other hand, will typically mean that a deal will be more likely to go through unmitigated.

The third is a supporting hypothesis. Controlling for the presence of economic nationalism, geopolitical competition between states *A* and *B*, competition concerns, and interest group pressure, it is argued that a foreign takeover will be least likely to face visible intervention by state *A* when any of the following conditions are met: the presence of an institutional investor, the ability to achieve a desired exit, fear of a less-friendly bidder, the national security concerns have been previously addressed, the deal is advantageous for another reason, or internal intervention is pursued (Figure 8). While resource and space constraints prevent a full statistical testing of this hypothesis, it will be examined qualitatively in Chapter 6 (which discusses those cases where governments do not intervene in foreign takeovers), and may prove fertile ground as an avenue for future research.

The first and second hypotheses *will* be rigorously tested, both quantitatively and qualitatively. They will be looked at qualitatively through an examination of ten critical cases and three illustrative supporting cases across all four categories of: (1) *unbounded* intervention, (2) *bounded*

Figure 8 Hypothesis #3

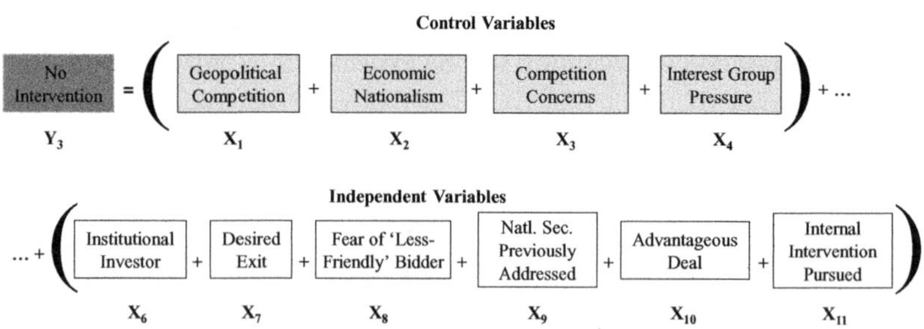

Figure 9 Critical cases

Critical Cases

Intervention Type	Acquiror	Country	Target	Country	Industry
Unbounded	CNOOC Ltd.	China†	Unocal Corporation	USA	Oil
Unbounded	Dubai Ports World	UAE	P&O Co.	UK	Infrastructure
Unbounded	PepsiCo Inc.	USA	Groupe Danone	France	Other
Unbounded	Check Point Software Technologies Ltd.	Israel	Sourcefire Inc.	USA	High-Tech
Unbounded	Macquarie Bank Ltd.	Australia	PCCW Ltd.	China	Telecom
Bounded	Alcatel SA	France	Lucent Technologies Inc.	USA	Telecom
Bounded	Lenovo Group Ltd.	China	IBM Corporation's PC Business	USA	High-Tech
Bounded	Finmeccanica* (Defense electronics div.)	Italy	BAE Systems plc	UK	Defense
Bounded	BAE Systems plc*	UK	United Defense Technologies	USA	Defense
None	Compagnie Générale de Géophysique (CGG)	France	Veritas DGC	USA	Oil & Gas (Seismic Data)
None	JP Morgan	USA	Troika Dialog	Russia	Investment Banking
Internal	Gaz de France SA	France	Suez SA	France	Electricity/ Gas/Water
Internal	Rusal*	Russia	Sual Group	Russia	Aluminum

† *The company is listed in Hong Kong.*
* *Abbreviated case included for illustrative purposes.*

intervention, (3) *no* intervention, and (4) *internal* intervention. These cases are listed in Figure 9.

The data will also be examined quantitatively through the use of categorical data analysis (CDA). Toward this end, a database was created of every cross-border M&A transaction in a set of sectors that states commonly associate with *national security* (Figure 10), which occurred in the six years following 9/11. There are a few reasons for adopting these parameters. First, the start date of the database was chosen because the security environment changed on September 11, 2001 in a manner sufficient to cause some states to be concerned with sectors of the economy that had previously not been identified with national security. The US, for example, now includes the "critical infrastructure" of the nation among such sectors. As the US is subject to the most foreign takeovers of any one country on a yearly basis (UNCTAD 2016b), it is important to limit the time frame in such a way that the cases can be considered comparable. The database ends in 2007, just before the beginning of the Great Recession, which had an immediate, negative, and severe impact on cross-border mergers and acquisitions activity globally.[42] The time period of the database thus offers a relatively stable

Figure 10 Commonly identified national security sectors (listed by ICB code)

Sector	Benchmark	Industries
Oil & Gas	0533, 0537	Oil & Gas Producers
	0573, 0577	Oil Equipment, Services & Distribution
Basic Resources (Industrial Metals)	1753	Aluminum
	1757	Steel
Industrials	2713	Aerospace
	2717	Defense
	2773	Marine Transportation
Telecommunications	6535	Fixed Line Telecommunications
	6537	Mobile Telecommunications
	6575	Satellite Telecommunications
Utilities	7535	Electricity
	7573	Gas Distribution
	7575	Multi-utilities
	7577	Water
Financials	8777	Investment Services (Stock Exchanges)
Technology	9537*	Software
	9572	Computer Hardware
	9576	Semiconductors
	9578	Telecommunications Equipment

* *Included only when the target company is known to retain a defense-related contract at the time of the transaction.*

Note: Sector, benchmark, and industry titles sourced from www.icbenchmark.com.

economic and security environment in which to test our hypotheses, though both of these environmental factors vary sufficiently during this period for the purposes of quantitative analysis.

Second, it is maintained here that the sectors listed in Figure 10 are those that are most often identified by nations with national security in the post-9/11 environment. As most states prefer to maintain a flexible approach to the scope of security, few choose to actually define or delineate those sectors they associate with national security, as already discussed. The economic sectors identified with national security have thus changed over time (Graham & Marchick 2006).[43] This list, therefore, does not attempt to be exhaustive, but seeks to represent those basic industries that both anonymous and written sources most commonly identify as posing security concerns vis-à-vis foreign takeovers today (see e.g., Graham & Marchick 2006; UNCTAD 2016b; Wehrlé

& Pohl 2016). Some sectors have been purposely left out because of the lack of identifiable (versus actual) intervention activity in recent years, making it difficult to accurately assess levels of government interference. Figure 10 identifies each sector used in this study according to its "Industry Classification Benchmark" (ICB; a coding system used to track M&A transactions).[44] Given the thousands of cross-border M&A transactions that took place globally during this time period, it was important for practical reasons to narrow the statistical inquiry down to those sectors where we are most likely to see intervention. The only case that arose in the course of my research that falls outside of these sectors for the time period of this database, the PepsiCo/Danone case, has been included in the critical case studies. The dynamics and findings should not change, however, if the hypotheses were to be tested against all sectors of the economy.

The cases are limited in scope to mid- to large-cap deals where the enterprise value of the target company is estimated to be over $500 million. This is largely because small-cap deals often do not receive the type of global press, analyst, sector, and database coverage necessary to ensure accurate coding of all of the variables involved in the creation of the database. Coverage for mid- to large-cap deals, however, is extremely good, allowing for comprehensive and accurate coding of these transactions.

Cases are also limited to those in which companies in the US, China, Russia, or one of the first fifteen members of the EU were the targets. This set of countries has been chosen for a number of reasons. First, and most importantly, they offer a wide range of approaches to government intervention in foreign takeovers. Second, they offer variance in that some of the first set are "advanced industrialized" societies, while China and Russia may be considered to be advanced *industrializing* powers. The inclusion of the latter is important to demonstrate that these hypotheses do not only hold for the most advanced Western industrial nations. At the same time, it does not make sense to include lesser developed nations among the cases examined here, because the developing world is subject to a separate set of dynamics within the process of globalization and interdependence that would make those cases less comparable. The advanced Western industrial states of Australia and Canada were not included in the dataset because their respective "national interest" and "net benefit" tests for FDI can make it difficult to disentangle when these states intervene on the grounds of national security from when they do so for more traditional economic protectionist reasons (e.g., to save jobs), making cases involving these countries less comparable.

Third, both the US and the EU belong to strong security communities, from within which foreign takeover bids are likely to originate. Furthermore, this activity flows in two directions within those security communities. US companies will take over EU companies, and vice versa, in the transatlantic security community. Within the community of the EU itself, foreign takeovers also occur without unidirectional flow. Russia and China provide an excellent contrast to this. Even though Russia may arguably maintain a series of strong alliances that resembles a security community, the nations within that community rarely engage in takeovers of Russian companies, but Russian companies will often seek acquisitions within its allied nations as well as without. The same is largely true for China.

Finally, it is important to include non-US states in the database because the theory of non-military internal balancing presented in this work is neither US-centric nor necessarily dependent on a unipolar environment. Cases involving the US do figure prominently in this study, as the US remains a hegemonic power, is the recipient of more cross-border M&A than any other country alone, accounts for roughly one-fifth of the value of cross-border M&A globally as a recipient target country (though this of course varies by year),[45] and has a highly institutionalized and sophisticated approach to addressing national security risks in the context of FDI. Yet, because the theory presented in this work is *not* US-centric or dependent upon a specific power context (uni-, bi-, or multipolar), it is also very important to examine not just those cases in which the US is being balanced *against*, but also those where the US might be balancing another state, or where balancing might be occurring against other states entirely, such as China, Russia, or France. In all, eighteen target countries are thus examined in the dataset, and five are covered in the critical case studies. Again, it would be an excellent area of further study to include a greater number of countries in the dataset, but this would have exponentially increased the number of cases studied beyond the point of feasibility for this work, without necessarily improving the picture or understanding sought herein.

For the purposes of this investigation, the parameter of cases was also narrowed to those examples of the purest form of cross-border M&A in order to allow for the clearest possible investigation of the relationship between the host state of the target company (state *A*) and the host state of the acquiring company (state *B*). In other words, cross-border cases were limited to those that took one of the forms represented in Figure 11.[46] In all, 209 cases were determined to fit these criteria, out of the 1,238 M&As that fit the other parameters of the database outlined earlier.

Figure 11 Cross-border case types[47]

State of Parent Company of Acquirer	State of Acquiring Company	State of Target Company	State of Vendor Company
(State *B*)	State *B*	State *A*	(State *A*)
State *B*	State *A*	State *A*	(State *A*)

Note: Certain values of the vendor and parent companies have been placed in parentheses to signify the fact that they may or may not necessarily be present in a given transaction.

Conclusion

The purpose of this book is to explain why states intervene in the foreign takeovers of companies on national security grounds, even within security communities founded on economic liberalism and integration. If the argument proposed in this chapter is accurate, the case studies and statistical findings should support the hypotheses presented here. For example, the cases are expected to support the conclusion that geostrategic concerns and economic nationalism are the best explanation for the use of such domestic barriers to foreign takeovers. I also expect to find that where geostrategic issues are the most important factor in determining whether or not domestic barriers are used, these barriers equate to a more intense form of non-military internal balancing of economic power, and the proposed takeover in question will usually be blocked. In this case, I expect to see that the home state of the target company perceives a large potential loss of relative power to the home state of the acquiring company should the bid go through, and that the relative cost of non-military internal balancing in this form is not perceived to be disruptive to the greater relationship between the two countries. I also expect to find that most of the cases that occur within the security community context, where geostrategic concerns are low, can be explained by the high presence of economic nationalism. Lastly, it is anticipated that the variables controlling for the alternative explanations (namely for concerns over competition and interest group presence) will be low in those cases where such domestic barriers are used. For example, one would anticipate a number of cases where those domestic interest groups that should be the most influential – i.e., economists, the market, and shareholders – are over-ruled or ignored by their own governments: governments who instead cast their actions in terms of national security. Such findings would support the idea that the primary hypothesis stated here may provide a more satisfactory explanation of the puzzle than could an interest group or other domestic politics explanation.

The phenomenon being studied here is of great significance, for a number of reasons. As discussed in the Introduction, the theory of non-military internal balancing presented in this book has implications for international relations theory, policymakers, and business alike. First and foremost, it provides an important addition to our understanding of power and how it is balanced in the international system – especially within the context of increased inter-state competition within the economic sphere. Second, explaining why states use intervention into foreign takeovers as a means of non-military internal balancing in the most unlikely of cases, i.e., within common security and liberal economic communities, will help deepen our understanding of the theoretical relationship between economic interdependence and levels of conflict within the international system. Third, if states repeatedly *overbalance* or miscalculate in their use of this particular tool of statecraft, there could be a potential impact on globalization.

Fourth, there are implications for international law, as efforts to create a multilateral treaty on foreign investment and foreign takeovers are continually thwarted by disagreement over how to handle sovereign intervention in key national security industries. Understanding when and why governments engage in such intervention would shed much light on this international legal process. Fifth, it is vital to understand the relationship between national security and the ownership of key industrial, technology, and energy companies, given state concern over resource competition and dependence on foreign oil. Sixth, the creation of domestic barriers by states to foreign takeovers is increasingly a matter of great concern for traders, investors, and economists, as well as for those states whose economies are affected by these actions. Lastly, in the process of trying to solve a previously unexplained empirical puzzle, it is hoped that this book will contribute to the literature on the political economy of international security.

NOTES

1 For a further discussion of these approaches, and a breakdown of how some states use multiple approaches, see Wehrlé & Pohl 2016, 10–16, and particularly Table 1 therein.

2 Like the second approach, states may use this type of review system to look at cross-border M&A in either a specific set of sectors or across the whole economy (Wehrlé & Pohl 2016, 11–16).

3 States do, however, agree that in relation to FDI, "essential security concerns are self-judging" (OECD 2009, 3).

4 For the full text, see the *Defense Production Act of 1950*, US Code 50, App. 2061 et seq.

5 These institutions include CFIUS, Section 721 of the 1950 DPA, and other associated foreign merger, acquisition, and takeover review processes in the US, as discussed in Chapter 3.

6 Graham and Marchick (2006) provide one of the most detailed investigations into the dynamics between national security and FDI through M&A in the US, and offer invaluable insights into this process.

7 Graham and Marchick note that concerns over espionage date back to the US' experience with Germany during World War I, when it was discovered that the Germans sought to control US companies (particularly in the vital chemicals sector) in order to gain technological, economic, and military advantages over the US (Graham & Marchick 2006, 2–18). They explain how "public and official attention to German investment intensified following a 1915 incident in which a German diplomat accidentally left a briefcase on New York's elevated transit. Materials found in the briefcase indicated that some German-controlled operations in the US were aimed at, or at least useful for, *enhancing German war capabilities, reducing Allied capabilities, or spying on the United States*" (Graham & Marchick 2006, 4, emphasis added). Significantly, this brought it home to US legislators "that at least some German investment in the US was meant to achieve sinister ends, even for cases in which the apparent purpose of the investment was purely for commercial gain" (Graham & Marchick 2006, 4).

8 Graham and Marchick claim that public concern over this issue, plus comprehensive confirmatory evidence provided to the government by the CIA and FBI, has affected the way Chinese takeovers are handled by CFIUS (Graham & Marchick 2006, 113).

9 As discussed in Chapter 3, *formal* vetoes are just one way in which a government can block a foreign takeover. Thus, the rarity of formal vetoes should not lull the reader into a belief that other forms of intervention taken to block a takeover are not a more common and frequent occurrence across the globe – for they are.

10 MAMCO did not hold classified government contracts, but was a contractor to Boeing, and held "some" technology "subject to US export controls" (Bush 1990). It was believed that the takeover was an effort by the Chinese government to obviate these control requirements and gain entrance into the industry in order to later pursue predatory practices (Interview 2006). CFIUS thus found "credible evidence that . . . the foreign interest exercising control [China] might take action that threatens to impair the national security" as a result of the deal, and President George H. W. Bush formally announced that the deal was prohibited on February 2, 1990 (Bush 1990).

11 In January 2006, Russia suspended natural gas supplies to the Ukraine in order to obtain that state's acceptance of higher gas prices (Nichol et al. 2006). Russia threatened to do so again in 2007, and then cut off supplies once more in January 2009 as the result of another price dispute. These disputes with the Ukraine often affected European supply more generally,

right itself. Alternatively, if state *B is* directly involved in the company pursuing the acquisition, then state *A*'s concerns will appear largely valid to the international community (even if the states involved are on the friendliest of terms). For, there would appear to have been some effort by state *B* to gain backdoor access to technology or resources in state *A*, over which state *A* did not desire to relinquish control.

31 For clarity, the host state of a target company is designated as "state *A*," the host state of the acquiring company as "state *B*" (or the sending state), the target company as "company *X*," and the acquiring company as "company *Z*."

32 An anonymous source has pointed out that once the US government is made aware of the security implications of a takeover it might have otherwise overlooked, the government then makes it quite clear to the interest groups involved that it will not be pressured into a decision in either direction. Interest groups are reminded of the institutionalized procedures for takeover reviews under US law, and that this process remains above their influence.

33 To reduce government action in any case to just the Head of State or Executive would be to ignore the complexity of the foreign policymaking process, and (in the US especially) would ignore the checks-and-balances systems that are part of this process for some governments. In each country, I examine the actions of the government as a whole, rather than just focusing on the Executive. In France, for example, I look at the actions of the Prime Minister, as well as the President, regulatory bodies, and parliament; for UK transactions, I examine the regulatory bodies as well as the Prime Minister, parliament, and royalty; and so forth. Though the Executive may take the final decision in many review processes, and often retains the right to make this decision regardless of the recommendations of the rest of its government, it would be wrong to assume that the opinion of the rest of the government is not, at times, taken into consideration. Moreover, in the US case, Congress can pass laws to try to "effectively" veto a transaction by lengthening the review process, or by denying funds for the review process, thereby participating in that process whether the Executive likes it or not (this may occur in other democracies as well). This is a good example of why it is important to study government response as a whole.

34 If the proposed bid were going to be financed through debt rather than (or in addition to) cash or stock, then the debt that had already been raised could be costly to maintain until the bidding process is over. There are also audience and opportunity costs associated with a lengthy bidding process, which the acquiring company may wish to avoid if they become too onerous.

35 There have only been four presidential vetoes of a transaction since 1988 (see Bush 1990; Obama 2012, 2016; US DOT 2008, 2009, 2013, 2017). Yet, from the beginning of CY 1988 to the end of CY 2007, there were 1,841 notifications of transactions voluntarily made to CFIUS, of which thirty-seven went to the "full investigation" stage and forty-seven were withdrawn from the process by potential acquirers, either during the initial review stage, before they could be taken to investigation, or during the investigation

phase, before the findings of the Committee could be sent to the President. After the passage of FINSA, the number and percentage of voluntary withdrawals increased, so that out of 782 total notifications made to CFIUS from 2008 to 2014, thirty-eight bids were withdrawn during the *pre*-investigation review, and a further forty-nine were withdrawn during the full investigation phase (author's calculations from US Department of Treasury data, compiled from: Graham & Marchick 2006, 57; US DOT 2008, 2013, 2016a). Yet, as Wallace and Armon (2005) point out, such numbers still "fail to capture CFIUS's real influence," as the threat of review and rejection often prevents companies from pursuing takeovers in the first place. This is important, because every deal that is visibly rejected by a country on national security grounds may indicate hundreds of others that were never even pursued due to potential opposition.

36 A special security agreement is an agreement that may be made between the US government and the foreign acquirer of a US company when that company has sensitive/classified facilities, programs, and/or contracts with the US government. It obliges the foreign acquirer to adhere to "all the requirements of any cleared firm in the NISP [National Industrial Security Program]" and would mean, for example, that while the "prerogatives of ownership [would be] retained by [the] foreign investor," the company's "decisions [would have to be] monitored by US Outside Directors," who would be required to have a certain level of security clearance with the US government (DSS 2008). For further information on special security agreements and the NISP, see the Defense Security Service's (DSS) website on industrial security: www.dss.mil/isp/index.html.

37 According to the DSS, a security control agreement can be used in those situations "when the cleared company is not effectively owned or controlled by a foreign entity and the foreign interest is entitled to representation on the company's governing board" (DSS 2016a).

38 According to DSS, both proxy agreements (PAs) and voting trust agreements (VTAs) can "be used when a cleared company is effectively owned or controlled by a foreign entity" (DSS 2016a). Both PAs and VTAs "are substantially identical arrangements whereby the voting rights of the foreign owned stock are vested in cleared US citizens approved by the Federal Government" (DSS 2016a). According to Reynolds (2004), a "foreign-influenced parent company will have limited authority over the company subject to the Proxy Agreement or Voting Trust and will be restricted even in its access to business information about the company." For further information on PAs, VTAs, SSAs, SCAs, and Board Resolutions, see DSS 2016a.

39 For a good discussion of this issue, see Smith 2006.

40 This term can have multiple definitions; the one used here is discussed further in Chapter 6.

41 For an excellent test of how this might be determined, see Moran 1993.

42 The database includes the population of deals (within the parameters discussed here) that were concluded (positively or negatively) between 9/11/2001 and 5/15/2007 (when initial access to some of the data sources ended, and coding began). More importantly, however, this time period was

2 The Numbers

Assessing the Motivations Behind State Intervention into Foreign Takeovers

Introduction

This chapter examines the theory of non-military internal balancing through the use of categorical data analysis (CDA). The specific type of CDA used here is the multinomial logit model (MNLM), which is highly valuable because it determines the probable likelihood that an individual outcome will occur (relative to a defined base outcome). Such models also illustrate how the change in one unit of a given independent variable x (such as economic nationalism) will result in an increased (or decreased) probability of a given outcome y (such as bounded intervention). This type of model is highly flexible and provides a comprehensive picture of the relationship between the individual independent variables and each of the considered outcomes.[1]

Toward this end, four MNLMs are used to evaluate the hypotheses on which this theory rests. MNLM I tests the primary hypothesis that government intervention into foreign takeovers chiefly depends on geopolitical and economic nationalist concerns in the host state of the target company (state A), controlling for the alternative explanations of economic competition concerns and interest group pressure. In order to explain the puzzle of why such intervention still occurs within security communities, MNLM II restricts the analysis of the primary hypothesis to those deals that take place within the security community context. MNLM III then tests the hypothesis against those cases that have occurred outside of such an environment. A comparison of all three models should thus provide deeper insight into the explanation behind the puzzle. Finally, MNLM IV evaluates the secondary hypothesis that the outcome of cross-border deals is clearly affected by government intervention on the part of state A.

The Variables

Each model uses the database of 209 cross-border M&A transactions specified in the previous chapter. In order to understand the dynamics

Figure 12 Variable sources

	Conceptual Variables	Proxy Variables	Type	Source
Explanatory Variables	*Geopolitical Competition*	Security Community	Dummy	CIA World Factbook 2001–07
		Relative Military Power	Scale	SIPRI Military Expenditure Database
		Resource Dependency	Scale	International Energy Agency (IEA): International Energy Balances of OECD Countries 2006 and International Energy Balances of Non-OECD Countries 2006
		Inward FDI	Scale	IMD World Competitiveness Yearbook (WCY) 2001–07
	Economic Nationalism	Nationalism	Scale	World Values Survey (WVS) 2001–04
		Pro-Globalization Sentiment	Scale	IMD WCY 2001–07
Controls	*Economic Competition*	Economic Competitiveness Index	Scale	IMD WCY 2001–07
	Interest Group Presence	Interest Group Position Index	Scale	IMD WCY 2001–07

behind these transactions and their outcomes, the database comprises variables that seek to approximate the concepts put forward in the primary hypothesis as closely as possible. It is important to understand, however, that cross-national and yearly data on these variables are not always available or complete. In certain instances, therefore, it has been necessary to use proxy variables to estimate the desired theoretical concept as closely as possible. Figure 12 explains how this was achieved.

Independent Variables

Geopolitical Competition

The concept of geostrategic concern was measured across four dimensions.

1. *Security Community:* A dummy variable was created to represent whether state *A* and state *B* were part of the same security community at the time of the deal in question. A security community is generally defined here in accordance with Adler and Barnett (1998), who argue that the formation of a common identity between states can eventually lead to the development of a norm of non-violence among those states. The result is a community in which participating states resolve their disputes with one another solely through the use of non-violent means, causing a sense of "we-ness" to develop (Adler & Barnett 1998, 7).[2] For the purposes of coding the database, security communities are more strictly defined as those in which this norm of non-violence has been demonstrated to be historically robust, whether through the existence of the highest level of mutual security agreements, such as the North Atlantic Treaty Organization (NATO), through the existence of treaties providing for the sharing of the highest levels of intelligence, such as the American, British, Canadian, Australian and New Zealand Multilateral Master Information Exchange Treaty (ABCANZ), or through membership in a highly integrated political and economic union, such as the EU. These communities are uncommon, and may not always take exactly the same form.
2. *Relative Military Power:* This variable roughly approximates the relative military power differential between both states involved in the transaction. Its purpose is to shed light on the extent to which state *A* might have felt threatened by state *B*, and to indicate when military power differentials might have played a role in causing a given state to seek alternative forms of balancing. It represents the ratio of the military expenditure of state *B* to that of state *A*.
3. *Resource Dependency:* This variable measures the general resource dependency of state *A*.[3] It was calculated in accordance with the method used by the International Energy Agency (IEA),[4] utilizing the yearly ratio of state *A*'s energy imports to its energy supply.
4. *Inward Foreign Direct Investments (IFDI):* This variable is meant to proxy the relative economic power position of state *A* by representing its IFDI. This measure is used because many political economists argue that it is the rapid or sudden increase in IFDI, rather than changes its net FDI position, that causes a state to react negatively – through protectionism or other means – to conspicuous foreign investment in its country (see e.g., Tyson 1992).

Economic Nationalism

1. *Nationalism:* A variable measuring the level of nationalism in state *A* has been included for two reasons. First, nationalism is often a strong

component of economic nationalism. The author strongly agrees with Helleiner and Pickel "that *economic* nationalism, like political or cultural nationalism, can be understood only if it is analyzed in the context of nation and nationalism in general, rather than as just another economic doctrine or ideology (the conventional economistic view)" (Helleiner & Pickel 2005, 12, emphasis in original). Second, comparable cross-national data on economic nationalism per se do not yet exist for many countries outside of the EU, and even within the EU, data are neither yearly nor complete. This variable, therefore, helps to round out an understanding of the theoretical concept of economic nationalism, while providing truly comparable data. Specifically, it represents the percentage of those survey respondents in a given state who said that they were "very proud" of their nationality (see WVS 2001–04).[5]

2. *Pro-Globalization Sentiment:* This represents the level of pro-globalization sentiment in state *A*. As high levels of anti-globalization feeling in a state are often associated with higher levels of economic nationalism, this variable acts as an excellent proxy for the latter concept. Furthermore, anti-globalization attitudes are often identified with the particular form of state action examined in this study, as state intervention into foreign takeovers is often associated with a desire to protect so-called "national champions." This variable thus represents the level to which respondents (business elites in state *A*) believed that "attitudes towards globalization [were] generally positive in [their] economy" (IMD 2007a, 6).[6]

Economic Competition

1. *Economic Competition I:* In the primary hypothesis, this variable is meant to control for the possibility that a foreign takeover may be blocked on competition, rather than national security, grounds. Data were not readily available for this variable on a case-by-case basis for all countries and within the limits of the author's resources. Moreover, it is a concept for which the creation of a single dummy variable would be inadequate to represent the complexities of the competition review process. The author thus leaves the detailed examination of this concept to the case study section, where it is more appropriately applied.
2. *Economic Competition II:* This variable seeks to control for a different theoretical concept, which also falls under the rubric of the word "competition." This is the extent to which state *A* is believed to be "competitive" in the international market as a state open to liberal economic business practices and foreign investment. Given the nature of the hypothesis, this variable offers another important statistical

Figure 13 Measures of economic competitiveness sourced from the IMD database

IMD Measures of Economic Competitiveness	
Relocation Threats of Production	"Relocation of production is not a threat to the future of your economy."
Relocation Threats of R&D Facilities	"Relocation of R&D facilities is not a threat to the future of your economy."
Policy Direction of the Government	"Policy direction of the government is consistent."
Legal and Regulatory Framework	"The legal and regulatory framework encourages the competitiveness of enterprises."
Adaptability of Government Policy	"Adaptability of government policy to changes in the economy is high."
Government Decisions	"Government decisions are effectively implemented."
Political Parties	"Political parties do understand today's economic challenges."
Transparency	"Transparency of government policy is satisfactory."
Public Service	"The public service is independent from political interference."
Bureaucracy	"Bureaucracy does not hinder business activity."
Bribing and Corruption	"Bribing and corruption do not exist in your economy."
Values of Society	"Values of society support competitiveness."

Note: Variable definitions sourced from IMD (2007a).

control to the data being examined here. Thus, an index of the perceived economic competitiveness of state *A* was made in order to create this variable. This index was formed by taking the average of twelve different measures of economic competitiveness provided by the IMD World Competitiveness Yearbook, which obtains these rankings by conducting a large-n survey of business elites worldwide on a yearly basis (see IMD 2007b, 2016). The IMD measures indexed for the purposes of this dataset are presented in Figure 13.

Interest Group Presence

1. *Interest Group Position Index:* The case study method is used in the following chapters to determine the presence of interest groups, as well as their effectiveness in blocking foreign takeovers, in each of the critical cases. Yet, such an investigation is not practical for the dataset,

Figure 14 Measures of interest group presence and position from the IMD database

IMD Measures of Interest Group Presence/Position in Society	
Labor Relations	"Labor relations are generally productive"
Shareholder's Rights	"Shareholder's Rights are sufficiently protected"
Interest Group Position Variable used in Dataset	
Interest Group Position Index	(Labor Relations + Shareholder's Rights)/2

Note: Variable definitions for Labor Relations and Shareholder's Rights sourced from IMD (2007a).

due to the lack of readily available and comparable data. The index variable used here, however, provides a useful approximation of the concept of interest group presence by measuring the general influence of relevant interest groups within state *A*. This was achieved by taking the average value of two separate measures of interest group position within these societies, again from the IMD World Competitiveness Yearbook (see IMD 2007b). These measures, outlined in Figure 14, arguably address two of the most critical interest groups involved in cross-border mergers and acquisitions. These are labor unions and shareholders: labor unions because they tend to be one of the more effective groups in voicing their opposition to takeovers and opposing them in costly ways, i.e., through strikes or negotiations, and shareholders for their ability to directly influence the outcome of public takeovers.

Specification of the Models and Expected Results

MNLM I

The first MNLM tests the primary hypothesis that state *A*'s intervention in the foreign takeovers of companies in its national security sectors will depend primarily on geopolitical competition and economic nationalism, controlling for economic competition and interest group presence. As previously specified, the independent variables tested as part of MNLM I are: security community, relative military power, resource dependency, nationalism, pro-globalization sentiment, economic competitiveness, inward FDI, and interest group position. The dependent variable in MNLM I represents the type of intervention, i.e., the form of non-military internal balancing, that state *A* chooses to utilize vis-à-vis the foreign takeover in question. This dependent variable, labeled *intervention type* (Y_1), has four value categories, as defined in Figure 15.

Figure 16 Values of dependent variable Y_2

		Deal Outcome (Y_2)
Conceptual Value	Numerical Value	Definition
Deal	0	Those cases in which the foreign takeover in question was allowed to occur apparently unaltered.
Changed Deal	1	Those cases in which the foreign takeover in question was (or will be) allowed to go through, but with alterations. This includes deals that were completed, announced, or pending.
No Deal	2	Those cases in which the foreign takeover in question was not allowed to take place. This category includes both those deals that were withdrawn after a formal announcement and those that were quashed at the stage of a verified market rumor.[9]

thus becomes the independent variable in this model. The dependent variable of MNLM IV, labeled *deal outcome* (Y_2), represents the actual outcome of the deal in question, and takes on the values noted in Figure 16. The results of MNLM IV are expected strongly to support the secondary hypothesis.

Results

The dataset of 209 cases utilized in MNLMs I–IV represents the population of cases of the type of cross-border deal specified in Chapter 1, rather than a random sample. It is interesting to note, therefore, that 158 of these cases (or 75.6%) occurred within the confines of a security community, and only 51 (or 24.4%) occurred outside of the bounds of such a relationship (see Figure 17). Thus, while those deals that crossed the borders of a security community are not rare, they do occur with a much lower frequency. These numbers are extremely important, because they illustrate the extent to which the globalization phenomenon is still largely confined to those states with close military and cultural ties. The notion of a truly globalized international economy, where global financiers can act unimpeded by the borders of such communities, has clearly not yet been realized.

This differential in "cross-border" deal type further evidences the fear that states experience when confronted by a potential takeover in a

Figure 17 Cross-border deal breakdown: the security community context 2001–07

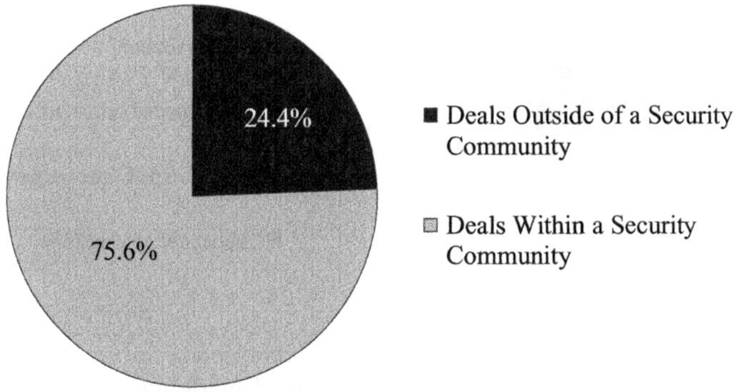

sensitive industry from a company that does not reside in an allied country. For these numbers do not include the large number of deals never even attempted by investment bankers, who shied away from economically viable acquisitions as a result of the domestic barriers created by governments to discourage takeovers originating from undesirable sources.

The fear of the acquisition of national champions or sensitive industrials by companies residing in non-allied countries has been intensified by recent concern over the rise of sovereign wealth funds (SWFs) and government investment corporations (GICs). Many political, economic, and market analysts view these funds as not only increasingly powerful within the world economy, but also as potential vehicles for the political goals of the states that control them. The "debate [is] grow[ing] among politicians and policymakers in the US and Europe who are increasingly fearful that some of these investors, including powerful [SWFs], are being driven by political motives, rather than purely financial ones" (Chung 2007a). At the same time, a report by the McKinsey Global Institute claims that these SWFs are among the "'power brokers' that are having an increasing impact on the world's capital markets," along with "Asian central banks, hedge funds, and private equity" (Chung 2007b).

Thus, it is not at all surprising that states may be more likely to intervene in a given deal in order to protect their national security interests when that deal does not take place within the environment of a well-developed security community. States may also be more concerned about those cases in which states *A* and *B* are engaged in intense geopolitical competition with one another, whether that competition is

Figure 19 *(cont.)*

	Y1: MNLM I (All Deals)	Y1: MNLM II (Deals Within Security Communities)	Y1: MNLM III (Deals Outside Security Communities)
Log pseudolikelihood =	−186.937	−125.355	−41.517
Number of Observations =	203	152	51
Wald chi^2 =	61.75	50.67	65.36
Prob > chi^2 =	0.000	0.000	0.000
McFadden's Pseudo R^2 =	0.107	0.157	0.292

by 7.9%. As nationalism increases from its minimum to maximum value, the chance of being in these categories increases by 16.7% and 11.7%, respectively. Figure 20 summarizes the effect of these variables on probability change in MNLM I (see Appendix B for the complete marginal effect tables).

Three indicators of geopolitical competition between states *A* and *B* – relative military power, resource dependency, and IFDI – approach significance in heightening the probability that state *A* will engage in high-bounded intervention. Increases in the IFDI and resource dependency of state *A* may therefore play a role in determining state behavior. Interestingly, so may a *decrease* in the relative power of state *B*. The results of MNLMs II and III, discussed in the next two sections, indicate

Figure 20 Probability change in MNLM I

Independent Variable		Average Change	0	1	2	3
Security Community	*0→1*	9.11%	16.67%	−6.86%	1.55%	−11.36%
Relative Military Power	*Min.→Max.*	23.13%	−26.75%	−6.65%	−12.86%	46.27%
	+/− s.d.	13.99%	19.06%	4.39%	−27.98%	4.54%
Resource Dependency	*Min.→Max.*	21.42%	−42.83%	13.47%	25.85%	25.85%
	+/− s.d.	7.49%	−14.98%	6.39%	6.90%	1.69%
Nationalism	*Min.→Max.*	14.20%	−19.70%	16.72%	11.67%	−8.69%
	+/− s.d.	9.71%	−14.17%	11.57%	7.85%	−5.24%
Pro-Globalization Sentiment	*Min.→Max.*	28.77%	41.45%	15.96%	0.14%	−57.54%
	+/− s.d.	5.48%	6.09%	4.88%	−1.67%	−9.29%
Economic Competitiveness	*Min.→Max.*	9.05%	−11.45%	−6.64%	0.15%	17.95%
	+/− s.d.	3.01%	−3.44%	−2.59%	0.25%	5.78%
Inward Foreign Direct Investment	*Min.→Max.*	11.71%	−5.47%	12.12%	−17.96%	11.31%
	+/− s.d.	6.64%	−4.51%	7.17%	−8.77%	6.11%
Interest Group Position	*Min.→Max.*	7.06%	1.50%	12.63%	−12.14%	−1.98%
	+/− s.d.	3.12%	−0.13%	6.23%	−5.11%	−0.99%

that, under certain conditions (namely within security communities), state *A* may feel more comfortable imposing domestic barriers to foreign takeovers when it is in an advantaged power position versus state *B*. Yet, it is also clear that when state *A* is in a position of weakness versus state *B*, state *A* will be more likely to engage in unbounded intervention.

Thus, when trying to understand what factors generally motivate states to engage in bounded forms of intervention, nationalism appears to be the most important determining factor. Geopolitical factors may also play a role, though their impact is less clearly defined.

In regard to unbounded intervention, MNLM I indicates that geopolitical competition and nationalism are the chief motivating factors in determining the behavior of state *A*. In fact, it can be said with 95% confidence that those deals occurring outside of the security community context were significantly more likely to result in state *A* engaging in unbounded intervention, rather than no intervention at all. For example, when states *A* and *B* are members of the same security community, the probability of state *A* engaging in unbounded intervention decreases by 11.4%. Furthermore, it can be said with 90% confidence that as the military power of state *B* increases relative to state *A*, state *A* is significantly more likely to employ a tool of unbounded intervention to block a foreign takeover. An increase of one standard deviation in the relative military power of state *B* increases the probability of state *A* using this category of intervention by 4.5%, but as relative military power moves from its minimum to maximum value, the probability of *A* engaging in unbounded intervention is raised to 46.3%. Together, these figures provide positive evidence that the motivations behind the behavior of state *A* will vary in accordance with its alliance relationship to state *B*.

In terms of economic nationalism, MNLM I also illustrates that a decrease in pro-globalization sentiment will significantly increase the likelihood of state *A* engaging in unbounded intervention, rather than no intervention at all. An increase of one standard deviation in the value of pro-globalization sentiment decreases the probability of unbounded intervention by 9.3%. In other words, as anti-globalization sentiment increases, the probability of unbounded intervention into foreign takeovers rises by 57.5%.

On the whole, therefore, elements of geopolitical competition and economic nationalism are found to play a clear role in motivating states to engage in this type of non-military internal balancing. Notably, none of the control variables registered as having a significant impact on *any* level of intervention that state *A* was likely to choose, indicating that the alternative explanations of interest groups and economic competition concerns cannot necessarily explain state behavior in this model.

Figure 21 Probability change in MNLM II

Independent Variable		Average Change	0	1	2	3
Relative Military	*Min.→Max.*	8.91%	17.82%	−2.88%	−14.80%	−0.14%
Power	*+/− s.d.*	19.69%	34.10%	5.09%	−39.39%	0.20%
Resource	*Min.→Max.*	25.55%	−49.14%	−1.95%	44.40%	6.70%
Dependency	*+/− s.d.*	6.25%	−12.51%	1.96%	9.45%	1.10%
Nationalism	*Min.→Max.*	10.23%	−19.20%	11.60%	8.86%	−1.26%
	+/− s.d.	7.00%	−13.27%	8.04%	5.97%	−0.73%
Pro-Globalization	*Min.→Max.*	36.01%	60.14%	11.74%	0.14%	−72.02%
Sentiment	*+/− s.d.*	2.77%	4.71%	0.83%	−2.80%	−2.74%
Economic	*Min.→Max.*	8.38%	10.33%	−12.76%	−4.01%	6.44%
Competitiveness	*+/− s.d.*	3.51%	5.72%	−5.35%	−1.68%	0.66%
Inward Foreign	*Min.→Max.*	10.05%	20.09%	−4.17%	−12.76%	−3.16%
Direct Investment	*+/− s.d.*	6.14%	12.28%	−2.90%	−7.87%	−1.51%
Interest Group	*Min.→Max.*	19.70%	−29.10%	39.36%	−10.30%	0.04%
Position	*+/− s.d.*	9.94%	−15.36%	19.86%	−4.52%	0.02%

MNLM II

Interestingly, none of the variables explored in MNLM II provide insight into why a state would be likely to pursue lower forms of bounded intervention. This phenomenon is likely to be explained by two factors. First, many cases of even low-bounded intervention are classified. Second, low-bounded interventions that occur within the confines of a security community are often not leaked to, or mentioned in, the press. This is because M&A activity is so frequent and regularized between these countries that the companies involved in these transactions see the government's actions as standard operating procedures, and may not feel the need to publicize them of their own accord.

It can be said at the 90% confidence level, however, that high-bounded interventions are significantly more likely to occur when the resource dependency of the target state is high and its levels of nationalism are high. This outcome suggests that elements of economic nationalism and geopolitical competition are again motivating factors for state behavior. The marginal effect of higher levels of resource dependency in state *A* resulting in high-bounded intervention is 13.2%, and a move from that variable's minimum to maximum value leads to a 44.4% increase in the probability of this form of non-military internal balancing. For nationalism, these numbers are 15.6% and 8.9%, respectively (see Figure 21; for the complete marginal effect tables, see Appendix B). Notably, as in MNLM I, relative military power is significant in the negative direction, indicating that stronger target states are likely to feel they have sufficient power to impose such mitigation measures on their allies.

Furthermore, it can be said with 99% confidence that unbounded intervention into foreign takeovers within security communities is significantly more probable than no intervention when there are lower levels of pro-globalization sentiment in the target state. (A one standard deviation change in this variable decreases the probability of state *A* engaging in this behavior by approximately 2.7%.) There is a great difference, however, in the value of this variable across countries.[10] Thus, it is important to note that as pro-globalization sentiment goes from its minimum to maximum value, the probability of state *A* engaging in unbounded intervention within a security community decreases by 72.0%. In other words, as anti-globalization sentiment increases (or economic nationalism rises) within state *A*, it is increasingly likely that state *A* will utilize a tool of unbounded intervention vis-à-vis a takeover deal emanating from within its own security community. This is in line with the expectation that economic nationalism will play a larger role within security communities, where geopolitical competition is clearly lower.

MNLM III

For the non-security cases examined in MNLM III, nationalism again proves to be a significant factor in increasing the likelihood that a state will engage in either low- or high-bounded intervention. For example, a one standard deviation increase in the value of this variable results in a 13.8% increase in the probability that state *A* will engage in low-bounded intervention, and a 9.7% increased probability that it will pursue high-bounded intervention (see Figure 22 and Appendix B). A change from the minimum to maximum value of the nationalism variable increases the chances of state *A* being in these categories by 33.6% and 10.9%, respectively. It is not surprising that this variable, which may be considered a precursor of economic nationalism, plays a role in state behavior here – especially when it is recalled that higher levels of nationalism in state *A* were associated with a significantly increased likelihood of high-bounded intervention in both MNLMs I and II, and of low-bounded intervention in MNLM I. Clearly, nationalism is associated with states that seek to protect their economic and national security interests by altering or mitigating cross-border deals in their favor.

Most significantly, however, MNLM III demonstrates the greater importance placed on the geopolitical relationship of states *A* and *B* in determining intervention type for non-security community cross-border

Figure 22 Probability change in MNLM III

Independent Variable		Average Change	0	1	2	3
Relative Military	*Min.→Max.*	47.13%	−77.53%	−5.14%	−11.59%	94.25%
Power	*+/− s.d.*	43.79%	62.44%	−23.07%	−64.52%	25.14%
Nationalism	*Min.→Max.*	22.80%	−45.59%	33.60%	10.90%	1.10%
	+/− s.d.	12.88%	−25.75%	13.80%	9.68%	2.27%
Pro-Globalization	*Min.→Max.*	18.70%	−37.39%	22.09%	9.27%	6.03%
Sentiment	*+/− s.d.*	8.18%	−16.35%	7.20%	5.47%	3.68%
Economic	*Min.→Max.*	6.81%	−12.96%	0.24%	−0.67%	13.39%
Competitiveness	*+/− s.d.*	3.03%	−5.76%	0.13%	−0.30%	5.93%
Inward Foreign	*Min.→Max.*	40.97%	−74.52%	45.62%	−7.41%	36.32%
Direct Investment	*+/− s.d.*	25.11%	−45.55%	16.58%	−4.67%	33.63%
Interest Group	*Min.→Max.*	49.82%	96.87%	−99.65%	1.12%	1.66%
Position	*+/− s.d.*	28.45%	56.89%	−37.68%	−4.87%	−14.34%

deals. To begin with, it can be said with 90% confidence that higher levels of IFDI in state *A* significantly increase the likelihood that state *A* will utilize low-bounded intervention in non-security community deals, rather than no intervention at all. Indeed, a one standard deviation increase in the level of IFDI in state *A* increases the probability that state *A* will use this tool of intervention by 16.6%. This, of course, illustrates the heightened importance that the relative economic power positions of states *A* and *B* play in determining even the lesser forms of intervention that occur outside of the security community context.

As with MNLM II, state *A* is significantly more likely to engage in high-bounded intervention as its military power relative to state *B* increases. Initially, this seems contradictory. As mentioned already, however, the likely explanation is that as state *A*'s power increases relative to state *B*, it may feel more comfortable engaging in a form of intervention that simply seeks to impose changes to a deal, rather than blocking it. In such a situation, state *A* may feel both that it is easier to impose conditions on a transaction that involves a weaker non-allied state and that more severe measures are unnecessary because of the less threatening nature of such a state.

In the category of unbounded intervention, we see that the theory is again borne out. If the acquirer's state (state *B*) has a higher level of military power relative to the target company's state (state *A*), then it can be said with 95% confidence that the target state's government is significantly more likely to intervene in this most strenuous of ways, rather than not at all. In fact, a one standard deviation increase in the military power of state *B* relative to state *A* increases the probability of

Figure 23 Cross-border deal breakdown by deal outcome 2001–07

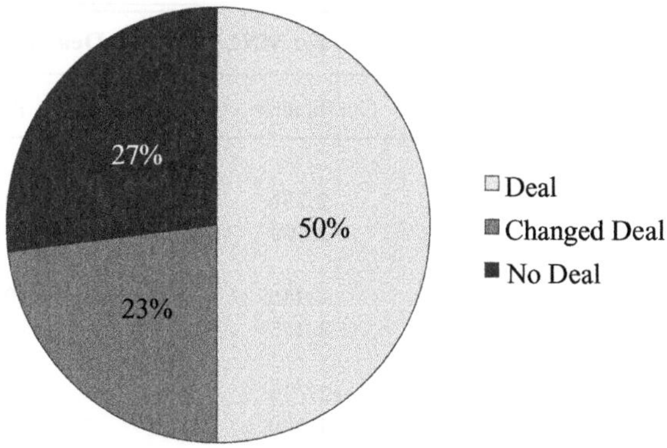

unbounded intervention on the part of state *A* by 25.1%. An increase from the minimum to the maximum value of the military power of state *B* relative to state *A* raises the probability of unbounded intervention on the part of state *A* by an astounding 94.3%.

Relative economic power proves to be an important element of geopolitical competition here as well, as higher levels of IFDI are shown to be significant in determining the probability of this course of action on the part of state *A*. A one standard deviation increase in the IFDI of state *A* raises the probability of unbounded intervention by 33.6%. On the whole, therefore, it does seem clear that outside of the security community context, foreign takeovers are more likely to be barred on the basis of geopolitical concerns.

MNLM IV

MNLM IV tests the effect of government intervention on the outcome of cross-border deals. Here, intervention type now acts as the independent variable, and the dependent variable is deal outcome, i.e., *deal*, *changed deal*, or *no deal*. Out of the 209 cases in the database, 104 deals went through with no apparent changes imposed by governments, 48 were mitigated in some way by the state in question, and 57 resulted in "no deal" (see Figure 23).

Significantly, the results of MNLM IV show clear evidence that the type of government intervention employed by state *A* will affect the outcome of the foreign takeover in question (see Figure 24). It may be said with 99.9% confidence that intervention type significantly affects the likely outcome of the dependent variable across each of its categories. Furthermore, as the level of government intervention increases, so do the chances that the deal will be barred or mitigated. For example, a

Figure 24 Multinomial logit model results: deal outcome 2001–07

	Y_2: MNLM IV (All Deals)	
Variable	Coefficient	*(S.E.)*
No Deal/Deal		
Intervention Type	2.736	(0.864)***
Constant	−1.600	(0.286)***
Changed Deal/Deal		
Intervention Type	2.945	(0.860)***
Constant	−2.033	(0.191)***
Deal/No Deal		
Intervention Type	−2.736	(0.864)***
Constant	1.600	(0.286)***
Log pseudolikelihood =	−162.227	
Number of Observations =	209	
Wald chi^2 =	12.660	
Prob > chi^2 =	0.009	
McFadden's Pseudo R^2 =	0.253	

† $p < 0.15$; * $p < 0.1$; ** $p < 0.05$; *** $p < 0.01$

one-unit increase in intervention type – i.e., an increase from no intervention to low-bounded intervention, or from high-bounded intervention to unbounded intervention – *decreases* the probability of an unaltered deal outcome by 111.3% (see Figure 25). Such a one-unit increase in the level of intervention, then, concurrently *increases* the probability of a "changed deal" outcome by 53.8% and raises the probability of a "no deal" outcome by 57.5%.

Figure 25 Probability change in MNLM IV

Independent Variable		Average Change	0	1	2
Intervention Type	*Min.→Max.*	49.97%	−74.96%	44.90%	30.06%
	+/− 1	74.20%	−111.31%	53.76%	57.54%
	+/− s.d.	72.92%	−109.38%	52.83%	56.55%

Conclusion

MNLMs I–III bear out the argument that intervention type is primarily motivated by geopolitical competition concerns and economic nationalism. Increased levels of nationalism (which can serve as a preliminary indicator of economic nationalism) in state *A* were associated with a significantly higher likelihood of low-bounded intervention in MNLMs I and III and of high-bounded intervention in all three models. This suggests that nationalism may motivate states to protect their interests by seeking to mitigate cross-border deals in their favor. Anti-globalization sentiment, which can be most clearly linked with economic nationalism per se, proved to be highly significant in increasing the probability of unbounded intervention generally, as seen in MNLM I, and even more significant within security communities, as shown in MNLM II. This finding indicates that economic nationalism may be a greater motivating factor for intervention than geopolitical concerns within security communities, where such strategic competition is by definition lower and occurs on a much longer time scale, and, consequently, where elements of economic power may be viewed as more important.

This idea is corroborated by the role played by geopolitical competition (approximated by relative military power) in MNLMs I–III. When state *A*'s military power was greater than that of state *B*, it was significantly more likely to engage in high-bounded intervention for deals both inside and outside of a security community, most likely because it felt more comfortable mitigating transactions in an advantageous power position. Yet, when the military power of state *A* was lower than that of state *B*, it was generally more likely to engage in unbounded intervention, as illustrated in MNLM I, and even more likely to do so outside of the security community context, as seen in MNLM III.

Other elements of geopolitical concern also play a vital role in determining intervention type. Higher levels of resource dependency in state *A* significantly increased the likelihood of high-bounded intervention within security communities. Furthermore, *outside* of security communities, inward FDI levels in state *A* played an important part in determining intervention type. For instance, when states *A* and *B* were not part of the same security community, IFDI was a highly significant factor in enhancing the probability that state *A* would engage in unbounded intervention to internally balance the relative economic power of state *B*.

It is also important to note that the models do not support the alternative explanations explored in the previous chapter, and controlled for in the primary hypothesis. The only instance in which a control variable neared statistical significance was in MNLM III, where interest group position was shown to approach significance in increasing the likelihood of low-bounded and unbounded interventions. As will become clear in the next chapter, however, interest groups are rarely able to affect a government's decision to intervene in a foreign takeover, even when they actively attempt to do so.

Finally, MNLM IV strongly supports the secondary hypothesis that intervention type significantly affects deal outcomes. As the level of government intervention increased, so did the chances that a deal would be mitigated or blocked. This is vital to the theory presented in this book, and is a result that could not have been as comprehensively tested through the case study method.

The numbers, therefore, clearly support the theory of non-military internal balancing. Moreover, the information provided in these models may offer a preliminary answer to the puzzle of why interventions occur within security communities. *Geopolitical competition and nationalism seem to motivate* ***bounded*** *forms of intervention, whatever the security community context. It is now clear, however, that in cases of* ***unbounded*** *intervention, economic nationalism may be a larger motivating factor within security communities, and geopolitical competition a larger motivating factor outside of that context.* The case studies that follow should provide additional evidence in support of the theory, and add further detail to these initial insights.

NOTES

1 The MNLM is also the most appropriate form of CDA for this investigation because the dependent variables of both the first and the second hypotheses are nominal. In other words, an ordered logit model would not be appropriate because neither of the dependent variables has an ordered set of outcomes, i.e., their outcome categories are not associated with a natural value hierarchy. This is because one cannot claim to know which type of government intervention or deal outcome is universally preferred. While the author recognizes the dangers of repeated intervention to the forward progress of globalization, not all cases of state intervention are necessarily or inherently bad, even if the general trend may be undesirable in the view of some analysts. For example, one might assume that "no intervention" is the "best" option within a liberal economic regime, but this may not necessarily be true given certain extreme geopolitical constraints and national security concerns. Furthermore, the cases being examined in this study go beyond the most entrenched areas of this regime. "Deal outcome" is also difficult to rank universally, for the preferred deal outcome of states and interest groups, and the best interests of the economy at large, may vary greatly from case to case. To truly understand the dynamics behind the puzzle and its hypothesized explanations, it is necessary to avoid placing value constraints on the categories of either dependent variable. The results of the tests can then be considered valid across more than one set of value systems, allowing for the creation of a more generalizable theory.

2 Adler and Barnett argue, after Deutsch, that there are two types of security communities: "amalgamated and pluralistic" (Adler & Barnett 1998, 5).

Amalgamated security communities are those in which states have become formally integrated or unionized under a "common government" rendering war between its previously autonomous parts unthinkable (Adler & Barnett 1998, 6). Pluralistic security communities, however, are not as formal, and rely more strongly on normative integration and common identity than on a formally structured relationship. According to Adler and Barnett, "states within a pluralistic security community possess a compatibility of core values derived from common institutions, and mutual responsiveness – a matter of mutual identity and loyalty, a sense of 'we-ness,' and are integrated to the point that they entertain 'dependable expectations of peaceful change'" (Adler & Barnett 1998, 7).

3 I would have preferred to analyze the resource dependency of state *A* on state *B* in each case. However, these data are not publicly available for all of the states examined in this database.

4 The resource dependency ratio calculation was provided courtesy of Riccardo Quercioli, Head, Non-OECD Countries Section, Energy Statistics Division of the IEA, on June 7, 2007.

5 These data were sourced from the 2001–04 World Values Survey. Question G006 in the survey asked respondents, "How proud are you of your nationality?" (WVS 2001–04). The value coded in the dataset represents the percentage of respondents who said they were "very proud" (WVS 2001–04).

6 In the IMD World Competitiveness Yearbook, this is variable 3.5.01: "Attitudes toward globalization," for which business elites in the sixty-one countries surveyed are asked whether "Attitudes toward globalization are generally positive in your society" (IMD 2007a). Scores are reported on a scale of 1 to 6 (with 1 being the least positive), which the IMD then recalibrates to a scale of 1 to 10 (IMD 2016).

7 For example, the following table provides the output of the Hausman IIA test for model I.

Hausman tests of IIA assumption (N=203)

Ho: Odds (Outcome-J vs. Outcome-K) are independent of other alternatives.

Omitted	Chi2	Df	P > chi2	Evidence
1	2.143	18	1.000	For Ho
2	0.313	18	1.000	For Ho
3	0.041	18	1.000	For Ho

8 There are only six cases in the database in which security community = 0 and the dependent variable = 3. In other words, there are only six cases of unbounded intervention outside of the security community context. It should be remembered that this is the population of such cases. However, the resource dependency of the states involved in each of these cases is quite close. Though resource dependency is a scale variable that ranges in value from 0.14 to 1.82, in four out of the six cases state *A* has a resource

dependency between 0.5 and 0.6. For detailed descriptive statistics of each of these different scenarios, see Appendix C.

9 It is extremely important to include those cases of market rumor that can be verified by both the Zephyr database and market intelligence. This is because they usually indicate instances in which companies or banks (whether purposefully or not) indicated interest in a merger or acquisition, only to find that there were difficulties facing its execution. It would be sheer folly not to include the most credible of these "rumors," because they are almost always true, and because governments and states do react to them. As will be seen, the PepsiCo/Danone case was technically a rumor, but the French government reacted to it vehemently, and with formal legislation.

10 See Appendix D for descriptive statistics of the variables used in the dataset.

3 Unbounded Intervention

The State and the Blocked Deal

Introduction

States may employ a variety of balancing strategies in response to a perceived threat to their relative position of power within the international system. This book argues that when the perceived threat to power is caused by the potential foreign takeover of a company in one of its national security industries, a state is likely to react using one of three non-military internal balancing strategies: *unbounded*, *bounded*, or *internal* intervention. The next four chapters provide a deeper explanation and examination of each of these forms of balancing, and qualitatively assess the theory through a series of cases studies.

The purpose of this chapter is to further specify the conditions under which a state might choose to engage in unbounded intervention. Toward this end, four critical cases are examined: (1) the rumored attempt of the US company PepsiCo to acquire the French food company Danone, (2) the attempted takeover of the US oil company Unocal by the Chinese company CNOOC, (3) the attempted takeover of the US software company Sourcefire by the Israeli company Check Point, and (4) the attempted takeover of the Chinese telecommunications company PCCW by Australia's Macquarie Group (Figure 26).

As with other forms of balancing, states face costs for both over- and underreactions to these potential changes in relative power,[1] even though they may not be fully cognizant that their proactive use of these tools could be categorized as "balancing." The next chapter will therefore focus on an instance of unbounded balancing by the US, which could also be considered an instance of "overbalancing," and thus an "outlier" case: namely, the US intervention into the takeover of P&O in Britain by DPW of the UAE (Figure 26).

Figure 26 Unbounded intervention: critical cases examined in Chapters 3 and 4

	Case 1	Case 2	Case 3	Case 4	Case 5
Acquirer Name	PepsiCo	CNOOC	Check Point Software	Macquarie	Dubai Ports World*
Acquirer Country	USA	China**	Israel	Australia	UAE
Target Name	Groupe Danone	Unocal Corporation	Sourcefire Inc.	PCCW	P&O
Target Country	France	USA	USA	China**	UK
Target Industry	Food & Beverage	Oil & Gas Producers	Software	Fixed Line Telecom	Marine Infrastructure
Deal Type	Acquisition	Acquisition	Acquisition	Acquisition	Acquisition
Deal Value (in $US thousands)	N/A	18,209,400	225,000	7,300,000	5,701,062 (Bid 1) 6,780,131 (Bid 2)
Deal Status	Rumor/ Informally Withdrawn	Withdrawn	Withdrawn	Rumor/ Informally Withdrawn	Bid 1 – Withdrawn Bid 2 – Completed
First Deal Date	February 12, 2004	March 3, 2005	October 7, 2005	June 20, 2006	October 31, 2005

* *The acquisition vehicle used for this deal was named Thunder FZE.*
** *The company is headquartered in Hong Kong.*

Defining Unbounded Intervention

Definition

The term "unbounded intervention" is used here to represent the most aggressive form of government interference into a cross-border merger or acquisition. Such intervention is defined by the *intention of government actors who, on the whole, seek to prevent a potential foreign takeover bid from reaching a successful conclusion.* Yet, government actors do not always act coherently, and on rare occasions the government itself may even be divided as to the best course of action. When trying to identify cases of unbounded intervention, therefore, it will be necessary to demonstrate that either a critical mass of government actors[2] seek to block the bid, or that crucial government players – i.e., those with veto power, or particular sway in the decision making process – wish to do so. In such cases, the opposition is often unable to prevent the unbounded intervention strategy from being carried out. In fact, the results from the secondary hypothesis indicate that intervention type and deal outcome are closely linked, and unbounded intervention strategies will usually result in the successful prevention of a foreign takeover.

Purpose and Motivation

The stated purpose of unbounded intervention will almost always be the protection of national security. Indeed, the right of states to intervene is based on the protection of companies whose loss or foreign control would pose an *immediate* threat to national security. It is important to note, though, that actors involved in this type of intervention may stretch the notion of "national security" beyond its traditionally defined bounds (see Introduction and Chapter 1). This is because government actors concerned with the relative power position of their state may have longer time horizons with respect to what they consider to be a "threat." They may also have more elastic definitions as to which companies should be placed under the rubric of the national security umbrella, especially if those companies are national champions considered vital to the state's economic power.

The first hypothesis tested here claims that government intervention into foreign takeovers is primarily motivated by either geopolitical concerns or economic nationalism. As the findings in Chapter 2 indicate, it should be expected that the respective prominence of each of these factors will vary in accordance with the systemic relationship between states *A* and *B*. In other words, the case studies should support the general idea that when states *A* and *B* are members of the same security community, economic nationalism will usually be the primary motivation behind unbounded intervention. Similarly, when states *A* and *B* are not members of the same security community, the case studies should show that geopolitical concerns play a greater role in unbounded intervention. In either situation, however, it is expected that state *A* is concerned with its power position relative to state *B*, and thus seeks to balance the potential increase in state *B*'s relative power that could result from a particular foreign takeover by preventing that transaction from occurring in the first place.

It is also important to recognize two other possible reasons that state *A* might employ a strategy of unbounded intervention, reasons that will be controlled for in the case studies. These are: the presence of interest groups who desire a negative deal outcome, and the presence of competition concerns on the part of a relevant economic authority. It is necessary to note, however, that while interest groups may raise alarms about a deal that could affect national security, it is expected that they will rarely affect the outcome of that deal, or the strategy with which state *A* chooses to handle it. It is also important to realize that in some cases a state may raise economic competition concerns at the same time that it flags national security issues, or that a relevant government agency may seek to veto a deal solely on competition grounds.

Means and Manner

Unbounded intervention involves the efforts of government actors to block a foreign takeover through formal, or "effective," means. A "formal block" is when a government, or a representative government agency, officially vetoes the deal on national security grounds. An "effective block" is when the acquiring company is convinced or pressured to withdraw/rescind its proposed bid for the target company through one of the following means:

1. The government and/or its agencies voice such significant concerns or reservations regarding the deal before the formal review process begins in the relevant regulatory agencies of state *A* that the acquiring company feels compelled to withdraw the bid in the face of overwhelming opposition, which it deems too costly to overcome.
2. The government forces the divestiture of facilities or subsidiaries involved in the transaction that reside in its country. This particular strategy may also be used by a third-party state involved in the transaction to block the sale of assets within its territory.
3. The government of state *A* institutes a lengthy review process in a relevant regulatory body from which the acquiring company does not believe its bid will successfully emerge. The company's cause for concern will likely be either that the review process has extended in time to a point where it is proving too costly for the company to proceed[3] or that the government of state *A* has indicated to the company that it is unlikely to emerge from the review process without triggering a formal veto.[4]

While it is possible that efforts to "effectively" block a specified transaction may not initially succeed, this is rare (for reasons outlined earlier and later), and a state can still decide to formally veto the deal in order to prevent it from being completed. In cases where the companies involved fail to notify the relevant national authorities before a transaction is completed, many countries also maintain the right to review a takeover after completion and to unwind it, in whole or in part, if it is deemed to pose a threat to national security.

Outcomes and Results

Unbounded intervention will usually lead the acquiring company to withdraw its bid, whether or not it has been formally announced. There are a couple of reasons behind this. First, even if there is a chance that state *A*'s position on the bid might be reversed, a company facing extreme government opposition will usually not have the time, money, or patience to surmount it. Second, a company is unlikely to desire any further negative publicity of the type that can result from such government opposition. Third, a company whose bid has been formally vetoed on national security grounds is often then branded as a "security risk" in future deals. Companies faced with severe government opposition will thus often withdraw from the bidding process before a formal veto can occur. Finally, if state *A*'s unbounded intervention strategy *does* result in a formal veto, it may not be possible for the company to reverse that decision through any means.[5]

Of even greater interest than the immediate deal outcome, however, is the impact that unbounded intervention is likely to have on the relationship between states *A* and *B*. At best, such intervention is viewed as a legitimate action by a state to protect a company from foreign control because of an immediate national security concern: an action considered a right of states, and which many states view as "fair play" even in the context of a free-market environment. Indeed, the relationship between the states involved usually remains largely unchanged, because such intervention is usually soon forgotten by states for the simple reason that M&A is associated with the private, rather than the public, realm. At worst, intervention may irritate another state into tit-for-tat behavior, causing it to respond similarly in the future.

State intervention into foreign takeovers may thus be considered a form of *non-military* internal balancing because, in addition to using non-military means, it rarely causes a *complete* disruption in the relationship between states *A* and *B*. Of all the forms of intervention discussed here, however, unbounded intervention is undoubtedly the most complete. Thus, if it is used improperly, i.e., if it becomes an instance of unnecessary balancing or overbalancing, it is the type of intervention most likely to produce a *temporary* antagonism between states *A* and *B*. Yet, even in such a case, as the DPW study in Chapter 4 shows, the internal and non-military nature of this strategy makes it unlikely to lead to a permanent disruption in the relationship between the states involved, such as the cutting of military or diplomatic ties.

Case Selection

The ten cases examined in this and the next three chapters are critical to understanding government intervention into cross-border M&A, as they have informed the way market analysts understand domestic barriers to foreign takeovers. These cases also represent a diverse population of states associated with both the target and the acquiring companies,[6] and each had a significant impact on the international merger market. A brief overview of why each of the cases included in this chapter is considered critical to our understanding of unbounded intervention as a form of non-military internal balancing is provided below.

The PepsiCo/Danone case is key to our knowledge of unbounded intervention, for two reasons. First, it is one of the rare instances in which unbounded intervention has occurred within the security community context, and can thus help us to understand how and why this might occur. As discussed in Chapter 5, bounded intervention tends to be viewed as a more satisfactory and useful tool of non-military internal balancing between closely allied states. It should be remembered that the database exhibited only eleven cases of unbounded intervention out of 158 cases of intervention within security communities as a whole. In almost every case, economic nationalism was the primary, and geopolitical competition the secondary, motivation for unbounded intervention.[7]

Second, though PepsiCo/Danone is clearly a case of unbounded intervention in terms of motivation and form, it has one unique feature that prevented its inclusion in the statistical database, and which makes it critical to examine qualitatively if we are to further our understanding of such balancing. For, though it is one of the more often cited examples of government intervention into foreign takeovers, the target company (Danone) hails from an industry that many states would not normally associate with "national security:" the yogurt industry. Food and agriculture were not included in the sectors covered in the statistical database, because there is little consensus over whether or not it should be considered a national security sector. Some countries do consider the agriculture and food sector to be critical infrastructure, and since the Danone case there have been several reviews of foreign investments into the takeovers of large agribusinesses for possible national security risks, though thus far no notable vetoes have been recorded in this sector on such grounds.[8] It was important to examine this case, however, because the French government adamantly argued that Danone's safety from foreign acquisition was a matter of national security, and promptly changed French FDI law to reflect its concerns. This case thus provides an excellent opportunity to examine the dynamics that result when such an unusual categorization is made.

Conversely, CNOOC/Unocal is a critically important instance of unbounded intervention *outside* of the security community context. This case provides a detailed example of a company, owned by the government of a rising power that has a stated policy of using M&A to gain control of vital resources, finding its attempted acquisition blocked primarily because the target company's state feared the geopolitical and national security implications of such a deal. It is also of interest because of its historical context, as unbounded intervention occurred with relative infrequency in the US before this case. The US had not previously sought to block British Petroleum's (BP's) purchase of Amoco in 1988 or Petróleos de Venezuela's (PDVSA's) purchase of CITGO in 1990, both of which were arguably of much greater economic importance. Thus, it is vital to understand why unbounded intervention was considered warranted in this particular instance.

The Check Point/Sourcefire case was included because it is a rare example of unbounded intervention within a security community that was primarily motivated by national security and geopolitical concerns, rather than by economic nationalism. Despite the extremely close relationship of the US and Israel (the countries involved), tensions existed over Israel's ability and willingness to adhere to US export control laws for technology in the sector in question.[9]

Finally, the Macquarie/PCCW case has been included as an example of unbounded intervention outside of the security community context, and is considered critical because it widens the geographical test of the hypotheses. In this case, the target company is Chinese, and the acquirer Australian. Certainly, it is the only example within the database of unbounded intervention being undertaken by either Russia or China within the time frame examined. This is primarily because these are what might be termed "capitalist autocracies," where the foreign acquisition of 100% of a company within the industries examined here is highly regulated and, if it is allowed at all, must often be undertaken with the cooperation of the government. Such strict regulations regarding this type of foreign investment mean that unbounded interventions are rarely necessary in these countries, because if the government doesn't indicate in advance that it wants a deal to happen in some form, companies are usually unwilling to risk the capital to pursue it. Indeed, the high degree of regulation within many industries in China and Russia already indicates a tendency toward internal balancing used to strengthen their strategic sectors relative to those of other states. The number of foreign acquisitions in these countries is also generally lower than in the EU or US, due to the uncertainties of their investment climate. It is still possible, however, for a foreign company to attempt a takeover in these "strategic industries," and it is important to understand how these governments will react, and what will motivate them.

Case 1: PepsiCo/Danone

The Story

On July 6, 2005, a rumor surfaced in the international equities market that the US beverage company PepsiCo was in the process of formulating a bid to acquire 100% of the French yogurt and water company Groupe Danone.[10] Talk of the rumor persisted throughout the summer despite Danone's insistence that they had not been approached regarding a possible takeover (Perri & Deen 2005), largely because of Pepsi's refusal to comment on the rumor either positively or negatively (Matthews 2005; Mercer 2005). International newspapers and wires kept the story going, naming inside sources who believed that the bid was real, or who claimed to know which banks were helping Pepsi to prepare its offer (see e.g., Brothers & Robbins 2005; Gay 2005; Schuman 2005). Meanwhile, "the French media reported rumors that [the takeover] was imminent – and even, wrongly, that the American group had already bought a 3% stake" (Gow 2005).

What followed was an almost immediate reaction on the part of the French government, which sought (with gusto) to prevent the takeover entirely. By July 19, a lower-level government official made the "concern" of the French government over such a "culturally awkward" deal known to the press (Zephyr 2005a). In the next two days, the French Prime Minister Dominique de Villepin publicly proclaimed Danone's status as a national champion, naming it one of the "jewels of [French] industry" (de Beaupuy & Vandore 2005) and claiming that the French government would protect its independent French status in order to "defend France's interests" (Vandore 2005a). At the same time, French President Jacques Chirac announced his concern over the possible deal, stating that the French government was "particularly vigilant and mobilized" to intervene if necessary, and stressing the role of the government in maintaining "the industrial competitiveness and . . . strength of its companies" (de Beaupuy & Vandore 2005).

It was not until July 25 that PepsiCo reported to the French market regulatory body (the Autorité des Marchés Financiers, or AMF) that it was not preparing a takeover bid for Danone "right now" (Perri & Deen 2005). This "denial" of the rumor, however, still clearly left open the possibility that Pepsi might make such a bid in the future. The result was that less than twenty days after the initial rumor surfaced, and without any formal bid having been announced by Pepsi, the French government signaled its intent to prevent a hostile foreign takeover of Danone through a series of actions that formed a coherent strategy of unbounded intervention.

First, the AMF became involved toward the end of the month by announcing that it would begin an investigation into the trading of Groupe Danone's shares (Vandore 2005b). This was because Danone's share prices had been fluctuating greatly, rising on reports of a takeover, and then falling sharply on July 25, when Pepsi denied an imminent bid (Gow 2005). The investigation was made at the behest of "the minority shareholders' defense group, ADAM," which "demanded a full-scale investigation to determine whether the rumors about Danone were the result of market manipulation and insider trading" (Gow 2005). The AMF echoed the widespread frustration that Pepsi's failure to clearly refute the rumor had a great effect on share price (AMF 2005). This investigation eventually had a great impact on FDI in France, as it prompted the so-called "Danone Amendment" to be passed into law in March 2006 (see Merger Market 2006). The new law "ultimately . . . aims to deter takeover bids that are either hostile or motivated by speculation, by [allowing the target company to] increase[e it]s capital through the issuing of stock purchase warrants" (EIRO 2006). Ironically, this amendment was attached to a law meant to provide for the domestic implementation of the European Takeover Directive, one of the goals of which was to reduce barriers to cross-border M&A within the EU (see European Parliament 2004).

Second, and more importantly, Chirac and Villepin announced in a government meeting on July 27, 2005 that France "must strengthen the measures to protect [its] key companies," and suggested that French law would need to be changed in order to protect its companies from such "hostile"[11] foreign takeovers (Vandore 2005b). Less than a year earlier, on December 9, 2004, the French National Assembly had already passed a "Reform Law" intended "to ensure that all foreign investments involving public order, public security, or interests of national defense were subject to official review" by the French government (Cafritz 2014, 1).[12] By August 31, 2005, amidst the PepsiCo/Danone rumors, French Finance Minister Thierry Breton announced that eleven "sensitive" sectors would be considered strategic and, therefore, that the government would be changing the law to protect companies in these industries from unwanted foreign takeovers in the future (de Beaupuy 2005). On December 31, 2005, the French government put this plan into action, passing an *anti-takeover decree* that gives it "the right to veto or impose conditions on foreign takeovers of domestic companies operating in as many as 11 sensitive industries" (Buck et al. 2006b). These include the industries dealing with:

> private security, if used, for example in nuclear or other secure installations; research or production of products that can be used in terrorist or chemical

> attacks; bugging equipment; information security; companies providing information technology security to government; dual-use technology for civilian or military applications; cryptology; companies entrusted with defense secrets; arms; certain sub-contractors to the defense ministry; and casinos, where the government is concerned about money laundering. (Buck et al. 2006b)

The French government notably broadened the scope of its strategic sectors list again in 2014, to help ensure government approval would be needed before the US company General Electric could acquire the French conglomerate Alstom,[13] adding industries related to the "security and continuity of supplies that are essential to public order or safety and national defence," such as water, energy, transport, and health (Hepher 2014).[14]

Both the French President and Prime Minister were strongly in favor of the 2005 anti-takeover decree as a result of their opposition to a possible bid for Danone by Pepsi, and, consequently, they used every opportunity to show their support for it during the furor caused by the rumor. They went out of their way to publicize their intent to "defend French interests" in a potential bid for Danone, and Villepin openly contended that France "must ensure that [its] companies have the same means to act and defend themselves as their foreign counterparts" (Vandore 2005b).

Thus, it is clear that even though the acquisition of Danone by Pepsi had not yet passed the rumor stage, the French government reacted to the potential bid with a virulent campaign to prevent its success. Furthermore, the French government sought, successfully, to carry out a strategy of unbounded intervention to block this potential cross-border takeover bid on the basis that it threatened the national interest and security. The question, therefore, is not only why did the French pursue this type of intervention, but also why did they pursue it in the context of the yogurt industry, which is not one that would normally be associated with "national security" in the traditional sense. The variables proposed in the primary hypothesis are explored in relation to the PepsiCo/Danone case in the sections that follow, together with an analysis of which variables provided the primary motivation behind the French government's actions.

Geopolitical Competition

Resource Dependency

While France is a resource-dependent nation, the US is not one of its primary sources of energy (see Encyclopedia of Earth 2007). France's resource dependency ratio, or the ratio of all its imported energy sources to its total energy supply, was 63% in 2005.[15] This is very close to the mean resource dependency ratio for the 209 cases in the dataset, which was 62%.

Relative Power Differential

Despite the fact that both the US and France are major powers, the relative power differential between them is vast. The US completely overshadows France in terms of relative military power. In 2005, US military expenditure was $504,638 million, which was over nine and a half times France's expenditure of $52,917 million.[16] Furthermore, this differential was increasing because the average growth rate of the US' military expenditure between 2001 and 2005 was 8%, while that of France was only 1%.[17] The differences are also stark in terms of relative economic power. US GDP in 2005 (at price purchasing parity, or PPP) was almost seven times that of France.[18] The relative economic power of the US was also increasing slightly vis-à-vis France at this time, with the average economic growth rate for the years 2001–05 being 5% for the US and 4% for France.[19] It is clear, however, that France was closer to the US in terms of relative economic power than it was in terms of relative military power. It would thus make sense at the time for the French government to seek to balance the US through means that would help enhance France's relative economic power position.

Overall Character of the Geopolitical Relationship

The US and France are formal military allies and members of a deeply integrated security community, a relationship formalized through their membership in NATO. At the heart of this alliance is Article 5 of the Treaty, which provides for the mutual self-defense of its members, who commit to treat "an armed attack against one or more of them" as "an attack against them all" (NATO 1949). Despite the end of the Cold War that originally gave it purpose, NATO's members have maintained the alliance and committed to strengthen it, and to redefine its mission. NATO remains the "essential alliance" for the US (Burns 2004), and France recognizes it as "a priceless asset that must be maintained in order to cope with current and future challenges and threats" (French Ministry 2008).

This being said, the relationship between the US and France within NATO is far from uncomplicated. France left the military arm of NATO in 1966 in order to pursue its own independent nuclear and military defense plans, largely because of disagreements with US policy and concerns that the US would not provide fully for the defense of France in case of a nuclear war (La Fondation Charles de Gaulle 2008). Since that time, France has contributed troops to Alliance operations such as Kosovo and Afghanistan, even when it was not officially part of NATO's military command. Chirac initiated a discussion to rejoin the NATO command early in his presidency, but his demands for rejoining were not met, and the discussion was dropped almost ten years before the 2005 PepsiCo/Danone case. In 2007, French President Nicolas Sarkozy made overtures to rejoin the military command of NATO, but France did not officially do so until April 2009, well after this case concluded.[20]

Strain within the US–French alliance arguably reached a height, however, following the invasion of Iraq in 2003. French opposition to the Iraq war was vociferous and unflagging, with threats of a French veto in the UN preventing the US from gaining full Security Council authorization for the invasion, and the acrimony of the discussion causing many to question the future of the alliance. This strain had not faded by the time of the PepsiCo/Danone case, and it was only with the later election of President Sarkozy that tensions began to ease.

As a result, there was a prevailing perception within France at the time that the US was a threat to international stability, not only because of its unilateral foreign policies, but, more fundamentally, because of its position as the world's only superpower. Though French public opinion of the US has been relatively low for some time, the Pew Global Attitudes Project (PGAP) found that it lowered dramatically after the Iraq War, falling from 63% in the summer of 2002 to 43% in June 2003 (Pew Global Attitudes Project 2003). Moreover, the French government has not been shy over its concerns with US *hyperpuissance*, a concept first put forward by then French Foreign Minister Hubert Vedrine in 1999 (Lieber 2005). The French strongly believe in "the need to counterbalance [US] power," and have "expressed under Chirac's presidency" the belief that "multipolarism is a better way to guarantee world security than unipolarism" (Tardy 2003). They feel that unipolar power is dangerous because of its ability to act beyond the constraint of international norms and agreements. The French have thus tried to establish themselves as the leaders of a self-styled effort to balance US *hyperpuissance* and return the world to multipolarity.

Within the confines of the NATO relationship, then, the potential exists for a certain level of strategic competition between the US and France. This competition largely focuses on the use of diplomatic and economic tools to balance US power. Within this context, it is not surprising that the French government might use a tool of unbounded intervention to prevent the takeover of one of its national champions by a US company. The use of such a non-military internal balancing strategy makes perfect sense within the context of France's desire to enhance its own power vis-à-vis the US, while at the same time maintaining an alliance with the US, which it believes provides more strategic benefits than costs.

Thus, while French and American security are formally intertwined, their relationship remains antagonistic because of the vast power differentials and historical differences between the two countries, which are resented by the French, and which were exacerbated by the US' unilateralist approach to Iraq. The French have a stated policy of seeking to balance US power, and, not surprisingly, chose to do so through unbounded intervention in the PepsiCo/Danone case. This can be interpreted as the French government protecting its relative economic power position vis-à-vis the US by defending one of its national champions (Danone) from a US "predator" (Pepsi).

The timing of the anti-takeover decree, and the acknowledgment that this case was the impetus behind the law, helped frame the protection of Danone as a matter of French national security. Chirac and other members of the French government painted Danone as a "key" company, "national treasure," and "jewel" of French industry, whose protection was of paramount importance not only to French "industrial competitiveness," but also to its "interests" (see Brothers & Robbins 2005; Corcoran 2005; de Beaupuy & Vandore 2005; Vandore 2005b). While the food industry was not protected in the final version of the law, there was speculation that it would be included as one of the eleven strategic sectors made "off limits" to foreign takeovers. The government also did nothing to dispel the belief that Danone would be protected until after the takeover rumors died down, when a French Finance Ministry official would only say that "Yogurt does not feature on our list" (Bennhold 2006a). However, under the provisions of the law, Danone itself was protected from a foreign takeover, because it also owned a casino – an industry that was protected at the time of this case, on the grounds that the government needed to monitor casinos and gambling to protect the country from money-laundering used for organized crime and terrorism (see PINR 2005). Casinos were later removed from the list of strategic sectors in a 2012 update of the 2005 Decree, reportedly under pressure from the EU Commission, though the wider gambling sector (excluding casinos) was retained on the list of strategic sectors for which the investments of non-EU foreign investors would be subject to review (Cafritz 2014, 3, 9).[21] France's government thus went to extraordinary lengths to ensure that a food and drinks company was associated with national security in order to effectively veto the potential transaction at the time, and to reinforce its "right" to veto such a deal in the future.[22] With all of this in mind, it remains true that the US and France are closer allies than many states in the world, and the underlying elements of geopolitical competition between them could not have been enough to cause this kind of virulent reaction on its own.

Economic Nationalism

As the birthplace of nationalism, and as one of the few true "nation-states," France retains high levels of national pride. In the last wave of the World Values Survey before this case, 37% of respondents in France claimed to be "very proud" of their nationality, and another 47% were "quite proud," making 84% proud of their national identity to at least some degree (WVS 2001–04).

Not surprisingly, the French are also well known for their economic nationalism. This is partially rooted in pride – 32% of French citizens claim to be proud of their nation's economic achievements (ISSP 2003). The virulence of their economic nationalism, however, is also rooted in a strong belief that globalization threatens not only French "culture and . . . identity," but also the health and vitality of the French economy (Gordon 2005). This belief is strengthened by the fact "that globalization directly challenges the statist economic and political traditions of the country" (Gordon 2005). For example, a 2005 World Public Opinion (WPO) survey of every G8 country but Japan asked respondents whether "the free enterprise system and free market economy [was] the best system on which to base the future of the world" (WPO 2006). France was the only country where more respondents disagreed with that statement (50%) than agreed that the free-market economy was a positive influence (36%) (WPO 2006). In a survey of fifty-four countries, French businessmen ranked second to last among those who believed that "attitudes toward globalization are generally positive in [their] economy," followed only by Venezuela (IMD 2007a, 2007b).[23] Such intense anti-globalization sentiment infuses every aspect of business in France, and was one of the primary reasons behind the French rejection of the EU constitution in 2005. Furthermore, the French associate the evils of globalization with "Americanization" (Gordon 2005; WPO 2006), explaining in part their virulent reaction to a perceived national champion being taken over by a US company.

The French government thus blatantly refused to allow one of its recognized national champions to become a victim of globalization in the form of a takeover by an American company. One observer even went so far as to proclaim "L'état, c'est Danone" (Corcoran 2005). France has had a history of subsidizing and protecting its companies from foreign control since the Cold War, but this case sent the government "into protectionist overdrive" (WSJ 2005a).

Villepin's stated policy of "economic patriotism"[24] throws the role that economic nationalism played in French opposition to the potential Danone takeover into stark relief. Simply put, this doctrine is an "industrial Maginot line" – a policy "designed to defend 'France and that which is French'... by declaring entire sectors of French industry off-limits to [foreign takeovers]" (Theil 2005; Economist 2006b). The French government even argued that this was not "protectionism," but a policy designed to counter similar policies "in the US and elsewhere" (Thornhill & Jones 2005). Most importantly, however, this policy of economic patriotism is considered by many to be a reaction to the rumors surrounding the possible takeover of Danone by Pepsi (see e.g., Franks 2006). Its formulation clearly demonstrates France's desire to balance the relative economic position of the US through unbounded intervention in this case, and to balance that of other countries in future like cases.

All of these facts combine to show that economic nationalism was indeed one of the primary motivations behind France's strategy of unbounded intervention in this case, and that this was exacerbated by tensions in the geopolitical relationship between the US and France. It is in the context of such virulent economic nationalism that the Pepsi rumor was able to trigger both legislation and the formalization of a new economic policy designed specifically to block a foreign takeover of Danone. Furthermore, these policies enjoy such strong support across government and public lines that it is unlikely they will change in the future.

Presence of Interest Groups

There were interest groups present in France that either opposed the PepsiCo/Danone deal or were likely to oppose it if given the opportunity to do so. Danone itself preferred "to remain independent," but was also reportedly looking for a domestic white knight to provide an alternative if Pepsi did make a formal offer for its company (Perri & Deen 2005; Schuman 2005). Danone Chairmen Franck Ribaud later suggested, however, that he did not actually want to see the government "sanctuarise" his company, because "sanctuaries are for relics, whereas Danone thrives on the competition it faces in all its markets" (Dairy Reporter 2006). Thus, the actual role played by Danone in the government's actions is somewhat opaque. Furthermore, the fact that the government reacted to the rumor almost immediately meant that shareholders (who would be the main stakeholders in such a transaction) didn't really have time to respond either positively or negatively to the deal.

It was also fairly clear that the interest groups normally associated with anti-globalization movements would protest against the deal due to fears that it would lead to job losses for French workers, and because of the company's iconic role in French economic identity. It was, for example, claimed that "France's Unions would . . . strongly oppose a PepsiCo deal," as would French farmers (Brothers & Robbins 2005; Corcoran 2005). This did, of course, play a role in the government's attitude toward the deal, and contributed to the unlikelihood that it would become more than a rumor. These interest groups, however, were largely motivated by economic nationalism themselves, and it seems clear that it was the general economic nationalist mood of the nation at that time, rather than the persuasive powers of any one interest group, that contributed to the rapidity of the French government's intervention. In the end, it was not the opposition of a particular interest group, but the staunch opposition of the French leadership combined with widespread opposition that prevented the rumor from ever becoming a reality.[25]

More importantly, the immediate groundswell of opposition to the deal did not come from the market, but from French government officials appalled at the notion that such a French icon would be bought by a foreign – and, equally important, an *American* – firm. As the preceding discussion of the general French tendency toward economic nationalism and the specific French policy of economic patriotism demonstrates, it is not surprising that the government in this case did not need the lobbying of a specific irate interest group or stakeholder to bring its attention to, or convince it of, the dangers of such a deal.

Competition Concerns

The issue of whether or not such a combination of companies would be monopolistic, or whether competition within the food industry would be affected negatively by such a takeover, was not a concern that was flagged by the government or the market in this case. This was largely because government efforts to block the deal on other grounds were so quick that the deal was scuttled long before it could move beyond the rumor stage.

Conclusions on PepsiCo/Danone

There is a distinct pattern of French government-led efforts to balance the relative economic power position of the US through a strategy of unbounded intervention in this case. This makes sense in the context of French efforts to balance American *hyperpuissance* as a whole. This strategy seems to be both purposefully and consciously implemented. Not surprisingly, the stock of French FDI abroad far exceeded that of FDI into France, in terms of both book and market value, in 2005 and 2006 (US DOS 2009). For, at the same time that the French have sought to protect their national champions from foreign takeovers, they have supported their "own companies [who] are active acquisitors" abroad (Parker & Thornhill 2005).

Case 2: CNOOC/Unocal

The Story

In 2005, the potential acquisition of the American Unocal Corporation by the Chinese government-owned CNOOC Ltd. caused an almost unprecedented reaction in Washington, where a widespread movement among members of the US government sought to block the foreign takeover through a strategy of unbounded intervention, allowing the American company Chevron to win the "war" for Unocal. All three companies involved were in the oil and gas industry, and Unocal was a recognized takeover target that, though relatively small as "the 9th largest oil company in the world" (Powell 2005), provided others with a unique opportunity to buy an independent company with wholly owned assets in Asia. Indeed, Unocal had relatively few assets in North America (mainly in the Gulf of Mexico) and Europe, but a number of prime assets in Asia (in Azerbaijan, Bangladesh, Indonesia, Myanmar, the Philippines, and Thailand), in addition to a number of joint venture (JV) projects in Asia (Unocal 2005; Greenwire 2005c). Meanwhile, CNOOC Ltd., an American listed company based in Hong Kong, was seeking to expand its asset base in Asia. The fit initially seemed obvious to the market,[26] though there were questions over whether CNOOC could afford Unocal. Yet, controversy ensued when it was realized by public policymakers that CNOOC Ltd. was 71% owned by the Chinese government-owned and controlled China National Offshore Oil Corporation.

The race for Unocal began early in 2005. CNOOC announced it was considering a bid for the company on January 7, and by March 3, Chevron had stated it too was contemplating mounting a takeover attempt. In early April, CNOOC withdrew itself from the bidding process amid the concerns of its non-executive board members, who were "troubled by the amount of debt" CNOOC would have to take on in order to complete such a deal (Timmons 2005). With the path seemingly clear, Chevron announced on April 4 its intention to buy Unocal for $18 billion in a debt/cash deal worth "an overall value of US $62.00 per share" (Zephyr 2005b, 2005c), for which it received approval from the Federal Trade Commission (FTC) of the US by June 10, and from the US Securities and Exchange Commission (SEC) by July 29. The race, however, was far from over, and on June 7, CNOOC once again "confirmed" its intention to make an offer for Unocal in the near future (AFP 2005a), a promise that it fulfilled on June 22 when it topped Chevron's bid with a *cash* offer of $67 per share of Unocal stock (Zephyr 2005b, 2005c).

Before continuing with this story, it is necessary to remember that in the US there are three major hurdles any foreign takeover must clear in order to be successful (Grundman & Roncka 2006). The first is a Foreign Ownership, Control or Influence (FOCI) review, in which the DOD Defense Security Service (DSS) investigates a transaction to ensure that it will not "result in unauthorized access to classified information or . . . adversely affect the performance of classified contracts" (DSS 2016b). This process was established in 1993 as part of the National Industrial Security Program (NISP) created by Executive Order 12829.[27] Like the CFIUS process, the FOCI review is classified, and it is unclear whether Unocal had classified contracts that would have triggered a FOCI review if it had accepted CNOOC's bid.

The second hurdle is a competition review provided for under the 1976 Hart–Scott–Rodino Antitrust Improvements Act, which occurs before a transaction is concluded. This review process, carried out by the FTC and Department of Justice (DOJ), with support from the DOD as needed, is "intended to protect competition and prevent transaction-specific adverse impacts on prices and innovation" (Grundman & Roncka 2006, 2).[28] As discussed later, the US government did not really display concern over a proposed CNOOC/Unocal deal on such competition grounds.

The third hurdle for foreign investors is the CFIUS process. As discussed in the Introduction, this national security review process for foreign takeovers was initially established by the Exon–Florio Provision of the 1988 Omnibus Trade and Competitiveness Act, which:

> amended Section 721 of the Defense Production Act of 1950 to provide authority to the President to suspend or prohibit any foreign acquisition, merger or takeover of a US corporation that is determined to threaten the national security of the United States. The President can exercise this authority under section 721 . . . to block a foreign acquisition of a US corporation only if he finds: (1) there is credible evidence that the foreign entity

> exercising control might take action that threatens national security, and (2) the provisions of law, other than the International Emergency Economic Powers Act do not provide adequate and appropriate authority to protect the national security. (US DOT 2007)

President Reagan also signed Executive Order 12661 in 1988, amending the Executive Order that originally established CFIUS (11858), and thus delegating his new presidential authority to investigate and review foreign takeovers to CFIUS. The Committee is headed by the Secretary of the Treasury, who at the time of this case was John Snow. In 1992, the "Byrd Amendment" to the 1950 DPA further stipulated that CFIUS be mandated to investigate proposed takeovers in which the acquirer was "controlled by or acting on behalf of a foreign government."[29] The national security review for foreign takeovers was thus referred to for a long time as the "Exon–Florio Process," and these provisions served as the backbone of foreign takeover law in the US until being updated by the Foreign Investment and National Security Act of 2007 (FINSA).[30]

FINSA was passed in response to Congressional concerns over the strength, transparency, and oversight of the CFIUS process following the CNOOC/Unocal and DPW/P&O cases examined in this book. FINSA and Executive Order 13456, respectively, once again amend section 721 of the DPA and Executive Order 11858. FINSA primarily clarifies the Exon–Florio process and makes it more transparent.[31] FINSA also notably increases the membership of CFIUS from the twelve reporting agencies it had reached by the time of the CNOOC/Unocal case[32] (adding the Secretary of Energy), and formally recognizes critical infrastructure as a national security concern in transactions covered by the review process. For the most part, however, FINSA simply provides for a "codification of [the] many existing informal practices" (Plotkin et al. 2009) already in play during this case and the DPW/P&O deal. Concern over critical infrastructure, for example, was already informally recognized in the DPW transaction, and the inclusion of the Energy Secretary was presaged by the CNOOC case. *Thus, though FINSA came after many of the cases examined here, it does not affect the theory, or the conclusions drawn from these case studies.*

Crucial to understanding the CNOOC/Unocal case is the CFIUS filing procedure and timeline for reviews, which has not changed since 1988. Filings with CFIUS are usually voluntary, with companies notifying the Committee once a preliminary or formal agreement has been reached for the transaction in question (US DOT 2007). When this notification is received, the review process begins; for most companies, this involves a simple thirty-day review of the transaction, but in cases where a national security issue is flagged, the Committee can conduct an "extended 45-day review," which must be followed by "a report . . . to the President, who must [then] announce the final decision [on the deal] within 15 days" (US DOT 2007). This means that ninety days is the maximum time allowed for a review (US DOT 2007). This time limitation is important because it gives foreign investors a time frame within which they can plan to have contingent funding and resources available for their transaction. One industry source has also pointed out that unexpected delays in the review process, especially those that might unofficially extend the ninety-day limit, can cause some foreign companies to lose short-term financing opportunities or force them to pay higher prices because of interest accrued on loans that may have already been in place for a deal. More importantly, however, and as the CNOOC/Unocal case will demonstrate, attempts to cause a delay in a foreign takeover transaction beyond the ninety-day process cause uncertainty and, therefore, a degree of risk that investors, shareholders, and board members of the companies involved are usually unwilling to accept. Understanding the details of this review process is thus integral to understanding what happened in the CNOOC/Unocal case.

The possibility of a Chinese government-owned company taking over a US oil company during a period of tense Sino-American relations and rising energy prices began to worry members of the US government, who quickly sought to deal with the issue both inside and outside the context of this highly institutionalized process for reviewing foreign takeovers under US law. By June 17, US Congressmen Duncan Hunter (R-CA) and Richard Pombo (R-CA) sent a letter to President Bush requesting that CFIUS investigate the potential ramifications of a CNOOC/Unocal deal because they were concerned that such a deal would threaten "US jobs, energy production, and energy security" (Timmons 2005). The latter issue was of significant concern to the congressmen, who "encourag[ed] Bush to consider the national security implications regarding the transfer of technology to China in the event of Unocal's acceptance of CNOOC's offer" (Bullock & Xiao 2005b). On June 22, only five days after the Hunter/Pombo letter, "Energy Secretary Samuel Bodman [confirmed] that a bid would be reviewed by [CFIUS]" (Gold et al. 2005). On June 23 – the same day that there was a hearing in "the Senate Finance Committee . . . on the evolving US–Chinese economic relationship"[33] – Senator Chuck Grassley (R-IA) announced that US "legislators [would] watch [the] CNOOC-Unocal" deal (Gold et al. 2005; Dow Jones 2005b). By the end of June, "41 members of Congress sent a letter to Treasury Secretary John Snow . . . asking that the potential transaction 'be reviewed immediately to investigate the implications of the acquisition'" (Graham & Marchick 2006, 131). On June 27, Congressmen Joe Barton (R-TX) and Ralph Hall (R-TX) wrote a letter to President Bush urging him to block a CNOOC takeover of Unocal because it "poses a clear threat to the energy and national security of the United States" (Orol 2005d; Barton & Hall 2005). Congress was thus beginning to lean toward a clear strategy of *unbounded intervention*, with the intent to block the deal one way or another.

This strategy was solidified on June 30 in two separate formal actions taken by the US House of Representatives. The first was the passage of House Resolution 344, sponsored by Congressman Pombo, which formally recognized congressional concern that a CNOOC/Unocal deal "threatens to impair the national security" (US House 2005c). This concern mostly emanated from a belief that, in an environment where the US and China were competing for energy resources and Sino-American relations were strained, the Chinese government might through its ownership of CNOOC use a Unocal purchase to gain control over much-needed energy assets, as well as over dual-use technologies that could have military applications. H. Res. 344, therefore, demanded that if Unocal and CNOOC did agree to a transaction, "the President . . . [would] initiate immediately a thorough review of the proposed acquisition, merger, or takeover" (US House 2005c). This resolution passed by a vote of 398–15.

The second action taken by the US Congress was the addition of Amendment 431 to H.R. 3058.[34] The purpose of this amendment, sponsored by Congresswoman Carolyn Kilpatrick (D-MI) and passed by a vote of 333–92, was to "prohibit the use of [Treasury] funds from being made available to recommend approval of the sale of Unocal Corporation to CNOOC Ltd. of China" (H. Amdt. 431 to H.R. 3058). This amendment was clearly a tactic to block a CNOOC/Unocal deal, because, had CNOOC and Unocal reached an acquisition agreement, a CFIUS review would have been triggered, and those funds required. H. Res. 344 mandated that such a review be "thorough," which would indicate a full forty-five-day CFIUS investigation, resulting in a report to the President, who would then have to give his approval or disapproval regarding the transaction (see H. Res. 344). This amendment, therefore, would have made it impossible for the President to give his approval under such a scenario, because the report would be delivered through the Chair of CFIUS, who is the Secretary of the Treasury, and who by definition would be using funds from the Treasury.

The high-profile concern generated by the deal caused the CEO of CNOOC, Fu Chengyu, to take the highly unusual step in late June of "writing to members of Congress expressing his company's willingness to participate in a [CFIUS] review" (International Oil Daily 2005c) and on July 1 of requesting that CFIUS review the transaction before an acquisition agreement had actually been reached with Unocal (Amaewhule 2005).[35] On June 30, Liu Jianchao, the spokesman for the Chinese Foreign Ministry, announced that "China wants to find a 'win-win' result," because "this issue is a commercial transaction between two companies, and a normal exchange between China and the US. It should stay free of political interference" (Dow Jones 2005a). In the beginning, CNOOC really believed that the US would not block the transaction as long as it marketed the deal, and its intentions, correctly. Chengyu, for example, was truly "confident [the] deal [was] politically viable" (AFX 2005a), once he made it clear that CNOOC's "all-cash offer [was] clearly superior for Unocal shareholders" and was "good for America," and that CNOOC would "protect Unocal's US jobs" (Gold et al. 2005).

Frustration on the part of the Chinese government at what it viewed as US "protectionism" soon began to show, however. In what is widely viewed as a critical slip in the campaign to win the race for Unocal, the Chinese Foreign Ministry made another statement on July 5, declaring: "We demand that the US Congress correct its mistaken ways of politicizing economic and trade issues and stop interfering in the normal commercial exchanges between enterprises of... [China and the US]" (Dow Jones 2005d). This statement only served to increase the fears of certain members of the US government that the Chinese government was guiding the CNOOC bid, and that such an offer did not necessarily have friendly motivations (Dow Jones 2005d).[36]

On July 13, the same day that it was reported CNOOC was contemplating making a higher offer in order to win over Unocal shareholders (Canadian Press 2005), the difficulties for CNOOC's bid intensified. First, CFIUS reportedly denied CNOOC's request for "a preliminary opinion on its proposed acquisition" (AFX 2005c). Second, the House Armed Services Committee held a hearing to review the "national security implications" of a CNOOC takeover (Dow Jones 2005c). The majority of witnesses at the hearing, and most members of the committee, believed such a takeover would be a threat to US national security (AFX 2005c), and Committee Chairman Duncan Hunter argued the deal was fundamentally "at odds with US interests" (AFX 2005c). Finally, Senators Chuck Grassley and Max Baucus (D-MT) sent a letter to the President expressing their concern over the possible CNOOC takeover, supporting calls for a formal CFIUS review of the deal if an acquisition agreement was made with Unocal (Grassley 2005). On July 15, Senator Dorgan (D-ND) introduced S. 1412, a piece of legislation that would have "prohibit[ed] the merger, acquisition, or takeover of

Unocal Corporation by CNOOC Ltd. of China" outright, if it had been passed (US Senate 2005).

Despite the hot political environment, Unocal was enticed by the possibility of a bidding war for its company, as well as the higher return for its shareholders that a courtship of CNOOC promised. Unocal's board and shareholders wanted the highest price at the lowest level of risk. Thus, on July 14, the board of Unocal "agreed that 'assuming neither Chevron nor CNOOC improved the financial terms of [their] proposed transaction[s], the board's inclination would be to withdraw its recommendation for the Chevron transaction'" (Natural Gas Intelligence 2005). When Chevron then raised its bid on July 19 to "an overall value of US $63.01 per share," Unocal's board not surprisingly recommended this new bid to its shareholders (Zephyr 2005d).

At this point, opposition to the deal remained strong within the US government and public. The hearing held by the House Energy & Commerce Committee reviewed the possible CNOOC/Unocal Deal on July 22. Senators Vitter (R-LA), Bayh (D-IN), Talent (R-MO), Coburn (R-OK), and Inhofe (R-OK) also sent a letter on this date,

> urging Senate Energy and Natural Resources Committee Chairman Pete Domenici (R-NM) and Ranking Member Jeff Bingaman (D-NM) to include language in the Energy Bill Conference Report that would require the Secretary of Energy, along with the Secretaries of Defense and Homeland Security, to study the implications of such a transaction before a formal review could begin. (States News Service 2005b)

By mid-June, 73% of Americans polled by the Wall Street Journal claimed to "'dislike' the potential [CNOOC] deal" (Voice of America 2005).

Throughout this period, the White House remained fairly neutral on the proposed foreign takeover, as is the norm in such cases. This was largely because it did not yet need to get involved, and likely because it probably was better to wait and see whether Unocal actually chose CNOOC over Chevron, rather than waste valuable political capital committing itself to a position at such an early stage in the process. The White House did make it clear, however, that a CFIUS review would be triggered if the CNOOC bid was chosen, and that it did not openly favor such a deal – indicating a desire for Congress and the Senate to do the dirty work of balancing in this case. Nevertheless, it was clear that the majority of the US legislative branch wanted to block a CNOOC/Unocal deal completely, and the muted response of the Executive branch would not fill CNOOC with confidence about the chances of obtaining approval for its proposed transaction.

Unocal, meanwhile, was still hoping for a bidding war, and continued to hold meetings with both Chevron and CNOOC during this time period, in the hopes of a higher offer. Though CNOOC's original bid was higher, the degree of political uncertainty surrounding it was much greater than Chevron's, which not only had FTC and SEC approval, but which (as a US company) would also not have to face the CFIUS process (see AFX 2005b; Reuters 2005b; Murray 2005). It was thus reported by July 26 that "Unocal management argued that increased risks of government approval and delay outweigh the differential on CNOOC's $67/share bid" (Taylor 2005). At the same time, it was reported that CNOOC might raise its bid for the company above $67/share, if Unocal met two demands (Taylor 2005). These were that Unocal: (1) "pay the $500 million break-up fee for terminating the [original deal with] Chevron" and (2) "take 'specific actions' to help 'influence the US congress' towards a deal with CNOOC" (Taylor 2005). Neither of these conditions would be particularly easy for Unocal to achieve, and the market roundly believed at this point that, while CNOOC still had a chance if it made a higher bid, the political risk of such a deal would probably be too much for either CNOOC or Unocal to accept. As one analyst put it, "the market [was] split" on "how to price political risk" (Natural Gas Intelligence 2005). One of Oppenheimer's analysts claimed that CNOOC "would not want to offer more money without assurances of success" (Taylor 2005).

Despite all of this, many observers in the market and the press still believed that CNOOC would raise its bid. For example, on July 28 it was rumored that "CNOOC Ltd. has drafted plans to increase its $67/share cash bid to more than $70/share, valuing Unocal at about $19.3 [billion], about $2 [billion] above Chevron's proposal" (Platts 2005). It was also believed that "Unocal's board would need a 10% premium from CNOOC, over and above Chevron's $63.01/share offer to compensate for risk that US Legislators and regulators would delay or even stop a CNOOC-Unocal merger" (Platts 2005). Rumors even surfaced as late as August 1 that CNOOC was waiting for Congress to recess to announce both a higher bid and a white-knight buyer for Unocal's US assets (Natural Gas Intelligence 2005). Either way, CNOOC's pursuit was dealt a strong blow that same day when the proxy firm Institutional Shareholder Services, "which can at times sway US takeover battles with its recommendations, said it was supporting Chevron because of the significant premium associated with the $17.5 [billion] offer, as well as the regulatory risks associated with CNOOC's bid" (Guerrera & Polti 2005).

In the following days and weeks, another crucial effort at unbounded intervention was made by the Legislative branch to block a possible

CNOOC/Unocal deal. On August 8, a piece of legislation introduced by Representative Joe Barton, the Energy Policy Act of 2005 (H.R. 6), was signed into law. This law included within it a provision for an extraordinary delay in the conclusion of any deal between CNOOC and Unocal – a delay that effectively killed the deal. Section 1837 of H.R. 6 required that a report be made to Congress assessing the national security implications of the issues relating to China's quest for energy, the use of foreign investment to satisfy those energy needs, and "reciprocity" issues, such as whether or not a US company would be able to purchase an oil company in China (US House 2005a). This section was the result of an amendment made by Congressman Pombo, who "admitted to reporters that his amendment was meant to effectively kill a potential CNOOC/Unocal deal" (Oil Daily 2005a). According to Senator Dorgan, who also supported the amendment, the main motivation behind the request for this study was the delay that it would cause (O'Driscoll 2005). H.R. 6 allowed 120 days for the completion of the report, and effectively mandated that CFIUS could not begin its review of a CNOOC/Unocal deal until twenty-one days after that, in order for its findings to be considered in the review process (US House 2005a; O'Driscoll 2005). Thus, this law ensured that there would be an excessive and onerous delay of 186 days (about six months) before the companies would officially be told if the transaction could be concluded.

Not surprisingly, CNOOC withdrew its outstanding bid for Unocal on August 2, 2005. Its stated reason for pulling out was "the political environment in the US," and the "unprecedented political opposition that followed the announcement of our proposed transaction" (CNOOC 2005). In fact, opposition to the deal was so intense that the Chinese government withdrew its support for the acquisition toward the end of the bidding process (Grimmer 2005). Tensions with the US were already high at the time, as discussed later, and "it was just not worth using up a lot of political capital over, especially with President Hu Jintao heading to the United States in September for his first visit" (Grimmer 2005). By August 10, Unocal held a shareholder meeting to assess the proposed merger agreement with Chevron, after which it announced the approval of Chevron's bid, and Chevron declared the deal complete.

The timeline of events in this case makes it clear that the Legislative branch's strategy of unbounded intervention forced CNOOC to decide that it was unlikely to be able to conclude the deal at all, much less do so in a timely and profitable manner. It was clear that many members of the US government felt the deal needed to be prevented, or blocked if necessary, on national security grounds. But what were their exact concerns, and what really motivated them, causing Congress to react the way it did to the possibility of a CNOOC/Unocal deal? Were geostrategic issues the main concern? It is clear that the context of the geopolitical relationship between the US and China at the time only intensified opposition to a deal that was never going to be easy in the first place because of the national security issues it raised. Indeed, "Washington attorneys familiar with the deal [said that] . . . CNOOC's biggest problem in Washington was that its attempt collided with US lawmaker's growing frustration with the US relationship with China on issues ranging from currency manipulation to trade reciprocity and intellectual property rights" (Kirchgaessner 2005). Or was the failure of the deal caused by "a variety of factors – economic nationalism, superpower rivalry, fears about declining US competitiveness, and worries about energy security – [which] blended into a potent mixture" to prevent CNOOC from taking over Unocal, as some (Molchanov 2005) claimed? The following section will assess the variables hypothesized to be the primary reasons behind unbounded intervention. It should show that while there were many variables influencing government action in this case, the geopolitical issues it raised were clearly the strongest.

Geopolitical Competition

China and the US were, in 2005, as they are now, geopolitical rivals with a highly complex, but mainly amicable, relationship. These states are neither military allies, nor members of the same security community. China is a major, and a rapidly "rising," power. The relationship between the two countries has long been complicated by each state's position on the status of Taiwan, which Beijing's seeks to reintegrate fully, while Washington seeks to defend the "status quo," thus treading a fine line between its commitment to a military defense of the island and its commitment to a "one China" policy (see US House 2004).

In the summer of 2005, when the CNOOC bid took place, there was a prevailing perception in the US that China was more than just an emerging power. Many saw it as a strategic rival, which had the potential to develop into a military threat in the future.[37] Thus, the DOD made clear in its Annual Report to Congress in 2005:

> The United States welcomes the rise of a peaceful and prosperous China, one that becomes integrated as a constructive member of the international community. But, we see a China facing a strategic crossroads. Questions remain about the basic choices China's leaders will make as China's power and influence grow, particularly its military power. (US DOD 2005, 4)

US unease over China's rapid growth and modernization was amplified by the fact that Chinese military spending is not very transparent (US DOD 2005). For, while the Stockholm International Peace Research Institute (SIPRI) reported its spending in 2005 as $40,300 million (SIPRI 2006), US DOD "estimates put it at two to three times the officially published figures" (US DOD 2005, 4). This means that China's average military growth over the five years leading up to this case may have been much higher than the already large estimates of 11.31%.[38] Yet, though this is far greater than the US' 8.19% average military growth rate over this same period, China's military spending still remained a far second to the US, which totaled $504,638 million in 2005 (SIPRI 2006).

The US continues to engage China economically, politically, and culturally, and trade between the two countries is highly interdependent. Yet, the relationship between them was strained in 2005 by China's growing economic power relative to the US. In relative terms, China's economy was far smaller at the time: China's GDP at PPP was about 50% of US GDP in 2005, or about 52% if you include Hong Kong and Macao.[39] Still, the undervaluation of its currency, the yuan (or renminbi), which some analysts then measured as being undervalued by more than 50%, implies that China's economy is larger than suggested by calculations taken from the official exchange rates, and by 2006 China's economy was the second largest in the world (CIA 2007). As with the examination of military growth rates, China's average economic growth rate outstrips that of the US for the five years before 2005, with China's being 12.13% and the US' remaining at 4.93%.[40] Not surprisingly, such figures contribute to US fears that China's relative economic power is growing rapidly.

At the same time, a number of other economic issues contributed to heightened tensions between the two countries. In 2005, China was seen by many as a nation whose financial actions would prove threatening to the future of the US economy. The trade deficit with China had reached $201,544.8 million in 2005 (US Bureau of the Census 2008). There was mounting US pressure placed on China during the summer of 2005 to revalue the yuan, as many in the US believed its undervaluation to be part of an economic policy designed to give China an unfair trade advantage (Preeg 2002).[41] The Chinese government did revalue the yuan by "2.1% against the US dollar" in July of that summer (CIA 2005, 2007), largely as a palliative measure against deteriorating US–Chinese relations during the CNOOC/Unocal bidding process. Other issues straining Sino–US relations at the time included disputes over intellectual property rights and "an escalating trade row" over Chinese export tariffs on textiles (Financial Times 2005a).

The geopolitical relationship between China and the US in the summer of 2005 was thus characterized by heightened tensions over a series of issues, making CNOOC's bid for Unocal more unpalatable to the US government than it might otherwise have been. Indeed, there was "a widening sense among politicians in both parties that China [was] reaping the benefits of free trade without playing fully by the rules," which observers rightly believed would make "steering [the] public debate away from politics . . . difficult" for CNOOC (Linebaugh et al. 2005). At the time, it seemed that the deal was only "raising political tension between two countries with an already strained relationship" (Kirchgaessner et al. 2005). Dick D'Amato, Chairman of the US–China Economic and Security Review Commission (ESRC), even went so far as to ask: "what in [the] relationship [with China] is working?" (Kirchgaessner et al. 2005). Congressmen Barton and Hall made clear their opposition to the CNOOC bid on the grounds that "the Chinese are great economic and political rivals [of the US], not friendly competitors or allies in democracy" (Alden & Kirchgaessner 2005).

Geopolitical tensions between the US and China were further sharpened by the fact that both countries were increasingly competing for access to energy resources, over which there were new worries about scarcity of supply. The US resource dependency ratio in 2005 was 36%.[42] Though the US was not dependent on China for oil,[43] China had recently become highly dependent on oil imports, and the two countries were now actively vying for new sources of supply (CIA 2008). Moreover, an April 2005 IEA Report may have raised fears about the scarcity of oil supplies at the time of the CNOOC/Unocal bid (Greenwire 2005c). All of this, of course, should be understood within the context that, at the time, "most of the world's oil fields [were] already believed to have been discovered, and many of those [were] in oil-producing countries such as Saudi Arabia that [were] off limits to public companies" (Gentile 2005).

In order to appreciate fully the effect of such geopolitical concerns, it is necessary to understand not only the stated rationale behind CNOOC's bid (and the Chinese government's original support), but also what the US government believed to be the *real* motivation behind it. CNOOC claimed that its deal rationale hinged mainly on the large gains to be made to its Asian asset portfolio: a "nearly 80% increase in reserves and a doubling of production," which had hitherto been deficient (FD 2005). According to CNOOC, the bid was one made by a commercial company for commercial reasons only. The company, furthermore, claimed that the Chinese government played no role in its decision to make an offer for Unocal.[44]

Yet, the deal did not necessarily make sense from a purely economic standpoint, for two reasons. First, CNOOC simply did not have the financial wherewithal to pull off its bid without the help of the Chinese government. It lacked the cash for such a high all-cash bid, and clearly needed its "state parent to foot the bill" (Lex 2005c). It was reported that "of the $16 billion in pledges the company has said it has received for its bid, $13 billion comes from state-owned Chinese entities, including $7 billion in long-term and short-term loans from CNOOC's parent China National Offshore Oil Corp" (Gold et al. 2005; see also FD 2005). Second, CNOOC's offer would be a financial burden to the company, as the Fitch Ratings Agency (among others) argued that it would negatively affect their credit rating (see AFX 2005b; PR Newswire 2005; Reuters 2005a). CNOOC's bid was thus perceived as another example of a Chinese company hungry for brands, resources, and assets that could outbid more traditional buyers because of the "extraordinarily cheap financing" it received from its government (Kirchgaessner et al. 2005).

Furthermore, despite CNOOC's claims of independent action, it was clear that the bid had the backing of the Chinese government. First, the government subsidy indicated to many observers that the deal was to a great extent "backed by a [Chinese] state keen for global influence and resources" (Lex 2005a). Second, CNOOC must have had state backing for the bid because all major foreign acquisitions made by Chinese companies were first required to receive Chinese government approval under Chinese law at the time.[45] Third, other observers verified that the Chinese government, whether tacitly or actively, was involved in the deal in some way. In fact, "all four of CNOOC's executive directors" were confirmed to be members of the Communist Party, and David Merjan of the mutual fund William Blair & Co. claimed that "it [was] clear that the Chinese Government [was] exerting... pressure on management" (Cheng & Ng 2005).

The geopolitical positioning of the two countries vis-à-vis world energy resources also forced US policymakers, for good or ill, to assume that CNOOC's bid for Unocal was part of a larger Chinese government policy of trying to gain access to oil resources abroad. A number of market and foreign policy analysts agreed that the Chinese government was using all means available, including the acquisition of foreign companies and the conclusion of JVs abroad through its state-owned national oil companies (NOCs), in order to meet energy demands at home, and to secure supply lines for the future.[46] James Sweeney, an energy economist and Director of the Precourt Institute for Energy Efficiency at Stanford University, publicly argued that CNOOC's bid for Unocal was about "security of supply" because "China want[s] to control supply themselves," and such a deal would arguably give them that control (Greenwire 2005b). The former Executive Director of the IEA, Robert J. Priddle, said at the time that China was "in a panic" because "they're relatively newly dependent on oil imports, and think they must do something to secure their own supply" (Blustein 2005). Similarly, an oil market analyst with Foresight Research Solutions claimed that the race for Unocal was "just round one in the fight for strategic energy resources" (AFX 2005b). McKinsey's Paul Gao maintained that the Chinese "government [was] pushing to create national champions to reduce dependence on foreign technology," giving it "a mandate . . . to look overseas for deals" that would help it accomplish this goal (Kirchgaessner et al. 2005).

Indeed, it was quite clear that the Chinese NOCs *were* busy actively concluding deals with companies in Canada, Sudan, and Venezuela, among other countries (see Greenwire 2005a; Chen 2005). The expansion of Chinese M&A activity during 2005 also included a number of big deals in the oil and gas industry (AFX 2005b). At the time of the CNOOC/Unocal case, for example, China Petroleum & Chemical Corp. was looking to buy the Canadian company Husky Energy Inc., and two separate Chinese companies (Synopec and CNOOC) bought stakes in Canadian oil sands development projects (Chen 2005; Reguly 2005). Such activity, as discussed later, heightened the fears of some in the US government that the Chinese government was using its NOCs to gain access to foreign oil reserves. Congressman Hunter, for example, was clear that part of his concern emanated from the fact that "China [was] in the business of making strategic acquisitions" (Orol 2005c) for the purpose of gaining access to both resources and technology.[47]

One of the fundamental issues for members of the US legislative branch, therefore, was *energy security*. A strategic competitor for natural resources was seeking to buy a US company with US assets when it was believed that there was a Chinese government strategy of systematically seeking resources through the use of the "free" market, and there was no guarantee that such a rival might not then take those freely acquired resources "off the market" in the future. For while market analysts generally assumed that CNOOC was only interested in the Asian assets of Unocal, there was no actual guarantee that CNOOC would sell off Unocal's American assets as promised. CNOOC had been vociferous about the fact that it was willing to give up Unocal's US assets in order to get through the CFIUS review process – a tactic that it fully expected to work.[48] However, CNOOC's advisor from JP Morgan, Charles Li, made it quite clear to investors that CNOOC had no intention of selling the US assets unless forced to by the US regulatory process.[49] Though the

US assets involved were relatively small in size, they were of symbolic importance in the context of a greater debate over whether a Chinese state-owned company might divert supplies solely to China in an energy crisis, pulling those reserves off the market and making them unavailable for purchase at any price. Priddle, from the IEA, claimed that a CNOOC/Unocal deal would not "change the price of oil, or the availability of oil," because these factors would be governed solely by the rules of supply and demand (Blustein 2005). Jerry Taylor of the CATO Institute made basically the same argument to a House Armed Services Committee hearing, claiming that even if China were to pull such supplies from the market, the US could replace them by paying for equivalent supplies from other sources (Kudlow 2005). The three other major witnesses at the hearing, however, completely disagreed with this assessment, instead arguing that the Communist regime was likely to divert those resources if necessary, that those resources would then be going to a rival, and that the market would not necessarily be able to fill the gap.[50] One of those witnesses, Thomas Donnelly, a member of the US–China Economic & Security Review Commission, believed "there [was] a fairly strong argument" for blocking the deal "not simply because Unocal is a national asset," but also because of "the strategic question of how China is approaching energy supplies" (Kirchgaessner et al. 2005). Indeed, the letter sent from Congressmen Barton and Hall to President Bush stated that "this transaction poses a clear threat to the energy and national security of the United States" (Barton & Hall 2005). Their argument was that:

> This sale would be a mistake under almost any circumstance, but it would be especially egregious at a time when energy markets are so tight and the US is becoming even more dependent on foreign sources of energy... US national energy security depends on sufficient energy supplies to support US and global economic growth. But those supplies are threatened by China's aggressive tactics to lock up energy supplies around the world that are largely dedicated for their own use. China has used its state-owned oil companies to advance this strategy, by buying up energy assets around the world without regard to human rights and environmental protection, in countries such as Sudan and Iran. And unlike other companies, these resources are not available to the global market. (Barton & Hall 2005)

Similarly, Congressman Hunter announced his "intention to oppose the sale" (International Oil Daily 2005b), which he saw as a security threat not only because China could try to block US access to Unocal's oil assets in Asia, but more fundamentally because it could shift the geopolitical balance of power in Asia. Referring to "investments by Unocal in pipelines running from Caspian sea oil fields through

Azerbaijan, Georgia, and Turkey," Hunter claimed that "China's purchase of Unocal would dramatically increase its leverage over these countries, and therefore its leverage over US interests in those regions" (Eckert 2005). Observers were also concerned that Unocal had terminals that were part of the US Strategic Petroleum Reserve (see e.g., Murray 2005; LA Times 2005).

Energy security, however, was not the only concern sparked by the geopolitical tensions between the two countries. Congress was equally concerned by a number of national security issues that were raised by the perception that the Chinese government backed such foreign takeovers in order to gain access to technology that had dual-use applications, thus helping China to enhance its military (or other forms of) power. Again, the text of Congressmen Barton and Hall's letter gives us an insight into the concerns of the legislative branch on this issue. They stated that:

> In addition to this obvious threat to our energy security, the acquisition of Unocal by a Chinese state-owned company poses other risks to our US national security. As a significant player in the US energy industry, Unocal uses a host of highly advanced technologies necessary for the exploration and production of oil and gas. Many of these technologies have dual-use applications. Given the potential military threat posed by China to our allies in Asia and our security interests, it is of the utmost importance that US export control laws be strictly applied to ensure that no sensitive technology falls into the hands of the Chinese government – or, through China, other, more dangerous regimes around the world – which can later be used to undermine our national security. (Barton & Hall 2005)

The SVP and CFO of CNOOC, Hua Yang, had likely confirmed some of these fears when he told investors during a conference call that the deal was desirable because it involved "technical advantages" such as "Unocal's leading deepwater drilling technology[, which] would extend CNOOC's exploration capability" (FD 2005). Yang also stated a desire "to retain substantially all Unocal employees" because they included "a highly skilled management and technical talent pool" that was "driving this technology" (FD 2005), confirming the general belief that CNOOC was as interested in Unocal's technology and expertise as it was in its physical assets.

In the end, there were five major technological and defense-related national security concerns raised during the bidding process. The first was Unocal's deepwater drilling technology. CNOOC was actually formed by the Chinese government "in the early 1980s to explore and develop undersea oil and gas fields" (Gold et al. 2005), but did not have the advanced technology Unocal possessed. In fact, the Research Director of the NBR Energy Security Program, Mikkal Herberg, foresaw that the Chinese company's bid would "incite a 'firestorm' in Congress" because of Unocal's "very good deep-water exploration skills, developed in projects off of Indonesia and Mexico that could have military applications," which "critics are likely to 'question letting . . . fall into the hands of the Chinese government'" (Cincinnati Post 2005). Richard D'Amato, Chairman of the US–China Economic Security Review Commission, made similar comments during the House Armed Services Committee hearing on the CNOOC bid (Orol 2005c). Second, the related underwater mapping capabilities Unocal possessed were also reportedly one of the causes of concern. "Trade and security analysts" at the time claimed that Unocal's "underwater terrain-mapping technology used for offshore oil exploration . . . might also be useful in navigation for the Chinese military's growing fleet of submarines" (Lohr 2005). The third concern was raised "in [an unpublished] letter to Energy Bill conference Committee Chairman Joe Barton" by Congressman Pombo, who "pointed out Unocal could have important technologies to access oil shale resources" (Oil Daily 2005a). The fourth issue was Unocal's alleged possession of a rare earth mineral mine that the US government would not want under foreign government control for strategic reasons, because the metals involved reportedly "have military functions for laser technology" (Orol 2005c). Congressman Joe Schwartz (R-MI), for example, showed his concern by stating: "these kinds of metal technology are important to our defense posture" (Orol 2005c). The final issue raised on pure national security grounds was related to US missile defense capabilities. This issue was, again, raised by D'Amato at the House Armed Services Committee hearing, when he "noted that Unocal has 14 offshore oil platforms in Alaska and the Gulf of Mexico that are near important US defense strategic facilities, an apparent reference to missile defense operations in those regions" (Orol 2005c).

In sum, the Sino-US geopolitical relationship in 2005 was mostly characterized by rivalry. Congress clearly defined energy security as a "national security" issue in this case *because* of that geopolitical context. It is also not surprising that within the context of these geopolitical and deal-specific concerns, many in the US government saw the deal as a Chinese "power grab,"[51] and therefore sought to intervene to block it outright. Despite this, both countries recognized their mutual economic dependence, and appreciated the need for constructive engagement, which led to mutual efforts and policies geared toward the maintenance of an overall amicable relationship. It was this recognition of mutual self-interest in a constructive relationship that eventually led the Chinese government to pull its support for CNOOC's bid for Unocal. This case, therefore, clearly shows that states can effectively use unbounded intervention, in line with the purpose of non-military internal balancing, to balance the power of another state without endangering the greater relationship between themselves and that state.

Economic Nationalism

The US is not usually associated with economic nationalism, yet as with many states there remain distinct pockets of such nationalism among members of the US government and its institutions. One source in the legal community that often deals with CFIUS cases pointed out that among all of the US government institutions, the only one that seems to continuously retain elements of economic nationalism is (perhaps not surprisingly) the Department of Commerce, which *is* one of the agencies involved in the CFIUS process. Thus, while national pride in the US is relatively high,[52] instances of economic nationalism in the US are usually fairly targeted and rare. Notably, they have largely been caused in the past by massive influxes of FDI from a particular state, as witnessed by the reaction and response in the US to the huge increase in FDI from Japan in the 1980s.

Some observers made comparisons between the Japanese case and the CNOOC bid, indicating a belief that economic nationalism might be to blame for government intervention (see e.g., Reguly 2005). Part of this was rooted in the fact that the CNOOC bid, if accepted, would have been "China's largest overseas investment ever" (Timmons 2005). Part can be explained in the context of a general expansion of overseas Chinese M&A activity, which included not only the oil and gas deals already mentioned, but also two recent high-profile Chinese purchases in unrelated US industries: Lenovo bought IBM's personal computing (PC) business in 2004 for $1.25 billion and Haier was bidding over a billion dollars for Maytag at the time of the CNOOC bid (Reguly 2005).[53] Thus, an element of economic nationalism may indeed have existed against Chinese investment generally, which was particularly aroused by this case, as it would have been the largest Chinese investment yet in a strategic industry in the US. In fact, it does seem true that this case marks the beginning of a period of somewhat increased economic nationalism in the US generally, at least relative to its previously low levels of that sentiment.[54]

There are some very important differences, though, between the US response to the CNOOC bid and its response to Japanese investment in the 1980s. First, unlike the Japanese in the 1980s, "Chinese companies seem more interested in industrial businesses than trophy assets" (Kirchgaessner et al. 2005). This was of more than symbolic importance, when many in the US government believed that the Chinese government had a policy of supporting/encouraging foreign takeovers through which it could gain technology and resources. This fact, and the geopolitical context between the US and China, made the influx of Chinese FDI much more worrying for the US government. Senator Schumer (D-NY), for example, pointed out that: "Japan was an ally, and Japan was fundamentally a smaller country than we are. [But] China is emerging as a dominant player, and at the same time, China isn't acting like one. It isn't playing by the rules" (Murray 2005).

It was for this reason that those concerned with the economic consequences of a possible CNOOC deal believed the issue was (or simply framed it as being) a matter of *economic security*. Certainly, there was a big push throughout the whole debate over the deal to change the way CFIUS defines national security, and to get economic security issues, such as oil, included in the definition (see Graham & Marchick 2006, 75, 172; Jackson 2007; Lohr 2005). On June 22, for example, Congressman Pombo said he did "not believe it is in the best interest of the US to have Unocal owned by the Chinese national government," as it could have "disastrous consequences for our economic and national security" (Greenwire 2005b).

It could be argued that this concern over economic security was an example of economic nationalism. "Some analysts," indeed, claimed that CFIUS was "being used as a weapon of economic nationalism" by some of the congressman involved (International Oil Daily 2005c). Other scholars, like Graham and Marchick, feared the inclusion of economic security in the national security criteria used by CFIUS could prompt the review process to "become even more politicized," and possibly allow "domestic companies to exploit the CFIUS process against foreign bidders" in the future (Graham & Marchick 2006, 143). Indeed, the July 1 House Resolution called on the deal to be blocked, given that "oil and natural gas resources are strategic assets critical to national security and the Nation's economic prosperity" (US House 2005c).

Despite this, it is important to understand that Unocal was never trumpeted as a national champion, and that the US does not really have a history of protecting national champions per se. As one observer poignantly noted: "Unocal is not an economic or cultural icon. For Americans it is holier than that; it's an oil producer" (Reguly 2005). Indeed, neither members of the US government, nor lobbyists, nor pundits, went so far as to call Unocal a national champion; it was a relatively small oil company that provided only a minor portion of the US oil supply. Moreover, the US did not block Chinese efforts to purchase Maytag or IBM, which could have been viewed as national champions in their industries. Within the oil and gas industry, furthermore, the US did not seek to block British Petroleum's (BP's) purchase of Amoco in 1988 or Petróleos de Venezuela's (PDVSA's) purchase of CITGO in 1990, which were arguably of much greater economic importance. In fact, unbounded intervention through CFIUS, or otherwise, was rare on the part of the US before the CNOOC case. For instance, at this time the only transaction to have been formally prohibited by the US President was, interestingly, when in 1989 the China National Aero-Technology Import and Export Corporation (CATIC) bought – and was ordered by the President in 1990 to wholly divest – the US company MAMCO Manufacturing (Bush 1990). The intervention was made "to protect national security," because MAMCO was the sole supplier of certain airplane parts in the US and CATIC was owned and operated by the Chinese government's Ministry of Aerospace Industry, which had clear ties to the Chinese military (Bush 1990). After that, one of the largest efforts made to block a deal before the Unocal case was when a Chinese military-owned company (COSCO) tried to lease terminal space at the former US naval base in Long Beach, California.[55] It would therefore be difficult to argue that the US has a history of supporting national champions against foreign takeovers, but clear evidence can be found of concern over Chinese state-owned corporations pursuing takeovers of US companies for national security reasons.

Thus, while there was an element of economic nationalism to the efforts of some members of Congress who sought to block the deal on the grounds of "economic security," these concerns were largely present and intensified *because* of the larger geopolitical context of the case. Furthermore, these concerns were consistently accompanied, and overshadowed, by anxiety over the national security issues just discussed.

Presence of Interest Groups

The majority of the lobbying in Congress for or against CNOOC's bid for Unocal was backed by either CNOOC or Chevron themselves. Indeed, once it became clear that the two would be battling for control of Unocal, both companies "hired public-relations firms to press their respective agendas" (Gold et al. 2005). As demonstrated in this section, Chevron's lobbying efforts played an undeniable role in making members of Congress aware of the national security issues posed by CNOOC's bid. Yet, it will also be argued that these lobbying efforts played on pre-existing national security concerns, and would not have resonated with Congress outside of the geopolitical context of this case.

Chevron was definitely the biggest and primary interest group actively lobbying against CNOOC's bid. The Vice-Chairman of Chevron, Peter Robertson, immediately declared that he felt Chevron was "competing with the Chinese government and . . . that is wrong," because "clearly, this is not a commercial competition" (Mouwad & Barboza 2005). Chevron went much further than scathing commentary, however. In fact, it was "Chevron lobbyists [who] helped draft language for at least one letter [that was] circulated by lawmakers to Treasury Secretary John Snow, [which] warns that CNOOC's bid for Unocal . . . challenges American jobs, energy production and national security" (Pierce & Newmeyer 2005). They also "provid[ed] Member offices with information to support th[ose] claims," and even helped "to gather signatures for the letter to Snow" (Pierce & Newmeyer 2005).

A history of campaign contributions to certain members of Congress by Chevron was also considered by many to have helped its cause. Californian representatives, where Chevron was based, obviously had a vested interest in looking out for the company (International Oil Daily 2005a). It is also important to note, however, that "both [Congressmen Hall and Barton] have received significant contributions from Chevron Corp. and Texaco" in the past (Orol 2005d). The Center for Responsive Politics had released information that "Barton received $19,000 . . . while Hall received $9,500" from these companies (Orol 2005d). It was also reported that Congressman Pombo had received $13,500 from Chevron (Alden & Kirchgaessner 2005). It is unlikely, however, that these contributions (the exact timing of which are unspecified) would alone have swayed these congressmen into such active opposition to the CNOOC deal. Many domestic companies that later end up in bidding wars with foreign companies contribute to lawmaker's campaigns, and yet it is extremely rare for those lawmakers to come out so vociferously against a foreign takeover.

Thus, it is highly unlikely that Chevron's lobbying could have been effective without there first being genuine national security and geostrategic issues for it to play upon. To be sure, it was reported at the time that "Chevron Lobbyists are finding a warm reception to the patriotic message they have been pitching on Capitol Hill, especially among Members with oil and gas interests in their districts as well as those with long-standing national security concerns" (Pierce & Newmeyer 2005). For example, Congressman Barton's spokesman Larry Neal responded to criticism over the congressman's position (raised because he had received donations from Chevron in the past) by saying: "Chairman Barton has consistently opposed advancing Chinese governmental interests" (Pierce & Newmeyer 2005).[56] Thus, the general consensus (not surprisingly) was that "while Chevron skillfully drummed up opposition to CNOOC's bid in Washington, it was merely tapping into already existing anti-China sentiment" (EIU 2005).

Outside of Chevron's lobbying efforts, there was one former policymaker in particular who lobbied vociferously against the deal, both as a witness at the House Armed Services Committee hearing and through press, TV, and radio interviews. This was Frank Gaffney, a former member of the Pentagon under President Ronald Reagan and, at the time, the head of the Center for Security Policy. Gaffney took a realist approach to the deal, arguing that China was not an ally and, as already mentioned, that he was worried it was using the deal to gain access to resources it would then make unavailable to the US in the future. While his arguments were well received at the hearing, they lost some support in the public when he lost his realist rational tone and went so far as to call those in favor of the deal "panda huggers" (Kudlow 2005).

CNOOC, however, had also hired a small army of lobbyists and advisors, which it used to counter the image Chevron painted of its intentions. CNOOC actually hired "three investment banks, a pair of media strategy groups, and four law firms" (Linebaugh et al. 2005). The firms hired to "manage the media firestorm" were "Public Strategies Inc., a firm with close ties to the Bush White House, and Brunswick Group, which handled the corporate meltdown at the energy company Enron" (Pierce & Newmeyer 2005). The law firms included Akin Gump Strauss Hauer & Feld, which also was reported to have close "connections to the White House" (Linebaugh et al. 2005; Pierce & Newmeyer 2005). Public Strategies diligently argued, as did CNOOC itself, that the transaction was meant to be a purely "commercial deal" (Gentile 2005). It was also reported that CNOOC's many lobbyists anticipated the arguments put forward by those against the deal,

> and prepared an aggressive response. CNOOC's Chairman immediately sent letters to every member of Congress and to the media. He argued that a Unocal purchase was not a threat to the US at all. Most of Unocal's assets are in Asia, not America. And CNOOC [would] sell whatever Unocal holdings are [in the US]. Unocal's US employees [wouldn't] have to worry either. CNOOC [would] not fire any of them, he wrote. (Davidson 2005)

CNOOC also had a variety of other interest groups on its side, which were not paid lobbyists, but which (for various reasons) had a vested interest in making sure that the bid was not blocked. The US Chamber of Commerce, the one institution from which we might possibly expect an economic nationalist response, publicly announced that it was not against a CNOOC bid for Unocal (Kirchgaessner et al. 2005). Indeed, a number of economic liberal groups were concerned that the market should be allowed to work. The National Foreign Trade Council, which wished to encourage more FDI from China, tried to speak out against the "paranoia" surrounding the deal (Kirchgaessner et al. 2005). Similarly, the National Association of Manufacturers had spoken out against "China's manipulation of its currency," but it maintained "a relaxed stance on takeovers" like many other business lobbies, which, again, welcomed such Chinese FDI (Kirchgaessner et al. 2005). Finally, Jerry Taylor, of the libertarian think-tank the CATO Institute, spoke out often against blocking the deal, usually arguing against Gaffney's position. In fact, he was the only witness at the July 13 Congressional hearing who believed the national security concerns were overblown (AFX 2005c), on the basis that the purchase would not pose a threat to US security because, among other reasons, the US would still be able to purchase oil on the open market.[57] Others who were advocates for the deal included Albert Keidel of the Carnegie Endowment, who argued that the US must:

> engage China in a rules-based global system, as the bedrock for our national military security... If we try to create a non-price based system for securing or guaranteeing energy resources or other scarce resources, we will be creating a climate that will force China into a similar posture. And that is dangerous, in a national military-security sense. (Voice of America 2005)

It should be noted that, despite all of this lobbying, two important and influential players in the case remained neutral. The first is the White House, which argued that it would reserve judgment on the deal until it received a report from CFIUS, when – and if – that process was triggered by a transaction agreement between CNOOC and Unocal (see Wright 2005).[58] Part of the desire to appear neutral may have been because Secretary Rice had previously served as member of Chevron's board (International Oil Daily 2005a). The Administration was very clear that the decision would be made on the merits of the national security assessment of the deal presented to it by the appropriate agency, and that it would not be swayed by interest group efforts.

The second group that remained neutral, and un-swayed by lobbyist pressure, was Unocal itself. As already mentioned, it was quite clear that Unocal's CEO Charles Williams wanted a bidding war, and was actively speaking to both companies throughout the whole process. "Unocal spokesman Barry Lane," for example, made it clear that "his company [was] not actively lobbying Congress on the issue, but [was] considering the CNOOC counter bid" (Pierce & Newmeyer 2005). It was also apparent that Unocal's shareholders, one of the most important interest groups in the takeover of a public company, wanted the highest price possible for the company, no matter who the eventual owner was. Two minority shareholders even went so far as to sue "[Unocal's] board of directors for a breach of their fiduciary duty to the shareholders, . . . contending that the directors failed to test the value of the company fully in the marketplace before hastily accepting Chevron's [original] proposal" (Amaewhule 2005), despite the board's comments that it would still consider CNOOC's later offer.[59]

There also did not seem to be any sort of true labor or union movement against the CNOOC bid, which might have been effective if it had been present. This was probably because of CNOOC's constant claims that it would "seek to retain substantially all Unocal employees" (FD 2005). CNOOC Chairman Fu Chengyu said that the deal would be "good for America," because CNOOC "[would] protect Unocal's US jobs" (Gold et al. 2005). The attorneys general of some states affected by the deal worried that the CNOOC bid might negatively affect Unocal pension plans and its promises on the environment (International Oil Daily 2005b).[60] Yet, these concerns were directed toward Unocal itself, not policymakers, and they did not turn into a widespread movement or seem to have any impact on the deal.

Thus, while some interest groups were pressing for the US government to block a CNOOC/Unocal deal – namely, those sponsored by CNOOC's competitor Chevron – these groups were not the primary motivation behind the US government's strategy of unbounded intervention. For there was an equal amount of pressure on the government coming from CNOOC's lobbyists, as well as from independent free-market and liberal interest groups. Furthermore, it is likely that even if the Chevron-sponsored groups had not lobbied against the deal, a number of these national security issues – especially those involving technology – would have been flagged in the CFIUS process anyway. Finally, Chevron was really only able to make lawmakers aware of existing national security issues involved in the deal, and was not able to coerce them into action. It would not have been able to have any effect on Congress if the geopolitical context of the deal had not been as it was, meaning that interest group presence – though it may have played a role in making legislators aware of the case earlier – was not the *primary* motivation behind government intervention into this foreign takeover.

Competition Concerns

Importantly, no real competition issues were involved with either CNOOC's or Chevron's bid for Unocal. Indeed, the Chevron/Unocal deal received competition clearance from the Federal Trade Commission by June 10, 2005, and no competition problems were expected to arise from CNOOC's alternative bid. "Marc Schildkraut, an attorney with law firm Heller Ehrman, said he [did] not see antitrust problems for the CNOOC-Unocal deal, commenting, 'It's extremely rare for the FTC to care about upstream deals'" (International Oil Daily 2005a). In fact, the only evidence of any concern on this issue comes from Charlie Crist, the Florida Attorney General, who wrote a letter to John Snow urging a review of the deal, because "[he was] concerned about the impact of increasing concentration in the petroleum industry on gasoline prices" (AFX 2005d). Yet, Snow's only comment on the deal was that it would be reviewed if the CFIUS process was triggered, and he did not evince any concern on competition grounds. Indeed, the general consensus of the market seemed to be that "whatever legal tools might be used to block a deal, antitrust probably won't be one of them," because "there is little to suggest an excessive concentration of ownership in the worldwide oil industry" (Orol 2005a).

Finally, it should be noted that the US is generally considered to be one of the most competitive economies in the international marketplace, in the sense that it is a state open to liberal economic business practices and foreign investment.

Conclusions on CNOOC/Unocal

Thus, it must be concluded that unbounded intervention in this case was primarily motivated by the geopolitical issues surrounding the Chinese state-owned company's bid for Unocal, and secondarily by economic nationalism. Interest group presence may have also played a much smaller, tertiary, role in motivating intervention. Yet, it is important to note that neither economic nationalism nor interest group presence would have had the effect that they did in the absence of the geopolitical context, without which those opposed to the case would not have been able to gain the support that they eventually found. Finally, competition issues did not seem to play any significant role.

Unbounded intervention in this case was, thus, clearly an example of non-military internal balancing. CNOOC's bid, and the presumed role played by its state-owned parent company, caused apprehension over the use by the Chinese government of its rising economic power to "buy" power in the form of companies that would supply it with resources, knowledge, and technology. Furthermore, certain members of the US government did not wish to allow China to win the "energy race" through the use of government-subsidized asset purchases that might result in control over vital resources. Therefore, intervention was about preventing a transfer in those forms of relative power from occurring. While this situation, in the context of increased Chinese FDI in the US, did arouse a certain amount of economic nationalist sentiment, intervention was *not* about saving a national champion (as it was in the Danone case). It was about intervening in a market transaction to prevent the loss of relative power to a strategic rival. For, while the CNOOC case was in process, Secretary Rice visited China and made it clear that the US government was aware of "a significant military buildup going on [in China], that is concerning, [and causing the US to] . . . have concerns about the military balance" (Rice 2005). Indeed, those who objected to the deal seemed to honestly believe that the sale of Unocal to CNOOC could lead to the transfer of military technology and of resources that could also eventually be used by the Chinese military. Others, as already mentioned, were concerned that ownership of the company would give the Chinese government more social power and influence in Asia, or even provide it with the ability to gain more power over Taiwan (see e.g., States News Service 2005a). As one member of the US–China ESRC noted, the US was not dealing with "a market economy," because "[China] see[s] resource acquisition as an integral part of their military plans. We need to look at it on the same basis" (Blustein 2005). Similarly, former CIA director James Woolsey called CNOOC's attempt to take over Unocal a "sharp elbow" (Eckert 2005) from a bully, and said that "anyone who believes this is a purely commercial undertaking . . . is extraordinarily naïve" (Ivanovich 2005).

Finally, the CNOOC/Unocal case provides an excellent example of unbounded intervention as *non-military* internal balancing. This is because the "balancing" was targeted and finite, and used a tool that was not expected to – and ultimately did not – damage the overall relationship between the two countries involved.

Case 3: Check Point/Sourcefire

The Story

On October 6, 2005, Check Point Software Technologies Ltd. (an Israeli company) made a mixed cash and share offer for Sourcefire Inc. (a US company) for about $225 million. At the time, both companies specialized in security software, and both provided software to the US government, making the deal seem like a smart fit to market and tech analysts alike.[61] The deal rationale provided by the companies was that

Sourcefire's intrusion prevention system (IPS) software (including a well-known open-source system called Snort) would complement and "strengthen Check Point's perimeter, internal, Web and endpoint security portfolio," allowing it to "expand" into the "fast-growing intrusion prevention and network awareness" business (Check Point 2005).[62] This rationale was well received, and the deal quickly gained the support of the "boards of both companies as well as Sourcefire shareholders" (Vaas 2005), after which it was subjected to an initial thirty-day CFIUS review and the Hart–Scott–Rodino anti-trust process.

On February 13, Check Point confirmed that CFIUS had decided to pursue a further forty-five-day investigation of the deal (Check Point 2006a), and that both companies were cooperating in that process.[63] Though the proceedings of the investigation itself are classified, and the Treasury Department refused to officially comment on whether or not the deal would have made it through the investigation unscathed, it emerged that several objections were raised to the deal while CFIUS performed its review (see Dagoni 2006; FD 2006; Lemos 2006).[64] The primary reported objection was against allowing a foreign company (any foreign company) to take control of a software company that provided computer network and systems security for a number of US government agencies, including the Federal Bureau of Investigation (FBI), the DOD, and the National Security Agency (NSA) (see Dagoni 2006; Greene 2006; Rothman 2006; Williams 2006). These agencies "expressed concern" that the deal "[put] their networks at risk" (Rothman 2006) and would have allowed Israel to "acquire sensitive technology" related to "the implementation of Sourcefire's anti-intrusion software 'Snort'" (Williams 2006). Peter Cooper, a Morgan Stanley analyst, claimed "CFIUS feared that the takeover would expose SNORT to manipulation by a non-US entity" and "that Check Point would shut down the open source software and limit accessibility by users," because "similar occurrences (unrelated to Check Point) had happened before" (Dagoni 2006).

Objections may also have been raised to Check Point, specifically. For, while the company had a "National Security Agency certification" and "has had success in US government security projects," some commentators questioned whether there was concern over the security of the company itself (McLaughlin 2006). One observer, for example, suggested that certain members of government might have had "a dim view of the close ties between key Check Point executives and the [Israeli Defense Forces], especially unit 8200," which handles signals and encryption intelligence (Dagoni 2006). Additionally, an industry source claimed at the time that "government contractors [had] told him that they [were] strictly prohibited from using Check Point software" (McLaughlin 2006).

Either way, it seems that enough concerns were raised during the CFIUS process to assume that the government's actions were tantamount to unbounded intervention. Throughout the process, it was clear that either the deal would be blocked or the requirements placed on both companies would be so onerous, and the delay to the completion of the deal so great, that Check Point would withdraw its offer voluntarily. For instance, "in private meetings between the panel and Check Point, FBI and Pentagon officials" made it obvious to the company that they "took exception to letting foreigners acquire the sensitive technology" (Williams 2006). Apparently, Check Point's "lawyers had tried to salvage the deal by offering to attach conditions intended to satisfy the Feds, despite execs feeling they were onerous," but "agreement could still not be reached" between the parties (Williams 2006). It was even reported that "the US [government] made the approval process so miserable for both parties that they threw in the towel" (Rothman 2006).

Thus, on March 23, 2006, Check Point announced that it was withdrawing from the CFIUS process, a week ahead of the recommendation the Committee was due to make to the President regarding the deal (Lemos 2006). CFIUS agreed to its withdrawal, and Check Point declared in a press release that it was now seeking a simple "business partnership" with Sourcefire, rather than continuing to pursue its acquisition of the company (Check Point 2006b; Dagoni 2006). Check Point also released a statement providing its rationale for abandoning the transaction, stating that "given the complex technology, the complexity of the process, [and] the current scrutiny of CFIUS, we have come to the conclusion that it may be simpler and better to pursue other partnership alternatives or take more time to work with the government" (Lemos 2006). Sourcefire's Chief Marketing Officer similarly blamed the pullout on "the complexities of the overall CFIUS process, the lengthy ongoing delays and the current climate for international acquisitions" (Chickowski 2006). One industry source believed that "the government" may have "put forward requirements that the companies found unacceptable" or that "CFIUS was dragging its feet" on purpose (Brockmeier 2006).

Yet, it was more than the costly delays and complex negotiations that scuttled the deal. For a number of analysts agreed that "the Bush Administration would have vetoed the Check Point... Sourcefire deal and that withdrawal from the acquisition was the only way for Check Point to avoid being branded a security risk" (Dagoni 2006). Thus, in the end, the deal was dropped because of unbounded government intervention:

multiple objections were raised by the government agencies that took part in the CFIUS investigation, the process was lengthy and difficult enough to be viewed as discouraging the transaction, and it was overwhelmingly believed that the deal would be blocked by the government at the end of that process.

Because Sourcefire's spokesman had mentioned the "current political climate," some observers blamed the government's intervention, and thus the ultimate failure of this deal, on the negative attitudes toward FDI raised by the DPW dispute, which was in full swing by the time Check Point withdrew from the CFIUS investigation.[65] Yet, the member agencies of CFIUS had raised objections to the deal long before the ports row began (Weisman & Schmidt 2006).[66] Furthermore, the nature and tenor of their concerns, which were not politicized by lawmakers as they were in the DPW transaction, suggest that the DPW dispute did not play a significant role in motivating government intervention in this case, as the software deal was unlikely to survive the CFIUS process anyway (see e.g., Brockmeier 2006). Indeed, the only role the ports dispute may have played was to contribute to the belief on the part of Check Point that its bid would be blocked by CFIUS, though it has yet to be proven that CFIUS can be swayed in its recommendations by political pressure, and enough reasons can be cited for the deal to have been blocked beyond the existence of a negative "political climate."

Geopolitical Competition

Though the US and Israel are not formal military allies,[67] the historical relationship between them has been extremely close, and is considered by many to constitute a security community (see Adler in Katzenstein et al. 1996, 434; Adler & Barnett 1998, 33). For, "even though there is no treaty obligation" between them, "President Bush has said several times that the United States would defend Israel militarily in the event of an attack" (Migdalovitz 2007, 23), a fact ensured by the close historical, diplomatic, and political relationship between the two countries.[68] As Adler points out, however, even this "special relationship" can be subject "to corrosive forces," and will, therefore, at times experience tension within it (Adler in Katzenstein et al. 1996, 434).

At the time of this particular transaction, for example, tensions between the two countries had only just begun to ease after a 2003 dispute over "Israeli arm sales to China," which caused the "annual interagency strategic dialogue" between the two countries to be suspended until November 2005 (Migdalovitz 2007, 29–30). And while Israel itself is obviously not perceived as a strategic competitor or general threat,

US government agencies remain concerned that its lack of cooperation on issues relating to US export control laws could negatively impact US national security.[69] Part of the problem has been that Israel is not a party to any of the multilateral export control regimes, and only "voluntarily adhere[s] to the Wassenaar Arrangement on Export Controls for Conventional Arms and Dual-Use Goods and Technologies" (Migdalovitz 2007, 32; SIPRI 2004). Just over a month before Check Point made it its bid for Sourcefire,

> the US DOD and the Israeli Ministry of Defense issued a joint press statement reporting that they had signed an understanding "designed to remedy problems of the past that seriously affected the technology security relationship and to restore confidence in the technology security area. In the coming months additional steps will be taken to restore confidence fully." (Migdalovitz 2007, 25)

Given this climate, it is not surprising that the US would be concerned about the purchase of a US company, which developed network security for its federal agencies, by an Israeli one. For, as one industry commentator noted, even among the closest of "allies, . . . all bets are off relative to source code" (Rothman 2006).[70] Indeed, a great deal of legitimacy would have been given to the concern that the sensitive code, which would have been purchased as part of this deal, might be passed on not only to the Israeli government, but also possibly to third-party governments that might be on less friendly terms with the US.

While it seems clear that these geostrategic concerns provided strong motivation for the US government's unbounded intervention in this case, it is unlikely that any of the remaining geopolitical factors to be examined in this section played such a significant role. First, it is unlikely that US resource dependency played any role in this case. The level of US resource dependency, while not low at 36.35% in 2005 and 37.68% in 2006, is also not excessively high compared to that of other nations.[71] Moreover, Israel is not a major supplier of energy to the US, providing just 0.04% of US imports of crude oil and petroleum products in 2005 and 2006 combined (EIA 2008c). Second, the relative power differential between the two countries is not only decidedly in the US' favor, but does not seem to be changing in any significant way. Unlike the US, Israel is not considered a major power, and it is also not considered a rising power. The five-year average economic growth rates of both countries remained largely similar.[72] Furthermore, Israel's military expenditure remained under 2.5% of that of the US, and its five-year average military growth rate actually declined during 2005 and 2006, while that of the US increased.[73]

Economic Nationalism

As discussed in the CNOOC case, the level of economic nationalism in the US was considered to be fairly low.[74] Sourcefire was never referred to as a national champion and, though it is very important to the government, it is an extremely small company.[75] Overall, the industry at the time seemed to believe the combination would be good for the technology involved, and for the industry as a whole (see McLaughlin 2006; Rothman 2006; Vaas 2005). The US is also "Israel's largest trading partner," and that trade is far from insignificant, totaling $29.9 billion in 2005 (Jones 2006; Migdalovitz 2007). This can partly be attributed to the US–Israeli free-trade agreement (Migdalovitz 2007, 21). Thus, it would not have made a huge amount of sense for the government to block the deal on economic nationalist grounds, and there seems to be no evidence available to show that this was a motivation behind its unbounded intervention.

Presence of Interest Groups

Finally, the control variable of interest group presence did not seem to provide a motivation for government intervention in this case, either. No evidence can be found of interest groups lobbying against the deal (outside of the government agencies themselves), and the only lobbying that does seem to have occurred was in favor of the deal. Though "Check Point had committed to an all out effort to lobby the committee for approval," its efforts were reportedly unsuccessful (Lemos 2006). In fact, the most powerful interest group in the US, the Israel lobby, would have been in favor of the deal. No reason can be found for the labor pool involved in the deal to protest either, as Check Point announced to the press that it "w[ould] be adding SourceFire's 140 employees to its own staff of 1400 and expect[ed] no layoffs" (Vaas 2005). Thus, in addition to the lack of evidence that this particular variable motivated government intervention, it is also highly unlikely that it would have done so.

Competition Concerns

Nor is there evidence available to show that competition concerns played any role in motivating government intervention in this case. The US concern with its competitive role in the international marketplace has already been explained in the CNOOC case, and is unlikely to have played any role here. Furthermore, there is definitive proof that anti-trust competition concerns did not affect this transaction in a negative way.

Check Point was "granted early termination" of the competition waiting period that is part of the Hart–Scott–Rodino process by both the FTC and the DOJ's Antitrust Division in November 2005 (Federal Register 2005), long before CFIUS even started its forty-five-day investigation.

Conclusions on Check Point/Sourcefire

Thus, we must conclude that it was national security concerns, motivated by specific geopolitical concerns, which were the root cause of unbounded government intervention in this case. It is rare for geopolitical concerns to be the primary motivating factor within the context of a security community relationship, and this case is critical because it demonstrates how and why this can occur. The US was worried not only about maintaining access to the Snort intrusion protection software created by Sourcefire (which was "open source"), but also over other Sourcefire systems used by the government (which were "not open source"), which would have been wholly owned by a foreign company if the transaction had been successful (Brockmeier 2006). Indeed, the US concerns over the deal seem to be legitimate given Israel's fairly lax approach to export controls of sensitive technology in the past. Thus, it can be concluded that the primary (and sole) motivating factor behind government intervention in this case was geostrategic concern.

Case 4: Macquarie/PCCW

The Story

On June 19, 2006, PCCW Ltd. (based in Hong Kong) confirmed that a consortium led by Macquarie Bank (of Australia) had made a preliminary offer for its core media and telephone assets for an estimated $5.15 billion (International Herald Tribune 2006a; Mitchell 2006; Zephyr 2006c).[76] The potential transaction came under fire almost immediately, as the Chinese state-owned China Netcom[77] raised major objections to the sale. At the time, China Netcom was the second-largest shareholder of PCCW, with a 20% stake in the company, as well as a "shareholder's agreement" that gave it control over any future sale of the company beyond a certain threshold (Fellman & Ong 2006).[78] The state-run company claimed on June 21 that it was not "willing to see any major changes to the asset structure of PCCW" (Fellman & Ong 2006), and it was reported only two days later to have "objected to any sale of PCCW's assets on the basis that the company is and should remain 'owned and managed by Hong Kong people'" (Lau & Mitchell 2006b).

China Netcom made it clear it would not approve of the sale to such a foreign consortium,[79] an action that had, at the very least, the tacit approval of the Chinese government. By June 27, it was reported that "China Netcom, the State-owned Assets Supervision and Administration Commission, and the Ministry of Information submitted reports to China's State Council about the bids for PCCW and are awaiting instruction" (Kwong 2006). Such actions made it apparent that the state-run shareholder would do what Beijing wished in the matter, and "most people involved in the PCCW saga think the Chinese government worked through China Netcom to scuttle the Macquarie and TPG Newbridge bids on nationalist grounds" (Dyer et al. 2006). The issue was greater than simply one of nationalism, however: the telecommunications sector is viewed as "a very strategic asset" in China, making the Chinese government "sensitiv[e] toward overseas ownership" in that industry (Chan & Fellman 2006).

Macquarie's consortium tried to overcome China's stark opposition by offering to incorporate China Netcom into the deal. By June 25, "Macquarie, seeking to make its bid acceptable to China, had offered China Network a 50% stake in a new Hong Kong phone company it planned to set up with the assets" purchased in the proposed deal (Mitchell 2006). Yet, this only seemed to cause more political problems, as the Hong Kong authorities were concerned it would only increase the "political and commercial clout" of Beijing in Hong Kong (Mitchell 2006). Similarly, it was argued that "China's perceived sensitivity over the sale of Hong Kong assets to foreign parties raises questions about whether there are in fact unwritten limits to the territory's economic and financial freedoms, which are guaranteed under its mini-constitution, the Basic Law" (Lau & Mitchell 2006a). This solution seemed unworkable not only for Beijing, but for Hong Kong as well.

Thus, it was not surprising when PCCW rejected approaches from both Macquarie and TPG on July 25. PCCW blamed the failure of the bids on China Netcom, because the company had, "in its capacity as a shareholder, . . . repeatedly indicated its opposition to such an asset sale" (Tucker & Mitchell 2006). By July 29, Rupert Murdoch told the press that China was "treating Macquarie as hostile invaders" (Lau 2006).[80] Indeed, the market widely accepts that the Chinese government would have blocked the Macquarie/PCCW deal if necessary, though this was in effect achieved through the objections of its company China Netcom.[81] As the following exploration of the motivations behind this behavior show, this was again a case of geopolitical competition and economic nationalism leading to state intervention in a cross-border acquisition.

Geopolitical Competition

Though their relationship is not necessarily negative, China and Australia are not allies or members of the same security community. Certainly, Australia is not really perceived as a threat to China, though there are points of tension and disagreement on issues such as human rights, intellectual property, and the treatment of Taiwan (Australia DFAT 2007b). Indeed, China is considered a major, and rising, power, while Australia is not, and China is clearly more powerful than Australia in both military and economic terms. China's five-year average economic growth rate was 12.09% in 2006, while Australia's was 4.94%, and Australia's PPP GDP in 2006 was only 9.28% of China's.[82] Similarly, China's five-year average growth rate of military expenditure was 12.35% in 2006, compared with Australia's 4.56% (SIPRI 2006). Considering that Australia's military expenditure was only about 27.87% that of China's at the time (SIPRI 2006), Australia had much greater concern for China's power than the other way around.

Furthermore, China's general level of dependence on energy imports was fairly low in 2006 at 0.14%, but there are some resource areas in which China recognizes the importance of its geopolitical relationship to Australia. First, China has signed two agreements with Australia on the transfer of nuclear material: the Australia–China Nuclear Material Transfer Agreement and the Nuclear Cooperation Agreement, which entered into force on February 3, 2006 (Australia DFAT 2007a). This is because China expected that it would soon be required to import uranium for the purposes of electrical generation in nuclear plants, as its own supply of nuclear energy is outstripped by demand (Australia DFAT 2007a). Australia's cooperation on this resource issue makes it seem more likely that China would wish to maintain a cordial economic relationship between the two countries.

Yet, China has also recently made it clear that it does not wish to become reliant on any individual country generally, or on Australia specifically, for natural resources. Only two years after the PCCW case, the Chinese government sought to block the acquisition of Rio Tinto by BHP Billiton, by purchasing enough shares of Rio Tinto in a "dawn raid" to achieve a 9% stake in the company, "mak[ing] it more difficult for BHP to buy Rio" (Bream et al. 2008). Though steel is a non-energy-related basic resource, it is vitally important to the running of any nation, especially one with a rapidly developing infrastructure and military. It was reported that "the Chinese government [was] dismayed at the prospect of a BHP takeover of Rio as it would give the combined company a virtual monopoly on iron ore supplies to China, which it fears would lead to higher prices and damage the country's economic growth" (Bream et al. 2008). The "dawn raid" was "a joint exercise" between "Chinalco, a state-owned mining company" and "Alcoa, the US aluminum group," which "spent $14bn in [the] move designed to block [the] planned $119bn takeover bid from rival miner BHP Billiton" (Bream et al. 2008). As one market source, who spoke on the condition of anonymity, confirmed, the primary mover behind the intervention was the Chinese government, whose concern over its source of steel prompted it to willingly (and greatly) overpay for the stake in order to prevent the takeover.[83] Thus, China is obviously quite willing to block M&A that threaten its access to or control over certain key industries and resources.

Furthermore, China exhibits a tendency to view most nations as strategic competitors – especially in geo-economic terms – irrespective of the historical details of their bilateral relationship. Thus, it would be difficult to imagine a scenario in which China's actions to prevent a foreign takeover were not at least partially motivated by this larger geostrategic concern and the desire to protect its position of power within the international system. As examined next, China's outlook means that economic nationalism is tied in this case to geopolitical competition.

Economic Nationalism

China and Australia have a fairly good economic relationship. Both are members of APEC and the East Asia Summit (Australia DFAT 2008). A free-trade agreement also exists between the two countries, and bilateral trade is one of the foundations of the relationship and of continued dialogue between them (Australia DFAT 2007b).

Despite this, however, economic nationalism in China is on the rise, and it is clear that economic nationalism played some role in the government intervention in this case. It is true that at this time the level of national pride in China was not overwhelming, at 24.7% (WVS 2001–04), and that pro-globalization sentiment was just above the median value of fifty-four countries surveyed in 2006, and on a similar level to the attitudes toward globalization in the US that year (see IMD 2007b).[84] Yet, in China, an unusually high disconnect exists between these measurements – determined through questions asked of the general population – and the actual levels of nationalism or economic nationalist sentiment present in the Chinese government, which still runs a large portion of the state's economy. Barry Naughton argued in his 2007 testimony to the US–China ESRC that there had been "a clear increase in economic nationalism" in China in recent years (US–China ESRC

2007).[85] In fact, there was widespread concern over "rising economic nationalism in China" at this time, not only among analysts and academics, but also among "senior officials from a number of countries" – especially in relation to recent Chinese opposition to the proposed foreign takeovers of Chinese companies (XFN 2006b; see also XFN 2006a; Morgan 2006).

There has also been a history of significant support for national champions in China since the 1980s (US–China ESRC 2007). That was when China began to "experiment with industrial policies . . . designed to strengthen larger firms and grow 'national champions'" (US–China ESRC 2007). While this policy weakened in the mid-1990s, experts agree that China seems to have resumed its support for national champions over "the past five years" (US–China ESRC 2007). Though the Chinese government never referred to PCCW as a "national champion" on record, the company held the majority of the telecommunications business in Hong Kong and was referred to as China Netcom's "cash cow" (Schwankert 2006), making it – at the very least – an important asset for a national champion, namely China Netcom.

Significantly, the Chinese government formally banned foreign investment in the telecommunications industry, and thus in companies such as PCCW, just months after the Macquarie bid was blocked, indicating the degree of sentiment against foreign takeovers in China at the time, and the negative reactions to deals such as the one being investigated here. In September 2006, less than two months after the Macquarie/PCCW transaction failed, the new Provisions for Mergers and Acquisitions of Domestic Enterprises by Foreign Investors, regulating foreign takeovers in China, came into force. Article 12 of these Provisions establishes the right to review foreign M&A that would establish control over Chinese companies that are in a "major industry, ha[ve] or may have influence on state security, or . . . [involve a] domestic enterprise owning [a] famous trademark."[86]

In addition to the new Provisions on Acquisitions, two separate Chinese government bodies that have played a significant role in protectionist policies against foreign takeovers – the State Asset Supervision and Administration Commission (SASAC) and the National Development and Reform Commission (NDRC) – issued new directives around the time of the failed Macquarie/PCCW transaction. First, the Chairman of SASAC announced in December 2006 that the Chinese state would "retain absolute control over [seven] sectors that are important to state security and economy," namely "telecommunications, . . . petroleum, . . . military-related industry, power and power networks, coal, civil aviation, and shipping," though some limited foreign investment would be allowed in some areas (Zheng 2007). This meant the Chinese government would maintain "more than 50% ownership stakes in the primary firms in those industries" (US–China ESRC 2007).[87] According to Naughton's testimony, this law "merely re-affirms the status quo" (US–China ESRC 2007), demonstrating that it was always unlikely the Chinese government would have allowed Macquarie to take control of PCCW. Second, in February 2007, it was reported that the NDRC wanted to create a body called the Joint Review Commission for Foreign Investment Sectors, which would review foreign takeovers in a large number of Chinese sectors (AFX 2007).[88]

It should also be noted here that by September 2011, the Chinese government had established a national "security review" for foreign takeovers, which – while loosely similar in form to the CFIUS process – retains a very different character. For example, the Chinese government Circular on the process states that the "content of [the] security review" will include not only "the effect of [the transaction] on the national security," but also its "effect" on "national steady economic growth" and "basic social living order."[89] (For a more detailed discussion of the Chinese FDI laws that have been introduced since this case, see Chapter 5).

Thus, it is clear that a high level of economic nationalism existed before, during, and after the failed Macquarie bid for PCCW: economic nationalism specifically targeted against foreign takeovers. It is also clear that telecommunications and media are particularly sensitive industries for the Chinese government when it comes to foreign takeovers for strategic reasons. The directives issued shortly after Macquarie's bid illustrate the Chinese government's desire to deter any such attempted takeovers in the future, and indicate its willingness to block those bids that are attempted. With all of this in mind, it is fairly obvious that economic nationalism – in addition to geopolitical concerns over their economic and military power – played a distinct role in motivating the Chinese to engage in unbounded intervention in this particular case.

Presence of Interest Groups

It is highly unlikely that interest group presence played a role in motivating intervention in this case. This is because the Chinese political system does not allow interest groups to flourish, and frequently crushes any such opposition to the will of the government. No interest groups were observed to be placing pressure on the government to block the deal at the time. Indeed, the only interest groups that seemed to appear in relation to the case represented members of Macquarie's consortium, and they were, obviously, in favor of the deal. This variable, therefore, can be ruled out as a motivating factor in this case.

Competition Concerns

As will be recalled, one form of "competition" that might be connected to China's actions has to do with whether or not China is believed to be "competitive" in the international market as a state open to foreign investment and business. It is fairly clear that, in certain industries, such as the telecommunications industry examined here, China is not open to such investment insofar as large-scale takeovers are concerned. Yet, China has made a distinct effort to encourage such foreign investment in other sectors, and even to encourage alternative forms of FDI in sensitive sectors, whether through JVs or co-sponsored projects. This is why the subjective economic competitiveness rating for China in 2006 was 4.58, just below the mean rating for the countries examined in the database. Though it does seem clear, in this case, that government intervention was connected to one of those areas it had "closed" to such competition.

On the other hand, competition concerns, as they are traditionally understood, are unlikely to have played a role in motivating government intervention in this case. At the time, several laws existed in China "incorporating antitrust provisions and prohibitions on anti-competitive conduct," but these laws were largely "fragmented, confined in scope, and rarely enforced" (Ha & O'Brien 2008; see Huang & Richardson 2005).[90] For example, in relation to merger controls to address anti-trust competition concerns arising from cross-border M&A, the 2003 Interim Provisions on Mergers and Acquisitions of Domestic Enterprises by Foreign Investors prohibited foreign takeovers that "might lead to over-concentration, impair fair competition, or damage consumers' interests."[91] But the Interim Provisions did "not specify any penalties . . . for non-compliance with the [law], and no follow-up activity appears to be taken in the vast majority of [cases]" (Ha & O'Brien 2008). Thus, China did not yet have a formal comprehensive anti-competition regime in place at the time of the failed Macquarie bid, of the type that was later adopted under the 2008 Anti-Monopoly Law (AML).[92] Even had there been one, there is no evidence to suggest that the proposed transaction would have caused an unwelcome concentration within the telecommunications or media industries, as Macquarie is an investment bank and not a telecoms company.

Conclusions on Macquarie/PCCW

The Chinese government's effort to block the takeover of PCCW by the consortium led by Australia's Macquarie through the actions of its State-run company China Netcom was primarily motivated by geopolitical and economic nationalist concerns that were deeply interrelated. In China, it seems to be more difficult to separate these two variables from one another, as economic nationalism in the M&A sector plays such an unambiguous role in the State's efforts to increase or maintain its relative power, at the very same time that it is trying to open up other areas of its economy under World Trade Organization (WTO) rules in order to enhance its international standing. Indeed, this remains one of the areas in which China can protect itself from unwanted FDI, as the "sensitivity" of the sectors allows it to engage in such protectionism with some measure of impunity and without fear of retaliation. Indeed, Macquarie's failed bid did not seem to cause any tangible damage to the overall relationship between Australia and China, though it may have discouraged similar attempts at investment from being made in the near future.

Conclusion

The four cases of unbounded intervention examined in this chapter provide excellent supporting evidence for both the theory of non-military balancing and the conclusions reached in Chapter 2. In keeping with the fundamental argument of this book, each case demonstrates that government interventions were usually motivated by either geopolitical or economic nationalist concerns, with one or the other being the primary and/or secondary motivation in every case. In further support of the conclusions reached in Chapter 2, geopolitical concerns were also the *primary* reason for unbounded intervention in every case where the two states involved were not members of the same security community. This includes the CNOOC/Unocal and Macquarie/PCCW cases, though the nature of China's capitalist autocracy does make geopolitical concerns and economic nationalism more difficult to disentangle in the latter.

Interestingly, the Check Point/Sourcefire case illustrates that geopolitical concerns can, under certain conditions, also be the primary motivator behind unbounded intervention within the security community context if, for example, the acquiring state raises very specific, and hard to avoid, security concerns regarding the takeover in question. In the Check Point/Sourcefire case, for example, the issue was Israel's history of lax adherence to export control laws in combination with a target company with extremely sensitive technology used by US government agencies.

Figure 27 Motivation matrix: unbounded intervention

Case	Geopolitical Competition	Economic Nationalism
Security Community Cases		
PepsiCo/Danone	Secondary	Primary
Check Point/Sourcefire	Primary	
Non-Security Community Cases		
CNOOC/Unocal	Primary	Secondary
Macquarie/PCCW	Primary	Secondary

Not surprisingly, the only case in which economic nationalism provided the primary motivation behind unbounded intervention was the PepsiCo/Danone one. Yet, it is important to note that, even in this case, geopolitical tension was the secondary reason for the government's desire to block the transaction in question. This suggests that geopolitical competition is usually present in some form or another when a state chooses a strategy of unbounded intervention over, say, one of "bounded" intervention (a point that will be explored further in Chapter 5).

Furthermore, the control variable of "interest group presence" was found to play only a minor role, and the control variable of "competition concern" no role at all, in the government's action in the four cases explored in this chapter. Indeed, interest groups were only moderately effective in raising awareness in the CNOOC/Unocal case. It is significant, however, that the role of interest groups was simply to alert government actors to pre-existing concerns, and was not a primary or secondary *motivator* of intervention, per se.

In sum, the four cases examined here provide clear support for the primary hypothesis and its supporting assumptions. Figure 27 summarizes the motivations for unbounded intervention uncovered in each of these cases.

Finally, each of these cases supports the secondary hypothesis that the type of intervention employed by the state would be closely correlated to the deal outcome. In each case, governments engaged in unbounded intervention, and in each case, the deal was either completely or "effectively" blocked.

NOTES

1 For discussions of the costs associated with over- and underbalancing in reaction to a change or threatened change in relative power, see e.g., Schweller 1998, 2004; Wolforth 1993; and Waltz 1979, 172.

2 As discussed in Chapter 1, it is important to understand that many different government actors ultimately contribute to a state's final stance on a specified transaction, from bureaucrats and civil service members, to members of a congress or parliament, to executive branches and ultimately to heads of government. For a more detailed explanation of why, please refer to Chapter 1, note 33.

3 If the proposed bid were to be financed through debt rather than, or in addition to, cash or stock, then the debt already raised could be costly to maintain until the bidding process is over. There are also audience and opportunity costs associated with a lengthy bidding process that the acquiring company may wish to avoid if they become too onerous.

4 As mentioned in Chapter 1, legal sources confirm that in the US, CFIUS and/or its member organizations will indicate to a company whether or not it is likely to emerge successfully from a CFIUS review or investigation. This is one of the reasons that the number of withdrawals during the review/investigation process is exponentially higher than the number of presidential vetoes of a transaction (of which there were only four from 1988 to 2017). For further details on the number of withdrawals during the CFIUS review process, see Chapter 1, note 35.

5 Many countries do allow for either an administrative and/or a judicial review of their own government's decision to block an investment on national security grounds; indeed, the OECD Investment Division's report found that of the seventeen countries examined, the laws of ten allowed for an administrative review, and sixteen for judicial reviews (Wehrlé & Pohl 2016, 40–2). However, the report also notes that, in practice, such appeals processes are rarely used, both because formal vetoes themselves are rare, and because where foreign investors and governments do not find common ground during or before the investment screening process, the investors will usually either bow out or "submit a revised proposal aimed at accommodating the security concern" (Wehrlé & Pohl 2016, 40–1). In the US, there is no right to either administrative or judicial review of a President's *decision* to formally veto an investment on national security grounds (Wehrlé & Pohl 2016, 42), though following the 2014 US DC Circuit Court of Appeals case *Ralls* v. *CFIUS*, "judicial review of constitutionally-protected due process rights may be available" to foreign investors whose investments are vetoed by CFIUS (ABASAL 2015, 214); for further details on the Ralls case, see Introduction, note 16.

6 Two examples have been included in which the target is from the US because the home states of the acquiring companies in each instance had vastly different political relationships with the US. Both these cases also faced an unusual level of politicization, sparking a worldwide debate about this particular form of intervention and arguably changing the discourse surrounding it.

7 It could be argued that the rankings of these motivations were switched in one case (the attempted purchase of the German company MTU Aero Engines by the American firm Kohlberg Kravis Roberts & Company (KKR) in 2003), because of the extremely sensitive nature of the target company's product and concerns that such a sale could make state *B* more dependent on state *A* for military technology in the future.

8 There have been recent cases of governments recognizing that there could be a link between FDI in some large agricultural companies and national security, arguably because the foreign takeover of a big agricultural producer could – in theory – raise the specter of a foreign power seeking to disrupt a nation's food supply or food security, as well as because of concerns raised in 2016 that industry consolidation through cross-border M&A could lead to an overall reduction in major agribusiness companies globally, with implications for the security and quality of supply. For example, in the US after 9/11, agriculture and food were included within the critical infrastructure to be protected by the Office of Homeland Security (see Moteff & Paromak 2004), and "on July 12, 2016 Senator Charles Grassley introduced S. 3161 to include the Secretary of Agriculture as a permanent member of the CFIUS and to include the national security impact of foreign investments on agricultural assets as part of the criteria the Committee uses in deciding to recommend that the President block a foreign acquisition" (Jackson 2016b, summary). CFIUS has also recently reviewed, but ultimately approved, a couple of foreign investments in this sector. For example, in 2013, the proposed takeover of the US company Smithfield Foods by the Chinese company Shuanghui International Holdings Ltd. was subjected to a full forty-five-day investigation following high levels of US domestic political opposition and concerns over food security, marking the first time the United States Department of Agriculture (USDA) was brought into the CFIUS process on an ad hoc basis, but was ultimately approved "without any conditions" (Carlson et al. 2014, 472). In 2016, CFIUS also reviewed the takeover of the Swiss agribusiness and seed biotech company Syngenta by the Chinese state-owned enterprise (SOE) ChemChina for national security risks, again bringing the USDA into the process, and again eventually approving the transaction (see e.g., Atkins & Weinland 2016).

9 It should also be noted that this case falls outside the technical parameters of the database, because its deal value was just below the $500 million dollar threshold used. It is included here, however, because even though its deal value was just a little low, market and research analysts believed it would have a significant impact on the prospects for future cross-border consolidation of companies in that particular sector of high-tech software. This case is also one of the few examples of a company pulling out of the CFIUS and bidding processes after the initiation of a full forty-five-day investigation in which the parties involved have been publicly identified. Thus, while the parameters set for the database were necessarily restrictive in order to increase the level of comparability among cases and to ensure the validity of the statistical results found, not all critical cases fit neatly within them. It is thus equally important to ensure that such significant cases are examined qualitatively and not discarded from consideration.

10 This story initially leaked when the news service *Dow Jones* cited "an advance copy of the French publication *Challenges*" (Matthews 2005).

11 A "hostile" takeover is considered to be one "which goes against the wishes of the target company's management and board of directors" (Investor Words 2008). The virulent tone of Jacques Chirac and Dominique de Villepin's

comments during the summer of 2005, however, suggests that they also considered "hostile" foreign takeovers to include those that have not been invited, or at least tacitly approved, by the government.

12 For the full text, see Article 30 of French Law No. 2004-1343 of December 9, 2004.

13 For a discussion of France's intent, see e.g., Carnegy et al. 2014; Shumpeter 2014.

14 Specifically, the industries added in the 2014 decree were: "a) Electricity, gas, hydrocarbon or other energy supplies b) Water supplies c) Transport operators d) Electronic communications e) Installations of vital national interest f) Protection of public health" (Hepher 2014).

15 This ratio of 62.60% for 2005 is consistent with the range of that same ratio from 2000 to 2004, which was between 60.96% (in 2001) and 63.38% (in 2000). Numbers used for these calculations were projected from past IEA data, sourced from IEA 2006. For the calculation used, see Chapter 2.

16 These figures are reported in constant 2005 US dollars by SIPRI (2006).

17 These numbers were calculated from data sourced from SIPRI (2006).

18 The ratio of US to French GDP PPP was 6.82. The numbers used for this calculation were sourced from the World Bank's World Development Indicators (WDI) database, reported in current international dollars (WDI 2008).

19 Numbers calculated from data from the WDI database (WDI 2008).

20 For further details on the timeline of French participation in NATO, see: www.diplomatie.gouv.fr/en/french-foreign-policy/defence-security/france-and-nato/.

21 As with other European countries' takeover laws, France now has different rules regarding the screening of investments from foreign investors of EU origin and those originating (ultimately) from outside the EU. In France, *all* foreign investments in *some* strategic sectors are reviewed. Narrower definitions of the remaining strategic sectors are then applied to EU-originating foreign investments than are applied for non-EU investors, in order to ensure compliance with "the case law of the European Court of Justice, which requires that measures restricting the free movement of capital within the European Union be narrowly-tailored to the protection of the public order or public safety" (Cafritz 2014, 2–6).

22 As discussed earlier (see Introduction, pages 4–5), European states maintain the individual right to veto foreign takeovers on national security grounds under the provisions of the 2004 European Takeover Directive and the Treaty of the European Union. See the European Takeover Directive (DIRECTIVE 2004/25/EC) and Chapter 4, Articles 63 (ex Article 56 TEC) and 65 (ex Article 58 TEC) of the Consolidated Versions of the Treaty on European Union and the Treaty on the Functioning of the European Union (2016/C 202/01).

23 In 2006, the IMD World Competitiveness Yearbook covered sixty-one countries, but for this particular variable, survey data were available only for fifty-four (see IMD 2007b).

24 It should be noted that "Villepin . . . was the first to coin the phrase 'economic patriotism'" (Betts 2005). From the beginning, he strenuously "urged his

compatriots to rally behind his concept of 'economic patriotism' to ensure they compete more effectively in a globalizing world" (Thornhill & Jones 2005). De Villepin declared: "I am absolutely convinced that France has exceptional assets and has nothing to fear from international competition. But our forces must be united, organized and mobilized so that we have the will to win together, business chiefs, social groups, the state and workers" (Thornhill & Jones 2005).

25 As one market analyst put it: "If I put myself in Pepsi's shoes, do I want to invest $30 billion in buying a company in France with President Chirac, the chairman, unions, and farmers hostile to the move? You'd be insane" (WSJ 2005a).

26 At the beginning of the bidding process, many market analysts and observers agreed that a CNOOC/Unocal deal would make sense insofar as the two companies' assets seemed to be a good fit for one another (see e.g., Chen 2005). There seemed to be a big difference between these analysts, who initially dismissed the national security concerns involved and focused on the financials of each bid, and policymakers, who emphasized them (International Oil Daily 2005b). This is not to say, however, that the market did not acknowledge early on that US policymakers would be wary of the deal. Not too long before the Unocal race, there was a scandal involving China Aviation Oil, which demonstrated the problems inherent in China's lax financial reporting requirements. Despite this, the market still believed that CNOOC could win because of the premium its bid offered to shareholders (AFP 2005b).

27 See Executive Order 12829. The American Bar Association (ABA) also provides one of the clearest explanations of the FOCI process (see Enix-Ross 2006).

28 Both FOCI and Hart–Scott–Rodino reviews can last anywhere from one to six months (Grundman & Roncka 2006).

29 For the text of the Byrd Amendment, see Section 837(a) of the National Defense Authorization Act for Fiscal Year 1993 (P.L. 102–484).

30 Executive Order 13456 was issued on January 23, 2008. After a period of public comment and analysis within CFIUS itself of the amendment requirements, the US Department of the Treasury (DOT) issued its final regulations on how the law would be implemented in practice on November 14, 2008, officially called the Regulations Pertaining to Mergers, Acquisitions, and Takeovers by Foreign Persons (see 73 FR 70702).

31 It does this, for example, by requiring CFIUS to provide "guidance on the types of transactions that the Committee has reviewed and that have presented national security considerations," and to provide an annual report to Congress with a comprehensive overview of their activities, in addition to briefings on individual cases when requested. For further details, see the Foreign Investment and National Security Act of 2007 (also known as Public Law 110–49, July 26, 2007).

32 Under Exon–Florio, these government agencies included "the Director of the Office of Science and Technology Policy, the Assistant to the President for National Security Affairs, . . . the Assistant to the President for

Economic Policy, . . . the [DHS], . . . the Secretary of Treasury, . . . the Secretaries of State, Defense, and Commerce, the Attorney General, the Director of the Office of Management and Budget, the U.S. Trade Representative, and the Chairman of the Council of Economic Advisers" (US DOT 2007).

33 The issues addressed at the hearing included "Beijing's currency-management practices [and whether they were] designed to give Chinese firms an unfair advantage over US companies in the world marketplace. Both Treasury Secretary John Snow and Fed Chairman Alan Greenspan . . . [testified]" (Gold et al. 2005).

34 For further details, see H.R. 3058 (US House 2005b).

35 As Amaewhule points out, the issue was all about timing, not only because CNOOC was facing "immense political pressure," but also because Chevron (its competitor for Unocal) had managed to move forward by several weeks the date on which Unocal's shareholders would vote on their bid for the company. This meant that CNOOC was left "with a mere five weeks to persuade Unocal's shareholders of the merits of its proposal," and even though the House legislation was "yet to take effect," CNOOC would be left "with very little room to maneuver," because even an early review could still take up to ninety days (Amaewhule 2005).

36 This statement had a deleterious effect on the situation. Congressman Pombo claimed it "only reinforce[d] the concerns expressed by the House last week. . . . If the Chinese are willing to tell the Congress of a free nation to get lost what assurance do we have that they wouldn't tell the free market to butt out too? I think the answer is 'no.' An investigation . . . of this deal is clearly warranted" (Dow Jones 2005c). Steve Hadley, National Security Advisor to President Bush, was also quick to point out that such an investigation would have happened anyway, but the statement did serve to solidify opposition and anger in Congress, ensuring that it would use its power to block a CNOOC/Unocal deal if need be (Dow Jones 2005c).

37 A 2005 Pentagon report, which came out before CNOOC came forward with its bid for Unocal, concluded that: "over the long term, if current trends persist, [the] capabilities [of China's Army] could pose a credible threat to other modern militaries operating in the region" (US DOD 2005, 4).

38 These numbers were calculated from data sourced from SIPRI (2006).

39 These numbers were calculated from the WDI database (WDI 2008) using GDP PPP in current International dollars. The GDP of China plus Macao and Hong Kong, divided by that of the US, equals 52.42%; without adding Macao and Hong Kong, it equals 50.32%.

40 Numbers calculated from the WDI database (WDI 2008).

41 Some economists, however, believed the push for revaluation was a grave mistake. Stiglitz and Lau, for example, argued in April of 2005 that "there is currently no credible evidence that the Renminbi is significantly undervalued, and an adjustment in its exchange rate at this time is neither warranted nor in the best interests of China or global economic stability" (Lau & Stiglitz 2005).

42 Numbers used for this calculation projected from past IEA data, sourced from the IEA (2006).

43 China is not among the top fifteen countries that import oil and petroleum to the US (EIA 2008a).

44 CNOOC's Chairman and Chief Executive, Fu Chengyu, said that his "company is driven purely by economics" and sought the acquisition for economic reasons, "not because the government asked us to do it" (McDonald 2005). He publicly stated that: "people need to understand that this is a purely commercial transaction driven by market forces" (AFX 2005a).

45 Kirchgaessner et al. (2005) point out that such investments needed to be approved by both the National Development and Reform Commission (NDRC) and the State Council.

46 The financial press was also keenly aware that this was part of CNOOC's motivation at the time. The *Financial Times*, for example, warned that: "CNOOC does not need this deal. But China . . . does. Unocal's . . . reserves would go a long way to meeting China's fast-growing liquefied natural gas demand. Unocal's Caspian assets would also satisfy a long standing – previously thwarted – Chinese desire to expand in that region" (Lex 2005b).

47 For a discussion of "China Inc.'s" use of state funds to pursue acquisitions of resources, see Fishman 2005, 294.

48 Hua Yang, SVP and CFO of CNOOC Ltd., confirmed this in a conference call. For a full transcript of that call, see FD 2005. It was also widely reported that CNOOC was ready to divest those US assets upon a Unocal purchase and to keep "US jobs" in order to make the deal more palatable to the US government and public (Gold et al. 2005).

49 See FD 2005.

50 One of those three witnesses was Frank Gaffney, who at the time headed that Center for Security Policy, but whom had also worked in the Pentagon during the Reagan Administration. Gaffney and Taylor took their debate beyond the hearing, but the difference between their positions largely boiled down to the fact that Gaffney did not believe that the market always operates freely, while Taylor argued that it would (see Kudlow 2005).

51 For commentary on this belief, see Lex 2005a.

52 In the last wave of the World Values Survey before this case, 71.1% of respondents in the US claimed to be "very proud" of their nationality (WVS 2001–04). Yet, while 86.71% of US citizens claim to be proud of their nation's economic achievements, the US is not always identified with economic nationalism (ISSP 2003).

53 Haier eventually withdrew its bid for Maytag, not because of government intervention, but because a bidding war increased the price beyond its means (Goodman & White 2005).

54 In 2005, the IMD World Competitiveness Yearbook covered sixty-one countries, but for this particular variable survey data were available for only fifty-one (see IMD 2007b). Pro-globalization sentiment was valued at 6.34 in the US in 2005, just above the median value of 6.22 among countries surveyed that year (see IMD 2007b). However, levels of pro-globalization sentiment had declined each year since an earlier reported high in 2002 (at the value of 7.20); in other words, anti-globalization sentiment in the US had risen slightly by 2005 relative to previous values (see IMD 2007b).

55 For further discussion of this case, see H.R. 3616 § 3601 (US House 1998); Iosco County Republicans 1999; and Walton 2008.
56 In a fit of frustration at the implication that the congressman had been "bought" by Chevron, his spokesman went on to state: "If you want the Chinese Government to own an American company, please do not contribute to the Congressman Joe Barton Committee, PO Box 1444, Ennis, Texas, 75120. Send your contributions to Communist Party General Secretary Hu Jintao, instead. If the Chinese government manages to buy Unocal, you're going to end up sending your money to Beijing anyway" (Pierce & Newmeyer 2005).
57 On whether or not such a deal would "deliver an oil weapon into China's hands," Taylor's response was "hell no" (AFX 2005c).
58 John Snow reiterated this position on July 9; see Bullock & Xiao 2005a.
59 This lawsuit did not gain any real traction, and as it was "not escalated to a class action lawsuit by all Unocal shareholders, the risks to the Unocal/Chevron deal remain[ed] minimal" (Amaewhule 2005). For full details of these two lawsuits, see Taylor 2005.
60 This included the attorneys general of California and Texas; see Oil Daily 2005b.
61 The US-based company Cisco Systems bought Sourcefire in 2013. For more information, see www.cisco.com.
62 At the time, Check Point was "best known for its firewall technology that defends networks against Internet attacks" (Lemos 2006).
63 The CFO of Check Point, Eyal Desheh, later said of the CFIUS process that "it's a dialogue with the government" (FD 2006).
64 The Chairman and CEO of Check Point, Gil Shwed, confirmed the company was "finding specific issues" in "dealing with the government," though he declared that he was unable to "share" what they were (FD 2006).
65 For example, see comments by Peter Cooper of Morgan Stanley in Dagoni 2006 and discussion in Lemos 2006 and Roberts 2006.
66 According to Weisman and Schmidt (2006), the DOD, DOJ, and DHS all displayed concern prior to the DPW/P&O case.
67 For, "although Israel is frequently referred to as an ally of the United States, the two countries do not have a mutual defence agreement" (Migdalovitz 2007, 23).
68 Some would argue that this position is also ensured by the high degree of political influence wielded by the Israel lobby within Washington; see Mearsheimer & Walt 2007.
69 A 2007 CRS report on Israel provides details of the particular sales that caused heightened tensions between the two countries and "angered the [DOD]" (Migdalovitz 2007, 25).
70 This observation was made in the context of discussing the difficulties Check Point was encountering in its attempt to purchase Sourcefire; Rothman (2006) argued that such protective actions were "not restricted to the United States. UK regulatory entities now have an issue with US company SafeNet buying nCipher, a UK encryption vendor."

71 These numbers have been calculated from data sourced from the IEA (2006).

72 For the US, it was 4.93% in 2005 and 4.96% in 2006, while Israel's was 4.40 and 4.98%, respectively. Numbers calculated from data from the WDI database (WDI 2008).

73 The US five-year average military growth rate increased from 8.19% in 2005 to 8.98% in 2006, while Israel's decreased from 5.96 to 3.79% during that same time period. Additionally, Israel's military expenditure was only 2.48% of that of the US in 2005, and 2.15% in 2006. These numbers were calculated from data sourced from SIPRI (2006).

74 In 2005 and 2006, the IMD World Competitiveness Yearbook covered sixty-one countries, but for this particular variable survey data were available for only fifty-one in 2005 and fifty-four in 2006 (see IMD 2007b). In the US, pro-globalization sentiment was valued at 6.34 in 2005 and 6.25 in 2006, above the median values (of 6.22 in 2005 and 6.21 in 2006) among countries surveyed in those years (IMD 2007b). Thus, though levels of pro-globalization sentiment had declined each year since a reported high in 2002 (at the value of 7.20), they remained within the average range (IMD 2007b), and economic nationalism was generally still considered to be low in the US relative to other countries.

75 Sourcefire only had 140 employees at the time of the failed transaction (Messmer 2006).

76 The announcement was apparently made "unilaterally" by PCCW "to spark a bidding war"; this tack seemed successful, as private equity group "TPG Newbridge entered the fray a day later" (Mitchell 2006), and by June 29 there was "interest" in the deal from Rupert Murdoch's News Corp., which reportedly contemplated joining Macquarie's consortium (Zephyr 2006c).

77 The China Network Communications Group Corporation is usually referred to as China Netcom or China Network.

78 This "shareholder's agreement" held that "PCCW needs China Netcom's permission to sell a stake of 25 percent or more in PCCW-HKT Telephone Ltd., the phone services unit, or a stake of 10 percent or more in PCCW Media Ltd., the pay television unit" (Fellman & Ong 2006).

79 An analyst from the Hong Kong based Atlantis Investment Management, Lui Yang, confirmed "[China Netcom was] really angry about this, as you can see from the fact they said something publicly" (Fellman & Ong 2006).

80 Murdoch reportedly argued that Macquarie "had been encouraged... by a middle-level Chinese official... But higher authorities appeared to take a different view on the transaction and did not want to see [Hong Kong]'s biggest fixed-line company... fall into foreign hands" (Lau 2006).

81 For discussion of this emerging consensus, see e.g., Dyer et al. 2006; Fellman 2006; Fellman & Ong 2006; Lau 2006; Lau & Mitchell 2006a; Tucker & Mitchell 2006.

82 Australia's GDP was just 8.93% of China's if you include Hong Kong and Macao in the figures. Numbers calculated from the WDI database (WDI 2008).

83 This information was passed on in a personal interview by a member of the financial industry, who wished to remain anonymous (Interview 2008b).

84 In 2006, the IMD World Competitiveness Yearbook covered sixty-one countries, but for this particular variable, survey data were available for only fifty-four (see IMD 2007b). In mainland China, pro-globalization sentiment was valued at 6.67, just above the median value (6.21) for that year, and not far off the US score of 6.25 (IMD 2007b). It should be noted that pro-globalization sentiment in Hong Kong itself was far higher, at 8.87: the highest in the survey at the time (IMD 2007b). However, the value for mainland China was used in this case, as it was ultimately the mainland Chinese government that de facto had the ultimate ability to veto investment in this case.

85 According to Naughton: "In the past five years, the Hu Jintao-Wen Jiabao Administration has resuscitated a broad array of industrial policies . . . that, taken together, represent a clear increase in economic nationalism" (US–China ESRC 2007).

86 For an English translation of the 2006 Provisions, see english.mofcom.gov.cn/aarticle/policyrelease/domesticpolicy/200610/20061003434565.html.

87 Furthermore, in the same month, China's State Administration of Radio, Film, and Television clarified that its policy at the time was "to temporarily not approve the creation of new joint companies" with foreign investors, instead limiting foreign investors' "activities to one-off co-operation projects" with Chinese media companies (Dickie 2006). This reinforces the idea that the PCCW deal was unlikely from the start, and that the Chinese government wanted to reaffirm its control over the media sector.

88 It was reported that the Commission would be given the authority to review deals in the following industries: "the military and national defense, power grid and power generation, oil and petrochemicals, telecommunications, coal, civil aviation, water transportation, banking and finance, steel and other metals, auto, heavy machinery and equipment, and electronics" (AFX 2007).

89 This definition of security review coverage comes from the Circular of the General Office of the State Council on the Establishment of Security Review System Regarding Merger and Acquisition of Domestic Enterprises by Foreign Investors (issued February 3, 2011). See also the Provisions of the Ministry of Commerce for the Implementation of the Security Review System for Merger and Acquisition of Domestic Enterprises by Foreign Investors (found in the Ministry of Commerce's No. 53 Announcement on August 25, 2011, and which took effect on September 1, 2011). English translations are available from MOFCOM at www.fdi.gov.cn/1800000121_39_0_1_6.html.

90 According to Ha and O'Brien (2008), these laws included the 1997 Pricing Law and the 1993 Anti-Unfair Competition Law, among others.

91 For an English translation of the 2003 Interim Provisions on Mergers and Acquisitions of Domestic Enterprises by Foreign Investors, see www.fdi.gov.cn/1800000121_39_1921_0_7.html.

92 There was a comprehensive *draft* Anti-Monopoly Law at the time of this case, but the actual Anti-Monopoly Law did not go into effect until August 1, 2008 (Managing Intellectual Property 2007). For a discussion of the 2008 AML, see Chapter 5.

4 Unbounded or Overbalancing?
An Outlier Case

Introduction

States do not always accurately assess the threat posed by another country, and such misperception can lead to potentially costly under- or overreactions to the reality of a given situation (see Christensen & Snyder 1990; Jervis 1976; Waltz 1979, 172; Wohlforth 1993; Schweller 1998, 2004). In other words, rather than appropriately balancing the actual threat to national power (which in this case would imply accurately assessing the threat posed by the foreign takeover, and choosing the appropriate level of intervention), states might instead under- or overbalance that threat (in this case, by engaging in an unwarranted degree of intervention, or not intervening enough).[1]

This chapter focuses on a case that is an example of such a costly aberration: the US intervention into the takeover of the Peninsular & Oriental Steam Navigation Company (P&O) in Britain by Dubai Ports World (DPW) of the UAE. This can be considered an instance of *overbalancing*, and thus an outlier case, because parts of the US government engaged in unbounded balancing against the UAE, in a situation where bounded balancing would have been sufficient to address any true national security concerns. The US and the UAE, though not members of a security community, were close allies in the War on Terror. Yet, two completely diverging views of the UAE emerged – one of it as a positive ally, and the other of it as a threatening power – that bifurcated the US government position. At the same time, a certain degree of economic nationalism arose against the deal. The result was that the powerful elements opposed to the transaction were able to block the US element of the deal and, thus, an act of overbalancing occurred, which had a temporarily negative impact on the relationship between the two countries. This is a unique case in terms of both US history and non-military internal balancing. It offers new insight into the primary argument put forward in this book and provides an excellent opportunity to examine the ramifications of such an overreaction.

Case 5: DPW/P&O

The Story

In fall 2005, DPW first indicated its interest in acquiring P&O. Owned by the Emirate of Dubai, DPW is a well-respected global ports operating company that at the time of this case operated fifty-one port terminals in thirty countries (Blitzer et al. 2006b). P&O was also a global ports operating company, which operated twenty-nine port terminals across eighteen countries. Combining the two companies seemed like a winning idea; with almost no competition issues emerging from the possible combination, a takeover would instantly "create one of the top three leading ports groups in the world" (Zephyr 2006a).

The initial public reports of a possible deal surfaced in the market on October 31, when P&O met with DPW for the first time (Paleit 2006; Zephyr 2006a). Yet, DPW contacted CFIUS on October 17, 2005, before even approaching P&O, knowing that any possible deal with P&O would be reviewed by CFIUS because DPW was owned by a foreign government, and because six of the P&O port terminals involved in the transaction were in the US (Paleit 2006).[2] Thus, long before any agreement had been reached and the CFIUS process officially begun, the relevant intelligence security agencies were able to start gathering information on DPW, and to "[review] the transaction with company officials" (Davis 2006). Notably, the various "US intelligence agencies" questioned by the Department of Homeland Security (DHS) did not find any "derogatory" evidence against the company (Davis 2006).

With the path seemingly clear, DPW made an offer to acquire 100% of P&O through its acquisition vehicle Thunder FZE on November 29, 2005, for £3.3 billion (Zephyr 2006a). On the same day, P&O's board of directors "unanimously recommended" that its shareholders accept the deal (Zephyr 2006a). By December 16, DPW had formally filed notice of the transaction with CFIUS, which began its formal review of the transaction the following day (Davis 2006; Paleit 2006). After conducting a thirty-day investigation of the transaction, and failing to find any significant national security repercussions, CFIUS approved the potential deal between DPW and P&O (Paleit 2006; Ylagan 2006). As part of the process, DPW signed a Letter of Assurance making certain concessions and promises to the US government, and providing rather unprecedented access of information to help US intelligence agencies in their efforts to ensure the security of the ports in question.

In the meantime, a rival bidder materialized from among the herd that had emerged to try and take over the only public ports operator of such size: PSA International Pte Ltd., which at the time was a minority stockholder of P&O (Zephyr 2006a). While other potential bidders, such as Hong Kong's Hutchinson Whampoa and the Singaporean SWF Temasek, fell by the wayside, PSA indicated that it was "willing to make an offer" on January 11, 2006, and by January 26 it had announced an offer worth almost £3.6 billion (Zephyr 2006a). DPW increased its own offer to £3.9 billion the next day, forcing PSA out of the running (Zephyr 2006a). By February 13, DPW's 100% acquisition of P&O was formally approved by the latter's shareholders (Paleit 2006), and it seemed the deal was almost done.

That week, however, turned out to be the beginning of what would become an intense and angry debate between US lawmakers and the Bush Administration over the deal. After discovering that a company owned by an "Arab" government would be buying seaport terminal operations in the US, lawmakers demanded that the President (and the member agencies of CFIUS) explain the rationale behind the approval for a deal that they believed posed a "potential national security threat" (Davis 2006; Paleit 2006). These lawmakers denounced the fact that two of the 9/11 hijackers had come from the UAE, and that money had been supplied to them through its banks. They pointed to the fact that the UAE was technically a member of the Arab League boycott against Israel and decried that nuclear material had once slipped through its ports. The implication of their statements was clear, though heavily misguided: they felt that allowing such a company to "control" operations at a US port would mean potentially laxer security standards that could lead to a future terrorist incident. A number of lawmakers, including Senators Charles Schumer (D-NY), Bill Frist (R-TN), and Hillary Clinton (D-NY), thus quickly promised to bring forward legislation in the coming weeks that would prevent the takeover.[3]

Members of Congress and the Senate not involved in the CFIUS process became aware of the deal largely through the lobbying efforts of a disgruntled US firm (Eller & Co.) that had operated a JV in stevedoring services in the port of Miami with P&O, and which feared it would lose business after the takeover was complete (Hitt & Ellison 2006a). With important mid-term elections coming up in November 2006, and President Bush's approval rating at an extremely low level, lawmakers seemed to seize the opportunity to look stronger than the Administration (and their opposition) on national security by registering their concerns over the transaction. Members of the US public became aware of the deal, and started to pressure lawmakers to stop it, once certain members of the media began to frame the takeover in a manner that played on post-9/11 fears. Spewing protectionist rhetoric and framing the story in an anti-Arab light, media figures such as CNN's Lou Dobbs and radio's Michael Savage are credited with having fanned a "grass-roots brush-fire" of opposition (Hitt & Ellison 2006b).

The Bush Administration was caught off guard by the media firestorm and the congressional backlash that emerged at this point. It was allegedly not until February 16 that President Bush was even made aware of the deal (Davis 2006). Upon learning about the case, President Bush was adamant that lawmakers should not intervene. On February 21, he argued: "They ought to look at the facts and understand the consequences of what they're going to do. But if they pass a law, I'll deal with it, with a veto" (Kuhnhenn 2006). This position had two primary bases. First, that the Administration and all of the government agencies related to security and intelligence were satisfied that the deal *would not* pose a national security threat following the initial CFIUS review. Scott McClellan, the White House spokesman at the time, argued that: "If this transaction were blocked, [it] would not change port security one iota. The Coast Guard and the Customs and Border Patrol remain in charge of our security . . . The Coast Guard remains in charge of physical security; the Customs and Border Patrol remain in charge of cargo security" (Dow Jones 2006h). He also pointed out that "there was a broader intelligence community assessment done as part of the review that addressed such questions, and there were no unresolved national security issues at the end of the process" (Dow Jones 2006g). The second basis for the President's strong stance in favor of the deal was that the UAE is a vital ally in the Global War on Terror, and the Administration had no desire to have it appear that the deal was being crushed because of perceived distrust of the Arab state. The President thus announced that he wanted those opposed to the transaction "to step up and explain why all of a sudden a Middle Eastern company is held to a different standard than a British company" (Hull Daily Mail 2006). In a meeting with the National Governors Association on February 27, he "stressed that the UAE is an important American ally," and that the "deal has foreign policy implications that must be considered" when weighing its merits (Feeney & Orr 2006).

Despite their frustration at the reaction, both the Administration and DPW itself sought to make lawmakers more comfortable with the deal. DPW tried to help the process by releasing the Letter of Assurance[4] it had provided to CFIUS on February 21, and, two days later, by "offer[ing] to delay taking operational control of terminals pending [the] outcome of discussions" (Paleit 2006). On the same day, however, the "Senate Armed Services Committee held [a] hearing" in which "Democrats charged the Bush [Administration] violated [the] law by not conducting an additional forty-five-day security review and fully informing congress" of DPW's intent (Davis 2006). At the same time, lawmakers – including Sen. Barbara Boxer (D-CA), Rep. Scott Garrett (R-NJ), and Sen. Schumer – continued to send letters to the President registering their discontent with the deal. Still, the Administration and DPW remained confident that such lawmakers would change their minds once they were given a chance to think about the deal and had all of the facts before them. Thus, they worked together to come up with a deal that would allow this to happen,[5] and on February 26 DPW formally requested that CFIUS conduct the full-length forty-five-day investigation of the proposed transaction (McAuliff 2006). In addition, the company "agreed to put up a temporary fire wall between itself and P&O's American operations, including Manhattan's cruise ship terminal, and Newark's vast container port" (McAuliff 2006).

Despite these efforts, a rush toward unbounded intervention by US lawmakers followed, as different congressmen and senators sought to go on record opposing the deal. On February 27, Sen. Susan Collins (R-ME) introduced S.J.Res. 32, otherwise known as "A Joint Resolution Disapproving the Results of the Review Conducted by . . . CFIUS into the Purchase of . . . P&O by . . . DP World," with Rep. Jane Harman (D-CA) introducing the resolution to the House the following day (US House 2006a; US Senate 2006c; Harman 2006). Over the course of the same two days, Sen. Schumer and Rep. Peter King (R-NY) also proposed related pieces of legislation (S. 2333 and H.R. 4807) in their respective chambers, which sought to mandate a further forty-five-day investigation of the DPW/P&O deal under the auspices of the Defense Production Act of 1950, which required that such an investigation "shall" occur if the acquiring company in question is owned by a foreign government (US House 2006d; US Senate 2006b). Also on February 28, Sen. Byron Dorgan (D-ND) attempted to go even further with S. 2341, subtly entitled "A Bill to Prohibit the Merger, Acquisition, or Takeover of Peninsular and Oriental Steam Navigation Company by Dubai Ports World" (US Senate 2006a). Finally, by March 7, Rep. Duncan Hunter (R-CA) had sought to use the issue as a springboard to address the greater issue of protecting critical infrastructure in general from such foreign takeovers with the introduction of H.R. 4881 (US House 2006c). Each of these different pieces of legislation was eventually referred to the relevant committee, which was the driving force behind the numerous House and Senate Committee Hearings on the subject of the takeover during the following weeks.

With no serious opposition to the deal arising in the UK, where P&O was domiciled, US lawmakers could only really affect the fate of the six US ports in question. The deal was thus formally completed, and P&O delisted, on March 9 (DPW 2006a). Yet, on the same day, the House "Appropriations Committee vote[d] 62-2 to derail the deal" (Paleit 2006). The same morning, President Bush met with Congressional leaders including Rep. Dennis Hastert (R-IL) and Rep. Frist, who made it clear that "there was no way to stop lawmakers from blocking" the deal because they had enough votes to override the promised presidential veto of any legislation seeking to do so (Kuhnhenn 2006). Donald Rumsfeld stressed the folly of this move, stating that: "from day one, they have been helpful to us. From 9/11 on . . . [the UAE] has provided direct assistance to the global war on terror" (Orr 2006a). Both the Administration and the UAE were thus increasingly concerned over the damage to their relationship that could arise from the "row" over this deal, largely because the national security concerns cited by those lawmakers opposed to the deal appeared to be at best unfounded, and at worst discriminatory and insulting. As discussed later, such an act of overbalancing, unlike a normal act of non-military balancing, had the potential to cause a temporary disruption in the greater relationship between the US and UAE.

In an effort to defray the issue, therefore, the "United Arab Emirates order[ed] DPW to relinquish control of the five US port terminal facilities" on March 9 (Paleit 2006). Sen. John Warner (R-VA), who had helped to broker the original agreement for an extra forty-five-day investigation, broke the news later that day on the floor of the Senate "on behalf of Dubai Ports World that it would transfer management of [the] six major US ports to an American company" (MEJ 2006).[6] The White House welcomed this development on the grounds that it seemed to calm the waters and would "give Congress a 'better opportunity to understand this deal'" (AFX 2006d),[7] but the Administration also made it quite clear to lawmakers and the general public that it would not change its mind about the transaction (Feeney & Martin 2006).[8]

Despite this agreement, Congress remained concerned. Some lawmakers worried that the "American entity" would simply be DPW's US subsidiary, leaving DPW in effective control of the operations. These congressmen wanted to ensure that the disposal of the port terminal leases in question was complete. Congress thus included a provision in §3011 of the Emergency Spending Bill (US House 2006b) introduced on March 13 that both (1) prohibited the President from using any of the funds in the bill to approve the transaction and (2) prohibited and nullified the "acquisition of any leases, contracts, rights, or other obligations of P&O Ports by Dubai Ports World" (US House 2006b). On March 15, therefore, DPW published a statement explaining how the disposal would proceed, which "appeared to satisfy the most prominent critics" of the deal in Congress (Blustein 2006; see CBS 2006). Finally, on December 11, 2006, DPW announced that it had divested the six US ports to the American International Group (AIG), ensuring that the ports would remain under American control (Guardian 2006).

Yet, though the eventual outcome was amicable, and the greater relationship between the US and the UAE remained strong, the initial ramifications of the "ports row" for that relationship were manifold. The US–UAE Free Trade Agreement talks, which had reached their fourth round before the takeover emerged, were stalled. On March 13, the UAE announced its intention to convert 10% of its foreign-exchange reserves from dollars to Euros, as a number of its public officials registered their anger and frustration at the intervention of US lawmakers into the P&O deal (Thornton 2006a).[9] The debate over the ports also had a lasting effect on US law. No matter what their stance on the deal, lawmakers in general were extremely unhappy that CFIUS did not pursue a lengthier review of the deal or have any special protections for "critical infrastructure." Long after the storm had passed, lawmakers continued to fight for CFIUS reform until FINSA was passed in 2007.

Significance as an Outlier

It is of vital importance to examine this case because of its very nature as an outlier. It is an aberration in the context of both the database as a whole and the history of US government intervention into foreign takeovers on the grounds of national security in particular. As shown in this section, there are a number of deeply interwoven reasons for this, but the end result is the misuse of the tool of non-military internal balancing.

It is first important to understand that the DPW case is arguably the most publicized example of government intervention into a foreign takeover in the US in recent memory. Graham and Marchick point out that this case "stands out" because of (among other reasons) its "highly politicized" nature, in which "the polemics surrounding the . . . case were especially raucous," and because "the case did not involve a direct purchase of a US firm, but rather an indirect purchase of US assets through one foreign firm acquiring another foreign firm" (Graham & Marchick 2006, 136–8).

This foreshadows another, more important reason why this deal is an "outlier," which is that domestic political factors seem to have outweighed the geopolitical ones in motivating certain congressmen and senators to pursue a course of unbounded intervention. Normally, within an allied relationship, even one outside of a security community context such as this, we would expect to see intervention motivated primarily by economic nationalism. Yet, P&O was not an American icon or a national champion; it was a British one, having played a critical role in the British Empire.[10] Furthermore, neither US jobs nor economic prosperity were threatened by the deal, which included only a tiny portion of US assets.

Thus, to block an acquisition originating from a close ally in the War on Terror on mostly spurious national security grounds that reeked of "anti-Arab sentiment," and to antagonize that ally to the point of potentially creating negative economic and military consequences, can only be explained as an anomaly, and a case of unnecessary and overbalancing. It was anomalous because it was the conflux of the desire of certain lawmakers to "score points" and look strong on national security at a time when they faced mid-term elections, and when the White House was extremely weak. Yet, the vast majority of US interventions are neither motivated by domestic politics, nor highly politicized – and this was, indeed, the most politicized case in the history of the US, much more so than the CNOOC/Unocal case of the year before.[11] It was a case of overbalancing, because the understanding of the geopolitical situation as conceptualized by those opposed to the deal was inaccurate – portraying a threat where it did not necessarily exist. For those few valid national security concerns that were raised by the deal, *bounded* balancing would have been sufficient, and would have been unlikely to lead to the tensions that *unbounded* balancing caused.

How, then, can one draw lessons from this deal that can impact our understanding of when and why governments will normally intervene in foreign takeovers? I argue that the reaction of most of the government – i.e., of the Administration, CFIUS, and its member agencies – is what we would normally have expected given the true parameters of the variables being examined in this investigation, namely the close alliance between the countries involved and the relatively low levels of economic nationalism at the beginning of this case. In turn, the intervention carried out by lawmakers, while anomalous in its motivations, would have been impossible to carry out if they had not been able to *contextualize* their concerns in terms of national security and geopolitical consequences in a plausible (or at least saleable) manner to the American public. It may thus be that in certain highly politicized cases with a large number of domestic externalities, the variables that normally provide the motivation for intervention may be used by policymakers to instead "frame," and sell, their concerns to a broader audience. Moreover, where there are instances of overbalancing such as this, the states involved will pay a certain price for their miscalculation. Thus, unlike the normal outcome of non-military internal balancing, where the greater meta-relationship between the states involved is unaffected, over- or unnecessary balancing can result in the possibility of a tension being created, at least temporarily, within that relationship.

Competition Concerns

The DPW/P&O deal did not face the possibility of being blocked because of economic competition concerns, for three reasons. First, the perceived economic competitiveness of the US, as with the CNOOC case, did not play a role in motivating lawmakers to try and stop the transaction. Second, the potential combination of the two companies did not threaten to create competition issues in the market. Though the deal did create the third-largest ports operator in the world, it was not expected to create a monopoly or threaten competition in any particular market. Alan Johnson, the US Secretary of Trade and Industry at the time, also confirmed that the deal did not pose a problem for competition (Lyons 2006). Third, despite the large number of foreign operators of US port terminals, a number of countries had recently charged the US with being guilty of not opening *enough* of its ports to foreign competition in the most recent Doha Round of the WTO meetings (Beattie 2006). In sum, this variable does not seem to have provided lawmakers with the motivation for their unbounded intervention into this deal.

Interest Group Presence

The DPW/P&O case is extremely interesting because there were a small number of interest groups actively pressing for both the UK and US to intervene and to block the deal. As illustrated in this section, these interest groups even achieved a certain amount of limited success in convincing lawmakers that the deal was a national security issue. Yet, it will also be argued here that their effectiveness in that respect was due to the domestic political factors and timing already discussed. The nature of this case as an outlier is, therefore, partly due to the elevation of this variable in terms of its importance in motivating state action; as expected, however, these interest groups are not the sole cause, reason, or justification for such intervention.

The first major interest group pressing for intervention in the deal was the Fort Lauderdale-based Eller & Co., which had a stevedoring JV with P&O based at the Port in Miami, and which "feared" the deal would ruin its future business prospects (Hitt & Ellison 2006a). Eller's campaign began with a completely unsuccessful attempt to lobby CFIUS, which – as is usual in these cases – remained unmoved by lobbyists' efforts (Hitt & King 2006). As we know, CFIUS did not find any national security issues with the deal that could not be resolved through certain agreements being made with DPW. After this clear failure, Eller started contacting lawmakers directly, and, according to a spokesman for Sen. Schumer, acted as "the canary in the mineshaft for many people on the Hill and in the media" (Hitt & King 2006). Its position as a "whistleblower," however, should be overshadowed in this analysis by the fact that it was only able to strike a chord with lawmakers seeking to either gain re-election, score points against the Administration, or distance themselves from the Administration. Significantly, Eller lost its attempt to block the deal through the legal systems of both the US and the UK.[12]

There were actually a few interest groups that sought to block, or at least mitigate, the deal through the use of the courts, including the Port Authority of New York and New Jersey, the State of New Jersey, and two groups of minority shareholders. The Port Authority sought the ability "to break the terminal lease that was held by P&O because of the transfer of ownership," on which it claimed it had not been consulted, and on which it claimed it had the final right of approval (Orr 2006a). Interestingly, however, the Port Authority did not base its lawsuit on any sort of national security concern: a spokesman for the Port Authority confirmed "it was a landlord-tenant dispute aimed at getting proper notification and information about who was going to be doing business at our port" (Davis & Jackson 2006). The case went to trial in the Superior Court of Newark on March 3 (Orr 2006a), and was unsuccessful. The State of New Jersey also tried to get "a federal judge to order an investigation into the deal, but the Bush administration had already agreed to the company's request for a forty-five-day investigation of the deal's potential security risks, and the judge said that review should be sufficient" (Frankston 2006).[13] The State of New Jersey also wanted to see confidential documents from the original CFIUS review relating to national security, but the judge refused the request on the grounds that he had no power to order such classified documents to be handed over to the state. Finally, two groups of "private holders of P&O securities objected to the deal, one saying the documents weren't detailed enough, and the other claiming the terms were unfair" (Singer 2006). This objection was registered in the British High Court at the same hearing that heard Eller's grievances, and, like Eller, the groups' concerns were dismissed and the deal was allowed to be completed in the UK (where P&O was based). Significantly, the "overwhelming majority of shareholders . . . approved the deal" (Singer 2006), demonstrating that one of the most important and powerful interest groups in such a takeover case was fully behind the transaction.

Additionally, two of the labor unions based at some of the six US ports affected by the deal protested against the takeover in a highly publicized rally on February 28, 2006 at the port in Newark, NJ. The International Brotherhood of the Teamsters (which provides the trucking services for the port) and the International Longshoreman's Association (which provides most of the dockworkers) joined forces to display their anger at the deal (Nussbaum 2006; Pacific Shipper 2006). Yet, excepting a minor demonstration in Los Angeles by another dockworkers union, such protests and rallies were not widespread, and not repeated.[14] The unions were protesting nominally because of fears over job security. However, one of the reasons why these protests were not more widespread was because it was clear that DPW did not intend to overhaul the existing staff used by P&O. The reason for the large rally in Newark was the proximity of that port to Manhattan, and continuing anger over 9/11 that caused many of the workers to resent the possibility of working for an "Arab" company. Unfortunately, the fact that the company resided in a country that is a vital ally in the Global War on Terror, and that the company itself had made unprecedented efforts to help US intelligence agencies in that war effort, seemed neither to register, nor to break through the "paranoia" that appeared to have taken hold of the workers.[15] Interestingly, workers at other ports seemed unworried by the takeover; at least, they seemed to realize that it would not really affect their daily lives, other than that they would be working for a well-respected company in the industry. The real reason why this rally was significant was because the protesters were joined by Senators Frank Lautenberg (D-NJ), Bob Menendez (D-NJ), and Schumer, who used the demonstration as a platform to show their own displeasure at the deal, while at the same time garnering support from an influential constituency in their districts.

It should be mentioned, however, that a number of interest groups, influential individuals, and companies were also lobbying on behalf, or in favor, of DPW. For example, as soon as DPW came under attack from members of Congress angry at the UAE's formal acceptance of the Arab boycott of Israel, ZIM, the leading shipping company in Israel, publicly backed DPW's bid for P&O (Condie 2006; Verjee et al. 2006).[16] This was largely because ZIM and DPW did a large amount of business with one another, despite the boycott, which is largely ignored by the UAE.[17] The global shipping industry in general was both extremely supportive of the deal, and shocked by the reaction that it caused within the US; the general feeling was that it was a mistake to view the deal as a threat to national security, and an even greater mistake to set a precedent for what reeked of unwarranted protectionism.[18] Other specific companies and institutions that backed the deal included APCP Worldwide,[19] Boeing,[20] and the American Business Group of Abu Dhabi.[21] Additionally, certain individuals voluntarily cast their weight behind the deal, including Thomas Freidman[22] and Oliver North (see Chanda 2006; US Fed News 2006a). At the same time, DPW hired retired Sen. Bob Dole (R-KA) to lobby Congress on its behalf (Pagnamenta 2006).[23]

It was not, however, just private companies and individuals who lobbied in favor of the deal. For example, the US Chamber of Commerce went on record saying that it "would lobby against any legislation that would give Congress the right to block such deals" (Kuhnhenn & Douglas 2006). Furthermore, while the Port Authority of New York and New Jersey was protesting against the deal, other US Port Authorities were happy to have DPW join the operators at their ports, mainly because the company had a reputation in the industry for having the best security equipment, and because of a strong belief that the takeover would not really affect day-to-day operations or personnel. For example, while the Port of New Orleans did not actively lobby for the deal, it did come out in favor of it publicly, as did representatives for the Port of Miami.[24]

Unfortunately, those interest groups lobbying in favor of the deal, or at least publicly pushing for it, were unable to overcome the fear-mongering rhetoric of those lobbying against it. As an EIU report makes clear, the attempts by these interest groups and by DPW to convince lawmakers that this transaction "posed no conceivable threat to US national security cut little ice – with congressional elections coming up in November, both Republican and Democratic members paid more heed to opinion polls" (EIU 2006). It also seems clear that at least one of the groups (like Eller) lobbying against the deal was successful in convincing lawmakers to object to it on so-called "national security" grounds. Yet, the fact that Eller was unable to persuade the relevant government agencies, which under law are meant to make the recommendation regarding national security for the review of the President, highlights the fact that it would not have been able to affect the takeover process under normal circumstances. Thus, it would seem that in this case, the control variable of "interest group presence" has played at least a minor role in motivating lawmakers to intervene in the deal. This role was only possible, however, within the context of such a highly politicized case.

Economic Nationalism

It is argued here that economic nationalism played a secondary role in the DPW case. The UAE (as discussed further later) is a strategic partner of both the US and the UK in the War on Terror and, therefore, we would normally expect that economic nationalism might play a much greater role than other factors in motivating unbounded intervention. Yet, in this particular case, not much evidence can be found of such an occurrence.

P&O was not protected on the basis that it was a national champion. As discussed in the CNOOC case, the US rarely evidences support for national champions, and in this case P&O was not even a US company, but a UK one. The US assets involved, which were actually leases to operate certain individual terminals within the context of six larger ports, could hardly be considered national champion material either, even though their safe operation is vital to national security.[25] Ironically, if P&O had been a national champion for anyone, it would have been so for Britain, given the company's long history and integral association with the trade of the British Empire. Yet, despite the occasional article in the *Daily Mail* or the *Independent* apathetically lamenting the great sell-off of British national assets and icons, no real movement arose against the deal on such grounds in the UK.[26] This is not surprising, given that the UK has relatively moderate levels of national pride (at 46.9%) compared to the US (at 71.1%) (WVS 2001–04). Interestingly, the UK's level of pro-globalization sentiment rose moderately over the course of the deal (see IMD 2007b),[27] and protectionist forces in the UK were largely ignored in favor of free-market principles.

Economic nationalism should have seemed an unlikely candidate for motivating action in this case. Though pro-globalization sentiment fell in the US during this time,[28] it was actually higher in the US than it was in the UK during 2005, when the ports row began, and remained above the median value of surveyed nations in the 2005–06 period (see IMD 2007b), supporting the notion that economic nationalism was overall generally low in the US relative to other countries. However, it might be argued that the same elements who reconceptualized and recast the geopolitical relationship between the US and the UAE for their own ends, also whipped up a certain amount of economic nationalism against the deal by playing on fears about economic security (a phenomenon that will be discussed to a greater extent later).

Geopolitical Competition

The special nature of this case mandates that we examine both the geopolitical relationship between the UAE and UK and that between the UAE and US. It can be shown that the UK, given the geopolitical context between it and the UAE, reacted to the takeover as we would have expected. Indeed, the British response largely supports the main hypothesis. The US, however, took a stance we would not have expected given (1) that the US was only a tertiary party to the deal, and (2) the geopolitical context between the US and the UAE. Ironically, the only way that the US response to the transaction can be truly explained is through an examination of how the geopolitical context between these two countries came to be politicized. It was this process that allowed two completely separate understandings of the relationship between the UAE and US to coincide: one in which the UAE represented a "foe," for those lawmakers seeking to block the deal, and another (more realistic) one in which it represented a close "ally," for those who sought to save the deal.

Degree of Resource Dependency

Neither the UK nor the US is particularly dependent on the UAE for any of its imported resources.[29] The UK is far more resource-dependent in general than the US: its resource dependency ratio was 54.83% in 2005 and 58.94% in 2006, compared to 36.35% and 37.68%, respectively, for the US.[30] Thus, if resource dependency played a role in motivating intervention, we would expect the UK to have intervened in the deal, rather than the US. As this did not happen, and as this issue was never really raised during the course of the ports row, we can safely dismiss the idea that resource dependency played a role in the upheaval that occurred in the US over the takeover.

Relative Power Differential

The UAE is not considered in the annals of international relations theory to be a "major power," like the US and UK, or even to be a "rising power" on the scale of China or India. In fact, while five-year military growth rate averages for both the US and the UK remained positive and in high territory in 2005 and 2006 (4.78% in 2005 and 4.08% in 2006 for the UK, and 8.19% and 8.98%, respectively, for the US), they were actually negative in the UAE, declining from −2.59% in 2005 to −2.67% in 2006.[31] The relative military power of the UAE to the UK is also fairly low, at a ratio of 4.26% in 2005 and 4.24% in 2006, while it is even lower in relation to the US, at 0.51% in 2005 and 0.48% in 2006.[32] Thus, neither the US nor the UK needed to worry about a rise in the conventional military power of the UAE during these years. Furthermore, the deal itself was located in an industry where a rise in asymmetric power capabilities, such as terrorist activity, would have been a more particular cause of concern.

Yet, while the UAE may have been declining as a military power, it was definitively rising as an economic power within the international system at this time. Over the previous decade, the UAE had become a financial center in the Middle East and abroad, and its SWFs had become a force to be reckoned with in the international financial system.[33] The five-year average economic growth rates for the UAE of 10.70% and 10.38% in 2005 and 2006 were almost double those of the US and the UK during those years.[34] Thus, at the time, the UAE was gaining economic power relative to the US and the UK, and some of the investments sought by its SWFs raised economic nationalist sentiment in certain countries.[35] Yet, the UAE's overall economy remained only a fraction of the size of that of the US or the UK, and, thus, its overall relative economic power remained fairly low and unthreatening. In fact, the UAE's GDP PPP totaled only 18.08% of the UK's in 2005 and 19.07% in 2006.[36] These numbers were even lower in comparison to the US, at 2.89% and 3.09%, respectively.[37] Again, if the reality of the geopolitical situation was as it was portrayed to be by those seeking to kill the deal, then we would have expected the UK to intervene rather than the US. The US should not have been motivated by this factor considering the context discussed here and the fact that the UAE is a good trading partner that the US has no interest in losing. Indeed, at the time of the deal, fears were expressed that "trade worth more than $8 billion between the US and the [UAE] could be jeopardized if a Dubai ports deal is blocked" (Reuters 2006e). The US and the UAE were even in the midst of negotiating a free-trade agreement when the row over the deal broke out – a free-trade agreement that the Administration believed was jeopardized by the dispute, and which it was determined to save. Thus, relative economic power *should not* have been a motivating factor behind the unbounded intervention in this transaction, but the lawmakers who intervened never seemed to have realized the true economic implications of their actions.

The Character of the Political Relationship

The UAE is a strategic partner to both the US and the UK in the Global War on Terror, but it is not a member of the highly integrated security community that exists between the US and the UK, nor a formal military "ally" in the traditional sense. Because of this, its role as an important, but relatively "new," friend and partner suffered from what might be termed a publicity problem in the US. Much of the American public and many of its lawmakers were sadly unaware of the fact that the relationship between the countries had strengthened considerably in the post-9/11 era, but everyone did seem aware that two of the 9/11 hijackers were from the UAE. The public perception issue was not as bad in the UK, however, where most of the general public was aware of the friendship between their country and the UAE, largely due to the economic activity between them and the heavy flow of tourists between the two countries.

Thus, the perception of the geopolitical "threat" posed by the UAE varied greatly between the US and the UK. Indeed, the position never even emerged in the UK media, parliament, government agencies, or courts that the UAE-owned company could pose a threat to British national security. In the US, obviously, the case was quite different: the government was neatly bifurcated in its opinion of the threat posed by the UAE and DPW.[38]

CFIUS, the Administration, and the defense and intelligence agencies clearly did *not* believe the UAE posed a threat to the US, because of the strategic importance of the country as an ally in the Middle East.[39] The Administration made it clear in late February that the country "is a staunch ally in the US war on terrorism and has worked to close the loopholes that allowed al Qaeda operatives to use it as a financial and logistics hub before the September 11th attacks" (Palmer 2006). In the post-9/11 period, the UAE has helped the US by "apprehending terrorists, ... providing tangible support for US military operations in both Afghanistan and Iraq," and giving the US military over-flight permission (US Fed News 2006a; Knight Ridder 2006).[40] The UAE also provides a vital port for the US Navy to dock and service its vessels (including aircraft carriers) in the Middle East, thus playing a critical role in the ability of the US to project its power in the region.[41] Reportedly, "it was this close cooperation" that convinced "CFIUS – to greenlight the transaction," and which in late February led Secretary of State Condoleezza Rice to assure the UAE that the "administration was confident" the deal would go through as planned (US Fed News 2006a; Daily Star 2006). When it became clear the deal was in jeopardy because of misconceptions over the relationship between the UAE and the US, a number of Administration and Defense Department officials weighed in to defend this important ally:

> Donald Rumsfeld, the Secretary of Defense urged the Senate not to follow the House move on the Dubai deal, saying that, while he did not know how the UAE would react, the country was a critical ally in a region strategically and economically vital to the US. His admonition was echoed by Condoleezza Rice, the secretary of state, who said it was crucial that "we treat this state as a valued ally." Gen John Abizaid, who oversees US operations in the Middle East, told Congress that the UAE had been "especially steadfast" in supporting the war on terrorism. "The port in Dubai is very important to the war effort," he said. (Kirchgaessner & Sevastopulo 2006)

These officials were clearly eager to ease any tensions created by the ports row in order to maintain and preserve this important alliance relationship.

Unfortunately, this public education campaign was belated and ineffective: those who did not understand the relationship between the two countries were easily swayed against the UAE, and hence DPW, by those who played on prevalent fears of terrorism to frame the UAE as an Arab country with "ties to 9/11." Members of the Senate and Congress continued to object to the deal on a number of grounds. To recap, their arguments against the UAE were mainly that two of the 9/11 hijackers originated from that country; that some of the money used in the attacks had passed through its banking system;[42] that it had formally supported the Israeli boycott; that it had allowed nuclear-related materials to be smuggled through its country;[43] and that it had been one of the only countries to recognize the Taliban before 9/11 (Cornwell 2006; Orr 2006a).

These same lawmakers then argued that DPW's takeover of the P&O port terminals in the US would endanger national security because the emirate-owned company might allow terrorists to breach the security of the port terminals, either unwittingly as the result of lax standards, or purposefully as part of some nefarious plot. The examples of this attitude are many. At the Teamster's rally in the Port of Newark, Senators Lautenberg, Menendez, and Schumer "said the deal would compromise the safety of the US and port workers" (Pacific Shipper 2006). At the rally, Sen. Menendez stated: "Our message is very clear, that the ports of the United States are part of the critical infrastructure that are a big part of security and they should not be in the operational hands of a foreign government" (Pacific Shipper 2006). This sentiment was echoed by Congressman Bill Young (R-FL), who later claimed that "one of the most vulnerable situations facing America is our ports of entry. Whoever's responsible for those ports of entry should be American. This is a national security issue" (Gawenda 2006). Similarly, Representative Virginia Brown-Waite (R-FL) claimed she "could not believe that officials at the Department of Defense could be so careless as to play Russian roulette with port security for the sake of a smooth business transaction" (Brown-Waite 2006). Senator Paul Sarbanes (D-MD) asked, "how could one reasonably question the fact that the Government of Dubai's control [over DPW, which would be operating] major terminals in some of the largest ports in the United States, 'could affect national security?' Port security is a major component of our defenses against terrorism" (US Fed News 2006b). He thus portrayed those who did not believe national security was in jeopardy as unreasonable or ridiculous. Others, such as Representative John Culbertson (R-TX), also tied the deal to the War on Terror, claiming: "the agreement would weaken America's border defenses and endanger our nation while we are fighting the war on terror" (Thiruvengadam 2006).

This type of argument was based on the often reiterated, and wholly misconceived, claim that DPW would be "buying" the ports themselves. For example, Senator Carl Levin (D-MI) argued: "I don't think we ought to fool the American people on what's going on here . . . if this [deal] takes place, Dubai owns these facilities" (Dobbs et al. 2006a). This argument seemed to take root, and to sway the American public against the deal, despite the persistent efforts of the Administration, a number of government agencies, and many present and former naval and Coast Guard officers, to explain that DPW was simply taking over the contracts and leases held by P&O, which allowed only for the *operation* of certain terminals within the context of the larger ports.

Other lawmakers took the argument further, framing the UAE as a geopolitical rival, and even as an enemy of state. Congressman Hunter, for example, argued vociferously against the deal on the grounds that the UAE was "a bazaar for terrorist nations" and a country "who you do not want close to American ports," not only because of its "lax security," but also because it (and thus DPW) would sell US port security to the highest bidder (Condie 2006; Kuhnhenn & Douglas 2006; Mathews 2006). According to Lou Dobbs, Rep. Hunter sent the President a letter stating that "a foreign owned company operating these ports could likely use its position to improve its understanding of security vulnerabilities at those ports" (Dobbs et al. 2006b). During the dispute over the deal, Rep. Hunter even used this platform to call for a ban on the foreign ownership of all companies and assets related to critical infrastructure,[44] and likened DPW's purchase of the British company P&O to the attempt in 1998 by the Chinese government-owned company COSCO (which had ties to the Chinese military) to take over a former naval base in the US port of Long Beach, which was blocked on national security grounds.[45] Such a comparison was especially damaging in the wake of the CNOOC case, which had also been somewhat politicized (though to a lesser extent),[46] framing the UAE as a geopolitical rival rather than the close strategic partner it was. Sen. Lautenberg went even further, framing the UAE as a foreign government to be "feared," when he said: "We wouldn't transfer the title to the devil, and we're not going to transfer it to Dubai" (Nussbaum 2006; Pacific Shipper 2006). In response to the idea that such a comment was racist, Lautenberg justified his claims by saying: "It's not anti-Arab. It's anti-enemy" (Nussbaum 2006). Congressman King similarly suggested that the "members of the [UAE] royal family," whom he believed might still be close to the Taliban and Osama bin Laden, could infiltrate DPW (Blitzer et al. 2006a). On Wolf Blitzer's CNN broadcast, Rep. King stated: "My concern is people working within the company, . . . people within the government who just four and a half years ago were allied with our sworn enemy" (Blitzer et al. 2006b). Not surprisingly, King (like many of the others just named) backed legislation that "would allow Congress to reject the Dubai Ports World transaction" outright (Kuhnhenn & Douglas 2006).

This framing of the UAE as a geopolitical rival, and even an "enemy," by the lawmakers who sought to block the DPW deal – in addition to the specific concerns they raised about port security – was in complete opposition to the view taken by the Administration, the Treasury, Commerce, and US security and intelligence agencies. CFIUS concluded by the end of its initial investigation that no national security concerns were sufficient to prohibit the deal or warrant a further full forty-five-day investigation. The DHS had been the only member agency of CFIUS to "protest" against the deal, and its "early objections were settled" once DPW "agreed to a series of security restrictions" in the Letter of Assurance it signed as part of the CFIUS process (Record 2006). In that letter, DPW promised to "adhere to strict security checks" and grant US government officials "instant access to company operational documents" (Griffin et al. 2006; Wolffe & Bailey 2006). The Coast Guard had also voiced concern in an internal memo circulated on December 13, 2005 over "intelligence gaps" during the initial CFIUS review,[47] but these were also addressed and satisfied by the end of it.[48] Thus, CFIUS "finished their formal review in mid-January with no public fanfare and no extended inquiry," and "approved the deal without dissent," as all of the government agencies involved in the process were by then comfortable with the takeover (Record 2006; Wolffe & Bailey 2006).[49]

Many of these government agencies even viewed the transaction as an opportunity to *improve* port security, as did most maritime and port security experts.[50] Indeed, Michael Chertoff, the Secretary of Homeland Security at the time, was in favor of the deal because DPW had agreed in writing to help the US government with security, and, since shipping companies only do that on a voluntary basis, it was a unique opportunity to enhance national security, not hurt it (Block 2006). Secretary Chertoff thus worried that this "unprecedented access that the [DHS] and other federal agencies would have to monitor the UAE shipping company's personnel and business records would 'evaporate' if Congress stopped the deal from proceeding" (Block 2006).

Moreover, DPW's security system was actually considered to be quite good.[51] It had already voluntarily implemented the Container Security Initiative (CSI). And it had a distinct interest in having good security for economic reasons: it needed to be trusted in order to expand its business, and security breaches could lead to costly disruptions and legal ramifications, in addition to loss of business.[52] The shipping industry itself even spoke out against the US lawmakers' attempts at unbounded intervention, in disbelief that the deal could be viewed as having a possible impact on international security.[53]

Additionally, many maritime and port security experts pointed out that the lawmakers' concern over foreign "ownership" of ports was misconceived, for four fundamental reasons. First, as mentioned briefly already, the ports were not being sold as part of the transaction. It is the "states, cities, and municipalities [that] own the ports" (Levans 2006). DPW was only purchasing "long-term contracts with port authorities" that would allow it to "assum[e the] operations of certain berths, stevedoring activities, and terminal operations from P&O at 22 US ports" (Levans 2006).[54] Thus, many agreed with the sentiment expressed by one "former member of the US Federal Maritime Commission" that "the reality is . . . this is really just a financial transaction . . . the controversy around this is political ignorance and grandstanding" (Thiruvengadam 2006).

Second, many foreign (and foreign government-owned) companies already operated in US ports without having caused any concern over national security. In fact, "some 80% of [US] ports are run . . . by foreign companies . . . some of whom you might argue are operated by foreign governments" (Hunter et al. 2006). The list of foreign companies operating US port terminals at that time includes AP Moller-Maersk Group (Denmark), Ceres Marine Terminals (Japan), Citgo Petroleum (Venezuela), COSCO (China), ISS (Dubai), Neptune Orient Lines (Singapore), Odfjell Terminals (Norway), and PSA (Singapore).[55] Furthermore, no objections were raised when DPW bought "the international terminal network of US-based CSX corporation" in 2005 (Urquhart 2006), nor was there any effort to block the purchase of the UK ports operator Inchcape Shipping Services (ISS) by the UAE-based private equity group Istithmar in January 2006 – at the same time the row over DPW's takeover of P&O began (Auger & Marashlian 2006). This is especially odd, given that ISS "provides security services to 12 US ports and the US Navy itself" (Auger & Marashlian 2006).

Third, the proposition put forward to ban all foreign companies from providing ports services was wholly impractical because of the international nature of the business[56] and the relatively small market share held within it by US companies (Cohn 2006). In fact, "the largest US firm, SSA Marine, is ranked ninth among global operators and has been mentioned as a takeover target itself" (Cohn 2006).[57] It is for this reason that the Administration "flatly rejected Senator Clinton's proposal to ban all state-owned foreign companies from owning terminal operations at US ports as uninformed and – quote – ‘totally unworkable’ . . . [and said that] to ban them would not only hurt the economy; it would hurt foreign relations too” (Griffin et al. 2006).

Finally, whether or not the companies operating and servicing the ports in question are foreign, the US government is ultimately responsible for providing security for those ports, and the greatest threats to their security usually hail from outside the port operating industry. In fact:

> the physical security of the port ultimately is the responsibility of the port authority. Port authorities must conform to security plans overseen by the US Coast Guard, which conducts regular compliance reviews. No matter who leases and operates a terminal, they are under the watchful eye of the coast guard and are subject to rules enforced by US Customs and Border Protection.[58] (Levans 2006)

It is true that port operators contribute to security by implementing the wishes of these agencies efficiently, and by providing them with intelligence. Yet, in an appearance on CNN, Christopher Koch, the President and CEO of the World Shipping Council, argued that “there is no evidence that terminal facilities operations conducted by foreign controlled companies are any less secure or in any way less compliant with security regulations or in any way less cooperative with US government security authorities than US controlled companies” (Dobbs et al. 2006c). Indeed, it should be recalled that as part of the deal, DPW had agreed to provide the US government with even greater levels of cooperation than a normal company would have done (foreign or otherwise). Additionally, the terminals retain “the same labor pool” regardless of whether a foreign or domestic company runs them, because the “dockworkers [are] hired through US Unions” (Thiruvengadam 2006; Wolffe & Bailey 2006). Experts also agree that ownership of operations is not the issue when it comes to security. For example, Stephen Flynn of the Council on Foreign Relations argued that, while he was “deeply worried about the security of our ports overall . . . this commercial transaction . . . ranks near the bottom of my security concerns, because the other gaps are so huge” (Scheiffer et al. 2006).[59]

Furthermore, even if national security issues did exist, lawmakers could have chosen to *mitigate* the deal through a strategy of bounded, rather than unbounded, intervention. This could have been achieved in a variety of ways, one of which CFIUS had already accomplished through its obtainment of the Letter of Assurance from DPW. Alternatively, CFIUS could have requested that DPW operate the ports through a subsidiary that was kept separate from the rest of the company and run by US citizens (Dow Jones 2006b).[60] Some lawmakers, such as

Rep. King and Sen. Collins, originally suggested this would be an acceptable solution to them (see Blitzer et al. 2006a). Yet, such thoughts were overtaken by the overwhelming movement to block the US-related aspects of the deal in their entirety.

Why and how, then, did this deal become one that lawmakers sought to block on so-called "national security" grounds? The preceding points seem to make it quite clear that, once DPW made the concessions and agreements requested by the DHS and other CFIUS member agencies, there should not have been any lingering national security issues over the transfer of operations from P&O to DPW at the ports in question. That there were still concerns – ones only weakly supported by the interest groups examined earlier, and which were not deeply rooted in competition issues, economic nationalism, or the reality of the geopolitical relationship between the two countries – makes this case a true outlier among all of the cases examined, not only in this chapter, but also among the population of 209 cases examined in Chapter 2.

In the end, the motivation behind the unbounded intervention in this case seems to have been an alternative understanding of the geopolitical relationship between the US and the UAE that was created by lawmakers and certain members of the media, which combined with the highly politicized nature of this case to contribute to the explosion of sentiment against the deal. It would seem that this alternative framing of the UAE as a potentially dangerous enemy, and of DPW as an Arab company controlled by that rival, was the result of (1) some lawmakers seeking to look "strong" on national security before an important election and, even more damagingly, (2) simple discrimination. For example, William H. Webster, a former federal judge, a former director of both the FBI and the CIA, and the Chairman of the Homeland Security Advisory Council at the time of writing, provided one of the clearest descriptions of this unfortunate process to a member of the press after attending a CSIS conference on DPW, who reported that:

> After the conference, Judge Webster spoke . . . [of] what may be an underlying reason for the recent furor. The relentless, politicized message of "protecting America from terrorists" may have come back to bite the Administration. Citizens have been convinced that they should fear Middle East terrorism as a result of this constant drum-beat of "keeping America safe." When they heard that an "Arab nation" would be "taking over our ports," they reacted. Members of Congress sensed this fear, and true to the political climate of today, smelled blood from a weakened White House in the water, and went full bore to show how vigilant they were in defending the nation . . . Senators and Representatives alike saw an opportunity to set themselves up for the next election's campaign ads; missing the real issue completely. (Forecast International 2006)

Indeed, many political observers of the ports row agreed that Congress seemed to be taking advantage of what looked like a golden opportunity to score political points.[61] Politicians were able to misconstrue the deal as a security issue by arguing (falsely) that total control over the ports in question would be ceded to the new owner and that the security for those ports would then be in the hands of that new "owner."[62]

The alternative vision of the geopolitical "stakes" was created over time by portraying "non-issues" as "issues." An excellent example of this was the reaction by certain senators and congressmen to the internal Coast Guard memo on DPW. Despite the resolution of the Coast Guard's initial concern, the memo was later leaked to the press as "proof" that the deal was a danger to national security, and for some time became a flashpoint in the controversy.[63] Senator Schumer, for example, proclaimed to the press that, "if this [wasn't] a smoking gun, it shows there may [have been] one undetected by the CFIUS committee" in the course of their initial review (US Fed News 2006c). There was, unfortunately, a public relations issue, as much of the concern raised by the memo could have been easily assuaged if it were not for the fact that the answers that most of the lawmakers sought were classified. Thus, the only lawmakers whose fears were eventually eased were those few who had security clearances high enough to be briefed on *how* the concerns in the memo were resolved.[64] Those lawmakers without this ability, however, did not believe the high-ranking Coast Guard officials who could only tell them that all of the issues *had* been resolved.[65]

In addition to this type of incident, the deal also became heavily politicized because certain members of the media were portraying it as one that involved a geopolitical rival. One observer points out that the media fanned a "grassroots brushfire" of opposition to the transaction (Hitt & Ellison 2006b). For instance, coverage of the deal skyrocketed after "the Associated Press framed the debate in a new way: [as] 'a company in the United Arab Emirates . . . poised to take over significant operations at six American ports as part of a corporate sale, leaving a country with ties to the Sept. 11 hijackers with influence over a maritime industry considered vulnerable to terrorism'" (Hitt & Ellison 2006a). Media figures such as Michael Savage, Michael Smerconish, and Lou Dobbs then continued to wage a media campaign against the deal (Hitt & Ellison 2006a; Mathews 2006; Wolffe & Bailey 2006).[66]

The American public was thus swayed against the deal over time by this "alternative" understanding and portrayal of the geopolitical stakes, which in turn placed constituent pressure on lawmakers to block the deal. Public opinion against the transaction therefore increased over time. On March 2, it was reported that "a Los Angeles Times/Bloomberg poll . . . [had] found that 58 percent of Americans oppose[d] the DPW deal," and by March 9 "a CNN/Gallup/USA Today poll" put that number at "66% of voters" (Sevastopulo & Kirchgaessner 2006; Yeager 2006). Indeed, observers at the time confirmed that "media portrayals of the port deal generated a wave of anger from Americans across the country that left lawmakers in Washington – by their own admission – following their constituents much more than leading" (Hitt & Ellison 2006a). Thus, constituent pressure on lawmakers to block the transaction became very heavy.[67]

Yet, some lawmakers originally opposed to the acquisition changed their mind once they had access to more information. Sen. Frist, one of the original opponents of the deal,[68] said that "he was more comfortable" with it by late February "because he had received more information" about DPW and the UAE after attending "classified intelligence briefing[s]" and "talking to the [DHS]" (Bohan & Cornwell 2006; Dobbs et al. 2006c).[69] Similarly, Governor Robert Ehrlich Jr. became more comfortable and moved away from his oppositional stance to the transaction once he learned more facts about it (Mosk 2006).[70] Unfortunately, not all lawmakers had the advantage of such high-level classified intelligence briefings, which meant that it was difficult for the Administration to change the opinion of a majority of those against the deal.[71]

There was also little to no resistance to the deal outside of the US on national security (or other) grounds. "None of the other countries including the UK, Australia, Canada, China, and India [were] especially worried about security issues once the P&O terminals in their countries [were to be] transferred to the new Dubai owners" (Urquhart 2006),[72] though India did voice concern over the competition effects of the deal in its country.[73] The country primarily affected by the transaction, the UK, welcomed the deal with "hardly a murmur of protest" and "surprisingly little uproar" (NPR 2006; Watson 2006; see also Pacific Shipper 2006; Whitfield et al. 2006). Indeed, the UK government made a point at the time of encouraging investment from the UAE, decrying US protectionism, and making it clear that it would not "protect UK plc from foreign bids" (Neveling 2006).[74]

As already mentioned, President Bush and his Administration did not believe that the DPW transaction posed a threat, because of the US alliance relationship with the UAE in the War on Terror (see Cornwell 2006; Orr 2006b). Furthermore, as Stephan Hadley pointed out, the deal "isn't a security risk" because "this is a company we know" (AFX 2006d). On the contrary, the Administration's greatest concern was that the dispute over the deal might damage the relationship between the two countries. Thus, at the very beginning of the row, "President Bush stressed that the UAE is an important American ally" and that "the port deal has foreign policy implications that must be considered (Feeney & Orr 2006). A small number of lawmakers agreed with this statement, including Representative Dana Rohrbacher (R-CA), who stated that "the real threat to national security is for the US to block the transaction and insult an ally that is a moderating influence in the Middle East" (Pacific Shipper 2006). Similarly, Senator John Warner helped to arrange the deal with DPW for the forty-five-day investigation, "call[ing] the ports deal diplomatically and economically vital to the United States" (Weisman 2006a). This seems to reflect an understanding that overbalancing in this case could potentially have damaged the relationship between the two countries, because it would imply the presence of a type of geopolitical competition that did not really exist.

President Bush thus stated he was "concerned about a broader message this could send" (Sun 2006). In particular, the White House worried the US would be sending the message that it was protectionist, and more specifically that it discriminated against foreign investment of Arab origin.[75] Many shared this concern. As Graham and Marchick note, "statements by congressional leaders from both parties were unusually strong, so strong that defenders of the deal could have credibly argued that anti-Arab sentiment was a factor in the statements" (Graham & Marchick 2006, 136). General John Abizaid stated he was "very dismayed by the emotional responses" to the deal, which he attributed to "Arab and Muslim bashing" (Federal News Service 2006). The EIU called "the DPW Affair . . . an unpleasant reminder of the enduring potency of anti-Arab sentiment" (EIU 2006). Some, like Lt. Colonel Kevin Massengill, representing the Dubai American Business Group, fought against the simplified characterization in the media of DPW as "an Arab Muslim company" that "is going to somehow have control of the port[s]" (Blitzer et al. 2006c).

The reaction in the UAE was mixed. T. B. McClellend, President of the Dubai-based consulting firm Center House, called the deal a case of pure "racism" (Hensel 2006a). Mohammed Sharaf, Chief Executive of DPW, argued it was a case of ignorance rather than of racism, claiming "it's a lack of information, a lack of understanding . . . the things that were said simply weren't the reality" (Teather 2006). Either way, many in the UAE agreed with the view of the *Gulf News* that "other foreign-owned companies run US ports – but they were not Arab. That is the message. And we got it" (Abdelsamad 2006). It seemed there was a widespread belief that "UAE companies will continue to face discrimination like DPW" (Sharif 2006).

This perceived protectionism caused a great amount of concern, not only in the Middle East, but also among the Administration and its supporters, who feared that it would lead to lower future levels of FDI from the UAE specifically, and from the Middle East in general (see Wallis 2006). Senator Warner, for instance, said of the deal that it was "going to establish a precedent, and it's got to be done in a way not to choke off other opportunities" (Weisman 2006a). Treasury Secretary John Snow worried that "the implications of failing to approve this would be to tell the world that investments in the United States from certain parts of the world aren't welcome" (Dobbs et al. 2006a). Wall Street leaders "published an open letter to the Senate Banking Committee" saying that they were "very concerned about proposals [to block the deal] that could impose harmful barriers to foreign investment" more generally (Litterick 2006).[76] In addition, a number of market "analysts voiced concern that the dollar may be vulnerable to the possibility that investment from the Middle East will dry up in the wake of news that US lawmakers have blocked the sale of P&O's ports to the Dubai Port Authority" (AFX 2006e).

A number of the Administration's fears proved to be warranted in the aftermath of the dispute. First, lawmakers attempted to pass legislation, such as H.R. 556, that would make the CFIUS process not only more stringent and comprehensive, but possibly more open to politicization (see Jackson 2007), causing Treasury Sec. Snow to say "that foreign investment is 'being put in jeopardy' by the bill" (Shinkle 2006). The DPW row is also widely viewed as having "set" an "unfortunate precedent... that if Congress raises a really big fuss about an individual takeover bid, it can effectively frighten off a foreign bidder" (Financial Times 2006b). Second, the dispute itself may possibly have had a negative impact on US port security, as it angered the very companies the US relies on to do voluntary security checks abroad (Lau & Mitchell 2006c). Third, as the White House feared, the reaction to the ports row in the UAE was sufficiently negative to have certain economic and political ramifications. While it will be quite some time before the exact effect on FDI from the UAE can be determined,[77] the leadership of Dubai did threaten in early March to decrease its investment in the US and in US companies as a result of the row (Mist News 2006; Tiron 2006).[78] It was soon clear, however, that there would be some definite effects. By July, for instance, the UAE announced its plan to "move 10% of its Dollar... foreign exchange reserves into Euros" and to move away from a dollar FX peg by 2010, in favor of a floating one (Khalaf 2006). The free-trade talks between the UAE and US were also "postponed" amid the dispute over the transaction, and later rescheduled for May 2006

(AFP 2006b, 2006d). This was attributed specifically to the fallout over the dispute, which led to "a determination on both sides to ride out the diplomatic and economic storms" before resuming the talks (Auger & Marashlian 2006).[79] The deal at the time was even reported to have negatively affected negotiations over the "open skies treaty" (Done 2006). The most damning report was made in the *Harvard International Law Review*, in which Abdelsamad argued that "the future looks grim" for the US–UAE relationship, as a "Gulf News poll" at the time had

> reported 64% of readers claimed the deal's dismissal "changed their opinion for the worst" regarding investment in the United States... The alienation of an essential trade partner and war ally in an increasingly anti-US region is bad for the United States and unnecessarily costly for US–UAE trade and diplomatic relations. (Abdelsamad 2006)

Luckily, the desire on the part of the Administration and the UAE to maintain and foster the relationship between the two countries was strong enough to overcome some of these negative impacts. It was clear that DPW was ordered to relinquish the ports by the Dubai leadership in order "to preserve" the US–UAE "relationship" (Lloyd's 2006).[80] A "UAE official" confirmed "it [was] a political decision to ask Dubai Ports to defuse the situation" (Cornwell 2006).[81] The US also clearly wished to repair any damage done to the relationship between the two countries. For example, "a senior defense official said the Pentagon would watch 'very carefully' to see whether the Congressional backlash over the ports issue would negatively impact the US–UAE military relationship," because "the Pentagon planned on making efforts to ensure the UAE understands the value the US places on the country as an ally in the 'war on terror'" (Alden et al. 2006c).

Indeed, the desire of the Administration to maintain good relations with the UAE may have been one of the reasons behind its support at that time for another UAE purchase of a UK company: that of the defense company Doncasters by the SWF Dubai International Capital. The fact that Doncasters owned "US plants that supply the Pentagon" (Mist News 2006)[82] meant there was a great potential for a negative reaction in Congress. Yet, it was observed at the time that the White House was "keen to patch up relations with the [UAE] following the failed takeover of British-owned P&O's port operations by [DPW]" because "the row has threatened to damage bilateral relations between the countries and undo lucrative US contracts" (Auger 2006).[83] And it was later reported that the "mood" between the US and the UAE did "improve with the successful conclusion of the purchase of... Doncasters," once "Bush gave his personal approval to the deal" and it "had been given the green light by... CFIUS" (Auger 2006). The Administration and CFIUS thus learned from the ports case to engage lawmakers early on, and to let it be known that a deal was being heavily scrutinized from a national security perspective,[84] in order to prevent it from becoming heavily politicized. There was a clear understanding on the part of not only the White House, but also some lawmakers, that the US had "overbalanced" against the ports deal, and that mitigation (i.e., *bounded* intervention) would have been sufficient to deal with any actual national security issues.

Conclusion

In sum, it was an alternative vision of the geopolitical stakes that seems to have motivated lawmakers (and the public) against the DPW/P&O deal. Though this "vision" was inaccurate, it was the primary motivator behind the actions taken to block the deal. Such cases are extremely rare, because such tremendously divergent understandings of the reality of a geopolitical relationship rarely coincide within one government. For, though it may be understandable for geopolitical rivalry to exist between two countries that are members of even the closest-knit security communities, like the US and France, that sense of rivalry is usually felt in some sort of universal manner, and does not necessarily question the basic premise of that friendship. In this case, however, the opinions and visions of the very basic nature of the bilateral relationship itself were completely bifurcated. Some of this may have been rooted in discrimination, some in "political grandstanding." Yet, it was the *politicization* of this case itself that allowed for such bifurcation of sentiment to persist, for an alternative understanding of the geopolitical ramifications of the deal to take root in public sentiment, and for a certain amount of economic nationalism to accompany it.

The DPW case also clearly indicates the price that states may pay for such an overreaction, and, thus, for the *misuse* of such a tool of non-military internal balancing. If the danger had not been miscalculated by lawmakers, and perhaps bounded (instead of unbounded) intervention had been undertaken, then no damage would have been done to the greater relationship between the UAE and the US. Even with this miscalculation, however, it is important to note that the resulting disruption to that relationship was temporary and ultimately not completely destructive.

Despite its status as an "outlier," the DPW case does evidence some support for the theory of non-military internal balancing, and is therefore useful to compare to the four cases of unbounded intervention examined in the previous chapter. First, in each of those four cases, geopolitical or economic nationalist concerns were the primary and/or secondary motivator for unbounded intervention. In the DPW/P&O case, the intervention eventually carried out by lawmakers was also rooted in these variables. It was simply that this intervention was rooted in an inaccurate conception of these variables' true values, as two distinct understandings of the geopolitical relationship between the US and UAE, as well as two separate values on the economic nationalism variable, had emerged within the US government. Indeed, unbounded intervention would have been impossible if those lawmakers intent on such action had not been able to contextualize their somewhat spurious concerns in terms of national security and geopolitical consequences in a plausible, or at least "saleable," manner to the American public.

Second, the cases in Chapter 3 demonstrated that, when the states involved were not members of the same security community, geopolitical concerns were the *primary* reason for unbounded intervention. Again, geopolitical concerns were arguably of primary importance in the DPW/P&O case, where even though the countries involved *are* strategic partners, they do not have a security community relationship, making it possible for some lawmakers to frame the UAE as a threat.

Third, "interest group presence" played only a minor role, and "competition concerns" no role at all, in motivating unbounded intervention in the cases in Chapter 3. And as with the CNOOC/Unocal case, interest groups were only moderately effective in raising awareness in the DPW/P&O case, where this variable was arguably affected by the unusually politicized nature of this aberrant case. Even then, the role of these interest groups was once again simply to alert government actors to preexisting concerns, rather than to be a primary or secondary *motivator* of intervention.

Finally, in each instance of unbounded intervention examined in Chapter 3, the transaction in question was either completely or effectively blocked. In this outlier case, the transaction as a whole was not blocked, because the objecting state (the US) was only a third party to the deal. Nevertheless, the US was still able to effectively block the sale of the assets on its national territory, offering some further support to the claim that intervention type is closely correlated with a deal's outcome.

NOTES

1 In an examination of the more traditional forms of military balancing, the neoclassical realist Randall Schweller explains that "appropriate balancing" implies an accurate assessment of, and reaction to, a given threat

(Schweller 2004, 10). "Overbalancing," however, "occurs when the target is misperceived as an aggressor but is, instead a defensively minded state seeking only to enhance its security"; which can result in "a costly and dangerous arms spiral" (Schweller 2004, 10–11). On the other hand, "non-balancing," which he argues can also in specific instances be considered "underbalancing," "may take the form of inaction, normal diplomacy, buckpassing, bandwagoning, appeasement, engagement, distancing, or hiding" (Schweller 2004, 11).

2 P&O owned port terminals in Baltimore, Miami, New Orleans, New York City, Newark, and Philadelphia, and "had lesser dockside activities at 16 other ports in the US" (Bridis 2006).

3 For example, on February 16, Sen. Schumer "holds a news conference to denounce the deal" (Hitt & Ellison 2006a). Sen. Clinton had promised by February 17 that "she [would] propose legislation to block deal," and by February 21, Sen. Frist claimed that "he [would] introduce legislation to ensure the deal is placed 'on hold' pending review" (Paleit 2006).

4 Normally, such documents remain classified and confidential unless the company involved decides voluntarily to release the information to the public. In the letter, written to DHS, "the company agreed to provide law enforcement, if asked, with information about its US operations, facilities, and personnel. It also agreed to provide federal agencies with any records in the US involving its foreign operations" (Block 2006). This was significant, because "since [9/11], federal law-enforcement and intelligence agencies have been trying to get inside information about global shipping operations" generally, to build better defenses against terrorists (Block 2006).

5 Reportedly, those involved were Senators Frist, John McCain (R-AZ), and Warner, as well as Al Hubbard, an Administration economic advisor, and Vin Weber, a lobbyist for the UAE (Dobbs et al. 2006a).

6 On March 9, DPW stated that it was told to make the divestment by the Ruler of Dubai and UAE Prime Minister Sheikh Mohammed Bin Rashid Al Maktoum, due to "the strong relationship between the [UAE] and the [US]" and a desire "to preserve this relationship" (DPW 2006b).

7 The Administration's efforts to sell "the 45-day probe as a chance to educate lawmakers" (Hitt & Singer 2006) seemed to backfire, however, as many lawmakers opposed to the deal resented the implication that they had not been doing their homework.

8 President Bush's National Security Advisor "told reporters the administration does not intend to use the [forty-five-day] delay to reconsider its approval of the sale," stating: "There's nothing to reopen. In terms of the . . . executive branch process, it's been completed" (Feeney & Martin 2006).

9 For example, Sultan Nasser Al-Suweidi, governor of the UAE Central Bank, said the US was "contravening their own principles . . . Investors are going to take this into consideration [and] will look at investment opportunities through new binoculars" (Thornton 2006a).

10 P&O was reportedly "once key to British Empire building" (Watson 2006).

11 Graham and Marchick agree on the latter point (Graham & Marchick 2006, 138), as do a number of industry sources and members of the legal community with whom the author has spoken.
12 For further details on these legal suits, see Harrison 2006; Rowe 2006; Tait et al. 2006.
13 Judge Linares, who presided over the case in the Newark District Court, reportedly said: "I am not going to order an investigation that everyone agrees is going to take place . . . I would have to assume the investigation will be a sham" (Brennan 2006).
14 The only other labor rally that received publicity was "a much smaller protest rally . . . held in Los Angeles by members of the International Longshore and Warehouse Union" (Pacific Shipper 2006).
15 For indicative comments by both the Intl. Longshoreman's Assoc. and the Teamsters, see Green & Cohn 2006; Nussbaum 2006.
16 ZIM's leadership formally endorsed the deal through the media, and through written statements to lawmakers. For example, its Chairman wrote to Sen. Clinton that "as an Israeli company, security is of the utmost importance to us . . . during our long association with DPW, we have not experienced a single security issue," and that DPW was a "leader with regard to security and works closely with us . . . to maintain the highest security standards in all its terminals" (Verjee et al. 2006).
17 Neither DPW, nor the UAE, seems to follow the boycott in practice (see Osler 2006; Verjee et al. 2006; Whitfield et al. 2006).
18 The row was denounced at the Port Productivity and Trans-Pacific Maritime conferences, and "leaders of the US transportation industry" also showed their support for the deal (McDermott 2006; Ward 2006). Supporters of the deal also included Scott Axelson, the Vice President of TraPac, Christopher Koch, the President of the World Shipping Council, and Matthew Rose, the Chief Executive of BSNF (see Ward 2006).
19 This firm gave DPW "strategic counsel and media support" (Crea 2006).
20 Boeing feared the UAE would cancel a large plane order as a result of the row (Tiron 2006).
21 As part of its lobbying efforts, the American Business Group of Abu Dhabi "sen[t] a delegation to Washington [in March 2006] to lobby 120 members of congress" (Reuters 2006e). Members appeared on CNN and spoke with the press; see Blitzer et al. 2006a; Reuters 2006e.
22 Friedman called the row "shameful" (Chanda 2006), and wrote a number of op-eds decrying the backlash against the deal.
23 DPW also hired other members of the lobbying firm Altson & Bird (Pagnamenta 2006).
24 See comments by the spokesmen for the Port of New Orleans (Chris Bonura) and the Port of Miami (Andrea Muniz) in Alden et al. 2006a, 2006b.
25 Whilc recognizing the importance of ports to US national security, a change in companies operating those ports does not necessarily threaten security. On the contrary, the US relies on foreign companies to cooperate to conduct security checks abroad, and to hand over vital intelligence. It is thus unclear how the change from P&O to DPW, which was globally envied for

its high-tech security system and internationally valued for its cooperation on intelligence, would have made the ports any less safe.

26 A number of articles discuss how too many UK "brands fall into foreign hands," and a *Financial Times* poll found "that more than two-thirds of the British public believe[d]" it was "outrageous" (Daily Express 2006). This suggests that certain sectors of the British public resented this fact, though not enough to try to make public officials change their free-market policies (for a list of the some of the UK's "most famous . . . icons that are no longer British," see Daily Mail 2006b).

27 The UK's level of pro-globalization sentiment went from a value of 5.83 in 2005 to one of 6.54 in 2006 (IMD 2007b).

28 Pro-globalization sentiment in the US went from 6.34 in 2005 to 6.25 in 2006 (IMD 2007b).

29 In 2006, the UAE supplied the US with only 0.06% of its total crude oil and petroleum product imports (EIA 2008c).

30 Numbers used for these calculations were projected from past IEA data, sourced from IEA 2006. For the calculation used, see Chapter 2, note 4.

31 These numbers were calculated from data sourced from SIPRI (2006).

32 These percentages were calculated from data sourced from SIPRI (2006).

33 Arab investment generally increased in the years before this deal, with the UAE, and the Emirate of Dubai in particular, demonstrating a meteoric rise in profile over that time. (For a list of its relevant SWF investments, see Reuters 2006b.) Despite Dubai's recent economic troubles, the UAE as a whole appears to have remained an active investor.

34 The UK five-year average growth rate was 4.76% in 2005 and 4.34% in 2006. The numbers for the US were slightly higher at 4.93% in 2005 and 4.96% in 2006. Numbers calculated from data from the WDI database (WDI 2008).

35 For example, the Dubai International Financial Centre (DIFC) was in talks for a while to obtain a large stake in Euronext, before it became clear that such a transaction would be blocked if the DIFC tried to take over the entire financial exchange, or even a majority stake (see Reuters 2006c).

36 These numbers were calculated from data sourced from the WDI database (WDI 2008) using GDP PPP, in current international dollars.

37 These numbers were calculated from data taken from the WDI database (WDI 2008) using GDP PPP, in current international dollars.

38 See, for example, the discussion in Jackson (2007, 19–20) on this issue.

39 Then Secretary of State Condoleezza Rice praised the UAE as "a strong ally" of the US – a sentiment echoed by then UAE Foreign Minister Sheikh Abdullah bin Zayed al-Nahayan (Daily Star 2006; Reuters 2006d). The UAE holds a unique position as an economic power considered benign by both Western and non-Western countries. This political position, combined with its "strategic position between China and India, the world's fastest-growing economies, and Europe and the US, its biggest consumers, . . . inarguably [give it] a trump card" (Watson 2006).

40 Defending the relationship, Yousef Al Otaiba, International Affairs Director to the UAE Crown Prince, pointed out on CNN that "the UAE contributed

forces to Operation Desert Storm. And we allowed US forces to base in the [UAE]. In 1993, we contributed forces to operations in Somalia. In 1998, we sent as many as 9,000 troops to conduct peacekeeping operations under the NATO alliance. We operated in Kosovo for over three and a half years" (Blitzer et al. 2006a).

41 According to the DOD, "more US warships are serviced . . . in Dubai than any other port outside of the United States" (Blitzer et al. 2006a).

42 On these two points, see also Blitzer et al. 2006b; Cornwell 2006; Wolffe & Bailey 2006.

43 Those against the deal pointed to a 2003 incident in which "66 high-speed electrical switches, which can be used to detonate nuclear weapons" passed through the country, and to comments by "a United Nations agency [that] said disgraced Pakistani scientist Abdul Qadeer Khan used Dubai as the headquarters for his nuclear black market" (Cornwell 2006; Mathews 2006). On Hardball with Chris Mathews, Rep. Hunter claimed he had "court documents that evidence the transfers of *bad stuff* through Dubai," referring to the switches (Mathews 2006). On his CNN show, Wolf Blitzer asked why "dangerous nuclear material, went through Dubai Ports World, the port here in Dubai from Pakistan to Iran and to Libya" (Blitzer et al. 2006b).

44 Congressman Hunter "wanted foreign firms to sell their investments in American ports, electricity plants and other infrastructure critical to US security," and "favor[ed] banning ownership by all foreign companies, not only government-owned ones" (Cornwell & Crawley 2006; Kuhnhenn & Douglas 2006).

45 Rep. Hunter did this in an appearance on Lou Dobbs' CNN show, saying, "We stopped that [transaction], even though the Clinton Administration supported it. We put that in as an amendment to the Armed Services Bill" (Dobbs et al. 2006b). Rep. Hunter felt supporters of such deals indicated that "you can do anything with free traders and with capitalists, because somehow that glazes our eyes and it blinds us . . . Let's stop it" (Dobbs et al. 2006b).

46 For a discussion of the "politicization" of the CNOOC case, see Graham & Marchick 2006, 128–35.

47 The memo from the Coast Guard Intelligence Coordination Center claimed that there were "many intelligence gaps concerning the potential for DPW or P&O assets to support terrorist operation," and noted "three areas where [such] intelligence gaps would prevent a thorough evaluation of the deal: operations, personnel, and foreign influence" (Hindustan Times 2006).

48 This point was verified after lawmakers tried to use the memo to claim the DPW deal was unsound. Clay Lowery, then Treasury Assistant Secretary for International Affairs, told the Senate Homeland Security Committee that "the concerns" raised in the memo had been "addressed and resolved" in the Letter of Assurance (PNG Post Courier 2006). Coast Guard Admiral Thomas Gilmore echoed this sentiment to the press, and the Coast Guard also issued a statement saying parts of the memo were "taken out of context" and that the "full, classified analysis" determined that the deal "[did] not

pose a significant threat to US assets in [US] ports" (PNG Post Courier 2006; Weisman 2006b).

49 Each of the "American intelligence agencies have told the White House that the change in ownership poses no additional risks" to national security generally, or to port security particularly (Stephens 2006). John Negroponte, then CIA Director, claimed he was "confident there's a low risk" posed by the deal, and that the CFIUS review raised "no red flags" (Dobbs et al. 2006c; Dow Jones 2006g). The Administration's spokesman, Scott McClellan, also told CNN that the "broader intelligence community assessment done as part of the review ... addressed such questions, and there were no unresolved national security issues at the end of the process" (Dow Jones 2006g).

50 Early on, "maritime security experts sided with the president" over the deal (Ambrogi 2006).

51 Wolf Blitzer reported that UAE customs authorities believed "their security is extremely tight and technologically advanced" (Blitzer et al. 2006a). More importantly, independent maritime experts agreed. For example, an ex-member of the US Federal Maritime Commission, Rob Quartel, working in private-sector shipping, argued: "From a security standpoint [the US] should be delighted, because [the UAE] have far more money to burn on security than anyone else" (Thiruvengadam 2006).

52 Coast Guard members also made this point during the debate (see Whitfield et al. 2006).

53 In addition to ZIM, numerous companies argued publicly that this was not a national security issue, including Seasecure, "the largest port security consulting firm in the country," and Dupuy Storage & Forwarding and Port Cargo Service, two warehousing service companies operating in New Orleans, a port affected by the transaction (see Buchanan 2006; Dobbs et al. 2006a).

54 As Oliver North pointed out, "the six ports ... aren't being 'sold to a foreign power' ... Nor is the sale a 'hostile takeover,' as one ill-informed television anchor described it" (US Fed News 2006a). Levans (2006) provides a detailed list of these ports at www.logisticsmgmt.com.

55 For further details on foreign port operators in the US, see Glanz 2006; Hensel 2006b; Urquhart 2006.

56 For instance, a Virginia Port Authority spokesperson said, "If you pulled the foreign shipping companies out of this port or any port, I don't know what we would do. It's as international a business as you can put your hands on" (Glanz 2006).

57 Similarly, "the biggest American container shipper is Matson Navigation Co. Inc. in Oakland, and it ranks 31st in terms of shipping capacity with 18 ships, ... Horizon Lines Inc., in Charlotte, NC with 16 ships, is the world's 35th-largest shipper" (Glanz 2006).

58 The Administration also tried to reiterate this point to the public, and Scott McClellan, who at the time was the spokesman for the Administration, said: "If this transaction were blocked, this would not change port security one iota. The Coast Guard and the Customs and Border Patrol remain in charge

of our security . . . The Coast Guard remains in charge of physical security; the Customs and Border Patrol remain in charge of cargo security" (Dow Jones 2006h). On this point, see also Berman 2006; Whitfield et al. 2006; Wolffe & Bailey 2006.

59 For more on Flynn's position, see Pine 2006. Similarly, Dr. Shashi Kumar, then Dean of the Loeb-Sullivan School of International Business and Logistics at the Maine Maritime Academy, claimed that "port security is a problem, but this (shift in control) is not going to change anything" (Berman 2006).

60 Some commentators expressed surprise that this more common route was not taken. For instance, Alan Sloan, Wall Street editor for *Newsweek*, said: "It's easy. You let the buyer own the whole company – but you don't let it control the strategically important business. That part is insulated from the rest of the acquired company and is controlled by a separate board of directors with impeccable national-security credentials. The new owner gets the financial benefits of ownership but can't exercise any control over the sensitive stuff" (Dow Jones 2006b).

61 Other commentators similarly observed that the White House had "created a climate in which economic xenophobia [could] be justified on spurious grounds" (Financial Times 2006b), and was now paying the price. Donna Brazile, a CNN political analyst, also noted that lawmakers' stance on the DPW deal was partially attributable to the fact that homeland security was "no longer an issue that the Democrats will allow the Republicans [to] control the dialogue on" (Blitzer et al. 2006b).

62 Sen. Clinton, for example, publicly argued that "we cannot cede sovereignty over critical infrastructure like our ports. This is a job that America has to do" (Guardian 2006).

63 The story broke when Sen. Collins "released an unclassified portion of the Coast Guard document during a congressional hearing on the takeover" (PNG Post Courier 2006). Senators Schumer and Olympia Snowe (R-ME) wrote a letter to Secretary Michael Chertoff around March 1, saying the "memo, in no uncertain terms, shows that the CFIUS evaluation of the DPW takeover was dangerously incomplete," and "the immediate initiation of the [full] 45-day investigation" was thus "warranted" (Hindustan Times 2006).

64 For instance, "among those who briefed the Armed Services Committee was Rear Adm. Thomas Gilmour of the Coast Guard," who "insisted he could answer questions on the [memo] only in a secret session to staff members with appropriate security clearances" (Weisman 2006b).

65 Admiral James M. Loy, Former Deputy Secretary of Homeland Security, and Rear Admiral Craig Bone, then US Coast Guard Director of Inspection and Compliance, both spoke at a CSIS conference on the deal; neither believed it would threaten national security (Forecast International 2006). Adm. Loy also wrote a couple of unsigned op-eds in favor of the deal in the *New York Times* and *Wall Street Journal* (Dobbs et al. 2006c). Other Coast Guard officials speaking out on the issue included Rear Admiral Thomas Gilmour and Vice Admiral Terry Cross. The latter went on record trying to calm the fears of some congressman, but they largely ignored his claims that though "much

work remains to be done . . . we're a lot more secure in our ports than we were prior to 9/11" (Dobbs et al. 2006b).

66 On February 13, three days after the appearance of that Associated Press article, Lou Dobbs became the first TV news anchor to frame the deal in a similar way (see Hitt & Ellison 2006a). He then continued his campaign against the deal, to the point that DPW refused to grant CNN any interviews (see Dobbs et al. 2006a, 2006b, 2006c, 2006d). Similarly, on February 13, "Michael Savage, a conservative radio talk-show host, also attacked the [deal]. Though [it] had received some newspaper attention before then, Mr. Savage's angry message raised early concerns inside the Bush White House about trouble ahead" (Hitt & Ellison 2006a; see also Wolffe & Bailey 2006). Such approaches continued, with TV personalities such as Chris Matthews continually referring to "the Arab company, Dubai Ports World" and applauding radio talk show hosts Savage and Smerconish for spreading the story (Mathews 2006).

67 James Carville pointed out on CNN that "the problem is that they can't seem to move public opinion on this. And if they don't move public opinion, they're not going to move Democratic or Republican senators. This thing has *the stench of being kind of fact-proof* right now" (Blitzer et al. 2006a, emphasis added).

68 The senator happened to be visiting a port for unrelated reasons when the story really broke, and he held a press conference there voicing his concerns over the transaction.

69 Sen. Frist changed his mind to such a degree that he eventually pledged to "not allow any related legislation on the Senate floor while the new inquiry is under way" (Bohan & Cornwell 2006).

70 He then declared that those opposed to the deal, such as his "opponent in [the mid-term election]," were "really behind the curve as far as the facts are concerned" (Mosk 2006).

71 Sen. Frist confirmed that getting such a briefing was not, at the time, something all members of the Senate could do "easily" (Dobbs et al. 2006c). The FINSA law (passed after this case) changed this; CFIUS is now required to supply such briefings to members of Congress when requested.

72 For further information on this point, see also Handelman 2006; Murphy & Norington 2006; Wilson 2006.

73 After the deal closed, India considered lowering the FDI levels allowed in some sectors. The DPW deal involved numerous ports in India, originally causing concerns that it might lead to the creation of a monopoly (Deshpande 2006; Shah 2006). Some further concerns were voiced months later by the Indian National Security Council over DPW's Indian operations, though these appear to have been satisfactorily addressed by DPW (Joseph 2006; Manoj 2007).

74 Then Prime Minister Tony Blair stated: "We strongly welcome Emirate investment into the UK, for example, Dubai Ports World takeover of P&O," and "I don't think you can ever allow issues like that to become a back door way into protectionism" (AFX 2006c; Blair 2006). Mark Warham, the Director General of the UK Takeover Panel, also claimed that "it was not the

responsibility of the panel to protect UK plc from foreign bids" (Neveling 2006).

75 President Bush said the nation had to "ask . . . what kind of signal does it send to say it's okay for a British company, but not okay for an Arab company to manage this port, when in fact, this same company manages ports all around the world" (Dow Jones 2006a).

76 Similarly, Dan Christman of the US Chamber of Commerce suggested the row could even "threaten South-East Asia's investment and trade with the US" (Han 2006).

77 The American Business Group of Abu Dhabi, for example, claimed investors would "now have to factor in a political risk premium into investments in the US" (Mist News 2006).

78 On March 9, it was reported that "members of Dubai's royal family [were] furious at the hostility" of US lawmakers to the transaction and were "saying: 'All we've done for you guys, all our purchases, we'll stop it, we'll just yank it'" (Tiron 2006). Moreover, it was reported that "retaliation from the Emirate could come against lucrative deals with aircraft maker Boeing and by curtailing the docking of hundreds of American ships, including US Navy ships, each year at its port in the [UAE]" (Tiron 2006).

79 Sultan bin Nasser Al Suwaidi, UAE Central Bank Governor, reportedly decided early on that "the issue would be raised on March 13, when the next round of trade negotiations [was] set to take place"; he said this was because the intervention by US lawmakers into the deal "is something that doesn't reflect well" on the US (Al-Bawaba News 2006). After that March 13 negotiation round was cancelled, Sheikha Lubna al-Qassimi, the UAE's Economy and Planning Minister, said the row had "raised 'certain questions on our side about the process of investment – because a major chunk of the FTA is related to . . . investment in the US,' but added that she was '100% confident' that the FTA deal will go through" (Auger & Marashlian 2006).

80 Edward Bilkey, COO of DPW, said in a press release that it was "because of the strong relationship between the UAE and the US, and to preserve that relationship, [that DPW] decided to transfer fully the operation of P&O Ports North America to a US entity" (Lloyd's 2006). Similarly, Sheik Muhammad bin Rashid al-Maktoum, the Emir of Dubai, "gracefully and generously declared that a financial deal will not be allowed to jeopardize present good relations with the US" (Ylagan 2006; see also Auger & Marashlian 2006).

81 The same UAE official said furthermore that "Our close ties with the [US] are important" (Cornwell 2006). Mohammed Sharaf, Chief Executive of DPW, also said that his company would "return to the [US] despite" the row, because it is "the world's largest economy. How can you just ignore it?" (Traffic World 2006).

82 The Doncasters deal would give "the [DIC] control of nine plants in the US. These produce turbine fan parts and airfoils for tanks and helicopters, among other things" (Auger 2006).

83 Indeed, the American Business Group of Abu Dhabi said at the end of April 2006 that "the Doncasters deal is now crucial" to the continued good relations between the US and the UAE (Mist News 2006).

84 The Bush Administration announced on March 3, 2006 that CFIUS was "conducting a 45-day review of the deal because security concerns had not been resolved in a preliminary probe" (Sevastopulo & Kirchgaessner 2006). This enhanced scrutiny was taken well in Dubai, probably because it was less politicized and more in keeping with the normal CFIUS process. Dubai International Capital's then Chief Executive, Sameer Al Ansari, understood this, announcing that "after what happened with Dubai Ports, the government is looking at this deal more closely" (Daily Mail 2006a).

5 Bounded Intervention
Mitigating Threats to National Security

Introduction

Bounded (like unbounded) intervention is a type of non-military internal balancing. Its primary objective is to balance another state's power, without fundamentally disrupting the overall diplomatic relationship with that other state. Bounded and unbounded intervention are also motivated by the same factors: i.e., economic nationalism and/or geopolitical competition concerns. The purpose of this chapter is not only to confirm the validity of the primary and secondary hypotheses posited in Chapter 1, but also to clarify how bounded intervention is different from unbounded intervention. In other words: what does it entail, and when and why will a state employ this balancing strategy?

This chapter begins by refining the definition of bounded intervention and identifying the government actions and methods that characterize it. The motivations for bounded intervention are then revisited, followed by an in-depth examination of two further critical case studies: the takeover of America's Lucent Technologies by France's Alcatel and that of IBM's American PC Business by China's Lenovo. Figure 28 provides an overview of these cases, which were chosen for their vital importance to a proper understanding of bounded intervention and their ability to provide further insight into the statistical results presented in Chapter 2. At the end of this chapter, it should be clear what bounded intervention is, what motivates it, and why governments choose to use it.

Defining Bounded Intervention

Definitions

The difference between bounded and unbounded intervention lies largely in degree, intensity, and intent. With *unbounded* intervention, the intent of the government in question is to block a deal through whatever

Figure 28 Bounded intervention: critical cases

	Case 6	Case 7
Acquirer Name	Alcatel	Lenovo Group
Acquirer Country	France	China
Target Name	Lucent Technologies	IBM Corporation's PC Business
Target Country	USA	USA
Target Industry	Telecom	High-Tech
Deal Type	Acquisition	Acquisition
Deal Value (in $US Thousands)	13,400,000	1,750,000
Deal Status	Completed	Completed
Deal Year	2006	2005

means are necessary. Further, the government believes such action is necessary to resolve its concern over relative power positions, regardless of whether it is economic nationalism or geopolitical factors that have motivated that concern. However, when the government believes the circumstances of a particular deal make it possible to resolve its concerns through a more limited form of intervention, it will often take the opportunity to exhibit restraint by using the *bounded* alternative instead. This is because bounded intervention is even less likely to produce antagonism in the general relationship between the states involved.

With bounded intervention, the state employs a restricted (and hence "bounded") strategy, the intent of which is simply to modify a cross-border deal in its favor, rather than to block it in its entirety. In other words, the state's intent is to allow the cross-border deal to occur, but in a modified form, which it has shaped. The means of modifying, or "mitigating," a deal naturally varies in accordance with concerns raised by the host government of the target company (state *A*). So, too, will the level of bounded intervention that the government feels it is necessary to employ. This section seeks to differentiate between the two levels of bounded intervention: high and low. It also identifies some of the methods governments have at their disposal to "mitigate" the negative effects of a deal in the interest of state security, as that state defines it, though the list of possible government concerns and solutions is theoretically endless.

A hypothetical example will elucidate the basic difference between high- and low-bounded interventions. Let us assume that state *A* is concerned by the inclusion of a certain corporate division in a cross-border transaction – perhaps because it retains government contracts, is the primary manufacturer of a significant piece of military technology, or plays an important role in the military-industrial complex of that state. There are a number of ways that state *A* might handle this concern, depending on the sensitivity of the technology involved, the nature of the government contracts, and the degree of concern that these factors raise vis-à-vis national security.

If state *A* is exceptionally worried about the implications of the inclusion of this corporate division in the transaction, as well as the intentions and reliability of the company and/or country involved in the takeover, it might choose a high level of bounded intervention. High-bounded intervention entails the imposition of severe or exceedingly restrictive changes on the transaction in question, and may even require unique measures. For instance, state *A* might pursue a formal arrangement by which the division in question remains entirely run and controlled by nationals of state *A*, allowing only the revenue of that division to go to the acquiring company in state *B*. Alternatively, state *A* might go so far as to request that the division be excluded entirely from the sale of the domestic company.

The government of state *A* may, however, choose to engage in a low level of bounded intervention if it feels that severe measures are unnecessary to protect its national security. Low-bounded intervention entails simpler, less intrusive actions, which are not necessarily unique to the deal in question. For instance, in the hypothetical transaction under discussion, state *A* might feel that it is an adequate solution to simply require the acquiring company to respect its export control laws, and not pass on the technology involved in the deal to countries it deems "unfriendly." Alternatively, if the acquiring company comes from a country that is a close ally and economic partner of state *A*, it may have already signed a comprehensive security agreement as the result of high-bounded intervention in a previous transaction. In that case, state *A* may simply rely on that previous agreement to resolve its concerns, necessitating only a low level of intervention in the current transaction.

A real-life example of this latter type of case would be when the UK's BAE Systems purchased America's United Defense Industries (UDI) in 2005. BAE Systems has purchased a number of US companies in the past through its US subsidiary BAE Systems North America. The US government had, in previous deals, asked BAE Systems North America to sign a comprehensive set of security agreements. Thus, one industry analyst has pointed out that when the BAE/UDI takeover occurred, only minimal intervention was required on the part of the US government because, even though UDI was a major government supplier with sensitive technology, the earlier agreements signed by BAE would allay the majority of the security concerns inherent in the UDI transaction.

No matter what level of bounded intervention a state chooses to employ, it will usually ensure that the modifications it makes to a deal are made legally binding upon the companies involved. In other words, the contracting parties (the acquiring and target companies) will be asked to sign a legal document (or series of documents) enumerating the ways in which the government has chosen to mitigate the negative effects of the deal, and confirming the contracting parties' willingness to be bound by those modifications and requirements. In the US, for example, the government is unlikely to be satisfied with such agreements unless it "believes that the risks it identifies can be managed" successfully through deal modifications and assurances agreed to by the acquiring company (Graham & Marchick 2006, 71–2). Indeed, in any country, in order to be satisfied with this more restricted form of intervention, the government must be confident that the changes made to the deal will effectively protect its national security and, in some cases, its economic position, if that state believes economic security to be tied to national security.

In summary, bounded intervention is a restricted type of intervention used as a form of non-military internal balancing, where the goal is once again to protect or maximize the economic and/or military power of the state, without damaging the greater meta-relationship between the states involved. Such intervention allows cross-border M&A activity to continue, while preventing foreign governments – through the market actions of companies that they may either wholly control or later gain influence over – from gaining access to sensitive technology or information, or from gaining control of resources, materials, and networks, that could eventually help to alter the economic and/or military power balance.

Different States, Different Means...

The exact method and means through which a bounded intervention is executed varies by country. For example, the level of institutionalization of the procedures for intervention, the tools available for intervention, and the formality of the agreements negotiated between the government and the companies in question can differ substantially depending on the country involved. Before moving to the case studies, it is therefore important for comparison to examine how bounded intervention is effected in four different countries – the US, China, Russia, and the UK – both during the case studies and at the time of writing. A brief overview is also provided of the overarching foreign takeover regimes in these countries (with the exception of the US, whose regime was comprehensively examined in Chapter 3, pp. 110–11), in order to place these different approaches to bounded intervention in context.

The United States

In the US, the foreign takeover review process, and therefore the process through which a deal might be mitigated, is highly institutionalized. Throughout the course of a proposed takeover for a US company, the foreign acquirer and the domestic target companies will regularly consult with CFIUS, often even before the formal review process begins. During the course of this interactive process, CFIUS may raise its concerns with the companies on an informal basis, allowing them to address an issue before it is formally raised as part of the Committee's official investigation. According to Graham and Marchick, the government agencies represented within CFIUS may also contact the parties directly. They explain, for example, that the DOD may "negotiate mitigation measures with the transaction party," "if [it] believes that the risks [to national security] it identifies can be managed" successfully through alterations to the deal, or through other assurances agreed to by the acquiring company (Graham & Marchick 2006, 71). They reveal that such measures "generally fall into four categories (in ascending order of restrictiveness)" (Graham & Marchick 2006, 71–2). These measures include: (1) some form of "board resolution" to ensure citizens of the target state remain involved in management, (2) the creation of a "limited facility clearance" to restrict foreign access to secure areas or technology, (3) a "Special Security Agreement (SSA)" or "Security Control Agreement (SCA)" that enumerates a series of security measures to be followed by the acquirer, and (4) a "voting trust agreement" or a "proxy trust agreement" (Graham & Marchick 2006, 71–2). CFIUS may, on its own, also impose mitigatory measures as part of a national security agreement, which it can ask the contracting parties to sign before recommending a deal to the President for approval. Such national security agreements may include onerous changes or modifications to a deal, or may seek more simple assurances that the company in question will adhere to US export control laws and other industrial and security regulations. More severe and involved actions are considered to be cases of high-bounded intervention. In rare cases, companies might be forced to divest a portion of the target company. On one extraordinary occasion, in the Alcatel/Lucent case examined in this chapter, the government reserved the right to force a future reversal of the takeover if the acquiring company fails to adhere to the assurances it made to the US government regarding measures to safeguard US national security.[1]

Thus, while the US process is not completely transparent, it is highly institutionalized and fairly straightforward to navigate for those companies that wish to make a deal work. Bounded interventions occur within a recognized, established, and coherent legal framework, which can easily be adapted to handle different threats to national security.

China

Relative to the US, the foreign takeover review process in China is not as highly institutionalized, predictable, or consistent (see e.g., Stratford & Luo 2015; US GAO 2008, 42–52). As China has moved toward a more open economy, and since its accession to the WTO in 2002, the Chinese government has sought to reform and clarify the FDI laws and regulations in its country in order to bring them in line with WTO members' expectations. Yet, the laws and regulations applicable to foreign investors can be difficult to follow, and can vary depending on the type of foreign investment made and the type of purchasing vehicle used to make it. In fact, by 2008, China reportedly had "more than 200 laws and regulations that involve foreign investment" (US GAO 2008, 45), and, by 2017, more than 1,000 of them (US DOS 2017). For example, the Company Law of the PRC,[2] the Takeover Rules,[3] and the Securities Law[4] apply to both domestic and foreign public M&A (Jian & Yu 2014, 2), while the basis for the body of regulations covering foreign M&A of Chinese companies lies in the 2002 Provisions on Guiding the Orientation of Foreign Investment[5] and the 2006 Provisions for Mergers and Acquisitions of Domestic Enterprises by Foreign Investors (amended in 2009).[6]

The 2004 Decision on Reforming the Investment System outlines the instances in which investment deals are "encouraged, restricted, and prohibited by the state," though it only provides general "guidelines" as to which industries might be included in these broad categories.[7] The Catalogue for Guiding Investment in Foreign Industries provides more detailed guidance on this topic. First released in 1995, the Catalogue has been reissued in 1997, 2002, 2004, 2007, 2011, 2015, and 2017 (CECC 2012; Koty & Qian 2017), and lists those industries that fall within the encouraged, restricted, and prohibited categories for foreign investment. In 2017, this included thirty-five restricted and twenty-eight prohibited industries, with the latter category including industries ranging from the mining of rare-earth metals to the retail of tobacco products.[8] In the past, it was assumed, but not explicitly stated, that foreign investors were generally permitted to invest in those industries not listed, with special rules for some regions and sectors (Qian 2016, 6–7). The 2017 Catalogue, however, explicitly states that it is now to be used nationwide as a "negative list for foreign investment."[9] This means that prohibited industries "are completely closed to foreign investment," and that restricted industries "are subject to restrictions such as shareholding limits, and must receive prior approval from MOFCOM." All other industries not appearing on this negative list now "do not require *prior* approval from MOFCOM," though they "are still subject to record-filing requirements" (Koty & Qian 2017, emphasis added). That being said, the Catalogue is far from simple or comprehensive, as particular regions and sectors may still have additional restrictions on foreign investment (see Koty & Qian 2017). Notably for our discussion here, the Catalogue generally "prohibits foreign investment in sectors that China views as key to its national security, . . . [but] does not prohibit investment for stated reasons, or define national security" (US GAO 2008, 44).[10]

Anti-trust competition review of M&A has also evolved and become more institutionalized over time, bringing with it more formal mechanisms through which the Chinese state can intervene in foreign takeovers on national security grounds. In the time period covered by the database (2001–07), China had several laws that included "antitrust provisions and prohibitions on anti-competitive conduct," but these were "fragmented, confined in scope, and rarely enforced" (Ha & O'Brien 2008). The 2003 Interim Provisions on Mergers and Acquisitions of Domestic Enterprises by Foreign Investors, and the 2006 Provisions that replaced it, prohibited foreign takeovers that would result in unacceptably high market concentrations or ultimately restrict competition, but the Provisions did "not specify any penalties," and in most cases there was "no follow-up" (Ha & O'Brien 2008). In 2007, the Chinese government passed a comprehensive Anti-Monopoly Law (AML), implemented in 2008, which in contrast includes broad powers to review the competition effects of both domestic and cross-border M&A transactions and institutes enforceable penalties for non-compliance with government decisions regarding a particular transaction (Ha & O'Brien 2008; Wang & Emch 2013). The Ministry of Commerce (MOFCOM), the National Development and Reform Commission (NDRC), and the State Administration of Industry and Commerce (SAIC) implement and enforce the AML, with MOFCOM handling merger control (Wang & Emch 2013).[11]

In addition to the ability to review a foreign investment on competition grounds, the 2008 AML notably included the first institutionalized regulatory mandate for the Chinese government to review a foreign investment on national security grounds, under Article 31 of its provisions.[12] Though, as demonstrated in the Macquarie/PCCW case, an informal process of intervention operated during the 2001–07 period covered in the database (see Chapter 3). China then established a more formal security review of foreign takeovers in 2011 with the Circular of the General Office of the State Council on the Establishment of Security Review System Regarding Merger and Acquisition of Domestic Enterprises by Foreign Investors[13] and the subsequent associated implementing provisions.[14] The 2011 Circular created a Joint Commission to undertake these reviews, led by MOFCOM and the NDRC under the oversight of the State Council (see US DOS 2017). This review process examines the "national security" implications of a proposed foreign takeover, as well as the potential impact of a transaction on "steady economic growth,... the basic social living order, and... the R&D capacity of key technologies involving national security" in China.[15] Deals subject to the security review process are those that involve

> acquisitions of a controlling interest in a PRC enterprise within a sensitive sector, such as key agriculture, key energy resources, key infrastructure, key transport systems, key technology and critical equipment manufacturing sectors, which may affect national security; or acquisitions by a foreign investor of any stake in a PRC military or military supportive enterprise, any enterprise located in the surrounding area of important or sensitive military facilities and any other enterprise which is of importance to national defence security. (Linklaters 2015, 37)

The Chinese national security review process is modeled loosely on the CFIUS process, with an initial review period, followed by a more extensive special review if a relevant government department believes the deal may affect Chinese security. Parties involved in the deal also file voluntarily for a review with MOFCOM, or the deal can be referred to MOFCOM for review by "other government agencies, or... third parties" (Jalinous et al. 2016, 5). Parties may not withdraw their application for approval under this review system without "MOFCOM's prior consent," however, and there is no administrative appeals process or avenue for judicial review of MOFCOM decisions (Jalinous et al. 2016, 6).

In China, both unbounded and bounded intervention are possible, though the level of formalization and institutionalization of the methods used to intervene has increased over time. The 2011 Circular, for example, now clearly provides that when a foreign acquisition or merger is believed to impact national security, MOFCOM or another relevant government department can veto the deal or modify it by "transferring related equities, assets or [taking other measures] to eliminate the effect of [the deal on] national security."[16] In other words, once a deal goes through the review process, MOFCOM can approve it, mitigate it (bounded intervention), or veto it (unbounded intervention). Moreover, if MOFCOM is made aware of a foreign takeover that has been completed without having voluntarily filed for approval, and it raises national security concerns, MOFCOM has the authority at that point to apply "sanctions or mitigation measures, including a requirement to divest the acquired Chinese assets" (Jalinous et al. 2016, 6). Once the foreign takeover is completed, the new entity must then register as a foreign-invested enterprise (FIE) (ABASAL 2015, 43–4).

It should be noted, however, that the approval process may vary according to the specific nature of the deal, as the acquisition of a Chinese firm can take place through a number of different routes and via various types of acquisition vehicles.[17] Most deals of the size and sector examined in this study *will* likely require government approval from MOFCOM,[18] though foreign investment in financial institutions is covered by a different set of regulations and approval authorities (see Chan et al. 2015b; Linklaters 2015), and some deals – depending on the size, vehicle used, and sector involved – may also require additional local and/or regional approvals (US GAO 2008, 46). There are also additional rules and regulations that might apply to foreign investments.[19]

It should be noted that further changes have been proposed and made to the Chinese foreign investment review process in 2015 and 2016 that, while offering further clarity to foreign investors, may also increase the opportunities for Chinese state intervention in both bounded and unbounded form. At the beginning of 2015, China released a Draft Foreign Investment Law looking at the possibilities for streamlining and reforming its foreign investment regime. It was in this Draft Law that China first considered extending national treatment to FIEs for investments beyond those restricted or prohibited in a negative list (US DOS 2016a), a policy that appears to have come to fruition with the 2017 Catalogue (US DOS 2017). The Draft Law also proposed changes to the national security review process, including a "broader scope of application . . . to *any* foreign investment that endangers or may endanger national security, regardless of structure and degree of control by the foreign investor" (Chan et al. 2015a, 6). In May 2015, the Trial Measures for the National Security Review of Foreign Investments in Pilot Free Trade Zones introduced a new security review process for the FTZs, likely as a trial for later national use, which broadened the definition of national security and widened the scope of security reviews "to include greenfield projects" (Stratford & Luo 2015, 3–4; US DOS 2016a).[20] In July 2015, the National Security Law of the PRC was adopted, which broadened the scope of national security reviews nationally, "to include an investment's impact on cultural security, information security, industrial security, military security, technological security, and territorial security, among others" (US DOS 2016a).[21] Further implementing legislation was not published at the time of writing (Jalinous et al. 2016), but it seems that all of these actions are intended to "reinvigorate the national security review system [and] seem to signal the awakening of a rather dormant regime that existed under the [2011] Circular" rules (Stratford & Luo 2015, 5).

In 2016, China also adopted and implemented the Decision of the Standing Committee of the National People's Congress on Amending Four Laws Including the Law of the PRC on Foreign-Funded Enterprises,[22] reforming part of the FDI system in China. It amends laws pertaining only to foreign investments made by FIEs[23] in permitted sectors not covered by the Catalogue, which now is treated as a negative list for investment made by FIEs (Ye 2016). This reform *does not* yet alter the national rules described earlier that apply to wholly foreign investors purchasing domestic Chinese enterprises (Cai 2016, 1; Livdahl et al. 2016, 2). The foreign M&A approval process, national security review process, and competition process under the AML, for example, remain in place at the time of writing. It is expected that reform may occur among these processes, but that such reform will allow for greater ease of FDI in those sectors desired by the Chinese state, while also allowing China greater maneuverability to block and/or modify deals to protect Chinese interests and the very "broad definition of national security" set out in the 2015 National Security Law (Stratford & Luo 2015, 5).

In sum, the purpose of all of these decrees has been to create a legal regime meant to protect China's strategic and economic security by ensuring the government's ability to modify cross-border deals to protect Chinese interests (see e.g., Stratford & Luo 2015; US GAO 2008, 42). The changes have not necessarily increased the transparency or efficiency of the review process, but have demonstrated a trend toward greater bureaucratic protection of China's self-defined strategic interests, in addition to a higher level of economic protectionism.

Thus, there is wide latitude for the Chinese government to engage in bounded intervention, and clearly identifiable means through which the state might mitigate a deal in order to reduce any perceived or potential threat to national security. MOFCOM, the evolving security review process, and various local reviews, all provide opportunities for the government to request that changes be made to a deal in order to place it in line with Chinese interests. The latitude for the government to make, or encourage, any modifications to a deal that it deems necessary is enhanced by the complexity of FDI legislation (see US GAO 2008, 42–50). Foreign investors can find it difficult to understand "when central versus local rules apply," or when particular regulations are more likely to be enforced (US DOS 2016a). Therefore, Chinese review authorities essentially have the latitude to decide how a deal must be structured in order for it to comply with Chinese strategic interest, if they desire to do so. Companies seeking approval for their transaction then have the choice whether or not to adjust to those demands. These conversations are rarely made public, however, helping to explain the extremely low levels of data available on bounded intervention in China.

Russia

The foreign takeover process is perhaps even less transparent and institutionalized in Russia. Officially recognized by the US and EU as a working market economy in 2002, Russia acceded to the WTO in 2012 and has been slowly opening itself to foreign investment over time. The 1999 Federal Law No. 160-FZ on Foreign Investment in the Russian Federation, in conjunction with the 1991 Investment Code, are intended to "guarantee that foreign investors enjoy rights equal to those of Russian investors" (US DOS 2016b). Yet, Russia has also "set foreign ownership caps in industries or individual companies in what are considered 'strategic' or sensitive sectors, including the power and gas monopolies, banking, insurance, mass media, diamond mining, and civil aviation" (EIU 2003, 14). The Russian government also maintains strategic stakes in what it calls "the natural monopolies," such as the oil and gas sectors, "for the sake of stability and national security" (EIU 2003, 10). In many instances, however, the laws surrounding foreign investment and ownership caps have "not always [been] enforced in practice" (US DOS 2015, 3), and the purchase of assets and the takeover of private companies have remained possible in some of the industries examined in this book.

During the time period covered in this book's dataset, from 2001 to 2007, the national security review process had not yet been formalized in law, and intervention into foreign takeovers was made on a case-by-case basis. For the industries covered, a fundamental requirement for a foreign takeover at the time was that it comply with Russian anti-competition rules, and thus that the "acquisition of more than 20% of a company's stock requires prior approval of" the competition authority (IFLR 2002). In the early 2000s, this was the Ministry of the Russian Federation on Antimonopoly Policy and Support to Entrepreneurship (MAP), which was replaced in 2004 with the Federal Antimonopoly Service (FAS). In 2006, Federal Law no. 135-FZ On Protection of Competition was adopted, which "reflected the existing system of antimonopoly regulation" (FAS 2015, 16).[24]

Yet, the attitude toward foreign investment arguably took a distinct inward turn in 2003/04 following the downfall of the oil company

Yukos. After that incident, Russian government intervention into foreign takeovers in these sectors tightened under then President, and later Prime Minister, Vladimir Putin. As one industry source noted, there was little formality to the review process at the Anti-Monopoly Ministry during this period, and takeovers of assets deemed to be strategic by Putin were often subject to an additional review by the relevant government authority or ministry (Interview 2008a). This appears to be clearest in the energy and natural resources sectors, where Putin has sought to maintain control over certain resources in order to use them as a tool for Russian policy and the furtherance of Russian power. Furthermore, by 2008, it was clear that any energy deal involving a foreign investor would only get approval if 51% of the new entity were to be owned, or designated to eventually be owned, by Russian citizens – a trend that seemed to affect other strategic sectors as well (Interview 2008a). This is clearly one rather blatant way in which the Russian government has sought to mitigate the proposed foreign takeovers of certain companies it believes to be tied to its nation's future security – a strategy which, at the time of writing, it still seems to employ in a variety of industries, companies, and circumstances.

An excellent example of this is provided by the 2007 EniNeftegaz-Arktikgaz case. In this case, a JV company (EniNeftegaz) owned by two Italian energy companies (Eni and Enel) bid for 100% of the assets of the gas production company Arktikgaz in a public auction. The Italian JV was allowed to take over the assets by the Russian authorities upon winning the auction, but it is clear that this was only allowed to happen because a preliminary deal had been forged with the Russian gas giant Gazprom, whereby Gazprom would eventually control the assets. The companies "negotiated" an agreement in advance whereby Gazprom retained "the option to buy a 51% stake in [Arktikgaz]" (Global Insight 2007). Furthermore, Dmitry Medvedev – then Chairman of Gazprom's Board, and President of Russia only a year later – was quick to announce "that Gazprom plans to exercise the option" to buy the controlling stake (Global Insight 2007). One member of the beleaguered Russian legal community made it plain that this was not a case of "open, free auctions but rather [of] organized sales at knockdown prices . . . with predetermined winners," where "in reality Gazprom," a Russian government controlled entity, "is the winner" (Global Insight 2007). This case highlights the desire of the Russian government to ensure that its most strategic companies remain domestically controlled, making it clear to foreign investors that foreign takeovers are only likely to be allowed to occur in strategic sectors when they have been mitigated in such a manner.

In 2008, just after the time period covered in the database, Russia adopted a more formalized national security review process for screening foreign investments in designated strategic sectors, but, importantly, the dynamics of Russian intervention into foreign investment appear to remain largely the same. In April 2008, Russia adopted Federal Law No. 57-FZ on Procedures for Foreign Investments in the Business Entities of Strategic Importance for Russian National Defense and State Security,[25] often referred to as the Strategic Investments Law. This law established a Government Commission for Control over Foreign Investments, chaired by the Russian Prime Minister, which must pre-approve foreign investments into designated strategic sectors and above particular ownership thresholds that vary by the type of foreign investor and sector involved. In other words, attempts by foreign investors to gain controlling stakes, much less complete ownership, over a company in an industry associated with national security in Russia must be approved by the committee. This law has been periodically amended, notably in 2011 and 2014, but again remains broadly consistent in its approach.[26] It was reported that "as of April 2015, 45 activities require government approval for significant foreign investment" (US DOS 2016b, 3). These include, but are not limited to: aerospace and defense sectors, such as the production and development of munitions, armaments, and aviation equipment; media and telecommunications, such as printing activities, broadcasting, and fixed-line telephone communications; energy and natural resources, such as nuclear energy and specially designated subsoil areas for natural resource extraction given federal status; and so-called "natural monopolies" (see Article 6, Strategic Investments Law; Syrbe et al. 2014, 2). It should be noted that under separate legislation in 2014, Federal Law no. 305-FZ simply caps foreign ownership of Russian media companies at 20% (US DOS 2016b, 3).

Investment thresholds triggering a national security review by the Commission for Control over Foreign Investments varies, as already mentioned, by type of investor and sector, with some of the latter subject to separate legislation. For state-controlled foreign investors, like state-owned enterprises (SOEs), investments in over 25% of a Russian company in most strategic sectors will trigger the need for a review, investments in over 5% of a subsoil block with federal status will trigger a review, and any "acquisition of over 50% is prohibited" in a strategic sector (Stoljarskij 2011, 79), making it virtually impossible for a foreign state-controlled investor to undertake a complete foreign takeover and merger in a strategic sector in Russia. For a private foreign investor, a review is generally triggered if over 50% of a company in a strategic industry, or over 25% of a subsoil block with federal status, is acquired;

review will occur at lower levels of investment if they result in influence or control over the decision-making processes in a company in a strategic industry (Stoljarskij 2011, 79; 2012, 2). Once a company files, its application is registered and examined to see if it is, in fact, necessary to proceed with a detailed review. The application is returned to the investor without further review if the investment is either clearly prohibited under the law or doesn't meet the requirements for review (Stoljarskij 2011, 81). If a review is required, and the investor does not withdraw from the process, an investment may be approved, denied (unbounded intervention), or mitigated (bounded intervention). In the latter case, "condition[al] consent [may be given] subject to the applicant's discharge of specific obligations," such as the "maintenance of specific production sectors, [or] the continued discharge of specific state orders" (Stoljarskij 2011, 81). Deals not submitted for approval are rendered "null and void," and the parties involved will be subject to penalties (Stoljarskij 2012, 2). Negative decisions by the Commission can be appealed in court under the Strategic Investments Law, but as of May 2014, no investors had yet done so (Syrbe et al. 2014, 7; Wehrlé & Pohl 2016, 70). From the establishment of the Commission and formalization of the national security review process in 2008,

> the Commission has received 395 applications for foreign investment (as of March 11, 2016). Of that total number, 150 were recognized as transactions for which approval was not required; 43 applications were withdrawn by applicants; and seven had not been completed. Of the 195 applications that the Commission reviewed, 183 were approved (93.8 percent), including 49 with certain conditions. Only 12 applications (6.2 percent) were rejected. (US DOS 2016b, 4)

While the outright veto rate is not too high, the restrictions in strategic sectors erect significant barriers to foreign investment of the type examined in this book – and a number of deals are clearly modified to ensure the continued control and influence of the state and the protection of national security in these sectors.

In summation, there is now a more regularized and somewhat more transparent process for the national security review of foreign investments in Russia, but the dynamics behind this process – intended to protect Russian control of strategic industries and companies, while encouraging the "foreign investment and technology transfer . . . critical to Russia's economic modernization" – has remained consistent over the time period covered in the database and up to the time of writing (US DOS 2016b). There is, after all, no published or public set of criteria used by the Commission in its review process to assess what might actually constitute a risk to nation security, giving the Commission extra leeway in how it approaches foreign investment in relation to state security and strategy, and making it difficult for investors to foresee which deals might be considered to have a "strategic element" (Syrbe et al. 2014, 1; Wehrlé & Pohl 2016 30). Moreover, concerns over the unpredictability of the process, and over a "Russian investment climate . . . marked by high levels of uncertainty, corruption, and political risk," also continue through to the time of writing, and "are unlikely to improve in the near term" (US DOS 2016b, 1; see Stoljarskij 2012; Syrbe et al. 2014).

The United Kingdom

The UK provides yet another example of the many different national approaches to bounded intervention that are possible. For the time period covered in this book, the UK has arguably represented one of the most open economies to FDI, though it is possible that this degree of openness may be subject to change in the future.

Until 2002, foreign M&A were subject to the 1973 Fair Trading Act (FTA), which supplied the framework for the competition review of all mergers in the UK. Section 84 of the FTA "set a broader public interest test" to be considered by those making decisions as part of this process, including, for example, whether a proposed transaction would have an effect on "maintaining and promoting the balanced distribution of industry and employment in the United Kingdom" (Seely 2016, 9). Toward the end of the FTA regime, however, "most merger decisions were already focused on competition" alone, rather than on wider considerations (Seely 2016, 9). The FTA was replaced in 2002 with the Enterprise Act, which, as of November 2016, provides the framework for the review process for all M&A in the UK. This act, as amended, establishes an anti-trust review that is triggered for deals that reach certain thresholds: transactions that would result in an entity with over £70 million in turnover, or which would have a post-transaction market share of over 25% (Seely 2016, 4). These competition reviews were originally handled by the Office of Fair Trading and the Competition Commission, and since 2014 have been handled by the body into which these entities were merged: the Competition and Markets Authority (CMA).

Section 58 of the 2002 Enterprise Act provides for the only instance in which the Secretary of State can intervene in the M&A review process. It "allows for the Secretary of State to intervene in mergers where they give rise to certain specified public interest concerns: specifically, issues of national security; media quality, plurality & standards; and financial stability" (Seely 2016, 3).[27] When the market share and turnover thresholds triggering the general merger review are not met, "the Secretary of State may [also] intervene in a very limited range of 'special public interest cases,'...where one of the enterprises concerned is a relevant government contractor...in defence mergers, or where the merger involves certain newspaper or broadcasting companies" (Seely 2016, 6). As in many other countries, concerns over national security or the public interest will trigger a further investigation, in the UK called a "phase 2 investigation," after which the Secretary of State makes the final decision over whether to approve the deal, prohibit it, or mitigate the concerns raised by the transaction by making it subject to certain "conditions related to, for example, security of supply or security of information" (Wehrlé & Pohl 2016, 72). The entire review process may take up to six or nine months, and decisions can be appealed through both administrative processes and judicial review (Wehrlé & Pohl 2016, 72). Interestingly, the 1975 Industry Act also "provides the UK government with the authority to intervene when the takeover of important manufacturing concerns by nonresidents is against the national interest" (GAO 1996, 40).

For the time period covered in this book, and up to the time of writing, the UK has not hesitated to engage in bounded intervention when it feels that it is necessary to preserve national security. Indeed, the Department for Business Enterprise and Regulatory Reform (BERR), and later its replacement the Department for Business, Innovation, and Skills (BIS), even maintained a list of the most serious potential "mergers with a national security element" on its website, and provided the legal documentation given to justify intervention in those cases, as well as documentation of the undertakings made by companies in respect to the conditions imposed on the deals.[28] While this list only seems to have related to those mergers in the aerospace and defense sector, despite clear evidence of intervention in other strategic sectors, such transparency regarding the details of bounded intervention, even in one industry, is extremely rare, and is a sign of the UK's valued commitment to an open FDI regime. In 2016, BIS was replaced with the Department for Business, Energy, and Industrial Strategy (BEIS), and this information can still be found using the search function on its website, or on the archived BIS website.

A good example of how bounded intervention is achieved in the UK is provided by the Finmeccanica/BAE case. In 2005, the Italian aerospace and defense company Finmeccanica sought to buy BAE Systems' avionics and communications businesses, which had a close relationship with the UK military community. The Secretary of State[29] determined the deal

> might adversely affect the public interest on national security grounds as a result of both the communications and avionics business transferring to the ownership and control of an overseas company. The MoD has identified two main areas of concern arising from this merger: the maintenance of strategic UK capabilities and the protection of classified information. (Boys 2005)

The government intervened and negotiated a solution with the two companies that helped to ensure those national security concerns would be mitigated, while still allowing the deal to occur. The changes made to the deal were that "the companies [would] . . . keep the businesses under the management of UK nationals [and] under the control of UK boards" (DMA 2005). Additionally, "the UK government [was provided] with 'golden-share'-esque guarantees that the businesses cannot be re-sold by Finmeccanica without its approval" (DMA 2005). Such agreements and remedies provide clear examples of how bounded intervention may be undertaken even by states with the most open of investment regimes.

Over past decades, the UK has prided itself on its openness to FDI, and only minimal evidence exists of *unbounded* interventions on the part of the UK government during the time period covered by the cases in this book (2001–07). Periodic public debates over the UK's openness to FDI have, however, coincided with unpopular potential and completed foreign takeovers of large UK companies. In 2006, a potential bid for the UK gas company Centrica by the Russian company Gazprom raised concerns over energy security, but the UK Prime Minister at the time reportedly "ruled out any possibility that UK ministers might actively seek to block" such a bid outright (Blitz & Wagstyl 2006; Seely 2016, 16) The 2010 takeover of the beloved UK chocolate company Cadbury by the US food company Kraft resulted in a vigorous public debate over foreign takeovers, led some Members of Parliament to call for the reintroduction of a public interest test for foreign investment, and resulted in some procedural modifications to the UK Takeover Code (Seely 2016, 16–26). And, "in May 2014, debate on the public interest test was rekindled by the plans of US pharmaceuticals company Pfizer to make a bid for the UK company AstraZeneca," due to fears over the impact it could have on the UK science and research base (Seely 2016, 30).

Shortly after the British public voted to leave the EU by referendum in June 2016, the soon-to-be Prime Minister Theresa May indicated that under her leadership the UK government would re-examine its foreign investment review system and look into the reintroduction of a broader public interest test that takes into account a wider range of factors than those specified in the 2002 Enterprise Act. Specifically referencing Cadbury and AstraZeneca in a speech on July 11, 2016, while running for leadership of the Conservative party, May said that

> a proper industrial strategy wouldn't automatically stop the sale of British firms to foreign ones, but it should be capable of stepping in to defend a sector that is as important as pharmaceuticals is to Britain.[30] (May 2016)

Yet, in September 2016, the UK government approved the Hinkley Point C nuclear power plant project, with significant investment from China and the French company EDF, after examining the national security implications of the foreign investment. Though this is a greenfield investment, and not a foreign takeover of the type examined in this book, it is notable for two reasons. First, the investment was mitigated through actions to ensure that EDF's controlling interest in the project could not be sold in the future without UK government approval, and the government also announced that it would take a golden share in *future* nuclear projects to make sure they could not be sold without approval (UK BEIS 2016). Second, as regards the national security review process for all foreign investment, including foreign takeovers, the government announced that:

> There will be reforms to the Government's approach to the ownership and control of critical infrastructure to ensure that the full implications of foreign ownership are scrutinised for the purposes of national security. This will include a review of the public interest regime in the Enterprise Act 2002 and the introduction of a cross-cutting national security requirement for continuing Government approval of the ownership and control of critical infrastructure. (UK BEIS 2016)

Changes to the national security review process, or the adoption of a broader public interest test for foreign investment in the UK, have not been made at the time of writing. Though, in a January 2017 interview, Prime Minister May said that the UK would "in due course . . . come up with some proposals" regarding the foreign takeover review process, and indicated that the focus would be on "national security and critical infrastructure," without referencing a public interest test (Parker 2017). It will be interesting to watch developments in this area. The introduction of a wider public interest test, to place conditions or block deals on the basis of issues like domestic job retention, is beyond the subject matter of this book. Other potential changes to the national security review process, however, such as the adoption of a broader understanding of national security that includes sectors like critical infrastructure, could bring the UK review process in line with that of countries like the US, and provide the UK with a more comprehensive approach to ensuring the protection of strategic assets through both bounded and unbounded intervention.

Summary

Differences exist in national approaches to the type of restricted intervention we associate with bounded balancing. The process for the review of cross-border M&A is more highly institutionalized among the Western advanced industrial states, which partially explains why we are more likely to see bounded intervention among the allies of the Western security communities. This is significant because higher levels of institutionalization allow allies to find alternative solutions to national security concerns, making it unnecessary for them to resort to other means, such as blocking a deal or throwing up such overwhelming opposition that the proposed acquirer voluntarily withdraws from the process. Low levels of institutionalization in states such as Russia and China – aside from the more closed natures of their markets, which pose a higher risk for investors – may also contribute to the low levels of cross-border deals in those states, especially in strategic sectors. This means we have even fewer examples of bounded intervention in these countries than we might otherwise expect.

Motivations for Bounded Intervention

As with unbounded intervention, bounded intervention tends to be motivated by economic nationalism and/or geopolitical competition. The findings in Chapter 2 indicate that the relative importance of these factors varies depending on the subset of cases under examination (Figure 29).

Figure 29 Bounded intervention: significant motivating factors

	Model I *(All Deals)*	**Model II** *(Security Community Deals)*	**Model III** *(Non-Security Community Deals)*
Low-Bounded Intervention	Nationalism		Nationalism Inward FDI
High-Bounded Intervention	Nationalism	Nationalism Relative Military Power *(Negative Direction)* Resource Dependency	Nationalism Relative Military Power *(Negative Direction)*

Generally, the variable associated with a significant increase in the likelihood of bounded intervention across all cases (MNLM I) is nationalism. As suggested previously, this finding might indicate that higher levels of economic nationalism in state *A* could *also* lead a state to protect its national interests through such measures. The analysis of the case studies that follow should help to demonstrate the accuracy of the assumption that economic nationalism is likely to play at least some role in a government's decision to employ bounded intervention.

When the population of cases was reduced to those that took place within the security community context (MNLM II), the significance of those factors representing geopolitical competition became apparent. As noted earlier, the probability of high-bounded intervention significantly increases when state *A* has higher levels of nationalism, resource dependency, and relative power.[31] Interestingly, relative military power is shown to be significant in the negative direction, which may indicate that under certain conditions state *A* might feel more comfortable imposing modifications to foreign takeovers when it is in an advantaged power position versus state *B*. Put simply, state *A* may not feel that it is necessary to use unbounded intervention to solve its security concerns when conditions allow for a solution to those problems through a more restricted form of intervention, which in turn helps to minimize political fallout from its actions. As will be demonstrated in the examination of the Lenovo case, this may remain true even when the acquiring state is a rising power.

In the subset of cases that occurred outside of the security community context (MNLM III), geopolitical factors again show their importance alongside nationalism. The statistical results show that low-bounded intervention was significantly more likely when state *A* had high levels of nationalism and inward FDI. The fact that IFDI is an indicator of the relative economic power positions of states *A* and *B* demonstrates that the concern over the relative geopolitical position of those states plays an important role in determining how state *A* will handle a foreign takeover that hails from outside of its security community. The results also show that high-bounded intervention was more probable in this subset of cases when state *A* had high levels of nationalism and relative military power. Military power is again significant in the negative direction, for reasons already explained.

It is evident that nationalism and geopolitical competition increase the likelihood of the restricted form of intervention identified here as "bounded intervention." As nationalism is used as a proxy for economic nationalism in the quantitative testing, the case studies that follow provide another opportunity to demonstrate the validity of this assumption and the importance of the role played by economic nationalism. The case studies also help to further refine our understanding of the role played by geopolitical competition in motivating this type of intervention. They focus on high-bounded intervention cases, which provide both a tougher test of the hypotheses and a greater opportunity to study the dynamics behind them in detail. Low-bounded interventions, such as those discussed earlier, do not provide the same opportunity to highlight these dynamics due to their more "routine" nature, as states are usually addressing more minor national security issues in such instances.

Furthermore, the case studies in this chapter elucidate the general conditions under which a state might feel more comfortable engaging in bounded, rather than unbounded, intervention. Bounded intervention is more common than unbounded intervention, with the former representing 29%, and the latter only 8%, of the total cases in the database. This may be because allowing foreign takeovers to be completed in modified form is even less likely than unbounded intervention to disrupt trade relationships or produce antagonism between the countries involved. In other words, it best accomplishes the goal of non-military internal balancing: to balance power without necessarily disrupting the greater meta-relationship at stake between the two countries.

Case 6: Alcatel/Lucent

The Context

Before delving into the Alcatel/Lucent case, it is important to understand where it stands in the context of the broader M&A market. This particular case involves a French company acquiring a US company in the telecommunications equipment manufacturing industry, which is part of the larger technology sector. Within the parameters of the database created for this investigation, sixty-eight US companies were targeted for foreign acquisition, and only *seven* of these deals occurred within this particular industry (see Figure 30). Of those, only one involved an acquirer from a country that the Correlates of War project does not classify as a member of the same security community as the US,[32] and that country was Sweden, which – though not a member of NATO – remains a very close NATO partner with significant economic, political, and cultural ties. This suggests that in the US, a foreign takeover in this industry is usually more likely to see successful completion when the acquiring company hails from a state with a close relationship to Washington.

Furthermore, of those seven cases, the US engaged in some form of intervention in almost every one: bounded intervention in five cases, unbounded intervention in one case, and no intervention in only one case. Significantly, there are indications that the US government would likely have engaged in some form of intervention in the latter instance

Figure 30 Dataset subset: cross-border deals between the US and France

Year	Acquirer *(French)*		Target *(American)*		Sector	Industry	Intervention Type	Deal Outcome
2003	Business Objects	FR	Crystal Decisions	US	Technology	Software	None	Deal
2006	Alcatel	FR	Lucent Technologies	US	Technology	Telecom Equipment	Bounded	Changed Deal
2007	Compagnie Générale de Géophysique	FR	Veritas DGC	US	Oil & Gas	Producers, Equipment, and Distribution & Services	None	Deal
2007	Capgemini US	FR	Kanbay International	US	Technology	Computer Hardware	None	Deal
2007	Schneider Electric	FR	American Power Conversion Corporation	US	Technology	Computer Hardware	None	Deal
Year	**Acquirer *(American)***		**Target *(French)***		**Sector**	**Industry**	**Intervention Type**	**Deal Outcome**
2002	Platinum Equity	US	Alcatel SA's European Enterprise Distribution & Services Business	FR	Telecom	Fixed Line Telecom	None	Deal
2003	PanAmSat Holding Corporation	US	Eutelsat	FR	Telecom	Satellite Telecom	Unbounded	No Deal
2002	Intelsat	US	Eutelsat	FR	Telecomm	Satellite Telecom	Unbounded	No Deal
2004	UGI Corporation	US	AGZ Holding	FR	Oil & Gas	Producers	None	No Deal
2005	Legg Mason	US	Permal Group	FR	Financials	Investment Services (Stock Exchanges)	None	Deal*
2005	Legg Mason	US	Permal Group	FR	Financials	Investment Services (Stock Exchanges)	None	No Deal*

* *In the first deal, Legg Mason acquired 80% of Permal; in the second, it failed to acquire the remaining 20% of the company.*

if the proposed bid had not been dropped before it was formally announced. The suggestion here is that even among allies, this sector is considered so strategically important that deals must at the very least be mitigated in order to ensure the protection of technology related to national security.

The Alcatel/Lucent merger is also the only instance in the dataset in which a French company even tried to buy a US company in this particular industry. In fact, in the dataset as a whole, there are only fifteen cases of a French company buying a foreign company in one of the target countries being examined here, and only five of those cases involved the purchase of a US company. Four of these five cases occurred in the technology sector as a whole, but only the Alcatel/Lucent deal involved the telecommunications hardware industry. This indicates that while takeovers in this subset of the technology sector have been rare, French takeovers of US companies in the technology sector as a whole are not. Figure 30 shows that French takeovers in the rest of the sector met with little resistance, highlighting the need to explain intervention in this case.

Significance

Beyond this market context, a number of factors make the Alcatel/Lucent merger a critical case. First, it is one of the most severe examples of high-bounded intervention. This is because the US government employed a mitigating tool now known as an "evergreen clause," giving it the ability to reverse the merger at a future date if it becomes dissatisfied with the new entity's adherence to the security agreement it signed as part of the review process. As the first known case in which such a method has ever been used, most market and research analysts consider it critical for understanding the nature of such intervention.

Second, this is also one of the clearest cases of bounded intervention available for study. Detailed knowledge of such cases is quite rare, because the mitigating measures taken by governments are usually classified. Thus, even when we know alterations are made to a deal, we normally only hear the details of those measures if they are voluntarily released by the companies or are leaked to the press. The wealth of information in this case is, therefore, important to study.

Finally, the case is critical to this investigation because it provides a better understanding of the role of bounded intervention within security communities. To understand how, it is necessary to momentarily return to a discussion of the statistical context illustrated in Figure 30. Out of the six attempts by US companies to buy French companies in any sector in the database, only one was successful. This reflects the high level of economic nationalism in France generally, and the geopolitical antagonism toward foreign takeovers by US companies in particular – as illustrated by the infamous PepsiCo/Danone case examined in Chapter 3. Conversely, the Alcatel/Lucent case is the only instance in recent history in which the US intervened when a French company tried to purchase a US technology company. As will be discussed, this is partly because of the timing of the Alcatel/Lucent deal, which came immediately on the heels of the DPW debacle and shortly after the CNOOC case, ensuring that economic nationalism would play a small but important role in the reaction of the US government. Yet, as will be shown, intervention was also triggered by geopolitical concerns. Indeed, the Alcatel/Lucent case is the only one in which a French company targeted a US company that was involved in classified government work and contracts, heightening the geopolitical implications of the deal for the US.

The case is thus critical because it helps to highlight something that the statistical investigation in Chapter 2 could not: that although economic nationalism will tend to play a significant role in cases of bounded intervention within security communities, such an alliance relationship does not necessarily preclude an important role for geopolitical concerns. In the PepsiCo/Danone case, French fear of US hegemony almost mandated such a foreign takeover be blocked. In this case, the US had less to "fear" from France, but France's desire to score a geopolitical coup against the US, its determination at the time to cast the US in a bad diplomatic light, and its disregard for certain US sanctions regimes ensured that the political tensions between the two countries would exacerbate the national security concerns raised by the sensitive nature of Lucent's work.

The Story

On March 24, 2006, rumors of a merger between Alcatel SA of France and Lucent Technologies of the US hit the newswires (Zephyr 2006b). The two companies had discussed a possible merger in 2001, but those talks had failed "over how much control [Alcatel] would have" of a new combined entity (Frost 2006). "Since then, however, Alcatel ha[d] grown faster than Lucent, giving it a clear upper hand in merger talks" (Frost 2006). Additionally, the sporadic bankruptcy rumors Lucent had faced in 2001 and 2002, as well as the periodic cutbacks and profit warnings it had suffered, made a merger with Alcatel now seem much more appealing (see McKay 2006a; Morse 2006).

Both Alcatel and Lucent were telecommunications equipment manufacturers in the technology sector.[33] Yet, while the majority of their business focused on the private sector, each company held defense contracts with its respective government, and each had divisions dedicated to the development of sensitive technology. Alcatel, for example, owned a stake in two satellite-manufacturing JVs, Alcatel Alenia Space and Telespazio, with Italy's Finmeccanica. Alcatel Alenia worked on sensitive projects such as the first iteration (Giove-A) of the Galileo Satellite (see Alcatel 2006b). Lucent, meanwhile, held a number of contracts with the US DOD that ranged from providing it with "classified technology" to supplying "telecoms equipment for the Iraqi reconstruction project" (MacMillan 2006). Lucent also owned and operated Bell Laboratories, an entity that for eighty years had conducted classified work for the US government: producing the transistor, the laser, and the touch-tone phone, while pioneering solar cells, cell phones, and the communications satellite (Alcatel-Lucent 2008; Reuters 2006a). Such pedigrees indicated that any deal between Alcatel and Lucent would raise national security concerns for both the US and France.

Not surprisingly, many analysts who felt the deal might make sense economically remained wary that its security implications could lead to failure if not addressed early, adequately, and carefully (see e.g., AFP 2006c; McKay 2006b; Morse 2006; Wickham 2006). Others believed that, even then, the deal might be blocked (see e.g., MacMillan 2006). Thus, while it remained only a rumor, analysts had already begun to contemplate the different ways the deal might be mitigated in order to satisfy both Washington and Paris. The most common suggestions and commentary assumed that, at the bare minimum, France would encourage Alcatel to sell its satellite divisions to another French company, such as Thales, and Lucent would need to protect Bell Labs by either divesting it, or creating a subsidiary that would be closed off from foreign influence (see e.g., Butler 2006; Dow Jones 2006c; McKay 2006a; Morse 2006). These hurdles were not low, but many market and industry observers believed that, if they were executed well, the merger would not be blocked unless it became "a political football" like the DPW deal (MacMillan 2006). Indeed, it was unlikely that France would completely block a deal that was largely in its favor, and that was viewed as a triumph for the French tech industry.[34] In the end, the lack of French cooperation geopolitically, combined with the need to protect classified materials and the rising protectionist sentiment in the US at that particular time, ensured the US government would at least intervene in a bounded fashion; and extreme politicization of the deal could have resulted in unbounded intervention.

By April 2, 2006, a definitive merger agreement was reached between the two companies valued at US $13.4 billion, giving Alcatel shareholders a 60% stake of the new combined entity and Lucent shareholders 40% (Zephyr 2006b). Because concerns over equality had quashed attempts by the two companies to merge in 2001, a clear effort was made to sell this as a "merger of equals" (MacMillan 2006). Hence, it was announced immediately that Lucent's CEO Patricia Russo would head the new combined company, and in return its headquarters would remain in Paris, its CFO would come from Alcatel, its COO from Lucent, and the new board of directors would be equally drawn from Alcatel and Lucent's existing board members (AFX 2006a). Yet, despite these overt efforts toward equal partnership, the market generally viewed and treated the deal as a foreign takeover of a US company by a French one (Intereview 2008b). Lucent was clearly the "junior partner" in the merger, and even M&A databases such as Zephyr classify the deal as an acquisition of Lucent by Alcatel (MacMillan 2006; Morse 2006; Zephyr 2006b). Thus, while the details of the French position will still be discussed, Lucent will be treated as the target company for the purpose of this investigation.

Unlike most of the cases examined in the previous two chapters, Alcatel and Lucent sought to address the national security implications of their proposed deal before it was even officially announced.[35] In France, Alcatel sought early on to push through a previously discussed arrangement whereby the French defense electronics company Thales would take Alcatel's stake in its satellite JVs in return for a stake in Thales (see TelecomWeb 2006c). This deal would both calm France's worries about sensitive technology being seen by foreign citizens and help the government protect the vulnerable French Thales from a takeover by the European EADS (see Dow Jones 2006d; Financial Times 2006a; TelecomWeb 2006c). In the US, Lucent issued a press release when the proposed merger was announced in order to calm fears over the future security of Bell Labs. The release stated that "the combined company [would] form a separate, independent US subsidiary under Bell Labs . . . to perform research and development work for the US government that is of a sensitive nature," and that Bell Labs would not be moved or its leadership changed (Lucent 2006). Lucent also announced it "ha[d] asked three experienced and distinguished members of the national security community to serve on the independent subsidiary's board, . . . subject to US government approval," namely former Secretary of Defense William Perry, former NSA Director Lieutenant General Kenneth Minihan, and former Director of Central Intelligence James Woolsey (Lucent

2006). These actions were meant to "black box" Bell Labs from foreign control and influence, allowing only the revenue from its activities to go to the new entity. Such special subsidiaries can alleviate national security concerns, allowing governments, that wish to do so, to mitigate foreign takeovers without having to block them outright. By announcing their willingness to create such a subsidiary early on, Alcatel and Lucent were trying to anticipate the problems their deal might face, and cast their intentions in a positive light. It was likely hoped this would alleviate existing geopolitical tensions between the two countries in order to prevent the kind of unbounded intervention that had been so recently faced by DPW and CNOOC in the US. The companies then "submitted a voluntary notice of the merger to CFIUS in August 2006" (Alcatel 2006a), and were reported to have worked (and cooperated) closely with that same body in order to resolve the US government's concerns (Dow Jones 2006e).

In order to properly understand the US reaction to the Alcatel/Lucent merger, it is necessary to examine the political context in the US at that time. This deal surfaced just after the heavily politicized DPW case, which unleashed a furor of congressional rhetoric about the threat foreign takeovers could potentially pose to national and economic security. Both economic nationalism and national security awareness were therefore abnormally heightened by this time, and were being manifested in a rush of legislation proposed to reform CFIUS and make the foreign takeover review process more stringent.

Not surprisingly, Congressman Duncan Hunter (R-CA), who had been vociferously against the DPW deal, came out early on against the Alcatel/Lucent deal (see AFX 2006b). In a letter to President Bush dated April 28, 2006, Hunter stated:

> I have several grave concerns about the potential merger . . . [that] arise in large part because Lucent Technologies and Bell Labs, a critical component of the parent company Lucent Technologies, conduct a significant amount of highly classified work for the United States government, including the Department of Defense. I am skeptical whether the current CFIUS process could provide adequate, verifiable assurances that such sensitive work will be protected. (Silva 2006a)

Both companies responded directly to Hunter's concerns, reiterating the precautions they had already announced regarding the future of Bell Labs. Yet, it was clear that Hunter no longer believed CFIUS to be an effective review body and was voicing his concerns in order to make CFIUS more accountable.

Another issue raised by Hunter, which the companies, interestingly, did not immediately address, was the fact that the merger "could result in transfers of sensitive technologies or information to several countries with which Alcatel has dealings, including [Myanmar], China, Cuba, Iran, North Korea, Sudan, and Syria" (Inside US Trade 2006a). This is significant for the discussion of geopolitical tensions that follows, because though the US and France are part of the same security community, long-standing tensions over French disrespect for US-led sanctions regimes proved difficult to overcome, making it highly likely the US government would intervene in some way in this case in order to protect the technology involved.

Despite these concerns, Congressman Hunter was largely alone in his desire to block the deal. In other words, his rallying cry for unbounded intervention was not answered in this case, because the French position as a formal ally made bounded intervention both more desirable for the US and more creditable within the international community. Unlike the Check Point/Sourcefire deal, it seemed possible that mitigation could satisfactorily address the geopolitical and security issues raised by this deal, because the critical technology concerned did not represent all of Lucent's business. Hence, it was reported that Hunter's message did not "resonat[e] with many other members of congress" and was not echoed by them (Inside US Trade 2006a). Indeed, "one private sector source" made it clear that Hunter's actions were an attempt "to politicize the CFIUS process," but "doubted [his actions] would impact a presidential decision on the CFIUS recommendation" regarding this deal "or on the broader debate over how to reform the CFIUS process" in general (Inside US Trade 2006b).[36]

By mid-September 2006, the Alcatel/Lucent deal had received most of the necessary regulatory approvals. The deal was approved by the boards of directors of both Alcatel and Lucent on April 2, and by the shareholders of both companies on September 7 (Zephyr 2006b). The merger also received anti-trust approval from the US Department of Justice on June 8, and competition clearance from the European Commission on July 24 (Johnson 2006; Zephyr 2006b).

It is clear, however, that the heightened protectionist sentiment post-DPW/P&O, the one-off factor of the CFIUS reform debate that DPW and CNOOC had triggered, and geopolitical tensions with France, did contribute to a more rigorous investigation of the Alcatel/Lucent deal within CFIUS. On October 6, it surfaced that CFIUS would engage in the formal forty-five-day investigation (in addition to the normal thirty-day review) of the proposed merger. In fact, Clay Lowery, the

Treasury Assistant Secretary for International Affairs, later testified before Congress in regards to the Alcatel/Lucent review that "CFIUS conducted one of the most rigorous and thorough investigations ever on a transaction before the committee" (Dow Jones 2006e).

These factors motivated the US government to engage in one of the most severe cases of bounded intervention in its history. It was announced on November 14 that CFIUS had concluded its review of the proposed merger, and on November 17 that President Bush had accepted CFIUS' recommendation to approve the deal, which by then included numerous mitigating changes requested by CFIUS and agreed to by both companies. It is likely that the proactive stance taken by both Alcatel and Lucent toward the mitigation of the US government's national security concerns helped them to navigate this process successfully, as did the fact that "CFIUS ha[d] been in contact with the companies even before the . . . formal security review process began" (Dow Jones 2006e). By November 30, 2006, the merger was officially completed, and the entity Alcatel-Lucent opened for business under its new moniker the next day.

Yet, it is important to understand that while this deal seemed to the general public to go through without a hitch, the US government actually did engage in one of the clearest and intense examples of bounded intervention of which the details are publically known. For, in addition to the proposed provisions made by the two companies regarding Bell Labs, which were adopted in the final agreement, the US government required Alcatel and Lucent to "enter into two robust and far-reaching agreements designed to ensure the protection of [US] national security": a "National Security Agreement and a Special Security Agreement" (TR Daily 2006). Though the exact details of these agreements are classified, it is assumed by the market that they covered the provisions made for the protection of Bell Labs and other classified work and contracts held by Lucent.

Furthermore, it was later confirmed that these agreements contained the evergreen clause mentioned earlier, allowing the US government to call for a reversal of the merger at any future date if it felt that the agreements were not being properly implemented. According to private-sector sources, such a clause had never been used before in the US, and many viewed it as highly detrimental because it might prohibit future FDI (Interview 2007). Thus, on December 5, 2006, the Business Roundtable, the Financial Services Forum, the Organization for International Investment, and the US Chamber of Commerce wrote to then Secretary of the Treasury Henry Paulson to "express concern over [the] so-called 'evergreen' . . . condition . . . attached to CFIUS' approval of the Alcatel/Lucent merger" (Inside US Trade 2006c). They pointed out that the serious nature of the inclusion of the evergreen clause lay in the fact that

> The bedrock principle of openness . . . is challenged when the Executive imposes conditions on investments that effectively allow it to re-investigate transactions, impose new conditions, and even potentially unwind the transaction at any time. That CFIUS sought to and, apparently, did impose this condition on the Alcatel/Lucent merger is a disturbing departure from the government's stated support for an open trade and investment regime. Such conditions can chill investment, make those who do invest more cautious about the types of commitments they are willing to give the government in the context of the CFIUS review and, ultimately, harm the economy. (Inside US Trade 2006c)

The text of their letter shows both how rare and how severe the nature of this particular bounded intervention was. For, it was apparent that the government did not intend to block the merger, i.e., did not intend to engage in unbounded intervention. However, it is also clear why this was a case of high-bounded intervention in the dataset, for this is the closest a country can come to blocking a deal without actually doing so. The investigation of the variables that follows shows that national security concerns combined with geopolitical tensions and economic nationalism to result in this outcome.

Geopolitical Competition

The overall US–French geopolitical relationship had not significantly altered since the PepsiCo/Danone case in 2005, though in the Alcatel/Lucent case the target company was American. France and the US remained part of the same security community, yet geopolitical tensions still existed between the two major powers. The US, of course, did not view France as a threat in the same overarching manner that France viewed US hegemonic power. However, France's stated desire to compete with the US for strategic power within the international system would necessitate that the US could not necessarily trust France in the same way it might other allies. Indeed, the French government remained opposed to the US stance on Iraq and Iran, and continued to do business with countries on which the US had imposed explicit export control regulations or strict sanctions regimes.

This deal therefore had very different geopolitical implications for France and the US. For the French, this takeover was seen as a great achievement for French economic power. Yet, because fears of American hegemony remained, the French government was careful to take steps that would protect its sensitive technology "from prying American eyes" (TelecomWeb 2006c). French President Jacques Chirac thus became personally involved in the deal, with the French government eventually backing a sale of Alcatel's satellite divisions to Thales, as already mentioned.[37]

For the US, the geopolitical implications of the deal had a tri-fold effect on government intervention. First, the geopolitical relationship between the US and France ensured that the deal would not be blocked outright, but rather that it would be mitigated if necessary. The US had no need to intervene in an unbounded fashion that would arouse French anger unnecessarily, and that would be likely to cause a resurgence in the tensions that had only just begun to ease. Given the sector and the countries involved, it is fairly obvious that US resource dependency did not play a role in this deal.[38] As the clearly more powerful country in terms of military and economic might,[39] the US also did not need to react to this case in the way that France had reacted to Pepsi's bid for Danone. Furthermore, there was a desire not to engage in the same kind of overt protectionist rhetoric or unbounded intervention for which France was so well known. For, if unbounded intervention had been used in this case, it would undoubtedly have caused the French (albeit somewhat ironically) to use their soft power to denounce the US as a protectionist country on the world stage, which was an unwelcome possibility following the wealth of such statements that had flowed in the wake of DPW and CNOOC. Hence, the Administration's statement that President Bush's decision in favor of the deal "demonstrates the commitment of the United States to protect its national security interests and maintain its openness to investment, including investment from overseas which is vital to continued economic growth, job creation, and an ever-stronger nation" (Silva 2006b). Also, the US still hoped at this point to obtain French assistance on such diplomatic fronts as the nuclear situation with Iran (see Wendlandt 2006). For such reasons, the market foresaw that there would be problems with the deal because of US–French politics, but there was a general belief that such problems could be overcome through the type of mitigation classified here as "bounded intervention" (Morse 2006).

Second, France's stated desire to enhance its geopolitical position vis-à-vis the US ensured that mitigation would be necessary. French geopolitical and economic aspirations, as well as its previous truculence toward the US on the world diplomatic stage, necessitated (at the very least) the rigorous protection of national security-related technology through measures such as the national security agreement and special security agreement that were eventually implemented as part of the deal. If unbounded intervention was not a seemly option for the US in this case, it was clear that bounded intervention of some form would be necessary. Furthermore, it was clear that France was engaging in similar mitigating measures in order to protect its satellite technology from the US through the sale of the Alcatel Alenia and Telespazio JVs. Hence, Congressman Hunter argued in his letter to President Bush that "the United States government must be able to protect its national security interests in at least the same manner as the French government" (Inside US Trade 2006a). On this particular point, at least, the rest of the US government seemed to agree with Hunter.

Finally, the French position of doing business with countries from which the US most wanted to protect its vital technology contributed to the severity of the mitigating measures that were eventually imposed. The need to ensure the security of the highly sensitive technology conducted at Bell Labs and involved in the government contracts held by Lucent would by necessity make the US mitigation procedures rigorous. Yet, given the outcome of the CFIUS review process and the implementation of the evergreen clause in the security agreements concluded between Alcatel/Lucent and the US government, it is clear that at least one of the other issues Congressman Hunter raised publicly was echoed confidentially within the CFIUS review process. This, of course, was the concern that the merger might "result in transfers of sensitive technologies or information to several countries with which Alcatel has dealings, including [Myanmar], China, Cuba, Iran, North Korea, Sudan, and Syria" (Inside US Trade 2006a). Indeed, upon the merger's completion, the new Alcatel-Lucent CEO Patricia Russo, a US citizen, announced, "I am forbidden by law from being involved in business in Iran . . . Clearly we have to respect US laws" that say "US citizens cannot participate in business done in US-sanctioned countries" (Optical Networks Daily 2006; Wendlandt 2006). The timing of her announcement implies that this was an issue raised within the CFIUS process. It was also followed by speculation, which was likely accurate, that the possibility of Alcatel-Lucent continuing to do business with Iran after the merger may have prompted CFIUS to include the evergreen clause that would allow the US to unwind the merger in the future (see e.g., Wendlandt 2006). Professor Antonia Chayes later commented that "if Alcatel were to actively pursue business with Iran it could create tensions between the US and France at a time when the US is trying to bring France into supporting sanctions against Iran" (Wendlandt 2006). Thus, tensions with France and the French position on Iran motivated the US to intervene in this case in order to protect its technology and national security. At the same time, however, the US desire to gain French cooperation on the Iranian issue and ease tension with its French ally ensured such intervention would be bounded rather than unbounded.

Economic Nationalism

Though economic nationalism had been relatively low in the recent history of the US, economic nationalism and national security awareness were abnormally heightened in 2006 in the wake of CNOOC's attempted acquisition of Unocal and the row over DPW. As already mentioned, this was highlighted by the large number of legislative and regulatory proposals put forward at that time both to reform CFIUS and to make the foreign takeover review process it oversees more stringent. US nationalism was, as usual, fairly high in 2006, at 71% (WVS 2001–04), and pro-globalization sentiment, while still above the median value among the fifty-four surveyed countries, was at the lowest level since its peak in 2002 (see IMD 2007b).[40] Rising protectionist sentiment was also clearly recognized in the US at the time (AFP 2006c), and some analysts feared that the deal "could yet fall afoul of political obstacles at [such] a time of heightened protectionism" (Frost 2006).

Furthermore, though Bell Labs, within Lucent, was not officially labeled or discussed within the national discourse as a national champion per se, it would certainly qualify as one because of the integral role its technology has played in the making of America as a superpower. It has provided some of the innovations in military, surveillance, and communications technology seen as vital to the protection, projection, and augmentation of that power's national capabilities. Thus, though the US has not traditionally supported companies as national champions, it is clear that the special role of Bell Labs in the American power structure helped to ensure that its work would be protected by the government from an unconditional foreign takeover, and that the deal would need to be altered to accommodate this fact.

Nevertheless, the transaction did not see the same kind of virulent reaction as did the DPW deal. This was largely because the Alcatel/Lucent deal was not heavily politicized, helping to stem the forces of economic nationalism that may have been present at the time. Only one member of the legislature, Congressman Hunter, was deeply opposed to the deal, and his true concern seemed to be the safety of the technology produced by Bell Labs and the possibility it would be sold on to unfriendly regimes, rather than opposition to the sale of the company as a complete economic entity. Furthermore, complete agreement existed in the market that these concerns and Hunter's activities would not be strong enough to block the deal as a whole (see AFP 2006c).

Thus, the real role of economic nationalism in this case was more indirect: its presence forced CFIUS to review the case more thoroughly than any other in US history (Dow Jones 2006e), and in this way it may have contributed to the decision to impose stricter mitigation measures than ever before in the form of the evergreen clause.

Interest Group Presence

Though a small number of interest groups opposed the Alcatel/Lucent deal, their pressure did not play an important or decisive role in prompting government intervention in this case. In part, this was because these groups were unconcerned with either geopolitics or the protection of a national champion, but instead opposed the deal on the grounds that those they represented would not be making enough of a profit. In France, "Proxinvest, a shareholder-rights consultant to leading French institutional investors, . . . advised [its] clients to vote against the . . . merger" on the basis that Alcatel was overpaying for Lucent (Matlack 2006). Meanwhile, in the US, "some Lucent shareholders . . . pursu[ed] a class-action lawsuit contending just the opposite – that they will get too little from the merger" (Matlack 2006). Significantly, this minority shareholder group's attempt to get a court order to postpone the shareholder vote was unsuccessful, and Institutional Shareholder Services, a powerful corporate governance/proxy voting services firm that provides research and recommendations on such deals, came out in support of this one (Les Echoes 2006). In the end, the shareholders of both Alcatel and Lucent approved the merger, as did the boards of both companies (Zephyr 2006b). Most importantly, at no time did any of these interest groups suggest that the US government should intervene in the deal in any way.

The only group that even suggested the deal "raises national security issues and should be referred to . . . CFIUS" was the "US Business and Industry Council lobbying group" (Jane's Defence Weekly 2006). Yet, this was also the same group that later came out against the inclusion of the evergreen clause in the security agreements that Alcatel and Lucent eventually signed with the US government. Thus, while it is apparent that this particular group may have desired some form of bounded intervention if it was deemed necessary for national security purposes, it certainly did not desire it on such a scale. Furthermore, in hindsight, it is clear that the Council's position was taken long after both companies were already in consultation with CFIUS because of the early recognition that some form of mitigation would be necessary for the protection of national security and the satisfaction of the geopolitical concerns already mentioned. It can be concluded that this particular lobbying group did not play a role in motivating government intervention in this case either.

Finally, the labor unions in both the US and France did not play a role in US government intervention on this occasion. It is true that the French labor unions were "upset" by Alcatel's plans "to do away with a 23 year-old practice of having employee representatives on its board" once the merger was completed (Gauthier-Villars 2006). Yet, this did not ultimately end up being an issue, and opposition quickly died down in France. Though heavy job losses were expected as a result of the merger (McLean 2006), it did not result in heavy union opposition. This is partly because the cuts were expected to take place in the US rather than France. If the scenario were reversed, union opposition would have been much more likely (see Sage 2006). Though labor groups and employees in the US were aware that most of the job cuts would take place in their country, they seemed more concerned over the fate of "health benefits and pensions" (McKay 2006c), and did not attempt to prompt the type of bounded government intervention that eventually occurred.

Competition Concerns

Anti-trust competition concerns also did not turn out to be an issue in this case. The EU Commission announced its approval of the "proposed transaction" on the basis that it "[would] not significantly impede effective competition" (EU Commission 2006a). This was because the companies, though "engaged in similar activities," were sufficiently "focused on different regions" (AFP 2006b). The US Department of Justice also "granted antitrust approval" to the deal on the basis that it did not raise any significant competition concerns (Johnson 2006).

Conclusions on Alcatel/Lucent

The preceding discussion of the variables illustrates that in the Alcatel/Lucent case, both geopolitical competition concerns and economic nationalism played a role in motivating bounded government intervention, and that the former factor played a more direct role than the latter. It has also been shown that competition concerns and interest group pressure did not play a significant role in motivating government intervention in this case.

Thus, the US was not intervening solely for reasons of heightened economic nationalism at that particular point in time, but because of geopolitical concerns that were exacerbated by the sensitive nature of Lucent's work. This fact shows the importance of both variables, highlighting a behavior that can be lost in MNLM I, where most cases of bounded intervention are associated with economic nationalism, and geopolitical concerns only near significance. The case supports the findings in MNLM II, which show that geopolitical factors can play a significant role in increasing the likelihood of bounded intervention within security communities, as can economic nationalism. Critically, this case demonstrates that even within security communities, geopolitical competition considerations can be of equal or greater importance compared to economic nationalism in motivating bounded intervention.

Case 7: Lenovo/IBM

The Context

The next case examines Lenovo Group Ltd.'s takeover of the International Business Machine (IBM) Corporation's PC business in 2005. Lenovo is a Chinese company whose majority stockholder is Legend Holdings Ltd., a holding company owned and controlled by the Chinese government. IBM, of course, is the pioneer of the original personal computer, and, in 2005, retained its position as the primary supplier of computers to the US government.

This case is critical for two reasons. First, the Lenovo/IBM takeover is an excellent example of an extremely rare case type. Chinese acquisitions of this size, and in the national security industries examined here, have only been attempted twice in the US between September 11, 2001 and May 15, 2007.[41] The first instance was the CNOOC/Unocal case of unbounded intervention examined in Chapter 3, the second the Lenovo/IBM transaction. Such cases have largely been viewed as threatening in the US, because the government of the rising Chinese power has openly stated its desire to use the market to gain power, influence, and technology for military and civilian use.

This case is also critical for testing the primary and secondary hypotheses, as it helps explain why two cross-border acquisitions between similar countries, and under seemingly similar conditions, might lead to dissimilar outcomes. For, while the CNOOC/Unocal case resulted in unbounded intervention and no deal, the Lenovo case only led to bounded intervention and a mitigated deal. Yet, both cases occurred in the same year (2005), and were therefore subject to the same general level of geopolitical tension and economic nationalism. How, then, can the different outcomes be explained within the context of the primary and secondary hypotheses?

The answer is that, while geopolitical concerns were once again the primary, and economic nationalism the secondary, motivation for intervention in a case that occurred outside of the context of a security community, specific elements of the case helped to ameliorate those variables in a way that ensured intervention would only take the form of bounded intervention. In other words, this case is critical because it enables us to examine the hypothesis in a way that strict statistical data testing cannot. The results of the multinomial logit function performed in Chapter 2 only confirmed that the presence of geopolitical competition and economic nationalism makes both bounded *and* unbounded intervention more likely than no intervention at all. This case study, however, in conjunction with the CNOOC case, can help us to understand why a government might choose one of these forms of intervention over the other.

The Story

On December 7, 2004, it was announced that Lenovo would acquire 100% of IBM's PC Division for a total consideration of $1.75 billion.[42] It seemed that despite "Big Blue's" traditional role as the flagship of US computer technology, the PC division had become its least profitable business, with its software development and consulting services divisions providing much higher margins. IBM was thus looking for a buyer for the division, and welcomed Lenovo's bid (see Hachman 2004). As will be discussed, no competition concerns were expected and the deal received an early termination of its anti-trust review from the Federal Trade Commission on January 7, 2005 (Spooner 2005a). Similarly, there was no real interest group movement against this deal. Shareholders were eventually won over, and US labor groups were largely unconcerned as it was clear that no real job losses would result from the takeover.

However, it was obvious early on that the deal would need CFIUS approval. This was both because of the industry involved, and because the majority shareholder in Lenovo was, and remains, the Chinese government, which owned 57% of Lenovo's stock through a government-owned and controlled holding company called Legend Group Holdings (Bilodeau & Kennedy 2005; Ramstad 2004). As a result, the companies "formally filed a notice seeking CFIUS clearance on December 29, [2004]" (Bilodeau & Kennedy 2005).

By January 24, 2005, the first report surfaced of concerns emerging within CFIUS on national security grounds in a widely read and cited Bloomberg article (see Bilodeau & Kennedy 2005). This article cited anonymous sources saying that "members of [CFIUS], including the Justice Department and Department of Homeland Security, [were] worr[ied] that Chinese operatives might use an IBM facility in North Carolina to engage in industrial espionage, using stolen technologies for military purposes" (Bilodeau & Kennedy 2005).

On the following day, three congressmen sent a letter to CFIUS urging it to conduct a more rigorous forty-five-day review of the deal because of national security concerns (Orol 2005e). They were three fairly powerful congressmen, whose input was likely be take into consideration by CFIUS: Duncan Hunter, Chairman of the House Armed Services Committee, Henry Hyde (R-IL), Chairman of the House International Relations Committee, and Donald Manzullo (R-IL), Chairman of the House Small Business Committee (Orol 2005e). Only Rep. Manzullo seemed to be truly motivated by what could be identified as economic nationalism. He feared the deal might provide China with control over the PC industry, or that China might be using "unfair" government subsidies in order to help Lenovo purchase IBM. As will be discussed further, however, the congressmen were primarily focused on the geopolitical concern that sensitive or dual-use technology might be transferred to a non-allied state, which could then apply it to military use. Given the Chinese government's own stated intent to use foreign takeovers for this purpose,[43] and its control over Lenovo, the idea was not far-fetched.

Despite this, the market was still somewhat surprised on January 27 when CFIUS extended its review to the further, and more intensive, forty-five-day investigation (see Moody 2005). For, while some analysts had expected the deal to result in stark unbounded intervention (see e.g., MPR 2005; WSJ 2005b), others truly believed that any security concerns could be dealt with in the initial thirty-day review (see Bilodeau & Kennedy 2005). This was because, though the PC business did involve some "high tech" aspects, and was once at the forefront of technology in the US, it was now considered to be relatively "low tech," in addition to "low margin," by some market analysts (see e.g., Blustein & Musgrove 2005; Sinocast 2005b). As will be discussed, however, the more optimistic analysts were not really thinking of the dual-use military applications of some of that technology, nor did they realize how seriously the US government seemed to take the Chinese espionage issue. IBM's PC business was located in Triangle Park, NC, where other IBM research and development projects were being carried out for the US government.

In the end, the government was able to work out a solution to these national security concerns with the cooperation of the companies involved. On March 9, 2005, IBM announced that the takeover "was cleared by the US government" at the end of the forty-five-day extended review (Moody 2005). It was reported that "Lenovo overcame US concerns that the Chinese government would use Lenovo's PCs and the US facilities for espionage" so successfully that CFIUS eventually agreed to "give the deal its unanimous consent" (Auchard 2005a; Moody 2005). The deal was officially completed on May 2, 2005. Though many of the exact details of the alterations made to the deal for national security reasons remain confidential, both the government and the companies publicly acknowledged such measures were put in place. Furthermore, the changes that were announced or leaked to the press, as discussed later, highlight the credence given to geopolitical concerns over espionage and technology transfers to non-allied states.

The investigation of the variables demonstrates that, as with the CNOOC/Unocal case, intervention in the Lenovo bid was primarily motivated by geopolitical competition concerns, and secondarily by economic nationalism. In other words, the presence of these factors made some form of intervention more likely than no intervention at all. In this case, however, the result was bounded rather than unbounded intervention because the specific aspects of the deal afforded the government the option to choose mitigation over an outright block, which was a more diplomatic solution to the protection of national security, and a more favorable one given the US' preference for open and engaged economic relations with China.

Interest Group Presence

No real interest groups were pressing for government intervention in this case. Though some of Lenovo's shareholders originally came out against the takeover, their concerns were soon overcome and they approved the deal on January 28 (Datamonitor 2005). Significantly, however, Lenovo's shareholders were worried that the deal would be blocked by the US government, or that a new combined entity might face difficulty in successfully combining the very different cultures of the two companies (ComputerWire 2005). In no way did they desire the US government to intervene, because it was clear that a successful deal would be to their benefit.

Labor groups were not incensed by the deal because the companies made announcements very early in the process that "no layoffs [we]re planned" and, furthermore, that "the deal w[ould] have a minimal effect on employment, benefits or compensation" (Cox 2004). This news seemed highly effective in quelling the initial fears of both IBM's and Lenovo's workers (Witte 2004; see also McMillan 2005).

One interest group did mobilize in favor of the deal: IBM. The company "hired consultants to help secure approval from CFIUS," one of whom was "Brent Scowcroft, the former national-security adviser to President George H. W. Bush and Gerald Ford" (Bilodeau 2005). It was also reported that IBM hired

> Bruce Mehlman, who served as President George W. Bush's assistant secretary for technology policy at the Department of Commerce until January 2004, and partners at DC-based law firm Covington & Burling . . . includ[ing] Mark Plotkin and David Marchick, a former deputy assistant secretary for trade policy at the State Department, according to federal lobbying records. (Bilodeau 2005)

These individuals were highly respected within the government and had an intimate understanding of the CFIUS process. Marchick, for example, wrote one of the only books on US government intervention into cross-border M&A on national security grounds, with Edward Graham. Though it is unknown what their exact brief from IBM entailed, it is generally thought that they were hired to help IBM and Lenovo navigate the CFIUS process successfully. Given the consultants hired, their expertise, and their current and former government positions, it is likely that the companies were advised on what mitigatory measures might be necessary to gain approval, rather than how to achieve the more unlikely "no intervention" outcome, as these individuals would also have been highly concerned with the preservation of national security in this case. In other words, they were likely hired to help the companies successfully navigate the process and achieve a bounded intervention outcome, rather than an unbounded intervention outcome, and it is fairly unlikely that they were pushing for no intervention. It is also important to note that they were reported to be serving in an advisory, rather than a lobbying, capacity.

Thus, there were no real interest groups pushing for intervention in this case, or attempting to prevent the US government from pursuing bounded intervention.

Competition Concerns

Similarly, economic competition concerns did not seem to factor into the Lenovo/IBM case. By January 7, 2005, the Federal Trade Commission declared "that it ha[d] granted Lenovo and IBM an early-termination ruling under the Hart-Scott-Rodino antitrust act" (Spooner 2005a). It was possible for the decision to be made quickly because there was no apparent evidence that the takeover would create a monopoly or anti-competitive concentration within the personal computer, or broader technology, industry. Thus, it seems clear that this was not a factor motivating bounded intervention in this case.

Economic Nationalism

As discussed in the CNOOC and DPW cases, the US is not always associated with economic nationalism, though distinct pockets of such nationalism do exist within some parts of the US government and its institutions, as evidenced periodically in its history. Displays of economic nationalism in the US have historically been targeted and rare, and have often been caused by distinctive massive influxes of FDI from a particular country, such as Japan in the 1980s. Nationalism was relatively high in the US in 2005, providing a solid base for potential economic nationalism.[44] Yet, the Lenovo bid came at the very *beginning* of China's notable surge in overseas investment and cross-border M&A activity; it would not be until later the same year that Haier[45] and CNOOC would both attempt large-scale takeovers in the US. Though some evidence can be found of antipathy toward Chinese FDI at this point, it is not nearly as marked or widespread as it was by the time CNOOC had made its bid for Unocal.

As also mentioned in the CNOOC case, the US has not traditionally shown great support or protection for so-called "national champions," and this attitude remained true in this case with IBM. Often called "Big Blue" in the media and press, IBM ostensibly makes a good candidate for a national champion. For decades, the company as a whole has stood at the forefront of the US technology sector, and it is viewed as "the original grand dame flagship of the industry" (Sullivan 2004). Its large market share, and its relationship with many government agencies, has made it an American icon.

At the time, some commentators and analysts noted the importance and significance of such an iconic brand as IBM being "sold to China" – but they were not incensed by the possibility, and were clearly not advocating either for or against intervention in this case. Some did, for example, ask "how... America's top PC maker end[ed] up as nothing more than lunch for an Asian Tiger" (Sullivan 2004). However, the focus was mainly on the fact that it was a momentous and historical deal, as it was "the first major Chinese acquisition of a Fortune 100 company," and clearly "a harbinger of deals to come" (Bilodeau & Kennedy 2005; Sullivan 2004). It seems that in the American psyche, "no brand is eternal" (Boston Herald 2004), an attitude that truly sums up the reluctance of the US government, and the public, to protect what would have been one of its national champions from a foreign takeover.

An icon does not necessarily translate into a national champion, and a single division of such an icon, even less so. It is important to reiterate here that IBM as a whole was not in danger of being taken over, only its "lower tech" PC division, and this was because IBM wanted to sell that part of the business, which had become a "drag on margins and profitability" (Hachman 2004; see also Blustein & Musgrove 2005). Market analysts were thus largely reported to believe that the White House's attempt to "foster cooperative economic ties with Beijing," combined with IBM's need and desire to get out of an unprofitable business, likely meant "that in the end Washington will allow the IBM/Lenovo deal to go ahead" (Blustein & Musgrove 2005). Of course, such a view was based on the inherent assumption that the larger geopolitical and national security concerns could be overcome through some form of mitigated intervention.

Despite this general lack of support for IBM as a national champion, however, there is some evidence that members of Congress believed the deal should be blocked on grounds that might be identified as economic nationalism. In the letter that Congressmen Hunter, Hyde, and Manzullo sent to President Bush, they were evidently "concern[ed] that Lenovo [would] have an unfair competitive advantage over US computer makers because the People's Republic of China subsidizes the company" (Orol 2005e). It should be noted, however, that Congressman Manzullo seemed to be the only one who was *primarily* motivated by such concerns. Certainly, Rep. Manzullo, known for "worr[ying] frequently about a . . . loss of US manufacturing jobs to China" (WSJ 2005b), was the only one to have publicly, and consistently, attempted to make an issue of the deal on these grounds. One of his representatives stated that Manzullo's concerns stemmed from a belief that "China gets a competitive advantage for many things because they are a nonmarket economy," and that "by selling IBM's PC Business to China, it could corner the global market on computers" (Orol 2005e). Such comments caused a sparse few, such as the China Business Strategy group (quoted here), to claim that the deal had met with resistance due to those "who oppose globalization and economic integration" (PZMN 2005). At the same time, "Manzullo insist[ed] that his campaign '[wa]s not protectionist'" because "his concerns might be unfounded, but he won't know unless Congress has more time to review the deal" (Kessler 2005). Despite this rather interesting logic, however, it is clear that Manzullo was mainly worried about the economic ramifications of the deal giving the Chinese undue control of, or advantage in, the PC market versus the US.

It also later surfaced that the US–China ESRC had sent a letter to Congressmen Hunter, Hyde, and Manzullo in which it advocated intervention in the deal. In the letter, the Commission reportedly

> made plain... [their] view, that the CFIUS mandate is broader than a technical security-minded technology transfer, export-control oriented event, and that in fact it implicates the defense industrial base, the national security capabilities of the United States in a broader sense... the bottom line is, in a sense, the security implications of the impact [of the deal] on the US economy. (Commission Vice Chairman Roger Robinson Jr. in US–China ESRC 2005)

This statement demonstrates the Commission's opinion that economic security and national security are intertwined, a position that has itself been tightly linked with protectionism (see e.g., Graham & Marchick 2006). The Commission was clearly also concerned by the increasing level of Chinese FDI, and Lenovo's bid for IBM was a prime example of China's efforts to become a "global player." In a later hearing, the US–China ESRC stated that because the "velocity and the size of those Chinese acquisitions [is] clearly on the rise," it "hope[d]" that there would "be an increasing use of the CFIUS process" (US–China ESRC 2005). Unfortunately, it is unclear whether the Commission's letter was sent to the three congressmen before or after they sent their own letter to the President advocating a further CFIUS investigation.

It is clear, however, that some elements of economic nationalism were present in this case, and that these may have acted at least as a secondary motivation for government intervention. CFIUS would be unlikely to seek alterations to the Lenovo/IBM deal on economic nationalist grounds alone, as previously discussed in other cases. Yet, it does seem that the three congressmen's letter, which included Rep. Manzullo's economic fears, did help ensure a forty-five-day CFIUS investigation. This, in turn, made it more likely that bounded intervention would occur, as it provided greater focus on the national security concerns discussed in the next section, and provided the opportunity for the government to seek changes to the deal that would allay those concerns.

It is important to note that though there is evidence of economic nationalism in this case beginning to be directed against Chinese foreign investment, as will be shown, it had not yet reached the level that it would in the later CNOOC case, when Chinese investment came to be viewed as more threatening to US economic security. It should be remembered, however, that even in the CNOOC case, more traditional geopolitical and national security concerns overshadowed those of economic security when it came to decisions regarding intervention. As discussed in detail in the section on that case, instances of unbounded intervention into the Chinese purchase of a US company have always entailed a heavy presence of traditional national and military security concerns, whether or not economic nationalism was present. The next section, on geopolitical competition, illustrates that the Lenovo/IBM case resulted only in *bounded* intervention because it was possible to mitigate such national security concerns, whereas this was not possible in the cases that resulted in *unbounded* intervention.

Geopolitical Competition

The level of geopolitical competition between China and the US was basically the same in this case as it was in the CNOOC case of the same year. In 2005, as today, China and the US were geopolitical strategic rivals with a highly complex relationship. China was positioned as a major power, with rising relative power in both the economic and military realms. This fact, combined with a widespread US government belief that China posed a potential future military threat, ensured that the intent of Chinese actions would be carefully examined. Disagreement over the status of Taiwan, worries over increasing Chinese military spending and their quest for natural resources, on top of the economic disputes over the valuation of the yuan and intellectual property rights, created constant tension between the countries at the very time that the Bush Administration was attempting to engage China diplomatically and economically. It was not surprising, therefore, that "while US officials such as [Treasury Secretary] Snow [had] called for closer ties between the two countries to foster trade, lawmakers such as Republican Senator James Inhofe of Oklahoma [had] raised objections to embracing China for security reasons" in 2005 (Bilodeau & Kennedy 2005). The Chinese government's intent to use cross-border acquisitions to increase its economic, and even military, power generally only intensified such fears.[46] With this in mind, the following discussion focuses on the specific geopolitical concerns that affected the Lenovo/IBM case. For a more detailed description of the general geopolitical relationship between China and the US in 2005, see the CNOOC/Unocal case in Chapter 3.

It should also be noted here that certain aspects of the geopolitical competition between the two countries led to a dissimilar outcome in the Lenovo and CNOOC cases, because of differences in the industries involved. The level of US dependence on oil and China's desire for ever-greater control over its own natural resource supply affected the type of intervention sought by the US government in the CNOOC case to a much greater degree than it did in the Lenovo one. In the CNOOC case, the target was an oil company with proprietary dual-use technology.

The likelihood of unbounded intervention was heightened because the purchase of Unocal by CNOOC would have meant complete control over a resource that was the focus of competition and contention, even if the deal could have been altered to prevent the transfer of the dual-use technology. Bounded intervention would not really have solved all of the national security concerns involved in that case. In the Lenovo case, however, it was possible, as will be shown, to effectively mitigate the deal in a manner that assuaged the national security concerns it raised. As the control over the PC business as a whole did not (in and of itself) pose a threat, and no resource was at risk, bounded intervention was a viable solution to the problem.

What were the national security concerns that were raised and intensified in this case by the level of geopolitical competition between the US and China?

The first concern that emerged was over the possibility that the Chinese government would use the facilities purchased in the takeover as a base for conducting both international and industrial espionage (see e.g., Bilodeau 2005; Bilodeau & Kennedy 2005; Blustein & Musgrove 2005; Orol 2005a, 2005b; Spooner 2005b; Tsuruoka 2005).[47] IBM's PC facilities were largely located in the industrial compound of Triangle Park, NC, where it had also stationed a number of its other business divisions. These included some IBM research and development facilities that do work "specifically" for the US DOD, making the security of these projects, and the park as a whole, of special concern to CFIUS (Orol 2005b). It was reported that "CFIUS . . . decided on January 27th to begin [the forty-five-day] formal investigation over concerns that the Chinese government will use Lenovo-made PCs and the company's new US facilities for espionage" (Bilodeau 2005). The same fear was voiced by Michael R. Wessel of the US government-sponsored US–China ESRC, who told the media that he had discussed this concern with the relevant government officials (see Blustein & Musgrove 2005). Well into the forty-five-day review, the issue seemed to remain at the forefront of the US government fears regarding the takeover. For, in late February, it was reported that the US DHS and Justice Department, both of which are represented in CFIUS, were still "question[ing] whether Chinese operatives could use the facility [in Triangle Park] . . . to engage in industrial espionage" (Bilodeau 2005).

The espionage issue seems to have been the primary focus of discussions between CFIUS, IBM, and Lenovo over possible mitigatory measures that could be taken to make the deal viable. It also appears that negotiations began long before the formal review process. They intensified when "agents from the US Secret Service and the Federal Bureau of Investigation inspected the Research Triangle site" in early February, leading IBM to "[offer] to take measures such as closing its buildings in the office park to access by Lenovo employees" (Bilodeau 2005). IBM apparently "balked at other demands," and "in a proposal that CFIUS considered [on February 23], the company refused to agree not to transfer any employees involved in research and development to the Research Triangle site and objected to some security measures, such as installing new safety doors" (Bilodeau 2005).

The concern over espionage was compounded by the fact that the Chinese government holding company that controlled Lenovo (Legend Group Holdings) had links to the Chinese military and the Chinese Academy of the Sciences. In fact, Legend Group "was established in 1984 by the Chinese Academy of Sciences, a government institution" that "plays a key role in exploiting technologies in China" (Bilodeau & Kennedy 2005; Tsuruoka 2005). Not surprisingly, this fact fanned "the fear [that] Lenovo might transfer sensitive technology it develops with IBM to China's military" (Tsuruoka 2005).

This argument ties in with the second concern: that Lenovo, and by extension the Chinese government, would be gaining access to dual-use technology that could be deployed for military purposes. The dual-use issue was among those raised early on by Mr. Wessel of the US–China ESCRC (WSJ 2005b) and William Triplett, a former member of the Senate Foreign Relations Committee (Tsuruoka 2005). This was because some of the PC components being developed by IBM at the time, such as super long-life batteries, could potentially have "military applications in the field" (Orol 2005a). Some observers also worried that IBM's microprocessor technology could be applied for use in missiles (Orol 2005a). Adam Segal of the Council on Foreign Relations summed it up well when he pointed out that the CFIUS investigation was "symptomatic" of the fact that "as China develops its more competitive civilian sector, there are pretty large concerns in the United States . . . about civilian technology bleeding over to the military side" (Tsuruoka 2005).

A third concern was that China would re-export dual-use technology to countries that were unfriendly to the US, such as Iran, given China's past history of flouting US export control laws (see e.g., Tsuruoka 2005; Rash 2005). One of the aspects of the Sino-US geopolitical context at the time that intensified national security concerns over the transfer of sensitive technology to China, beyond its position as a strategic rival to the US, was China's poor record of adhering to US export control laws. In January of 2005, the tension over this issue was heightened when the US government "imposed penalties" on eight "of China's largest companies" for exporting technology that would assist "Iran's efforts to improve its ballistic missiles" (Sanger 2005).

Finally, there may also have been a fear that the Chinese government and/or military might use the Lenovo acquisition to gain backdoor access to US government computers. IBM provided PCs to a number of government agencies. Yet, China was at the time "blacklisted" (along with Iran, Iraq, and North Korea) by the US Trade Agreements Act (TAA), meaning that the US government was not supposed to use Chinese suppliers (Aitoro 2005).[48] Many analysts believed that the issue of supply would be easily obviated, because it was likely that the PCs would still be assembled in the US, or ignored. The worry over the security of that supply, however, remained. Mr. Wessel, again, pointed out that

> IBM has "other facilities" in North Carolina "that do R&D . . . so the issue is not just the making of boxes; it's how the networks work. IBM has service contracts throughout the government and (knowledge about) how one networks these computers gives one not only the opportunity to do reverse engineering, but greater opportunities to hack in." (Blustein & Musgrove 2005)

Thus, there was likely also concern that the Chinese government could arrange backdoor access to computers provided to the US government by Lenovo.

Eventually, a number of measures were agreed upon between CFIUS and the two companies as part of the US government's strategy of bounded intervention to alleviate the national security concerns rooted in the geopolitical tension between the US and China at this time. In order "to win federal approval . . . Lenovo employees working at IBM's manufacturing and design facility in Raleigh, NC, [had to] be housed in a separate building on campus" (CMP TechWeb 2005). By March 9, it was revealed that the "staff working in the Research Triangle Park, North Carolina, area w[ould] be relocated to a central facility that [was] sold by IBM to Lenovo and is located in the same industrial park" (Auchard 2005a). This modification to the deal was obviously intended to protect the security of the IBM government R&D projects at the park, and to prevent opportunities for espionage. Though a number of modifications were apparently made to the deal as a result of government intervention, these changes are among the few that were made public by the companies.

Overall, neither IBM nor Lenovo appeared upset at the mitigation measures required by the government, likely because they were fairly reasonable and simple given the concerns voiced. In fact, the new CEO of Lenovo, Mr. Ward, told reporters that "everything that CFIUS asked of us was perfectly reasonable" (Auchard 2005a). Thus, bounded intervention was an option in this case because it was possible for mitigation to alleviate the national security concerns without losing the cooperation of the companies involved, and without having to block the deal as a whole.

Conclusions on Lenovo/IBM

The discussion of the variables in the Lenovo/IBM case clearly shows that geopolitical competition was the primary, and economic nationalism the secondary, motivation for bounded intervention in this case, resulting in a changed deal. Once again, interest group pressure and economic competition concerns did not play an active role in guiding government intervention. This result is in line with the primary hypothesis, and with our expectations as a result of the statistical findings from Chapter 2. In other words, given the presence of economic nationalism and geopolitical competition in a case that took place outside of a security community context, we expected to see some form of intervention, either bounded or unbounded, rather than its absence.

The preceding examination of the variables also helps us to understand something that the statistics did not: why we saw *bounded* intervention into the Lenovo takeover, when the ostensibly similar CNOOC case resulted in *unbounded* intervention. The result of the Lenovo/IBM takeover differed from that of the CNOOC/Unocal one because, in the latter instance, bounded intervention would have not been as successful an option for the government. The issue there was that Chinese control over Unocal in and of itself became associated with the struggle for control over resources, and politicization of the deal made it difficult for bounded intervention to appear to be enough to alleviate fears that the Chinese company's intent was nefarious. With Lenovo, it *was* possible to mitigate national security concerns in a way that could not be accomplished in the CNOOC case. In the Lenovo case, the company being purchased was relatively "low tech" for a "high tech" industry, it was losing money rapidly, IBM wanted to exit the business, and there was a viable government strategy for protecting the technology that was deemed to be at risk of espionage in other parts of the company. Control over resource access was not at stake, and it was possible to solve the national security concerns posed by the deal *without* having to block the deal as a whole. In other words, bounded intervention in the form of mitigation strategies is likely to occur when the circumstance of the deal make it a viable option for the government to pursue, without jeopardizing its security. Few states would want to employ unbounded intervention unless it was considered absolutely necessary, because, though unbounded intervention will not damage the relationship between two countries in the same way other balancing techniques might, bounded intervention is even less likely to create tension between states. This is because, though it is done on the basis of national security, it is pursued in a manner that is unlikely to negatively affect valuable trading relationships, and that is often seen as an amicable compromise to a difficult problem. It can also be a matter of timing, for after the US government's perceived need to block both the CNOOC/Unocal deal, as well as the Hutchinson Whampoa deal, there was likely an even greater desire to seek a compromise in this case, where compromise was possible, in order to ease fears of anti-FDI sentiment among Chinese and other foreign investors.

Conclusion

The purpose of this chapter has been to provide a deeper understanding of the nature of bounded intervention. First, the definition of bounded intervention was refined. A state can effect a policy of bounded intervention by engaging in restricted forms of intervention into foreign takeovers, by mitigating the parts of the deal it deems dangerous to its national security and strategic position. An examination of the foreign takeover review processes in the US, China, Russia, and the UK established that different states will employ different tools and methods to alter a deal, and that the modifications made will naturally vary in accordance with the concerns that the deal raises. This discussion also examined the possibility that bounded intervention may occur more frequently within security communities, where the review process through which such deals are mitigated is more highly institutionalized and regularized.

Second, the case studies confirmed that *both* economic nationalism and geopolitical competition concerns can play a significant role in increasing the likelihood of bounded intervention. Additionally, economic competition concerns and interest group politics did not seem to have a great effect on behavior in either case. This provides clear support for the primary hypothesis. Though the statistical results in MNLM I only showed nationalism to be significant when examining the entire population of cross-border cases, MNLMs II and III demonstrated that the significance of geopolitical factors emerges alongside nationalism when the cases are restricted to subsets of either security community or non-security community cases. In the Alcatel/Lucent case, bounded intervention was demonstrated to have been motivated both by a heightened economic nationalism at that particular point in time in the US, and by geopolitical concerns that were exacerbated by the sensitive nature of

Lucent's work (which involved classified government contracts). This was a case that took place within the context of a security community, highlighting the fact that one should not discount the possibility of geopolitical competition among allies. In the Lenovo/IBM deal, which took place outside of a security community context, bounded intervention was primarily motivated by geopolitical competition between the US and China, and by concerns arising from the potential for the deal to be used as a springboard for espionage; economic nationalism was a secondary motivation. It should also be noted that in both cases, economic nationalism did prove significant, rather than just nationalism alone, demonstrating that the use of the latter as an indicator of the former in the statistical analysis is not off base.

Third, in both cases the type of intervention chosen by the government affected the outcome of the deal in question, supporting the secondary hypothesis. In both cases, the decision to utilize bounded intervention for balancing purposes resulted in a modified (or "changed deal") outcome.

Fourth, both of the cases examined helped to clarify something that the statistical modeling could not: under what conditions a state will choose to employ bounded, instead of unbounded, intervention. This study has clearly demonstrated that both forms of intervention are a more probable outcome than "no intervention" when geopolitical concerns and/or economic nationalism are present in high levels. Yet, bounded intervention is more common than unbounded intervention, with the former representing 29% of total cases, and the latter only 8%.[49] So, why do states choose one over the other? *They do so because allowing these foreign takeovers to be completed in modified form is even less likely to disrupt trade relationships or produce antagonism between the countries involved than is unbounded intervention.* In other words, it best accomplishes the goal of non-military internal balancing: to balance power without necessarily disrupting the greater meta-relationship at stake between the countries involved. Thus, if state A feels that restricted intervention can adequately address the problems presented by a foreign takeover, it may prefer to engage in bounded intervention, which is largely seen as a more desirable outcome by economists (because the market is not completely disrupted) and tends to be viewed as a more creditable action by the international community (which tends to see unbounded intervention as protectionism, no matter what its motivation).

This was certainly true in the Alcatel/Lucent case, where it was viewed as possible for mitigation to satisfactorily address the geopolitical and security issues raised by the deal, because the critical technology concerned did not represent all of Lucent's business. Additionally, the position of France as a formal ally made bounded intervention more desirable for the US. These dynamics were also present in the Lenovo/IBM case, where it was possible to effectively mitigate the deal in a manner that assuaged the US government's concerns, largely because giving the Chinese control over the PC company as a whole did not, in and of itself, pose a threat. This is in stark contrast to the CNOOC/Unocal case examined in Chapter 3, where the likelihood of unbounded intervention was heightened, because allowing the purchase of Unocal would have entailed giving the Chinese complete control over a resource that was the focus of state competition and contention, even if the deal had been altered to prevent the transfer of the dual-use technology. Therefore, it can be concluded that bounded intervention is more likely to occur when the circumstances of a given foreign takeover make a restricted intervention strategy a viable option for the preservation and/or maximization of security and power.

NOTES

1 This provision, known as an "evergreen" clause, was part of the security agreement between the US government and the companies involved. It is believed that such a clause has never been used before in a US security agreement regarding a cross-border acquisition (TelecomWeb 2006a), indicating that new forms of mitigation may be emerging.

2 The Company Law, first adopted in 1993, has been periodically revised, e.g., in 1999, 2004, 2005, and 2013, with the latter revision coming into effect in March 2014. For an English translation of this law as amended in 2013, see www.fdi.gov.cn/1800000121_39_4814_0_7.html#_Toc381707436.

3 The Takeover Rules date from 2006, and were amended in 2012 (Jian & Yu 2014, 2).

4 The Securities Law, which dates from 1998 and was amended in 2014, is "the basic statute governing securities-related activities in China" (Jian & Yu 2014, 2).

5 Before this point, the primary law covering FDI of this type was the 1995 Provisional Regulations for Guiding the Direction of Foreign Investment. The Provisions on Guiding the Orientation of Foreign Investment, Decree of the State Council of the People's Republic of China, No. 346, was released on February 11, 2002 and entered into force on April 1, 2002. It replaced the State Council's Interim Provisions on the Guidance of Foreign Investment Directions, originally released in June 1995. For an English translation of the 2002 Provisions, see www.fdi.gov.cn/1800000121_39_2169_0_7.html.

6 The 2006 Provisions for Mergers and Acquisitions of Domestic Enterprises by Foreign Investors was originally introduced in draft form in March 2003 as the Interim Provisions on Mergers and Acquisitions of Domestic Enterprises by Foreign Investors, and was then updated with the No. 6 Decree of the Ministry of Commerce PRC on Promulgation of the Provisions on Mergers & Acquisitions of a Domestic Enterprise by Foreign Investors on

June 22, 2009, in order to bring it in line with the 2007 Anti-Monopoly Law. For English translations of the 2006 Provisions and the 2009 Decree, respectively, see http://english.mofcom.gov.cn/aarticle/policyrelease/domesticpolicy/200610/20061003434565.html and www.fdi.gov.cn/1800000121_39_4115_0_7.html.

7 It is inferred that investment is permitted in those areas not covered by the 2004 Decision on Reforming the Investment System. For an English translation of the Decision, see www.fdi.gov.cn/1800000121_39_1465_0_7.html.

8 For an English translation of the 2017 Catalogue, see http://www.fdi.gov.cn/1800000121_39_4851_0_7.html.

9 China had been under pressure for some time from other countries, and investors, to adopt a less complicated "negative list" system for foreign investment, in which only items on the list are prohibited or restricted. China first adopted a negative list for its Free Trade Zones on April 8, 2015 (see the Circular of the General Office of the State Council on Issuing the Special Administrative Measures (Negative List) for Foreign Investment Access to Pilot Free Trade Zones). For a period of time after this, it was unclear whether the Catalogue was to be considered a negative list for the rest of China (Ye 2016), but this has now changed with the 2017 Catalogue (see Koty & Qian 2017, as well as the English translation of the 2017 Catalogue, www.fdi.gov.cn/1800000121_39_4851_0_7.html).

10 For example, as in previous versions, the 2015 Catalogue specifically prohibited investment projects that might "endanger the safety and performance of military facilities." (See, e.g., www.cov.com/files/upload/Blog_Insert_Foreign_Investment_Catalogue_Redline_Comparison.pdf.)

11 According to Wang and Emch (2013), the NDRC is additionally "responsible for ... price-related conduct, [and the] abuse of dominance and ... administrative powers ... that eliminate or restrict competition," while "[SAIC] has enforcement powers for other anti-trust cases falling outside the jurisdiction of MOFCOM and NDRC."

12 For an English version of the 2008 AML, see http://english.mofcom.gov.cn/article/policyrelease/Businessregulations/201303/20130300045909.shtml.

13 For an English version of the Circular of the General Office of the State Council on the Establishment of Security Review System Regarding Merger and Acquisition of Domestic Enterprises by Foreign Investors, see http://english.mofcom.gov.cn/article/policyrelease/aaa/201103/20110307430493.shtml.

14 The associated implementing regulations are the Provisions of the Ministry of Commerce for the Implementation of the Security Review System for Merger and Acquisition of Domestic Enterprises by Foreign Investors, Announcement No. 53 of the PRC's Ministry of Commerce, originally made on August 25, 2011. For an English translation of these Provisions, see http://english.mofcom.gov.cn/article/policyrelease/aaa/201112/20111207869355.shtml.

15 See Article II of the Circular of the General Office of the State Council on the Establishment of Security Review System Regarding Merger and Acquisition of Domestic Enterprises by Foreign Investors, February 3, 2011.

16 See Article IV (VI) of the Circular of the General Office of the State Council on the Establishment of Security Review System Regarding Merger and Acquisition of Domestic Enterprises by Foreign Investors, February 3, 2011. See also Article 7 (3) of the 2011 Provisions of the Ministry of Commerce for the Implementation of the Security Review System for Merger and Acquisition of Domestic Enterprises by Foreign Investors, which states that "where a merger with or acquisition of a domestic enterprise by a foreign investor has already produced or may produce a serious impact on national security, based on the review opinion of the Ministerial Panel, the Ministry of Commerce shall, along with relevant departments, terminate the transaction of the parties concerned or take measures such as the transfer of the equity or assets in question or other effective measures so as to eliminate the impact of such merger or acquisition on national security." It remains to be seen, however, how this new provision will be implemented in practice.

17 For a discussion of the different types of acquisition vehicles that a foreign company might use to merge with, or acquire, a Chinese entity, see ABASAL 2015, 6–7. Though there are additional acquisition and taxation regulations that apply to each different type of investment vehicle, the national security review regime in China discussed in this chapter will "generally apply" regardless of the type used (ABASAL 2015, 7).

18 This review process was formalized in the 2003 Interim Provisions for Mergers and Acquisitions of Domestic Enterprises by Foreign Investors and the later 2006 Provisions for Mergers and Acquisitions of Domestic Enterprises by Foreign Investors, as such deals became more commonplace. Reviews seem to have occurred on a more ad hoc basis before 2003, conducted by the Ministry of Foreign Trade and Cooperation (MOFTEC), which MOFCOM has since replaced.

19 For example, a foreign investor acquiring companies listed on the stock exchange will be subject to the Administrative Measures on Strategic Investment in Listed Companies by Foreign Investors, while one seeking to invest in state-owned enterprises (SOEs) will be subject to "special rules for acquiring state-owned enterprises" (Qian 2016, 6), though it is highly unlikely that a 100% acquisition of an SOE would be allowed by a foreign investor, at least at the time of the cases examined in this book. Other foreign investment laws of possible relevance, depending on the type of investment made, include those covering the different types of FIEs: the Law of the PRC on Foreign Funded Enterprises, the Law of the PRC on Chinese-Foreign Equity Joint Ventures, and the Law of the PRC on Chinese-Foreign Contractual Joint Ventures, among others (see US GAO 2008, 45). For an English translation of the 2006 Administrative Measures on Strategic Investment in Listed companies by Foreign Investors, see http://english.mofcom.gov.cn/aarticle/policyrelease/domesticpolicy/200604/20060401971375.html.

20 National security under the Trial Measures is linked to "investments in military, national defense, agriculture, energy, infrastructure, transportation, culture, information technology products and services, key technology, and manufacturing" (US DOS 2016a).

21 The English translation of Article 59 of the National Security Law was sourced from http://chinalawtranslate.com/2015nsl/?lang=en.

22 For an English translation of the Decision of the Standing Committee of the National People's Congress on Amending Four Laws Including the Law of the PRC on Foreign-Funded Enterprises, see www.fdi.gov.cn/1800000121_39_4849_0_7.html. This was followed shortly by the Interim Administrative Measures for the Record-filing of the Incorporation and Change of Foreign-Invested Enterprises. For an English translation, see https://hk.lexiscn.com/law/law-english-1-2951857-T.html.

23 The laws amended include the Law of the PRC on Foreign Funded Enterprises, the Law of the PRC on Chinese-Foreign Equity Joint Ventures, and the Law of the PRC on Chinese-Foreign Contractual Joint Ventures.

24 For an English translation of this law, as amended in 2016, see http://en.fas.gov.ru/documents/documentdetails.html?id=14737.

25 For an English translation, see www.wipo.int/wipolex/en/text.jsp?file_id=188843#LinkTarget_243.

26 The 2008 Strategic Investments Law, Federal Law No. 57-FZ, was updated in December 2011 with Federal Law No 322-FZ, and again in November 2014 with Federal Law No. 343-FZ. For more information on these updating laws, see Nikiforov & Maximenko 2014; Stoljarskij 2012.

27 It should be noted that the Enterprise Act was amended in 2008 to include financial stability in the list of specified public interest concerns. This addition was made in light of the global financial crisis generally, but more specifically because it "allowed the Secretary of State to intervene directly in the takeover of HBOS, the UK's largest mortgage lender, by [another British bank] Lloyds TSB," which raised a number of competition concerns, but which was also deemed by the Secretary of State to be good for the overall financial stability of the UK given the economic conditions at the time (Seely 2016, 6–7).

28 For the archived version of the BIS website displaying the list of "Mergers with a National Security Element," see http://webarchive.nationalarchives.gov.uk/20090609003228/http://www.berr.gov.uk/whatwedo/businesslaw/competition/mergers/public-interest/national-security/index.html.

29 Before 2007, the full title of the Secretary of State was the Secretary of State for Trade and Industry, when the relevant government department was the Department of Trade and Industry. In June 2007, the Department of Trade and Industry was replaced by the BERR, and the title of the position changed to the Secretary of State and Industry. In June 2009, the BERR was replaced by BIS, which was in turn replaced by BEIS in 2016, and the relevant title became the Secretary of State for Business, Energy, and Industrial Strategy.

30 Notably, "on the same day as the Prime Minister's statement, Japan's SoftBank announced a £24 billion bid for the Cambridge-based tech company ARM Holdings" and made legally binding undertakings to the UK government to do things including protecting UK jobs (Seely 2016, 42–3).

31 As the reader will recall, none of the variables provides insight into why a state would be likely to pursue lower forms of bounded intervention within the security community context, a phenomenon most likely to be explained

by two factors. First, many cases of even low-bounded intervention involve actions and agreements that are considered classified information in many countries – the public only learns about them if there is a press leak, or if one of the companies involved releases the information. Second, low-bounded interventions that occur within the confines of a security community are often not mentioned within the press, as M&A activity is so frequent and regularized between these countries that the companies involved in these transactions see the government's actions as standard operating procedure and, thus, may not feel the need to publicize them of their own accord.

32 In other words, they are not classified as a Type I ally of the US, because there is no formal treaty relationship for the provision of their mutual military defense.

33 Both were at the time classified by the industry benchmark number 9578, placing them in the technology sector and telecommunications equipment industry.

34 Reportedly, "the announcement of merger talks between Alcatel and Lucent . . . was greeted with quiet satisfaction in Paris, where the assumption is that the French group will effectively swallow its US counterpart . . . The Alcatel/Lucent talks appeared to have the blessing of the French authorities. They are confident that the headquarters would remain in France, enabling them to comfort Gallic public opinion by presenting the new group as French" (Sage 2006).

35 For reports of the companies meeting to discuss proposals for dealing proactively with these recognized issues, see e.g., McKay 2006a; TelecomWeb 2006b.

36 For example, as Chairman of the House Armed Services Committee, he tried to have a public hearing on the proposed merger, but was eventually forced into holding a closed hearing because of the classified nature of the discussion (Inside US Trade 2006b).

37 It became clear early on that the French government supported the sale of Alcatel's satellite divisions to Thales in order to protect sensitive technology from the US; see TelecomWeb 2006a. At the same time, "German Chancellor Angela Merkel and French President Jacques Chirac . . . met and agreed that EADS should take a stake in Thales" under a scheme that would allow EADS to sell its satellite arm to Thales as well (TelecomWeb 2006c). Thus, in an odd twist, the French government wanted the sale of Alcatel's satellite JVs, but opposed any sale that did not include EADS (of which it owns 15%) (AFP 2006a; TelecomWeb 2006c). In the end, the deal between Alcatel and Thales was approved (Aviation Week 2006), with the general understanding that Thales would remain open to future talks with EADS over its satellite assets.

38 The 2006 US general resource dependency ratio was around 0.38; though this is not low, the US did not depend on France for natural resources such as oil and gas. France was not among the top fifteen importers of oil and petroleum products to the US; the US only imported a tiny fraction from

France (26,736) of its 5,003,082 thousand total imported barrels of crude oil and petroleum products in 2006; see EIA 2008a; 2008d.

39 France's military power relative to the US was only 10.04% in 2006, and US military power was rising at a rate of 8.98%, while that of France was rising at only 1.13%. Similarly, the relative economic power of France to the US was relatively low, with French GDP PPP being only 14.82% of that of the US in 2006. Interestingly, the growth rate of both countries was closer, with the five-year average economic growth rate registering at 3.38% for France and 4.96% for the US. Numbers calculated from SIPRI (2006) and the WDI database (WDI 2008).

40 In 2006, the IMD World Competitiveness Yearbook covered sixty-one countries, but for the variable "Attitudes towards globalization" survey data were available for only fifty-four (see IMD 2007b). In the US, pro-globalization sentiment was valued at 6.25 in 2006, above the median value of 6.21 among countries surveyed that year, but the lowest it had been in the US since 2002, when it was valued at 7.20 (IMD 2007b). While economic nationalism was generally still considered to be low in the US relative to other countries, it had arguably spiked there by the time of this particular case in the second half of 2006, which occurred in the wake of the 2005 and early-2006 US cases examined in Chapters 3 and 4.

41 The Hutchinson Whampoa/Global Crossing case can be instructive in our understanding of these two cases, as it provides another example of unbounded intervention into the takeover of a US company by a Chinese one. The Whampoa case, however, cannot provide a pure comparison to either the Lenovo or the CNOOC case, because Hutchinson made its bid for Global Crossing in conjunction with the Singaporean company STT. In other words, it cannot be classified as a "simple" cross-border takeover of the type examined in the database created for this book, because the acquisition involved two purchasing companies from different countries.

42 The $1.75 billion figure comprises half a billion in Lenovo equity, which became IBM's stake in the new entity, and $1.25 million in cash (Market News Publishing 2004; Zephyr 2007a).

43 For further details on this point, please refer to the CNOOC/Unocal case in Chapter 3.

44 It should be recalled from the CNOOC case that in the 2001–04 wave of the World Values Survey, 71.1% of US respondents claimed to be "very proud" of their nationality (2001–04). Yet, while 86.71% of US citizens claim to be proud of their nation's economic achievements, the US is not always identified with economic nationalism (ISSP 2003). Indeed, though levels of pro-globalization sentiment had been declining since 2002, it was valued at 6.34 in the US in 2005, which was above the median value of 6.22 among the fifty-four countries for which survey data were reported on this variable in that year (IMD 2007b).

45 The Haeir Group (China) bid for Maytag (US) in 2005.

46 For example, see McKinsey & Co.'s analysis in Financial Express 2004.

47 It should be noted here that some people found these concerns to be "overwrought": examples of "anti-Chinese" sentiment rooted in geopolitical

(rather than economic) competion (see Blustein & Musgrove 2005). Yet, the fear apparently had a basis in past US experience. For, "15 years [earlier], the Washington Post [had] revealed that the Chinese government was secretly owner of a number of retail outlets and restaurants frequented by government officials" (Rash 2005). Apparently, "these businesses existed as a means of funneling Chinese spies into the US, and as a way to keep tabs on unsuspecting government officials" (Rash 2005).

48 The act provides that "the government can spend taxpayers' money with certain countries that are considered friends to the United States and whose products, therefore, qualify for an exception to the government's preference to acquire only domestic end products" (Aitoro 2005).

49 It is important to remember that the number of bounded intervention cases may be larger than the estimate provided here, as the actual existence of most of these forms of mitigation is meant to be confidential in any one case, and their content classified. Thus, we only know of the existence of these forms of mitigation if they have been made public through a press release made by one of the companies in question, or if news of their existence has been leaked to the press. This may affect the statistical results slightly, but this is an acceptable reality because it means we can largely assume that any correlation found in the database is in fact much *stronger* than the statistical results indicate.

6 Non-Intervention and the "Internal" Intervention Alternative

Introduction

The database contains 131 cases of *non-intervention*, which means that for a majority (62.68%) of the population of cross-border cases examined in this study, there is no evidence of direct government interference through either *bounded* or *unbounded* intervention. Yet, in a small number of cases, the target state may have obviated the need for such behavior by engaging in *internal* intervention. In other words, the state actively fosters an alternative domestic merger or acquisition for the vulnerable company, in the hope of precluding the completion, and in some cases the initiation, of the foreign takeover it believes to threaten its power and/or survival (i.e., national security).

Fostering a better understanding of both these forms of state behavior is important, as each one has a potentially significant impact on the validity of the theory proposed in Chapter 1. This chapter is organized as follows. Part I looks at the dynamics behind non-intervention, including: (1) a discussion of the value of negative cases for hypothesis testing, (2) an examination of two key instances of non-intervention, (3) an analysis of the population of non-intervention cases, and (4) observations on the mitigating circumstances that may cause states to pursue this strategy over others. Part II examines the phenomenon of internal intervention. This section provides a more detailed discussion of the nature of such behavior and its relationship to traditional understandings of internal balancing in international relations theory, and concludes with a detailed case study.

Part I: Non-Intervention

Non-Intervention, Negative Cases, and Hypothesis Testing

Instances of non-intervention serve as "negative cases" for the primary hypothesis. If the basis of this hypothesis is that a high presence of either economic nationalism or geopolitical concerns can explain the motivation behind unbounded and bounded government intervention into cross-border M&A, then one would expect the majority of non-intervention cases to be characterized by either a lack, or very low levels, of these factors. The cases that provide the best test of the hypothesis, however, will be those in which “the dog did not bark;” in other words, those cases in which one would expect bounded or unbounded intervention, based on the presence of high levels of economic nationalism in the target state and geopolitical competition between the parties, but this did not occur.

Selecting negative cases for the purpose of hypothesis testing is a particularly difficult task in international relations theory. Too often, scholars choose to ignore the proverbially quiet dog, rather than become mired in methodological difficulties. In order to obviate that potential quagmire, the author has chosen to utilize insights from two of the most highly respected approaches to this issue.

First, the next section briefly examines the two most relevant non-intervention cases, chosen on the basis of insights from Mahoney and Goertz’s “Possibility Principle” (Mahoney & Goertz 2004; see Skocpol 1984). Fundamental to this approach is a belief that negative cases should be selected on the basis that they exhibit similar values on the independent variables to the positive cases, and that a positive outcome was, as a result, “possible” in these cases (Mahoney & Goertz 2004, 653–4). Thus, each of the cases examined in this part of the chapter could have resulted in a positive outcome – i.e., in bounded or unbounded intervention, because of the presence of a high level of economic nationalism and/or geopolitical competition – but did not. The lack of intervention, expected by the primary hypothesis in these cases, thus requires explanation. It should be noted that the approach of these scholars has been adapted slightly due to the probabilistic nature of the hypotheses in this book and the use of continuous independent variables (see Appendix F for a full description of how this was achieved).

The subsequent section employs an alternative approach to negative case selection that supports the inclusion of all cases, rather than limiting cases on the basis of the *possibility* of positive outcomes. This approach contends that all cases, both negative and positive, within a well-defined population should be used for hypothesis testing. The fundamental point is “that if researchers define the population carefully and appropriately, each case in the population contributes to causal inference and is therefore useful” (Seawright 2002).[1] This argument would seem to be especially true in this study, where there may be additional circumstances that affect a state’s choice not to intervene in a given case. While they may be beyond the bounds of the primary hypothesis, such conditions are important to an understanding of the overall theory of non-military internal balancing of this type, and may provide important insights for future research and testing. For, though it is not feasible or desirable to include detailed case studies of all 131 cases of non-intervention, it is possible to make some general observations about interesting trends that occur within that population.

Relevant Negative Cases

This section aims to confirm the accuracy of the hypothesis against the hardest negative case tests that could be raised against it. In each case, a non-intervention outcome results despite the apparent presence of the independent variables hypothesized to motivate intervention. Yet, the fundamental assumption of the primary hypothesis is that these factors cannot have a true effect unless the deal is seen to pose a real or perceived threat to national security. In the sectors examined in this study, the lack of such a real or perceived threat is actually quite rare when these two factors are present at extremely high levels; but it can happen, and in those rare instances where it does, one must turn to qualitative analysis to understand what appears to be a deviation from the hypothesis. Once that is done, it is quite clear that the primary hypothesis can be confirmed.

Case 8: CGG/Veritas

The French geophysical services and software business Compagnie Générale de Géophysique (CGG) announced on September 5, 2006 that it had agreed to acquire the American seismic data services company Veritas DGC. The deal was completed on January 1, 2007 without ostensible US government intervention.

One might have initially expected intervention in the transaction, because it fulfills certain criteria of the primary hypothesis. On the surface, the case appears structurally identical to the Alcatel/Lucent case of the same year. It involves a French company acquiring a US company in a strategic sector. The US government was exposed to the same degree of economic nationalism domestically, and was dealing with the same level of geopolitical tensions with France. In fact, it was this similarity of environment, and the presence of motivating factors for intervention, which led CGG and Veritas immediately and voluntarily to file the acquisition for review with CFIUS.

Yet, in the Alcatel/Lucent case, there *was* an unprecedented level of bounded intervention on the part of the US government. In this case, there was no intervention of which the public was made aware. How, then, can we explain the difference in government strategy in these cases, when the levels of economic nationalism and geopolitical competition are ostensibly the same?

The answer is simple, but can only be found through a qualitative examination of the case itself. Despite the presence of these broad factors, no national security issues specifically attenuated the takeover of this particular company. CFIUS wrote a letter to Veritas on November 16, 2006 confirming that it "had concluded its [preliminary thirty-day review], having found no national security issues sufficient to warrant further investigation" (Veritas 2006, 29). From Veritas' filing with the SEC, it also seems safe to assume that neither company was asked to modify the conditions of the transaction by either CFIUS or the US President (Veritas 2006, 298). CFIUS does not, of course, make the details of its deliberations public. So it is difficult to determine exactly why the takeover of Veritas did not raise any major flags, despite the fact that seismic data are generally important for oil exploration and for the military, which uses it, for example, to monitor compliance with bans on nuclear warhead tests. When asked, one equity research analyst pointed out that it was "presumably" because "either nothing material in terms of state security contracts or use of their technical capacity by US forces" existed or remained within Veritas (Interview 2008c). In other words, no proprietary technology was at risk in the transaction that would negatively affect US defense, and the purchase of Veritas did not threaten US control over any kind of finite resource.

It should also be noted that the control variables in this case did not affect the intervention outcome. First, though the US government did investigate the deal in accordance with the Hart–Scott–Rodino Antitrust Improvements Act, it did not find any competition concerns related to the takeover (Zephyr 2007e). Second, interest groups did not play a significant role in affecting the US government's stance on the takeover. The shareholders and boards of directors of both companies supported the takeover, as was required for its successful completion, on the basis that the economic rationale was sound, significant "complementarities" were present, and new opportunities for growth would be created (Zephyr 2007e). No major interest groups – shareholders, unions, political, or others – emerged in strenuous opposition to the merger. Yet, none of these facts seems to have swayed the US government's decision not to intervene in this case.

Thus, though the broad independent factors of geopolitical competition and economic nationalism were present, no specific national security concerns were raised by the deal, making government intervention unlikely, rather than likely. This is important, because it helps to highlight the fact that the primary hypothesis *assumes* geopolitical competition and economic nationalism will only lead to intervention in foreign takeovers when either a genuine, or at least a plausible, national security concern is raised by the proposed takeover. As mentioned in Chapter 1, a government requires the presence of such a concern that it can point to as the reason for that intervention. Such a concern makes geopolitical competition relevant, and economic nationalism acceptable, in motivating government response. The lack of intervention in this case therefore confirms the primary hypothesis.

Case 9: JP Morgan/Troika Dialog

Rumors circulated the markets and newswires on August 28, 2006 that the US investment bank JP Morgan was considering an acquisition of the Russian investment bank Troika Dialog. As Western banks were seeking to expand into Moscow's markets, Troika's position as one of the older non-state-owned banks made it a fairly attractive takeover target. Troika's suitors included not only JP Morgan, but also the US bank Citigroup, the Swiss investment bank Credit Suisse, and even the Russian government-owned Vneshtorgbank (VTB) (see Prince & Baer 2006; Busvine 2006).

The Russian government did not ostensibly intervene in this case, despite the presence of geopolitical competition between the US and Russia, and of economic nationalism within Russia in 2006. Indeed, at this time, geopolitical tension between the US and Russia was increasing over a series of issues, ranging from US involvement in Iraq and Afghanistan to the initial failure to agree upon the bilateral US–Russian protocol needed for Russia's bid for accession to the WTO (see e.g., Aslund 2006; Rutenberg & Kramer 2006). Furthermore, there was also a fairly high degree of anti-globalization sentiment in Russia in 2006 (see IMD 2007b).[2]

Once again, however, there was no direct national security concern related to this potential takeover, despite the fact that it was occurring in a sector generally considered to be strategic. Troika's independence from the Russian government gave it the opportunity during that time to search for the economic option for its company's future from a purely fiduciary outlook, to the point where it was able eventually to reject the state-owned VTB's offer on the basis that the price was too low (see Busvine 2006). In the banking and financial services sector, an independent company is unlikely to be seen as an issue of national security unless (1) it is a national champion, (2) it is fundamental to the health and/or identity of the national economy, or (3) times of severe economic crisis require the active retention of capital and banking resources within the domestic economy. As Troika did not meet any of these conditions in the generally optimistic investment and economic climate of 2006, it was unlikely that the Russian government would intervene. Even economic nationalist sentiment in Russia at this point was focused on national champions in the natural and basic resource sectors, and was unlikely to spill over to the financial services sector in order to protect a company that was not really seen as a national champion, and thus not necessarily a matter of national concern.

Finally, neither interest group pressure nor competition concerns seem to have played a role in Russia's decision not to intervene in this case. Neither factor emerged as an issue in response to the rumored takeover. They were not even mentioned by reporters, analysts, members of government, or the companies themselves in their discussions of the potential deal.

Once again, this case confirms the primary hypothesis. Government intervention did not occur – despite the general presence of the motivating factors of economic nationalism in the target state and general geopolitical competition between the countries involved – because there was no national security concern inherent to the takeover in question. It should also be noted that this particular proposed foreign takeover never made it past the "rumor" stage. This is because the management of the company, which had a controlling interest in Troika, decided not to sell on the basis that it desired to stay an independent Russian bank, and therefore protected itself temporarily from a potential takeover by affecting a large employee stock purchase (Syedain 2007). In this way, the company itself also voluntarily obviated the true issue. The intervention outcome might have been different if this had not happened, and if the Russian government had decided to identify Troika as a national champion that it was necessary to protect on national security grounds.

Overview of the Negative Case Population

The purpose of this section is to provide a more general analysis of the negative case population within the dataset.

Primary Hypothesis

The quantitative testing of the dataset in Chapter 2 supported the primary hypothesis. The result of MNLM I demonstrated that a state was less likely to intervene in a foreign takeover, in an unbounded or bounded manner, when geopolitical tensions and economic nationalism were low.

The notion that low levels of geopolitical friction between states make direct intervention less likely seems borne out by an examination of the population of negative cases in the dataset. MNLM I confirmed that state *A* was significantly *less* likely to use unbounded or bounded forms of intervention (i.e., it was more likely not to intervene) when state *B* was a member of the same security community. In fact, 79% of the non-intervention cases took place within the security community context, and of that 79%, 83% of cases resulted in a completed and unmitigated deal. (This observation is striking when compared to the fact that of the 65% of unbounded intervention cases occurring within the confines of a security community, 73% were successfully *prevented* from resulting in any deal at all.) For the 21% of non-security community cases of no intervention, MNLM III showed that state *A* was significantly less likely to intervene if its military power was greater relative to that of state *B*.

Furthermore, it seems clear that direct intervention is *unlikely* to occur when levels of economic nationalism are very low. MNLM I demonstrated that, across all cases, intervention was significantly less likely when pro-globalization sentiment in state *A* was high. At the same time, MNLM II proved that the significance of this relationship, between low-levels of economic nationalism and non-intervention, was even stronger for deals that took place within a security community.

The phenomenon of "non-intervention" may, however, have some additional dynamics, which will be useful for understanding the implications of non-military internal balancing, and which may provide avenues for future research. It is important to note that these observations do not contradict the primary hypothesis proposed here, but may instead add to its explanatory power.

Mitigating Circumstances Identified in the Population of Negative Cases

It appears that, in each of the cases in the dataset where geopolitical competition concerns and economic nationalism are exceptionally high (whether quantitatively or qualitatively examined), non-intervention usually is the result only when the exact deal in question can still not be perceived as posing an unacceptable problem for national security. However, there also seem to be six "mitigating circumstances" that emerge from this population, which appear to ameliorate issues/deals that could potentially be seen as national security concerns – *if* the state wants to make an argument to that effect.

1. *Bid from an Institutional Investor*

A state may be more open to a foreign takeover, despite the presence of the hypothesized motivating factors, when the acquirer is an institutional investor. An institutional investor may be generally defined as "a bank, mutual fund, pension fund, or other corporate entity that trades securities in large volumes" (FINRA 2008). However, the true nature of the institutional investor is captured by the fact that it must be a "third-party professional," whose purpose is to act as a "fiduciary investment capital allocation organization" on behalf of a client (Interview 2008d).[3]

The data provide some interesting facts regarding this type of investor. Of all the 209 cases in the database, forty-nine involved potential acquirers that may be classed as institutional investors. The government of the target company in question chose *not* to intervene in thirty-nine (or 80%) of these forty-nine cases. Only ten resulted in some form of government action. Half of these remained at the level of low-bounded intervention. Of the remaining five cases, three involved high-bounded interventions, and only two led to unbounded interventions on the part of the state. This means that only 10% of institutional investor bids resulted in these less routine, and more intense, forms of government intervention.

This tendency toward non-intervention into foreign takeovers that are proposed by institutional investors indicates that governments may perceive such actors as less threatening than other types of potential acquirers. This might be because institutional investors are usually considered to be pure market actors with a fiduciary responsibility to act impartially in the best interest of their clients, i.e., to be motivated by financial, rather than political, gain.

Granted, some institutional investors may be more political than they seem at first glance. Indeed, SWFs, state banks, and other state investment funds qualify as institutional investors, despite their connection to the state. The rise in power and quantity of SWFs over the last decade has been frequently discussed as having a potentially political impact, for example, because, though many continue to be innocuous market actors, some are viewed as potentially having political motivations for their investment choices. For example, one hedge-fund analyst pointed out that some SWFs very simply "have a more political mandate from inception (like Russia, Libya, etc.) than others" (Interview 2008d). He argued that, based on "the criteria of: (1) sources and target recipients of funds, (2) mandate and oversight of capital allocation, and (3) forms of investments, [one could] array a spectrum of public/funded institutions . . . from the most like a profit-maximizing fund manager to the least" (Interview 2008d). This range would appear as follows:

> (1) pension/retirement trusts for public employees, taxpayer entitlements' trusts, etc., (2) sovereign wealth funds, (3) regulatory trusts (e.g., the Pension Benefit Guaranty Corporation and the Federal Deposit Insurance Corporation), (4) the World Bank [and other] multi-lateral lenders (e.g., the Inter-American Development Bank and the European Investment Bank), (5) the International Monetary Fund, and (6) Central Banks. (Interview 2008d)

Banks that are state-owned, controlled, and run, he argued, are much more difficult to categorize (Interview 2008d).

Thus, while there is a clear connection between non-intervention and acquirers that are institutional investors, the highly varied nature of this type of investor suggests that further research into this correlation is required.

2. *Desired Exit*

A state may also be more open to a foreign takeover, despite the presence of the hypothesized motivating factors, when it involves the purchase of a company that has actively and willingly placed the "for sale" sign in its window, i.e., when the takeover resolves a company's desire to voluntarily exit the marketplace. There are many reasons for a "desired exit" of this nature. The company may no longer be viable, it may have difficulty competing in a particular sector, it may have been put up for sale by a parent company that thinks its margins are too low or by a parent company that needs to concentrate its resources elsewhere. Whatever makes the target company pursue such a strategy, it does seem to have a distinct and ameliorating effect on intervention.

Across the full database of 209 cases, twenty-seven can be classified as a desired exit. In twenty-one (or 78%) of those twenty-seven cases, the target company's government chose *not* to intervene in the takeover. Of the remaining six cases, there were *zero* instances of unbounded intervention, only one of high-bounded intervention, and the remaining five cases involved only low-bounded intervention. Thus, there seems to be a very clear trend that desired exits only rarely lead to intervention, and that when they do, the intervention will tend to be of the more moderate low-bounded variety.

There is a fairly simple explanation for this behavior. If a company desires an exit – because it is no longer a viable concern or because its parent company cannot afford to operate it, or no longer wishes to do so, for whatever reason – then the company will need to find either a domestic or an international buyer. If that company is vital to national security, say because it is the sole producer of an important piece of military equipment, then the state has two preferred options:

1. It can hope for a domestic company to step in and take over the target, or it can actively facilitate such a domestic merger through internal intervention, as discussed in Part II of this chapter. (Remember that in this scenario, the state's actions are classified as non-intervention because it has not intervened directly to stop or alter a proposed foreign takeover from a specific company.)
2. It can allow the target to be taken over by a foreign company, but modify the deal in its favor in an effort to protect its national security interest in the company. Clearly, this may not be the preferred option for some states, but it will likely be a much better alternative than the complete failure or disappearance of the company, the continued function of which it perceives to be vital to national security. In this case, the state would rather have the company bought and continue to operate, than go out of existence all together.

The Chinese government, for instance, did not intervene in 2006 when the US networking equipment manufacturer 3Com Corporation took over the JV company it had originally established in China with the Chinese telecommunications equipment manufacturer Huawei. This is an extremely interesting example, because when Huawei attempted to acquire 3Com only a year later, CFIUS found significant national security concerns involved in the transaction, and the US government eventually sought to stop the proposed transaction through unbounded intervention. Yet, in the earlier case where the Chinese JV was the target, the Chinese government did not react as the American government later did. This was because, despite tension between the US and China, and China's stated efforts to protect its strategic telecommunications companies from takeover, Huawei (and China) had already gained the technology it originally sought through the JV, and wanted to leave the project, making its sale a desired outcome.

3. *Fear of a Bidder from a Less Friendly Country*

Another circumstance that might influence a government's decision to either *not* intervene, or to do so at only the low-bounded level, is when the proposed foreign acquirer is seen as coming from a "friendlier" country than that from which alternative possible bidders might originate. Again, this remains true even in the presence of perceived national security issues heightened by the presence of geopolitical competition and economic nationalism. While such an occurrence is rarer, and more difficult to identify and code on a consistent basis, than the previous mitigatory circumstances examined here, its effect on intervention outcomes is undeniably clear.

One need only look, for example, at cases like the takeover of Arcelor by the Indian steel manufacturer Mittal Steel. Arcelor was another steel manufacturer, based in Luxembourg, but really seen as a French company. Mittal's bid for Arcelor was rejected out of hand twice in early 2006, primarily because of virulent resistance from European leaders, who argued the takeover would be dangerous for the security of the region. Here, there was a definitively strong presence of economic nationalism, as well as geopolitical competition concerns aroused by India's rising status as an economic power. Yet, these leaders did a dramatic about face when the Russian company Severstal emerged as an alternative bidder. Despite the initial unbounded intervention by the French government, the deal was eventually allowed to proceed unaltered, rather than have Arcelor's steel production come under Russian control. This is not surprising, given the fact that Russia already controlled a large proportion of this particular resource, and had recently proved its willingness to use control over another resource (i.e., natural gas) as a means to demonstrate its power over its neighbors.

4. National Security Concerns Previously Addressed

Governments are also highly unlikely to engage in high-bounded or unbounded intervention when the national security concerns inherent to a particular target company's takeover have already been addressed in some way. For example, this may mean that the foreign acquirer has already signed a stringent national security agreement (or the equivalent thereof) with the target state, or that the companies may have already agreed among themselves to divest or "black box" the division of the company that is identified as related to national security.

This particular mitigating circumstance may not have as great an effect in those target countries where economic nationalism is present in *extremely* high levels, as the governments of such states may not wish to recognize the fact that a national security concern has already been addressed, but may instead wish to raise it for more political reasons. Yet, in those instances where geopolitical competition is the main motivating factor of intervention, unbounded or high-bounded intervention is less likely when the national security issues have already been dealt with in some way.

In other words, if the companies have arranged to "take care" of the national security-related aspects of the deal before the formal bid is made, or as part of the merger agreement, and have done so to the satisfaction of the target state, intervention is unlikely. This is often true even in the face of moderately high levels of economic nationalism or geopolitical tension.

Alternatively, if the companies have not made such arrangements, but the acquirer has a proven track record of acquisitions in strategic sectors in the target country, and has previously signed a national security agreement[4] or similar contract with the target state that obligates it to adhere to certain security precautions and laws, and which can be adapted to the current takeover, then low-bounded intervention will ensure this adaptation is made. In such a case, though the general geopolitical relationship between the states involved may be good, the deal is still identified as having implications for national security and power that must be dealt with. As discussed in Chapter 5, this was the case when the UK's BAE Systems took over United Defense Industries (UDI) in the US. BAE Systems had a subsidiary, BAE Systems North America, which was to be used for the takeover, and which already had a series of stringent national security agreements with the US government, as well as a track record of honoring them. Thus, though the deal involved the takeover of a premier US defense company with multiple government contracts, the US only needed to engage in low-bounded intervention to update these agreements. It stands to reason, however, that if the previous agreements signed by the acquirer can be perceived to cover the new proposed takeover, no intervention will be considered necessary.

5. Deal Strengthens Industrial Base/National Security

Another mitigating circumstance that will increase the chance of non-intervention or low-bounded intervention is if a deal is actually considered to be advantageous to national security, or is perceived to strengthen national security and/or the defense industrial base in some way (see Grundman & Roncka 2006; Moran 1993). For example, Grundman and Roncka argue that there are twenty possible variables that might affect a company's chance of survival of the US government review process of foreign takeovers, and seven of these are related to whether or not the deal can be seen as contributing to the health of the defense industrial sector (Grundman & Roncka 2006, 8).[5] A deal might, for example, increase the competition among companies in the production of a good considered vital to national security (e.g., semiconductors). Alternatively, it could provide the state in question with access to a resource that it desperately needs (e.g., uranium or natural gas).

Such considerations will, probably, be more common when the potential acquirer is a close ally, for it is unlikely that a bid originating from an "unfriendly" country would be perceived as contributing positively to the target state's defense sector. Furthermore, there may already be some degree of integration of the defense industrial base among close allies, and this may be viewed as preferable on the basis that it widens the scope of competition, and thus enhances the opportunities for the development of new technologies, while offering the possibility of lowering the price of such advances.

It is important to note, however, that alliance relationships are unlikely to matter if a deal is still considered to pose a significant national security risk or to have a highly negative impact on the defense industry. This partly explains, for example, why the US was willing to allow the takeover of UDI by BAE Systems, but would be unlikely to allow the same company to take over a business like L-3 Communications. UDI arguably needed to be revitalized. The situation would be viewed differently for a company like L-3, however, which holds sensitive government contracts integral to national security, and the takeover of which would appear to have no immediate benefit to the health of the defense communications and technology sector.

6. State Pursues the Internal Intervention Option

Finally, one very particular instance should be mentioned in which economic nationalism and/or geopolitical competition concerns are present, along with a clear national security concern, but state *A* still does not intervene in the deal itself. This is when the state decides instead to pursue a course of "internal intervention" in order to counter the threat posed by the deal. (It should also be noted here that if a deal (Z) supports state *A*'s efforts toward internal intervention in another case (Y), then state *A* will obviously not intervene in deal Z.) The dynamics behind the strategy of internal intervention are fully explained in Part II of this chapter.

Secondary Hypothesis

The secondary hypothesis posits that the type of intervention chosen by the government of state *A* will affect the deal outcome. If this is true, we would expect to find that, barring unforeseen circumstances, deals would go through unaltered if government intervention did not occur.

Once again, the numbers seem to support this hypothesis (see Figure 31).[6] Of the 131 cases of no intervention in the database, 102 deals (or 77.86%) were completed, all with ostensibly no changes or modifications. (See Figure 32 for a breakdown of deal outcomes by sector in all cases of non-intervention.)

Only twenty-nine (or 22.14%) of the cases of no intervention still resulted in a failed deal. Some unforeseen factors account for this. First, one of the companies involved may have had a change of heart or have been forced to pull out, either for financial reasons or because of intractable shareholder opposition. Second, the government of state

Figure 31 Non-intervention and the secondary hypothesis

Intervention Type	Deal Outcome	Number of Cases
No Intervention	Deal	102
	Changed Deal	0
	No Deal	29

Figure 32 Non-intervention cases: outcome breakdown by sector

Sector	**Industries**	**Completed Deals** (Total = 102)	**Failed Deals** (Total = 29)	**All Non-Intervention Deals** (Total = 131)
Oil & Gas	Oil & Gas Producers Oil Equipment, Services & Distribution	24	5	29
Basic Resources	Aluminum Steel	9	2	11
Industrials	Aerospace Defense Marine Transportation	7	4	11
Telecommunications	Fixed-Line Telecommunications Mobile Telecommunications Satellite Telecommunications	18	2	20
Utilities	Electricity Gas Distribution Multi-Utilities Water	15	6	21
Financials	Investment Services (Stock Exchanges)	18	5	23
Technology	Software Computer Hardware Semiconductors Telecommunications Equipment	11	5	16

Note: Sector and Industry titles sourced from www.icbenchmark.com.

Figure 33 Non-military internal balancing: M&A intervention options

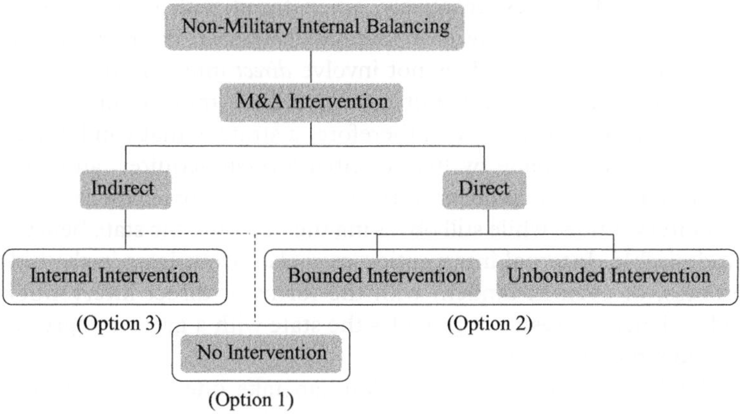

A might have made it clear to the parties that it would intervene in the deal if it went any further, without allowing that information to become public. Finally, state *A* might not have had to intervene in the deal itself in order to create an effective barrier to its completion. Instead, the state may have obviated the issue by choosing what I have termed the *internal intervention* option.

Part II: Internal Intervention

There are times when market analysts become aware that a company is susceptible to a potential takeover long before any potential "suitors" emerge. In such circumstances, the company in question, and the state in which it is domiciled (state *A*), may have a fairly long window of opportunity in which to assess its options, and to determine who might seek to buy the vulnerable target. If the company is viewed as a strategic asset, or a national champion, the government of state *A* may decide to monitor the situation closely.

If a foreign bidder then emerges for the vulnerable target, or if it is believed one will do so in the near future, the government of state *A* has three options (see Figure 33). (1) If the foreign bidder is not perceived as threatening, for one of the reasons already discussed, the government may decide not to intervene. (2) If it is believed that the potential foreign acquirer, and the deal that they propose, poses a potential threat to national security, state *A* may choose to intervene *directly* into the proposed foreign takeover through a strategy of either unbounded or bounded intervention, once the deal has solidified. These first two choices were analyzed in the primary and secondary hypotheses proposed in this work. (3) Alternatively, when faced with such a threat, state *A* may choose to engage in a strategy of internal intervention. As will be shown, this strategy does not involve *direct* intervention into an unwelcome proposed takeover, but instead utilizes more indirect tools to accomplish a similar goal. It is, therefore, a strategy that can be used *before* a formal bid is made by the potential foreign acquirer, and even before a rumored suitor has been verified, in order to preempt the need for direct intervention, while still obviating the outcome the state believes to be undesirable. Internal intervention may also occur later in the bidding process, or even in tandem with the forms of direct intervention analyzed earlier. As a result, it provides the state with a greater degree of latitude and strategic flexibility.

As defined here, internal intervention can take one of three forms. First, it can mean that the government proactively seeks, encourages, and then supports a domestic company to act as an alternative bidder for the vulnerable target. Such a company would then act as a "white knight:" a welcomed and friendly bidder that would fend off a hostile (and, in this case, foreign) bid by either acquiring or merging with the target. The Gaz de France (GdF)/Suez case study that follows examines this form of intervention, as it is the most interesting and useful for our discussion of this particular form of non-military internal balancing. (In that case, a French government-sponsored "white knight," GdF, stepped in to merge with the French power company Suez, which was feared to be susceptible to an unwanted foreign takeover.)

Second, the government might aggressively encourage domestic investors and/or companies to purchase a large stake in the target in order to promote a high level of cross-shareholding. Such a strategy can help a vulnerable entity to defend itself from a takeover later, assuming that those new domestic shareholders will vote against the unwanted potential foreign takeover bid. The German government, for example, was active in promoting cross-shareholding between Porsche and Volkswagen (VW) (one of its national champions) in order to prevent VW from being acquired by a foreign company. Indeed, the promotion of cross-shareholding to protect strategic sectors is popular in a number of European and Asian countries, such as France, Italy, Spain, and Japan.

Third, state *A* might promote or support a merger (that it would normally block on competition grounds) of two weaker domestic companies in order to create a national champion. Such a national champion would not only be less susceptible to a foreign takeover, but would also, arguably, provide other economic benefits. Russia's government, for example, is believed to have played a strong hand in the consolidation of the Russian aluminum companies Rusal and Sual in order to prevent these companies from becoming liable to a future foreign takeover. After the Rusal/Sual tie-up, it then supported a further merger with Glencore (of Switzerland) in order to create "the world's biggest aluminum producer" (Pavliva 2007), but only on the understanding that the majority of the new company would remain in Russian hands. Oleg Deripaska, the owner of the newly merged entity United Company Rusal, has openly said that he is even prepared to "'give up' the company to the state if the Russian government asked for it," because he "[does not] separate [him]self from the state" and "[has] no other interests" (Pavliva 2007). Such statements clearly indicate that the company remains under the definitive influence and control of the Russian government.

Internal Intervention as a Tool of Non-Military Internal Balancing

Internal intervention is, therefore, one potential means of non-military internal balancing. It allows the state to protect those sectors it deems vital to national security from foreign ownership and control, when such an outcome would be potentially detrimental to its relative power position and rank, or to its future survival. For example, internal intervention offers one possible way to obviate a potential foreign takeover that would place a highly sensitive industry, or vital and scarce resource, in the hands of a known political/military competitor and/or rising power. Ally and foe alike, therefore, might be targeted by such a form of intervention, as both have the potential to change or challenge a state's relative power position in a world where economic, political, and military power are inextricably linked, though challenges to state survival are obviously most likely to come from previously identified foes.

Like any other tool of non-military internal balancing, internal intervention is a strategy that allows the state to maintain (or maximize) the economic and military power necessary for state survival, and is a response to a specific threat – real and/or perceived – to relative power. It, too, like the types of intervention discussed in the previous chapters, qualifies as form of internal balancing, because it is a "move to increase economic capability" (Waltz 1979, 118) as part of the wider effort to preserve and/or maximize power in response to a challenge to that power. It is non-military in nature, because this balancing tool is also chosen for its ability to maintain the greater meta-relationship at stake between the states involved, as it is unlikely ever to lead to a truly negative or irreversible disruption in such a relationship.

On first appearance, this internal form of intervention may appear to be the most similar to the "economic component" of traditional internal balancing as defined by Brawley (in Paul et al. 2004). Yet, while it can be a tool connected to a direct "increase [in] military strength" (Waltz 1979, 118) or an "arms race" (see Brawley in Paul et al. 2004, 85), it may also simply be part of a more general strategy that seeks to counter threats to other areas of economic power vital to a state's overall power, position, and long-term survival. The temporal frame and cadence of the internal intervention strategy may also be very different from more conventional forms of internal balancing. In other words, while internal balancing has traditionally been understood to be a response to an immediate, or near-term, threat to power, the type of intervention discussed here may be part of a strategy to balance a challenge to power that may not threaten survival for many decades to come.[7]

The author is not arguing that the dynamics behind *internal* intervention can be fully explained by the primary and secondary hypotheses posited earlier. Though the factors motivating the desire to intervene internally may be similar to those hypothesized to influence the direct forms (unbounded and bounded) of government intervention in most cases, there *may* be additional factors governing this particular type of state behavior under certain circumstances. It must be stressed here that internal intervention is an *alternative* to direct intervention into a cross-border acquisition, and its *indirect* nature may make it subject to other domestic political factors.

Furthermore, while all governments retain the right to engage in direct intervention (bounded or unbounded) against a takeover they deem threatening to their national security, not all governments are necessarily willing to engage in internal intervention, which is seen by some states as aggressively anti-free-market behavior. Other nations, however, such as Russia, France, Italy, Germany, and Spain, have been more open in their willingness to help vulnerable national champions find domestic saviors. Economic nationalism may therefore play a larger role in this type of intervention.

Either way, the case study that follows is meant only to explore the possibility that internal intervention may be motivated by the same factors of economic nationalism and geopolitical competition that have been found to have such a great effect on bounded and unbounded intervention. Remember that the primary hypothesis tested in the previous chapters is meant only to cover *direct* intervention into a foreign takeover. The purpose of this section, therefore, is simply to provide insights on the basis of the primary hypothesis, which should enable a better understanding of the relationship between internal intervention and other forms of non-military internal balancing, and should contribute to the formation of a more complete hypothesis governing such *indirect* forms of intervention in the future.

Case 10: GdF/Suez

The merger of the French energy companies Suez SA and Gaz de France (GdF) is one of the most striking examples of internal intervention over the last decade. Initiated as an effort by the French government to protect Suez from a hostile takeover by the Italian energy company Enel, the deal took over two years to complete, and pitted the French and Belgian governments against that of Italy. It stands as a testament to the lengths that a government will go to in order to fend off a foreign takeover it perceives as threatening, even before such a takeover is formally attempted. It also clearly demonstrates how state power can be employed, and balanced, though the market. An overview of this case is provided, as well as an examination of its connection to the factors examined in the primary hypothesis and a discussion of how it exemplifies balancing through internal intervention.

The Story

The saga began in the middle of February 2006, when it became clear that Enel was likely to place a bid for Suez in the near future. At this point, the CEO of Enel, Fulvio Conti, confirmed that his company might be interested in a hostile takeover of Suez, in order to gain control of the electricity assets held by its Belgian subsidiary Electrabel (Freeman 2006; Thornton 2006b). The company then released a statement on February 25, indicating it was considering different options for "expanding abroad," and specifying France as one of the countries in which it was "examining . . . opportunities" (Enel 2006).

The reaction of the French and Belgian governments was immediate and forceful. On the very same day as Enel's press release, the French government took two major and definitive steps. The first was to take preventative action by actively fostering a domestic merger between Suez and GdF, which was still a French state-controlled entity. GdF was France's leading natural gas supplier at that time, and the combination would create a national champion whose size and ownership structure would be significantly strengthened against a foreign takeover (see e.g., Dempsey & Benhold 2007; Ng 2006). Concern over Suez's vulnerable position had already led Thierry Breton, the French Minister for Economy, Finance, and Industry, to ask in September 2005 that the companies "draft a merger plan" (Robin 2006). Then, "less than one hour after Enel['s announcement]" on February 25, "the top management of Gaz de France and Suez met together with the French [Prime Minister] and approved a friendly merger between the two groups," which would have the explicit "support of the French and Belgian governments" (Freeman 2006; Roden 2006). The timing and speed of this official announcement sent a clear signal to any potential foreign bidders for Suez that the French government preferred a domestic partner for the company. This message was clearly received by Enel's CEO, who rightly called the action "a pre-emptive maneuver to shield the country's utilities from foreign takeovers" in general (Freeman 2006).

In the second step, the French government made it clear, through public statements and personal communication to the Italian government, that it would not allow Suez to be taken over by Enel specifically. The then Prime Minister of France, Dominique de Villepin, immediately called his "Italian counterpart Silvio Berlusconi to express his opposition to any Suez takeover" (Freeman 2006). Indeed, Villepin's opposition was vehement. He was widely reported to have said that a "hostile bid from Enel would be considered as an '*attack on France*'" (Chassany 2006, emphasis added). Such language is more than mere French rhetorical style, for it clearly shows that the French government considered the speculated bid to be a potentially serious threat to French economic and political power.

The Italian reaction to this position was equally pronounced. Berlusconi, for his part, initially requested "the French government to be impartial in the face of Enel's takeover bid" (International Herald Tribune 2006b). When it was apparent that that was not going to happen, the Italians' frustration became more pronounced. The Italian government cancelled a meeting between its "Industry Minister Claudio Scajola . . . [and] his French counterpart Francois Loos to discuss energy and competition" (Freeman 2006). Scajola declared publicly that "the political and economic destiny of the European Union will be compromised if neo-protectionism prevails" (Freeman 2006). For, the Italian Minister, not surprisingly, viewed the French move as one of pure protectionism, despite the fact that there were obvious strategic implications for France of such a takeover (to be examined in detail later). Scajola's stance, however, was followed by some rather unfortunate rhetoric referencing World War I, which did not strengthen the Italian position in French eyes. Italy's Economic Minister Giulio Trementi stated on the same day: "We still have time to stop European Union states from building national barriers. If not, we risk the impact of August 1914" (International Herald Tribune 2006b). The (perhaps unintended) bellicosity of this statement only seemed to make the French more wary. The Italians also registered a formal complaint with the European Commission over the proposed combination of GdF and Suez, in an effort to have it stopped.

In the end, however, the French achieved the creation of a new national champion (now called GdF Suez), and the Italians were forced to back down. As will be discussed in greater detail shortly, a foreign takeover of Suez was unacceptable to France for reasons of both economic nationalism and geopolitics. Yet, as will also be examined, the threat was diffuse and not necessarily specific to Italy. An act of internal balancing through internal intervention was thus required, because it would strengthen the French position against this type of threat from *any* external actor. At the same time, France's overall relationship with Italy was not truly damaged. Despite the Italian government's official rhetoric and frustration, it was unlikely such a disagreement could permanently damage an otherwise healthy diplomatic relationship, and Italy was eventually mollified both politically and economically.

Setting the Stage: Geopolitics and Economic Nationalism

Both geopolitical considerations and economic nationalism played a strong role in motivating the French government's decision to intervene in this case. The following analysis will review the position of the companies within the framework of France's strong economic nationalism, while also showing that the country's reaction had important geopolitical underpinnings.

As one of the world's top diversified utilities companies, Suez provided a large proportion of the electricity, natural gas, water, and waste management services in France. This provision of vital resource and energy services made Suez of special interest to the French government at a time when many European countries were seeking to consolidate their control over the provision of domestic utilities.[8] Competition in the recently liberalized European utilities market was (and has remained) fairly low, and Neelie Kroes, then European Commissioner for Competition Policy, made it a top priority to change that situation when she acceded to her post in 2004 (see Kroes 2008). Her push for legislation within the European Parliament introduced significant structural reforms to Europe's energy markets, and led to a race among European companies, and the governments that often controlled them, to consolidate control and resources before the proverbial "doors" were opened to further competition and new market entrants (Interview 2006; Scott 2008).

At the same time, the French and Italian governments were made highly aware of the dangers of natural gas dependence. Just under two months before the proposed hostile takeover of Suez by Enel, Russia had flexed its geopolitical muscle through its control over natural gas resources. On January 1, 2006, the Russian state-controlled oil company Gazprom cut off natural gas supplies to the Ukraine for almost four days following an alleged dispute over a rise in prices. The Ukraine was believed to have fought back by siphoning gas from that headed to Europe (BBC 2006). Whether this was truly a case of "siphoning" or a result of other technical difficulties, the cut-off had a deep impact on Europe, which saw a significant reduction in its natural gas supplies. The French supply of Russian gas fell by 25–30%, and the Italian supply by 24% (BBC 2006), the true impact of which is understood when one recognizes that between 2006 and 2007, Russian natural gas exports accounted for 20% of French and 25% of Italian domestic consumption (EIA 2008b). The event seemed to impact deeply on both countries' desire to gain access to alternative supplies of natural gas, as well as their desire to bolster their own domestic natural gas companies.

The specter of Russian control over natural gas not only helps explain Enel's initial search for foreign expansion opportunities, such as a Suez takeover, but was also a motivating factor for France's internal intervention throughout the duration of this case. By December 2006, Russia was threatening to take similar action against Belarus, which in turn threatened to siphon exports of Russian gas destined for Europe in retaliation (Osborn 2006). The dispute between Russia and the Ukraine over natural gas was revived in October 2007, and Russia again cut off supplies to the Ukraine in January 2009. Once more, whether intentionally or not, this caused a noticeable disruption in supply to continental Europe, demonstrating European concerns about Russia's control over the resource were well founded.

The French government, and the companies themselves, clearly saw the potential loss of strength in the natural gas sector as a source of geopolitical concern. The GdF/Suez merger prospectus clearly stated that the tie-up was largely motivated by the "greater geostrategic challenges associated with the security of European energy sources" (GdF Suez 2008). The primary problem was that

> The European Union is currently dependant on imports for 55% of its natural gas needs. By 2020, it is estimated that imports will account for 85% of European Natural Gas requirements. Norway and two countries outside of Europe (Russia and Algeria) account for a significant share of current supplies and the future resources that will supplement those supplies are relatively concentrated in a few distant countries (particularly the Persian Gulf). (GdF Suez 2008)

The Belgian government, whose country relied heavily on both Suez and GdF for its natural gas and electricity supplies, shared this concern. Suez's subsidiary Electrabel generated 92% of the electricity, and provided 70% of the natural gas, in Belgium (Roden 2006). At the same time, GdF, through its subsidiary Segeo, owned one of the larger gas pipelines in Belgium. Thus, it was not particularly surprising that the Belgian state supported the proposed merger of GdF and Suez. It had no national champion of its own to support, but the proven relationship with the French companies was highly satisfactory, whereas the Italian company Enel was an unknown quantity.

This geopolitical competition over resources and economic power combined with high levels of economic nationalism in France to spur the vigorous response of the French government as a whole. The PepsiCo/Danone and Alcatel/Lucent cases demonstrate that economic nationalism was high in France during this period.[9] Indeed, France has never been shy about its desire to protect its markets or its national champions through the stated policy of "patriotisme économique." In this particular case, the European Commission specifically decried the use of "nationalist rhetoric" on the part of both the French and Italian governments (Times 2006). This case also came at a time when the French government had only recently announced its plan (in 2005) to protect the eleven sectors it deemed to be strategic, which included the energy sector. Furthermore, French Prime Minister de Villepin and Economic Minister Breton were consistently open about their desire to create a national champion that would have European reach through the merger of GdF and Suez.

The French government also ensured that the new "national champion" would remain under state control by taking a golden share in the newly formulated entity. A golden share is a special issue of stock that gives a government certain final veto powers over decisions made about the company in question. The Merger Prospectus of GdF Suez makes it clear that "the purpose of this golden share is to preserve the essential interests of France in the energy sector to ensure continuity or security of energy supplies" (GdF Suez 2008). The Prospectus also makes it clear that natural gas supplies were the primary energy concern of the French government in this case.[10]

It is also important to note that the geopolitical threat was more diffuse in this case than it was in the cases examined in previous chapters. There was likely some level of concern that Italy's natural gas sector would soon fall under greater Russian control, and therefore increase Europe's dependence on its supplies. This concern emanated from Russia's stated desire at that time to gain greater market share in Italy's gas distribution network. In general, however, it was not specific geopolitical tension with

Italy, or a specific difference in the relative economic or political positions of France and Italy, that seems to have aroused French concern. Rather, it was the general concerns over France's economic position, and over its control of resources ahead of further deregulation by the European Commission, that were primarily at issue.

Alternative Explanatory Factors: Interest Group Presence and Competition Concerns

In the final analysis, neither interest groups nor competition concerns proved to be a significant factor in motivating French intervention in this case.

First, the French unions did not significantly affect the outcome of government intervention because, even though their opposition to the combination of GdF and Suez held up the completion of the merger, it never completely threatened to derail it. The French unions were vociferously against the GdF/Suez deal because it would mean the privatization of GdF and, thus, the loss of a number of employee protections and privileges (see e.g., ICEM 2006; International Herald Tribune 2008). GdF's unions initiated a brief strike against the proposed combination in June 2006 (Kanter 2006). They were also able to cause delays by requesting, through a court-stay, more time to review the deal before providing their official opinion on it (International Herald Tribune 2008). The outcome, however, was never placed in jeopardy by this action. This was because the "official opinion" required by the union under French law was only a legal formality for completion; the eventual negative opinion given by the unions did not (and was not expected to) stop the merger (International Herald Tribune 2008; Roden 2008). Thus, while the French unions were not in favor of a GdF/Suez merger, they would probably have taken similar steps against any action that would have privatized GdF. Their opposition was not enough to affect the French government's decision.

Second, the powerful interest groups of the various shareholders in both companies that could have tried to block the deal did not do so, largely because they agreed with the French government on the threat posed by an Enel takeover. In the end, the boards and shareholders of both companies approved the merger in 2008. The major shareholders of Suez at the time were reported to be very close to the French government (Roden 2006). Market analysts believed that when Suez shareholders voted to enact a "poison pill" against a potential Enel takeover in May 2006, their actions were politically motivated because of their proximity to the government (Roden 2006). Even the shareholders of GdF (beyond the French state itself, which owned a majority of GdF stock), who were not threatened by a hostile foreign takeover, voted in favor of the deal. Perhaps it is most telling that they did so despite the fact that many equity research analysts believed the terms of the deal were unfavorable for GdF (Roden 2006). Shareholders were thus largely in favor of the merger, and it seemed that this was a political response to the threat identified by the French government in a hostile Enel takeover of Suez.

Finally, though the European Commission was initially concerned by the potential effect of the deal on competition, these problems were eventually easily resolved by two small asset disposals. The European Commission decided to investigate the proposed merger of GdF and Suez to ensure that the combination was not detrimental to energy competition in Europe. This investigation was *not* conducted in response to Italy's objections that the deal was protectionist.[11] In the end, the Commission "found that the deal would have anticompetitive effects in the gas and electricity wholesale and retail markets in Belgium and in the gas markets in France" (EU Commission 2006b). It determined, however, that these effects could be sufficiently assuaged by "structural remedies": primarily "the divestiture of Distrigaz and SPE and Suez relinquishing its control of [the] Belgian network operator Fluxys" (EU Commission 2006b). These disposals were effected before the deal was completed in 2008, with Distrigaz being sold to the Italian energy company Eni, which may have provided some mollification for the Italian government. Furthermore, though the European Commission has generally sought to reduce the level of golden share ownership within member states, on the basis that it is anti-competitive in nature, the Commission did not object to the inclusion of a golden share for the French government in this particular case. In fact, the European Commissioner for the Internal Market and Services, Charlie McCreevy, wrote a letter to Minister Breton in September 2006, which "made clear that the decree establishing the golden share did not contain any 'contentious' elements that would merit legal action" on the part of Brussels (Buck et al. 2006a). McCreevy reportedly attributed this to the fact that "France . . . managed to draft a decree that meets the Union's strict criteria for such special rights" (Buck et al. 2006a).

Conclusions on GdF/Suez

High levels of economic nationalism and geopolitical competition in this case combined to make a foreign takeover of Suez identifiable with a threat to French power and security, and thus made intervention of some kind extremely likely. As the threat was more diffuse in this case, an act of internal balancing through internal intervention was required, because it would strengthen the French position against this type of threat not only from Italy, but also from any future external actor.

This act of internal intervention also appears consistent in cause, purpose, and effect with more traditional notions of internal balancing. The cause was an identified threat to security and power, here in the form of a foreign takeover of Suez. The purpose and effect were to counter that threat through internal economic and political measures, which would enhance the future French power position in this area. In this case, that was achieved by the support of a domestic merger that created a national champion (GdF Suez) that the French government could control through a golden share, and which increased the French position in the natural gas sector, enhancing not only France's national capabilities, but also its economic power.

At the same time, the goal of using non-military internal balancing to maintain the greater meta-relationship between the two countries was also achieved. Though Enel and the Italian government were forced to back down from their position, the overall relationship with Italy was not truly damaged. Despite the Italian government's official rhetoric and frustration, it was unlikely that such a disagreement could permanently damage an otherwise healthy diplomatic relationship, and they were eventually mollified both politically and economically.[12]

Conclusion

Part I of this chapter demonstrated that the primary and secondary hypotheses concerning the motivations behind direct intervention into foreign takeovers still hold once the population of non-intervention, or "negative," cases has been examined. This was achieved by testing the hypotheses against the "hardest" negative case. In other words, against a case where the outcome was non-intervention despite the presence of the high levels of economic nationalism and/or geopolitical competition hypothesized to motivate intervention. Two such cases were examined, CGG/Veritas and JP Morgan/Troika Dialog, and it was demonstrated that, in each, a fundamental assumption of the hypothesis was missing: there was no real or perceived threat to national security, despite the fact that each case took place within what are normally considered to be strategic sectors. Though the lack of such a real or perceived threat is rare in such sectors, it does occur, and when that happens, non-intervention will tend to result, notwithstanding the presence of economic nationalism or geopolitical competition. This is because, in a generally liberal international economy, it is difficult to make a case for intervention without at least a plausible national security reason for doing so, and states are unlikely to pursue such a course of internal balancing unless they believe it to be necessary.

The first part of the chapter also posited that, in addition to the primary and secondary hypotheses, there may be six potentially mitigating circumstances that make non-intervention, or at least low-bounded intervention, a more likely outcome. These are when: (1) the proposed acquirer is an institutional investor; (2) the target is pursuing a desired exit from the marketplace; (3) state *A* fears a less friendly bidder will otherwise emerge; (4) the national security concerns inherent in the deal have been previously addressed; (5) the deal strengthens the defense industrial base; or (6) state *A* instead pursues the internal intervention option.

Part II of this chapter discussed the alternative, and indirect, form of non-military internal balancing that is internal intervention. The GdF/Suez case was examined to illustrate the possibility that economic nationalism and geopolitical competition also play a role in motivating this type of intervention. It was demonstrated that, at least in this case, the French government's actions seemed to be a clear internal balancing response to an imminent and identifiable external threat to French relative power and security. Though the purpose of this work was to test the hypothesis focused on direct forms of intervention (bounded and unbounded), this case study helped to demonstrate that the hypothesis does potentially hold for indirect (i.e., internal) intervention, and further testing might provide a fruitful avenue for future research.

NOTES

1 It should be noted that Seawright (2002) focuses on hypotheses "testing necessary and/or sufficient causes." This particular study is more probabilistic in nature, as necessitated by the quantitative logit-model testing of a multinomial outcome. Yet, Seawright's observations are still of great value here. He also concentrates on sampling techniques, but this is not necessary here as the population examined is already relatively small.

2 In other words, pro-globalization sentiment was low in Russia in 2006: it was valued at 4.87, which was well below the median score of 6.21 among the fifty-four countries for which there were survey data available in that year (IMD 2007b).

3 The author has chosen a broad definition of the term that gets at the essence of the idea, but which is more widely applicable across countries. This is because the term "institutional investor" is frequently used but rarely defined by governments, which often have slightly different definitions from one another. For example, in the US, an institutional investor is essentially an

accredited investor, as defined by the SEC (for a complete definition, see SEC 2008). In the UK, the equivalent is a *market counterparty*, as defined by the Financial Services Authority (for a complete definition, see FSA 2008).

4 In non-American cases, "national security agreements" may be given another name, but they are essentially contractual documents that obligate the acquirer to agree to certain security precautions and laws as desired by the target state.

5 Please refer to Chapter 1, pp. 47–8 for a more detailed description of these variables. It should also be noted here that Theodore Moran has argued from the public policy perspective that CFIUS should employ a test for the ability of a deal to contribute to the health of the defense industrial base that goes far beyond that which already apparently exists (see Moran 1993).

6 It should be noted that there is little utility in using Mahoney and Goertz's Possibility Principle to test the secondary hypothesis, as there is only one independent variable, and the correlation between it and the dependent variable is very strong. Instead, an examination of the population as a whole is both more useful and more enlightening.

7 See Brawley on the distinction between the temporality of "balancing now" versus "balancing later" and its implications for the "economic component" of internal balancing (in Paul et al. 2004, 85–8).

8 It should be noted that this process of consolidation and the desire to create national utilities champions remains ongoing within mainland Europe, and is in constant tension with the European Commission's efforts to make the European energy market more competitive.

9 As mentioned in the PepsiCo/Danone case, French businessmen ranked second to last in terms of pro-globalization sentiment (followed only by Venezuela) among the fifty-four countries for which survey data were available for this variable in 2006 (IMD 2007b).

10 The prospectus states that "the assets concerned by the French state's veto rights conferred by the golden share include: natural gas transmission and distribution pipelines in France; assets related to natural gas distribution in France; underground natural gas storage facilities in France; liquefied natural gas facilities in France" (GdF Suez 2008).

11 The European Commission made it clear early on in the process that "it would [intervene] only if the planned merger between Gaz de France and Suez broke competition rules" (Times 2006).

12 The two countries' formal alliance within the European Union made it difficult to make too much of the issue. The French deal also eventually ensured that the Italians got access to the Belgian market, through a side deal, which had initially prompted the idea of an Enel/Suez takeover. More importantly, the Italian government needed France's political alliance/clout in the EU to get some economic reforms that it needed approved (Roden 2007).

Conclusion

The Theoretical Context

Bretton Woods marked the beginning of a liberal economic order, establishing a global system founded on free-market principles. Its purpose was not only to deepen economic interdependence in order to help the West and the world realize the absolute gains that attend free trade, but also – through the deepening of such ties – to lower the likelihood of future conflict within the international system. The order was intended to be durable, institutionalizing the economic and political values of the West in a manner that would outlast the eventual decline of the country that had thus far forcibly defended it – the US (see Ikenberry 2001).

Over the past decade, however, there has been a notable trend in state behavior that one might not expect in this context. For, though cross-border M&A has proven to be one of the foundation stones upon which the liberal economic order rests, there has been a surge of state intervention into this type of financial transaction on national security grounds. Significantly, this behavior is not unique to any one country or group of countries; it is not a "Western" or a "non-Western" phenomenon. Yet, many observers find it surprising that states are intervening against "foreign" takeovers originating from within their own security communities – communities founded not only on the historical sense of "we-ness" that emerges from exceptionally close long-standing alliances, but which are also often rooted in a commitment to economic liberalization and, in the case of the EU, integration.

The purpose of this book has been to explain this simple puzzle: to understand why states are engaging in such behavior not only against their strategic and military competitors, but against their closest allies as well. Because existing theories cannot fully explain this behavior, I present a new theory that builds on the insights of structural and neoclassical realism. Beginning from the realist assumption that states living in anarchy will compete for power and seek to balance challenges and threats to their relative power through either internal or external means in order to ensure their own survival, I also recognize that this struggle for power among states will not always be played out in the military or diplomatic realms. For, though nuclear weapons have decreased the likelihood of a major power hot war, the competition for scarce resources and technology is arguably on the rise. *Thus, one can expect that conflict will increasingly occur in the economic realm, and that some states will try to take advantage of the interdependent relationships that arise from economic globalization through FDI.*[1]

Some states *will* use the market to try to gain economic and military power through companies they control. China has long been known to acquire (through companies it influences or owns) foreign companies in order to gain control of and/or access to their technology and resources, or for the simple purpose of conducting espionage (Graham & Marchick 2006, 100–17). Russia has made no secret of its desire to use the M&A market as a way to gain access to, and the right to distribute, natural resources abroad. Additionally, as sovereign wealth funds (SWFs) increase in terms of their power, wealth, and scope of activity, it raises concerns that some SWFs may not always be subject to the same market-based motivations as other financial actors (Lenihan 2014). *As a result, states are increasingly vigilant in their efforts to ensure that cross-border M&A transactions do not make them dependent on other states, or pose a threat to their position in the international system.*

This is not to imply that the insights of neoliberal institutionalists or liberal economists are wrong. States clearly recognize the value of the absolute gains that free trade and international cooperation can bring, as demonstrated by their efforts to reduce barriers to global trade through the WTO. Yet, there is a difference between agreeing to trade goods and services without the imposition of tariffs and the willingness to allow, for example, a domestic company that makes your air force's fighter jets to be taken over by a foreign company.

It is for this very reason that states have refused to give up the right to block cross-border mergers or acquisitions that they believe pose a threat to their national security, even if the result of such transactions would be otherwise beneficial for their economy. As a result, and because governments reserve the right to identify the nature of such threats on their own, states have been largely unable, or unwilling, to agree to a multilateral treaty governing cross-border M&A, making this one of the last remaining arenas in which such economic power competition and conflict can play out without violating international law.

Figure 34 Case study findings: unbounded and bounded intervention

	Cases	Motivation	
Intervention Type	**Security Community Cases**	**Geopolitical Competition**	**Economic Nationalism**
Unbounded	PepsiCo/Danone	Secondary	Primary
	Check Point/Sourcefire	Primary	
Bounded	Alcatel/Lucent	Primary	Secondary
	Non-Security Community Cases		
Unbounded	CNOOC/Unocal	Primary	Secondary
	Macquarie/PCCW	Primary	Secondary
Bounded	Lenovo/IBM	Primary	Secondary

Non-Military Internal Balancing

This study has demonstrated that governments will intervene in foreign takeovers that they believe challenge or threaten their relative power, using such intervention as a tool of non-military internal balancing. This intervention will either be *unbounded* (direct action aiming to block the deal), *bounded* (direct action to mitigate the negative effects of the deal), or *internal* (encouraging domestic-based actions and outcomes that obviate the need for direct intervention into a specified deal). The exact form intervention takes, and the motivations behind it, vary with the nature of the relationship between the countries involved and the exact nature of the threat posed by the transaction in question.

This work has also shown that *geopolitical competition* and *economic nationalism* are the primary motivating factors behind direct government intervention into foreign takeovers of companies in national security industries. This argument assumes that, in each case of intervention, an element of the specified takeover can be legitimately construed as posing a national security risk, before these factors come into play. Alternative explanations of state behavior were also controlled for and examined. Statistical analysis confirmed that the presence of geopolitical competition and/or economic nationalism in a particular country increases the likelihood that it will engage in either unbounded or bounded intervention. Neither interest group presence nor economic competition proved to be generally significant, demonstrating that these factors do not provide an adequate alternative explanation for such action.

These findings were substantiated in the case studies (see Figure 34 for a summary of the direct intervention cases examined in Chapters 3–5).

Both geopolitical competition *and* economic nationalism proved to be the motivating factors behind state action in both cases of bounded intervention and in three of the five unbounded intervention cases examined; and in one case of unbounded intervention, geopolitical concerns *alone* proved relevant. Even the outlier unbounded intervention case (DPW/P&O) offered some support for the primary hypothesis. In that case, an unusually high level of politicization of the deal allowed two values of economic nationalism (one high, one low), and two alternative understandings of the geopolitical relationship involved, to emerge within the same state. Certain lawmakers were therefore able to believably couch their concerns – whether justified or not – in terms of national and economic security, and the US-related aspects of the transaction were blocked. The hypothesis also held in both cases of non-intervention. In addition, even though the hypothesis was formulated to explain *direct* forms of intervention (and further analysis is thus necessary), the final case examined in Chapter 6 indicated that the hypothesis may even help to explain cases of *internal* intervention.

For the theory to hold, it was also important to show that intervention type actually affects deal outcomes. The statistical data confirmed that this could be said to be true with 99.9% confidence, and that as the degree of government intervention increases, so too do the chances of a deal being mitigated or blocked. As predicted, each case study of an *unbounded* intervention resulted in a *no deal* outcome, and both cases of *bounded* intervention led to *mitigated deals*. Additionally, in both cases of *non-intervention*, where the state did not believe the deal to raise any national security concerns, the transactions proceeded unaffected as expected, with one completed and the other leading to a management buy-out.

Significance

The Puzzle Revisited

The answer to the puzzle seems to lie in a few discoveries. First, it is important to recognize that intervention within the security community context will only rarely take the unbounded form. Across all cases, intervention will most often take the *bounded* form. For the total population of cases examined in this study, the bounded intervention rate was 29%, compared to a rate of only 8% for unbounded interventions. Significantly, when these numbers were broken down, it was confirmed that the rate of unbounded intervention is even lower in security communities (at 7%) than it is outside them (where the rate is 12%).

I found that this lower rate of unbounded interventions within security communities might be explained by a number of factors. One is that the review process through which cross-border deals are mitigated is often more highly institutionalized in the countries that are coded here as being members of a strong security community, which may make bounded intervention more effective and reliable in the eyes of those states. A more fundamental reason for the lower level of unbounded intervention within security communities, however, is simply that within that context, such drastic measures of state action are rarely considered necessary.

This brings us to the second finding. Economic nationalism will, for the most part, play a greater role than geopolitical competition in motivating unbounded intervention within the security community context. This is because the geopolitical tensions within such relationships are *usually* very low, and therefore cross-border transactions within those contexts are less likely to pose intractable national security threats. In other words, any national security issue that originates from geopolitical concerns in this situation can *usually* be resolved through mitigation of the deal in question. Geopolitical tensions or concerns will only rarely be so acute within a security community context that they alone motivate unbounded intervention. Instead, high levels of economic nationalism will normally be the primary motivator of unbounded intervention in this situation.

However, it is also important to understand that geopolitical competition *can* still play a role in explaining intervention within the security community context, under certain circumstances. The statistical analysis demonstrated that geopolitical competition would significantly increase the likelihood of *bounded* intervention within security communities. This finding was supported by the Alcatel/Lucent case, where geostrategically based national security concerns were shown to be the primary motivator of bounded intervention. Furthermore, intractable geopolitical competition and geostrategic concerns, of a nature that cannot be resolved through bounded intervention, can still occur within security communities. In such situations, these concerns can be the secondary, primary, and/or sole reason for *unbounded* intervention within a security community. As mentioned earlier, this is likely to occur in cases such as Check Point/Sourcefire, where the nature of both the concern and the transaction makes unbounded intervention the only option for achieving non-military internal balancing and protecting national security, despite the close relationship of the countries involved. An unusually high level of economic nationalism may also exacerbate an existing geopolitical tension within a security community, as occurred in the PepsiCo/Danone case.

Thus, the answer to the puzzle becomes clear. The puzzle asked why states would engage in ostensibly protectionist behavior not only against their strategic and military competitors, but also against members of the same security community founded, in part, on economic liberalism. It has been argued here that these acts of intervention can be more clearly understood once they are identified as a tool of non-military internal balancing. This form of internal balancing is focused on immediate challenges to long-term military and/or economic power; challenges that can come in the form of a foreign takeover initiated from non-allied and allied countries alike. Yet, the tool of balancing used – in this case, government intervention into those foreign takeovers – can be tailored to respond to the difference in the level of threat. It was found that the most serious form of intervention, unbounded intervention, is only rarely used within security communities. The ability of states to employ a *bounded* form of intervention, in an institutionalized and routine manner, helps explain how intervention is possible within the security community context. The fact that such internal balancing as a whole is *non-military* in nature explains why even unbounded intervention has become possible and permissible within a security community. The end goal of such balancing is to protect and preserve power *without* disrupting the greater meta-relationship at stake between the two countries involved. Hence, even unbounded intervention – though generally more intense and serious – is unlikely to create any long-term rift within a security community relationship on its own.

Even within the EU – a security community founded on economic liberalism and integration – states pursue this strategy of internal balancing to gain (especially economic) power and position within the context of that greater relationship. That government intervention into foreign takeovers, undertaken for the preservation of national security, is seen as a right of the state, and is not prohibited under international law, makes it in many ways one of the last areas in which states can intervene in the international market in order to preserve their economic and military power. Considered in such a light, it is not surprising that states within close alliance relationships might use this form of balancing, perhaps either to balance a state whose rising power they think could prove destabilizing to the alliance over the long term, or to preserve or gain a leadership position for themselves within that alliance. The interventionist behavior of Germany and France, and even Spain and Italy, provides an excellent example of this strategy being employed within the EU. Events such as the UK's 2016 referendum decision to leave the EU highlight the tensions that can exist beneath the surface of even the closest of alliances.

Where intervention becomes truly shortsighted is when it is fundamentally misused and becomes a case of over- or inappropriate balancing, as occurred in the DPW/P&O case. Such cases, where intervention is almost universally perceived as unwarranted outside the target state, are especially impolitic and imprudent because they are either (1) seen as a case of pure economic protectionism with no true national security foundation, or (2) viewed as being antagonistic to the sending state. In either case, the goal of non-military balancing is lost, and there is the potential for a disruption in the meta-relationship between the states involved and, as discussed in the next section, for a negative impact on the economic system as a whole.

Conflict, Competition, Economic Interdependence, and Systemic Change

The theory and findings presented in this book should also shed additional light on the relationship between economic interdependence and conflict. As discussed at the beginning of this work, Waltz (1993) suggests that realists should expect conflict – especially economic conflict – to potentially increase with interdependence. Even Keohane and Nye (2001) recognize that "conflict will take new forms, and may even increase" as interdependence deepens over time. Yet, both of the theoretical approaches represented by these authors (realism and complex interdependence theory, respectively) are underspecified concerning the intensity and form such conflict is likely to take.

The theory presented in this book shows the value of reconciling the insights from these two approaches. For, competition does take an increasingly economic form, but – especially within security communities that are also highly economically interdependent – such competition must also take a novel form. It might be that as interdependence increases within the EU, for example, traditional forms of economic conflict (such as tariffs) disappear, and new ones (such as intervention into foreign takeovers) rise to take their place. This may be especially true when these new tools have the ability to appear less confrontational and sweeping. In fact, it might be that states are not only finding new ways to deal with the competition for economic power, both within and outside such interdependent relationships, but also that the progression of these relationships necessitates this evolution. Thus, government intervention of the type examined here is, in many cases, truly vital to the protection of national security *because* of the more open environment for cross-border M&A.

This can be viewed positively, as it demonstrates an attempt by states to balance power shifts internally, and in a non-military fashion, in order to avoid more serious forms of conflict further down the line. Certainly, the findings *did* confirm that, for all cases of intervention in the database, with the exception of the outlier case, a legitimate state-defined national security concern was attached to the affected transaction. The findings also demonstrate a preference among states for dealing with such national security concerns through deal mitigation (bounded intervention) where possible, rather than through continual attempts to block disadvantageous deals (unbounded intervention).

The evidence presented in this book thus confirms the need for theorists to have a more holistic understanding of power and national security. Conflict and competition do not disappear when the likelihood of major power war is relatively low. Instead, competition among great powers (and even second- and third-order powers) may simply take a non-military form. This scenario illustrates the value of recognizing that other forms of power become important for determining great power "rank." This does not just mean recognizing the usefulness and necessity of social power and soft power, it also means an acknowledgment of the increasing relevance of economic power. This is particularly true if one believes that one of the next major sources of conflict in the international system will be the scarcity of vital natural resources (NIC 2008, 63), or control over the next big technological breakthrough.[2] Such competition is likely to be played out in the economic sector in the future. Indeed, cross-border M&A is a front line in the battlefield over some vital aspects of economic and military power. Intervention into such transactions takes on an important role as a form of internal balancing, for the very reason that some states will attempt to use foreign takeovers as a way to take advantage of interdependent relationships and gain control over resources, technology, information, critical infrastructure, and other strategic sectors of the economy.

For instance, recent evidence shows that states are using foreign investment into the US to achieve such goals, and to increase their power relative to that country. In three out of its last four annual reports to Congress, CFIUS disclosed the US intelligence community's assessment that "there may be," or that "there is likely," such "a coordinated strategy among one or more foreign governments or companies to acquire US companies involved in [the] research, development, or production of critical technologies for which the United States is a leading producer" (US DOT 2012, 23, 2015, 26, 2016a, 29). CFIUS has regularly pointed out that other "coordinated strategies may go unobserved due to limitations on intelligence collection, or may be hidden or misconstrued because of foreign denial and deception activities" (see US DOT 2009, 28, 2010, 19, 2011, 25–6, 2012, 23). Moreover, credible evidence of industrial espionage by foreign governments seeking access to critical US technology was found in each year since reporting began in 2008 (see US DOT 2008, 2009, 2010, 2011, 2012, 2013, 2015, 2016a; US NCIX 2006).[3]

While the unclassified versions of these reports do not specify *which* foreign governments or companies are suspected of such activities, many countries have, for example, shown concern over certain types of foreign investment from some Chinese companies. These concerns are not surprising given stated Chinese policy, which makes no secret of a government-led industrial strategy that involves using foreign investment to the state's advantage. Within the wider context of its "going out" strategy,[4] the Chinese government openly encourages outward foreign investment that might help it "mitigate the domestic shortage of natural resources" or gain access to "internationally advanced technologies" (UNCTAD 2006, 210). More to the point, such investments are often state-directed or coordinated by companies that, if they are not state-owned, frequently have government-appointed or affiliated executives (Salidjanova 2011, 4). China also often supports these investments by offering incentives to companies that make them, or by providing cash and credit from state banks, SOEs, and SWFs to help finance these deals (Lenihan 2014, 242–5; UNCTAD 2006, 210).

As discussed throughout this book, countries like the US, Australia, Canada, and Germany have therefore blocked or mitigated those Chinese investments that appear to pose a risk to national security, balancing against specific targeted threats to relative power. Concerns have been raised over investments made by two Chinese telecoms firms in particular, Huawei and ZTE, because of their suspected links to the Chinese government, history of attempted purchases of sensitive companies, and lack of transparency (US House 2012). A 2012 investigative report to the US House Intelligence Committee determined, for example, that the US "must block" foreign investment involving these companies because of the "threat" they pose "to US national security interests," and that the US "should view with suspicion the continued penetration of [its] telecommunications market by Chinese telecommunications companies" (US House 2012, vi). Similarly, a 2013 report by the Chair of the UK Parliament's Intelligence and Security Committee (ISC) raised national security concerns over the involvement of Huawei in that country's critical telecommunications infrastructure (ISC 2013). Beyond these specific companies, the national security risks raised by other proposed Chinese investments have ranged from the proximity of potential acquisitions to sensitive military installations, to the information, technology, or resources possessed by the target companies involved. For instance, in October 2016, the German government withdrew its initial approval for the takeover of the German chipmaker Aixtron by the Fujian Grand Chip Investment Fund because Aixtron "owns technologies relevant to national security" and Grand Chip's consortium of investors included those with suspected ties to the Chinese government (Chazan & Wagstyl 2016). As discussed in the Introduction, President Obama notably vetoed Grand Chip's proposed acquisition of the US business of Aixtron by Grand Chip just two months later, in December 2016, over similar national security concerns (see Obama 2016; US DOT 2016b). And less than a year later, President Trump vetoed the purchase of Lattice Semiconductor by an acquirer determined to be supported and funded by the Chinese government, on comparable grounds (see US DOT 2017). In late 2016, it was reported that Germany is considering strengthening its own legal and regulatory regime for the review of foreign investment affecting national security, and is also "pushing for new EU rules that would allow member states to protect companies working in strategic sectors from Chinese approaches, especially when the acquirers are linked to the Chinese state" (Chazan & Wagstyl 2016). Similarly, the UK revealed in 2016 that it is considering changing its system for screening and assessing foreign investment following a national debate over the national security implications of Chinese investment in the UK's Hinkley Point C nuclear power project, even though that investment was eventually approved.[5]

All of this should be understood within a wider context, in which the global distribution of economic power is undergoing a fundamental shift. The US has had the largest economy of any *single* country in the world – by a wide margin – since the end of the Cold War (as measured by GDP in current USD), being roughly similar in size to that of Europe.[6] But there has been a dramatic shift in the fortunes of the developing world, and especially of the BRIC countries of Brazil, Russia, India, and China, in the 21st century. While the global financial crisis and the collapse in commodity prices dampened the growth trajectory of many of the BRICs, and Russia's growth has faced the additional drag of the economic sanctions imposed on it in 2014, China remains on course to displace the US as the world's biggest economy by 2050.[7] Though China faces its own internal economic challenges,[8] and GDP is only one very basic measure of economic power,[9] it is nevertheless a powerful indicator of China's potential rise in relative economic power vis-à-vis the US, Europe, and Russia. At the same time, China's increasing activity in the South China Sea in the 2010s, and Russia's engagement in Ukraine and

Syria in the same period, show a willingness by these countries to test boundaries in the military sphere. Though long-term changes in military power are harder to predict, it will be difficult (without groundbreaking innovation or technological change in the West) for the US and Europe to maintain the positions of economic power they currently enjoy given (among other factors) the maturity of their economies and the demographics of their populations.

The looming possibility of systemic change implied by these trends only intensifies the need to understand the types of competition and balancing discussed in this book. For, as the US is faced with the possible loss of its primacy, the world may be moving toward a system that is truly multipolar. This work began from the premise, after Nye, that the system was unipolar in the military realm and multipolar in the economic one. But it is quite possible to envision that we are on the cusp of systemic change – and that the system will be multipolar in both realms in the not too distant future. This change should *not* affect the theory of non-military balancing posited here, which was designed to hold regardless of the polarity of the international system. Such a scenario may, however, lead to an increase in the type of competition and balancing examined in this study. Thus, recognizing the importance of the economic component of power, the tools of non-military balancing available to states, and when and why such balancing might occur only becomes more important.

Resurgent Economic Nationalism and Non-Military Internal Balancing

The mid-2010s saw a rise in nationalism in a number of advanced industrial and industrializing states. To name but a few, these have included Japan, Russia, India, and China in the East, and the US, UK, France, and Hungary in the West. Many of the nationalist movements in these countries have been linked to a resurgent economic nationalism, often in combination with one of the many variants of populism.[10] Foreign and economic policy in China under President Xi Jinping, for example, has focused on "realizing the great rejuvenation of the Chinese nation" (Wang 2016). In Japan, Prime Minister Shinzo Abe's economic program, often referred to as Abenomics, has been likened to "economic populism" (see Stewart & Wasserstrom 2016). In the US, the election of President Trump marked a victory for a populist movement notable for its emphasis on nativism, as well as anti-free trade and anti-globalization sentiments. The UK's decision to leave the EU, though the result of an array of political factors, was partially attributable to anti-immigration sentiment and growing feelings of economic nationalism within Great Britain. Nationalist and populist movements in France, Germany, Hungary, and the Netherlands evidence similar themes. It is unclear the degree of success these movements will ultimately achieve, or how long they will last, but it is clear that they will have an impact on geopolitics, and that the rise in economic nationalism associated with them will have an impact on non-military internal balancing.

The theory presented in this book suggests that when a particular merger or acquisition is recognized to pose a legitimate potential national security risk, a higher level of economic nationalism in the target state contributes to a greater likelihood that it will intervene in that particular transaction under certain circumstances. Cumulatively, higher levels of economic nationalism within the international system could therefore trigger a higher level of, albeit legitimate, intervention into cross-border M&A globally. In particular, we might expect states to intervene in foreign takeovers that originate from within their own security communities to a greater extent than we might otherwise expect without the heightened presence of economic nationalism. This is a situation for which both the public and the private sectors may need to prepare, but which will not necessarily lead to a chilling economic or political effect on the international system.

The danger would be if economic nationalism spills over, under populist leadership and amidst nationalist fervor, to lead states to *abuse* or *misuse* this tool of non-military internal balancing. In such a scenario, it is possible to envisage a state blocking or vetoing a transaction on national security grounds when the national security risks involved could have, instead, been mitigated by simply modifying the transaction. In other words: in such a scenario, it is possible to imagine states overbalancing by employing *unbounded* balancing where *bounded* balancing would have sufficed. Worse still would be a state intervening in a foreign takeover when there are no justifiable national security concerns present, but still citing national security as the reason for intervention. Both actions would be examples of overbalancing and miscalculation that could result in costly economic, political, and diplomatic outcomes for the states involved, or for the international system as a whole, if such behavior were to become widespread.

The systemic effects of such behavior could be magnified if it were to originate in the US, the leader of the liberal economic order from its inception at Bretton Woods, or the EU, which has thus far been a staunch ally and supporter of that order. This is not to say that the liberal economic order would not survive – the order is highly institutionalized and durable, and therefore likely to survive this and other challenges (see

Ikenberry 2001; Nye 2016). Such behavior on the part of the leaders of the liberal economic order could, however, be enough to stay or slow the pace of globalization that we might have otherwise expected to see under its umbrella.

Globalization and Government Intervention into Foreign Takeovers

It is vital to realize the impact that this tool of non-military internal balancing could potentially have on the forward progress of globalization if it is misused. Cross-border M&A has become one of the main engines of globalization, and that position should not necessarily be threatened when non-military internal balancing of the type studied here is used appropriately. Yet, unnecessary or *overbalancing*, of the type witnessed in the DPW/P&O case, can carry a heavy cost for the states involved, and if the mistake is repeated by a widespread number of states, the impact can be systemic.

The misapplication of this intervention tool in an *individual* case means that the goals of non-military internal balancing will not be met, and, therefore, that it could potentially lead to a strain on the economic, or worse the diplomatic, relationship between the countries involved. For, such action is likely to be viewed as either antagonistic or unnecessarily protectionist. If a country gets a reputation for such behavior, it will unintentionally ward off future deals and other forms of foreign investment – including those investments the state might desperately need. Such actions could lead to potentially lower levels of M&A more generally for that country, or for that particular industry – because, if the potential cost of a transaction is seen as insurmountable or unprofitable, it will not be attempted in the first place.

The *widespread* misuse or abuse of state intervention into foreign takeovers could also have a potentially negative impact on cross-border M&A activity globally. Repeated politicization of foreign takeovers could, for example, contribute to a backlash against globalization more broadly. In conjunction with (or as a result of) already heightened anti-globalization sentiment in a number of states worldwide, this could lead to a deceleration of economic integration and interdependence, with all of the attendant negative economic effects and foregone gains of trade and investment that would entail.

Economic Crisis and Non-Military Internal Balancing

In times of economic crisis, the issue of the correctly calculated use of non-military internal balancing is even more acute, because the potential costs of miscalculation are magnified. The failure to strike a balance between an open system of foreign investment and non-military internal balancing could certainly result in unforeseen consequences. As already discussed, depending on the states involved, and the degree and intensity of the problems triggered, overbalancing could contribute to a slow-down in cross-border M&A levels globally, impacting on globalization and, potentially, the growth of the countries involved.[11]

The issues examined in this work are of particular concern in light of the current economic climate, where the stability of the international economy already faces a number of challenges. The sudden and severe contraction in the credit market in 2008 meant that many states needed to nationalize failing banks and bail out foundering companies in order to stabilize their economies. Combined with potential deflation, the situation raised the possibility of currency crises in Europe and Asia. The general lack of ready financing and capital within the system during the crisis also had an unmistakable impact on cross-border M&A, whose numbers severely declined at its onset, and are only just beginning to approach pre-crisis levels. In fact, "global merger volume dropped by almost a third in 2008, ending five years of deal growth" (Hall 2008). By 2015, cross-border M&A globally had still not recovered to the record highs of the pre-crisis period, reaching only 70% of the value and 83% of the volume of 2007 levels. In such a situation, states need to be careful not to misuse the tool of intervention in a manner that would impact the international economy by shrinking M&A values and volumes even further.

It is important to understand that lower global levels of cross-border M&A will not change the *role* that unbounded, bounded, and internal intervention play as a tool of non-military internal balancing. For, it is true that there was a higher level of both intervention and M&A in the recent period of pre-crisis economic prosperity, but that correlation may correspond to the evolving nature of power and/or the fact that there were simply more opportunities for the world to take notice of such activities. Either way, it can be expected that economic competition will only intensify in future times of scarcity. As private-sector M&A activity levels off, it will be government-subsidized, owned, or controlled companies that have the cash and financing to pursue cross-border deals. Indeed, a number of SWFs provided liquidity during the recent global financial crisis by making substantial investments or taking stakes in troubled banks and financial institutions, though these were not 100% acquisitions or takeovers (see Bortolotti et al. 2009; Lenihan 2014). Thus, one should not be surprised to see an increasingly high proportion of government activity within cross-border M&A during future economic downturns, especially given increasing state involvement in the banking sector. As a result, there may even be a rise in the use of foreign takeovers to enhance state power and a corresponding increase in the use of government intervention into such actions as a form of internal balancing.[12]

Policy Implications

States that wish to strengthen the foundations of the liberal economic order must make a choice to use such tools of balancing wisely and judiciously – especially in times of financial crisis or widespread resurgent economic nationalism. The general gains from FDI are vital to a state's economic power; so, if that economic power is important to them – and it clearly is – policymakers will have to find a balance moving forward between intervention into foreign takeovers and encouragement of them. If governments find themselves, in times of either severe competition or prosperity, using the intervention tool more often, then they must do so prudently.

This may mean increasing the institutionalization of the intervention process where possible, and making it more transparent so that potential acquirers know what to expect. The US, for example, has arguably already moved toward better transparency of the intervention process. The Foreign Investment and National Security Act of 2007 (FINSA), which went into effect in October of 2007,[13] amends previous US law regulating foreign acquisitions of US assets in such a way as to further clarify not only the review process and procedures for foreign acquirers, but also the national security criteria on which transactions will be judged.[14] One of the effects of the new regulations implemented under FINSA is that they arguably make the process more user-friendly, both for the US in terms of achieving its national security goals and for the companies that seek to navigate the CFIUS process successfully (see e.g., Plotkin et al. 2009). In other words, making the review process less opaque should be good for business. Transactions will not drop in numbers because of fears that intervention will occur when *necessary*, but they will drop in the face of the inappropriate use of intervention.

Largely in response to the need to foster such good practice following the rise of intervention on national security grounds, the OECD began its Freedom of Investment process in 2006. This provides an ongoing forum for policy coordination and information exchange among over fifty governments.[15] As part of this process, in 2009 the OECD Council adopted the Guidelines for Recipient Country Investment Policies Relating to National Security. As in treaty and custom, these Guidelines recognize that "essential security concerns are self-judging" and that "each country has a right to determine what is necessary to protect its national security" (OECD 2009, 3). At the same time, they encourage and

> recommen[d] that, if governments consider or introduce investment policies... designed to safeguard national security, they should be guided by the principles of nondiscrimination, transparency of policies and predictability of outcomes, proportionality of measures and accountability of implementing authorities. (OECD 2009, 2)

As states become more open to foreign investment generally, and as the political environment and security context evolve, adopting such principles will help states to navigate the challenge of walking the tightrope between openness and safeguarding both national security and power.

Concluding Thoughts

The theory of non-military internal balancing provides valuable insights for theorists and policymakers alike. On the theoretical front, the solution to the puzzle explored in this book contributes to our understanding of the political economy of international security, and provides international relations theory with yet another take on the relationship between conflict, competition, and interdependence. For the businessman, this theory may help to show where transactions are more likely to be accepted, and where they are not. For governments, a better understanding of the type of behavior examined here should contribute to a lower level of miscalculation and misunderstanding in their relations with other states regarding these matters.

For policymakers, this book has highlighted some of the true limits of globalization. This is key, because a member of a government that wishes to promote a deepening of global economic integration will need to understand where that is possible, and where it is not. Additionally, a more complete understanding of government intervention into foreign takeovers could help policymakers to avoid an unnecessary slowdown of globalization, which would have a negative impact on the economic welfare of all states. Given the nature of the recent global economic crisis, higher global levels of (economic) nationalism, and the potential for a systemic change in the balance of power in the near future, the US and other Western states may seek to re-examine how to institutionalize their values for the future. This is not only because they may not be the dominant powers in the next system, but also because the next list of great powers is likely to include countries such as Russia and China, whose economies are not yet completely liberalized. In such a scenario, understanding the limits of the free market, as demonstrated by the theory presented here, may contribute to the West's ability to entrench liberal economic principles in the next iteration of the international economic order.

NOTES

1 For further discussion of economic conflict arising out of interdependence, or how states might use economic interdependence to their advantage, see e.g., Gilpin 1981, 1987, 2001; Hirschman 1945; Moran 1993; Shambaugh 1999; Tyson 1992; Waltz 1993, 1999.

2 For a discussion of the effect that different types of technological advances could have on the future of the international system, see NIC 2012, 83–97.

3 For example, in 2008, it was reported that "foreign government entities – including intelligence organizations and security services – have learned to capitalize on private-sector technology acquisitions" (US DOT 2008, 38). Moreover, "some governments have established quasi-official organizations, either in the United States or in their home countries, to facilitate contact with overseas scientists, engineers, and businessmen" (US DOT 2008, 38). Notably, Russia and China were cited in the Annual Report to Congress on Foreign and Industrial Espionage as "the most aggressive" in such industrial espionage efforts, accounting for "much" of this activity "since the Counterintelligence Community first began systematically tracking foreign technology collection efforts in 1997" (US NCIX 2006, iii).

4 This policy is primarily intended to "promote the international operations of capable Chinese firms" to improve both "resource allocation" and "international competitiveness" (UNCTAD 2006, 210).

5 Following a national debate over its potential national security implications, the UK government approved the Hinkley Point C Project on September 15, 2016, while at the same time announcing that it "will impose a new legal framework for future foreign investment in Britain's critical infrastructure, which will include nuclear energy and apply after Hinkley" (UK BEIS 2016). In an earlier (July 11, 2016) speech, given just before she became the UK Prime Minister, Theresa May intimated that "a proper industrial strategy wouldn't automatically stop the sale of British firms to foreign ones, but it should be capable of stepping in to defend a sector that is . . . important . . . to Britain" (May 2016). By October 14, 2016, the UK Parliament's House of Commons Library published a briefing on the UK government's emerging industrial strategy, which it noted included "stricter merger and acquisition rules, with more emphasis on a 'public-interest test' for foreign take-overs" (Rhodes 2016, 3). The Library also released a briefing paper on September 1, 2016 (while the UK government continued to review its policy on foreign takeovers), which provides a targeted history of the UK M&A regime, past UK public interest tests, movements to adopt a new public interest test, and the debate and developments surrounding this (see Seely 2016).

6 These estimates were calculated using World Bank Development Indicators data, which show that the difference between the US share (i.e., percentage)

of global GDP and the EU's remained below 10% from the end of the Cold War to 2015 (WDI 2016).

7 While many observers agree China's economy will surpass that of the US by about 2050, exact growth estimates, measures, and projections vary. For example, Wilson and Purushothaman (2003) project China's GDP, in US dollar terms, will surpass that of the US by 2041, while Hawksworth and Chan (2015) argue that, in market exchange-rate terms, it will surpass that of the US before 2030. For a discussion of the effect of economic sanctions on the Russian economy, see Feaver & Lorber 2015.

8 For a discussion of some of the internal domestic challenges faced by China, see Chapter 2 of Bergsten et al. 2006 and Mallaby 2015.

9 For a discussion of different measures of economic power beyond GDP, see e.g., Cox 2012; Nye 2011; Subramanian 2016.

10 For a discussion of the populist movements in the US, Europe, and Asia, their connection to economic factors, and their differences, see e.g., Kazin 2016; Mudde 2016; Stewart & Wasserstrom 2016; Zakaria 2016.

11 See the discussion in the Introduction, pp. 20–21, as well as Kekic & Sauvant 2006; NIC 2004, 2010, 2012.

12 For a discussion of the use of SWFs by some states to make acquisitions that enhance state power, and the potential use of non-military internal balancing by receiving states in response to these activities, see Lenihan 2014.

13 As discussed in the Introduction, FINSA amends section 721 of the Defense Production Act, and went into effect on October 24, 2007. After a period of public comment and analysis within CFIUS itself regarding the amendment requirements, the US DOT issued its final regulations on the law on November 14, 2008.

14 For a further discussion of FINSA and its implications, see e.g., Plotkin et al. 2009; US DOT 2008, as well as Chapters 1 and 3 of this book. It is also important to remember that the new FINSA regulations do not materially affect the case studies or conclusions drawn as part of this study. The primary function of FINSA is to clarify procedure and codify certain existing realities already addressed within this book (such as the addition of "critical infrastructure" as a national security concern). FINSA does not, however, materially change the CFIUS process.

15 The OECD Freedom of Investment process has already held twenty-four roundtable meetings on topics ranging from "Freedom of Investment, National Security and Strategic Industries" to "Freedom of Investment for Green Growth"; see www.oecd.org/daf/inv/investment-policy/oecdroundtablesonfreedomofinvestment.htm.

Appendix A: Alternative Independent Variables Considered

A number of domestic variables were considered when formulating the theory presented in this book, but were not included in the final hypotheses for the reasons outlined in this appendix. Indeed, throughout this project, colleagues, reviewers, and critical friends were kind enough to suggest the inclusion of a number of potential variables. The most notable among these included: the role of *electoral politics* in government intervention; the role of *racism* in government intervention; the presence of *competing bidders*; and the *ownership structure* of the acquirer. My aim was to create as parsimonious a theory as was possible on a complex subject. I therefore ultimately decided not to include variables that proved to be insignificant and/or whose inclusion as controls did not improve the explanatory power of the case studies or the fit of the statistical model.

Electoral Politics

I tested, but ultimately chose not to include, a variable on *electoral politics*. I initially considered this variable as a means of testing whether or not government interventions into foreign takeovers are correlated to the electoral calendar and/or are politicized to the advantage of politicians who are candidates in upcoming elections. Over the course of my case study research, however, I did not find electoral or partisan politics to have a significant impact on M&A interventions. This may be because in most cases it is difficult for a politician to use intervention of this type to "score electoral points" unless his or her constituents are *already* concerned about the geopolitical ramifications of the deal, or full of economic-nationalist zeal. Cases of intervention into cross-border M&A also rarely enter the public consciousness, and, even in cases of a formal veto, the general voting public is rarely brought into (or even aware of) the debate over intervention in the first place.

Let us consider the PepsiCo/Danone case, and the role played by the Franco-American clash over the Iraq War (see Chapter 3). This "clash" became a factor in government intervention as part of a wider geopolitical tension and rivalry between two allies (see Chapter 3, pp. 104–5). While intervention may have resonated in terms of electoral politics, the actions of the French government, even with its excellent "soundbites" on the issue, were more widely reported in the *Financial Times* and other financial outlets, such as Bloomberg, than in the French popular press. It would be difficult to determine what effect intervention had on a later election, or whether that played a role in the calculus of those involved in the French government – though I think it highly unlikely as a sole motivation, based on those I interviewed. Rather, the desire to balance US power in this instance was a genuine, albeit secondary, motivator of intervention, as was the healthy dose of economic nationalism that was the primary motivator of intervention at the time. Both of these factors may have been politically useful to some politicians, but I did not identify disingenuous instrumental advocacy of intervention for the purposes of electoral politics in this case. Even were that to be the case, it would be difficult for politicians to use intervention to their electoral benefit without the pre-existing condition of wider geopolitical concern or economic nationalism.

Indeed, the only case study where I found electoral politics to be of any real import was in the DPW case (see Chapter 4), where a handful of senators seemed to be raising the issue as part of an electoral strategy, aware that it would resonate with existing economic nationalist feeling within their particular constituencies. (Importantly, this was *not* true of all of the senators or of the other government stakeholders who came out against the deal). What the behavior of these few senators did contribute to, however, was the type of politicization that I argue makes this an outlier case. From my research, and based on those I interviewed, it became clear that this was historically the only extant case of M&A intervention to become this heavily politicized, making its dynamics unique. As discussed in Chapter 4 (pp. 164–6 and 172–86), this had negative consequences strategically (and politically) for the US, because it led to a strategic overreaction and, thus, overbalancing. I would have considered including levels of *politicization* of an individual transaction as a control variable if the frequency of such an occurrence were greater, but at this stage it does not appear generally significant across the history of government intervention into cross-border M&A, or across countries.

Racism

I also considered including *racism* as an explanatory variable. In my research, however, I came across only rare and isolated incidences of racist comments by individuals (see e.g., Chapter 3, p. 130 and Chapter 4, p. 175), and the individuals making these comments did not, themselves, seem to affect the nature or status of government action or intervention. Rather, greater scrutiny of the foreign investments emanating from particular countries seems to result from perceptions that they might be "threatening" to national security because of a recent rise in those countries' relative power, combined with noticeable increases in the influx of FDI coming from them (see e.g., the discussion in the Introduction, pp. 7 and in Chapter 1; Graham & Marchick 2006; Meunier 2012; Tyson 1992). This is, however, different from racism, which though it may very well underlie threat perception in *some* outlier cases (see e.g., Chapter 4, p. 182), was not a consistent feature in the general debates over intervention and threat perception during the time period examined in this book.

Competing Bidders and Ownership Structure

Additional alternative explanations include the existence of a *competing bidder* (domestic or foreign) and the *ownership structure of the acquirer.* While I did not have the resources to include competing bidders as a variable in the statistical dataset, I do discuss their role in the case studies. In terms of direct government intervention on national security grounds, however, the only place where competing bidders realistically entered the equation were as interest groups lobbying against a particular acquirer, which is already accounted for in the control variable of *interest group presence*. Inclusion as an independent variable would, thus, run the risk of double-counting the effect of competing bidders on intervention.

Before finalizing my theory, I also tested the dataset and case studies for the impact of the *ownership structure* of the acquirer, and did not find it to be a significant variable, or to improve the fit of the model. There are a number of reasons for this, the most notable of which is that the ownership structure of a company alone may not necessarily account for the level of influence a foreign government actually has (or is perceived to have) over that company at a given point in time. The Chinese company Huawei, for example, is not a SOE, but is largely perceived to be heavily influenced by the Chinese government, especially in terms of its foreign acquisition strategy (US House 2012). Ultimate ownership of a company can also be difficult to fully discern from the outside, as it can easily be hidden through the use of shells, holding companies, and other means. As discussed in the case studies, ownership structure of the acquirer *is* an important factor. But it is also one that I believe is already accounted for in the independent variable examining *geopolitical competition* in each deal, and that is taken into account in the discussion of the specific national security concerns raised in each transaction (which can include state ownership of the acquirer). Having *ownership structure* as a separate variable could thus, again, potentially lead to double counting. To the extent possible, I did do some alternative tests for the impact of some ownership structures, such as SWFs, that might be seen as more likely to lead to interventions. But, again, this did not turn out to be statistically significant as an explanatory or control variable, and seemed to be overshadowed (and encompassed) by the variable of geopolitical competition in the case studies for each transaction in question. This may be because different SWFs have different agendas and remits, and the SWF (and state behind it) that is of geopolitical concern to one country may not be of concern to another. As discussed in Chapter 6, however, the one ownership structure that I think might be correlated to lower levels of intervention is that of institutional investors. Though testing the variables raised in Chapter 6 is beyond the remit of this particular book, it could potentially provide a further depth of understanding on this overall topic.

Appendix B: Descriptive Statistics of Variables in MNLMs I–IV

Figure 35 Descriptive statistics of variables in MNLM I

Independent Variable		Average Change	0	1	2	3
Security Community	*0→1*	0.09112	0.16672	−0.06863	0.01552	−0.11361
Relative Military Power	*Min.→Max.*	0.23133	−0.26748	−0.06653	−0.12864	0.46266
	+/−1/2	0.00373	0.00502	0.00115	−0.00747	0.00129
	+/− s.d./2	0.06995	0.09528	0.02194	−0.13989	0.02268
	Marginal Effect	0.00373	0.00502	0.00115	−0.00747	0.00129
Resource Dependency	*Min.→Max.*	0.21416	−0.42832	0.13471	0.25855	0.25855
	+/− 1/2	0.10910	−0.21819	0.09054	0.10371	0.02394
	+/− s.d./2	0.03746	−0.07492	0.03195	0.03451	0.00846
	Marginal Effect	0.10954	−0.21907	0.09377	0.10048	0.02482
Nationalism	*Min.→Max.*	0.14197	−0.19701	0.16722	0.11671	−0.08693
	+/− 1/2	0.24762	−0.33287	0.27597	0.21927	−0.16237
	+/− s.d./2	0.04854	−0.07087	0.05784	0.03923	−0.02620
	Marginal Effect	0.25897	−0.37918	0.30942	0.20852	−0.13876
Pro-Globalization Sentiment	*Min.→Max.*	0.28770	0.41447	0.15956	0.00138	−0.57540
	+/− 1/2	0.02696	0.02992	0.02401	−0.00825	−0.04568
	+/− s.d./2	0.02742	0.03044	0.02440	−0.00837	−0.04647
	Marginal Effect	0.02636	0.02888	0.02385	−0.00842	−0.04431
Economic Competitiveness	*Min.→Max.*	0.09046	−0.11453	−0.06640	0.00145	0.17947
	+/− 1/2	0.01765	−0.02019	−0.01512	0.00145	0.03385
	+/− s.d./2	0.01507	−0.01720	−0.01294	0.00126	0.02888
	Marginal Effect	0.01739	−0.01974	−0.01504	0.00151	0.03327
Inward Foreign Direct Investment	*Min.→Max.*	0.11714	−0.05466	0.12120	−0.17962	0.11308
	+/− 1/2	0.00062	−0.00043	0.00068	−0.00082	0.00057
	+/− s.d./2	0.03320	−0.02253	0.03584	−0.04387	0.03056
	Marginal Effect	0.00062	−0.00043	0.00068	−0.00082	0.00057
Interest Group Position	*Min.→Max.*	0.07062	0.01497	0.12627	−0.12145	−0.01979
	+/− 1/2	0.01774	−0.00073	0.03549	−0.02911	−0.00565
	+/− s.d./2	0.01558	−0.00065	0.03116	−0.02554	−0.00497
	Marginal Effect	0.01774	−0.00081	0.03549	−0.02901	−0.00567
Pr(y|x)			0.70996	0.16820	0.07593	0.04591

	Security Community	Relative Military Power	Resource Dependency	Nationalism	Pro-Globalization Sentiment	Economic Competitiveness	Inward FDI	Interest Group Position
x=	0.74877	5.51068	0.60780	0.49742	5.88792	4.84877	77.77100	6.73209
sd(x)=	0.43479	17.37460	0.34215	0.18765	1.01634	0.85710	53.23630	0.87822

Figure 36 Descriptive statistics of variables in MNLM II

Independent Variable		Average Change	0	1	2	3
Relative Military Power	*Min.→Max.*	0.08911	0.17821	−0.02880	−0.14799	−0.00143
	+/− 1/2	0.00449	0.00786	0.00108	−0.00897	0.00004
	+/− s.d./2	0.09847	0.17050	0.02546	−0.19695	0.00099
	Marginal Effect	0.00448	0.00785	0.00107	−0.00897	0.00004
Resource Dependency	*Min.→Max.*	0.25547	−0.49141	−0.01954	0.44398	0.06697
	+/− 1/2	0.09469	−0.18939	0.02297	0.14820	0.01822
	+/− s.d./2	0.03127	−0.06253	0.00978	0.04723	0.00552
	Marginal Effect	0.08794	−0.17589	0.02849	0.13208	0.01531
Nationalism	*Min.→Max.*	0.10227	−0.19198	0.11596	0.08858	−0.01256
	+/− 1/2	0.18518	−0.34529	0.19624	0.17412	−0.02508
	+/− s.d./2	0.03502	−0.06637	0.04018	0.02987	−0.00367
	Marginal Effect	0.18386	−0.34863	0.21159	0.15614	−0.01910
Pro-Globalization Sentiment	*Min.→Max.*	0.36010	0.60135	0.11742	0.00142	−0.72019
	+/− 1/2	0.01329	0.02258	0.00400	−0.01351	−0.01307
	+/− s.d./2	0.01385	0.02353	0.00417	−0.01401	−0.01369
	Marginal Effect	0.01254	0.02134	0.00375	−0.01364	−0.01145
Economic Competitiveness	*Min.→Max.*	0.08383	0.10326	−0.12758	−0.04009	0.06441
	+/− 1/2	0.02059	0.03340	−0.03136	−0.00983	0.00779
	+/− s.d./2	0.01757	0.02858	−0.02675	−0.00839	0.00655
	Marginal Effect	0.02057	0.03376	−0.03132	−0.00982	0.00738
Inward Foreign Direct Investment	*Min.→Max.*	0.10046	0.20092	−0.04167	−0.12764	−0.03161
	+/− 1/2	0.00059	0.00118	−0.00029	−0.00076	−0.00014
	+/− s.d./2	0.03069	0.06139	−0.01449	−0.03933	−0.00757
	Marginal Effect	0.00059	0.00118	−0.00029	−0.00076	−0.00014
Interest Group Position	*Min.→Max.*	0.19701	−0.29097	0.39364	−0.10304	0.00037
	+/− 1/2	0.05846	−0.09037	0.11682	−0.02656	0.00011
	+/− s.d./2	0.04971	−0.07679	0.09932	−0.02262	0.00009
	Marginal Effect	0.05809	−0.08963	0.11606	−0.02656	0.00012
Pr(y|x)			0.77787	0.15374	0.06215	0.00625

	Relative Military Power	Resource Dependency	Nationalism	Pro-Globalization Sentiment	Economic Competi-tiveness	Inward FDI	Interest Group Position
x=	6.26355	0.64045	0.49901	5.81662	4.90296	76.45350	6.73955
sd(x)=	18.28520	0.35198	0.19037	1.03735	0.85326	51.37000	0.85166

Figure 37 Descriptive statistics of variables in MNLM III

Independent Variable		Average Change	0	1	2	3
Relative Military Power	*Min.→Max.*	0.47126	−0.77529	−0.05137	−0.11587	0.94253
	+/− 1/2	0.00994	0.01143	−0.00614	−0.01373	0.00845
	+/− s.d./2	0.21897	0.31222	−0.11533	−0.32261	0.12572
	Marginal Effect	0.00990	0.01136	−0.00613	−0.01367	0.00844
Nationalism	*Min.→Max.*	0.22795	−0.45591	0.33595	0.10897	0.01098
	+/− 1/2	0.48887	−0.94099	0.94437	0.03336	−0.03675
	+/− s.d./2	0.06438	−0.12876	0.06902	0.04839	0.01135
	Marginal Effect	0.31879	−0.63758	0.30040	0.26355	0.07363
Pro-Globalization Sentiment	*Min.→Max.*	0.18695	−0.37391	0.22093	0.09266	0.06032
	+/− 1/2	0.04427	−0.08854	0.03934	0.02949	0.01971
	+/− s.d./2	0.04088	−0.08175	0.03601	0.02736	0.01838
	Marginal Effect	0.04255	−0.08510	0.03539	0.02937	0.02034
Economic Competitiveness	*Min.→Max.*	0.06814	−0.12960	0.00236	−0.00668	0.13393
	+/− 1/2	0.01770	−0.03365	0.00074	−0.00175	0.03466
	+/− s.d./2	0.01514	−0.02879	0.00064	−0.00150	0.02965
	Marginal Effect	0.01762	−0.03350	0.00075	−0.00175	0.03450
Inward Foreign Direct Investment	*Min.→Max.*	0.40968	−0.74522	0.45621	−0.07415	0.36316
	+/− 1/2	0.00191	−0.00343	0.00108	−0.00039	0.00274
	+/− s.d./2	0.12554	−0.22773	0.08291	−0.02334	0.16816
	Marginal Effect	0.00191	−0.00343	0.00108	−0.00039	0.00274
Interest Group Position	*Min.→Max.*	0.49825	0.96866	−0.99650	0.01125	0.01659
	+/− 1/2	0.15071	0.30143	−0.20371	−0.02469	−0.07303
	+/− s.d./2	0.14223	0.28446	−0.18840	−0.02437	−0.07169
	Marginal Effect	0.11195	0.22390	−0.10172	−0.03229	−0.08989
Pr(y|x)			0.85855	0.02041	0.03871	0.08233

	Relative Military Power	Nationalism	Pro-Globalization Sentiment	Economic Competitiveness	Inward FDI	Interest Group Position
x=	3.26682	0.49271	6.10042	4.68725	81.69770	6.70988
sd(x)=	14.24750	0.18105	0.92834	0.85651	58.81650	0.96164

Figure 38 Descriptive statistics of variables in MNLM IV

Independent Variable		Average Change	0	1	2
Intervention Type	*Min.→Max.*	0.49975	−0.74962	0.44900	0.30063
	+/− 1/2	0.37102	−0.55653	0.26882	0.28771
	+/− s.d./2	0.36460	−0.54690	0.26414	0.28276
	Marginal Effect	0.41042	−0.61563	0.29701	0.31862
Pr(y|x)			0.32086	0.28953	0.38961

	Intervention Type
x=	0.65550
sd(x)=	0.97861

Appendix C: MNLM III and Resource Dependency

For those cases in which security community = 0, the descriptive statistics for resource dependency are as follows:

Figure 39 Descriptive statistics of the resource dependency variable in MNLM III

	Descriptive Statistics				
	N	Minimum	Maximum	Mean	Std. Deviation
Resource Dependency	51	.14	1.82	.5105	.29308
Valid N (listwise)	51				

		Resource Dependency			
		Frequency	Percent	Valid Percent	Cumulative Percent
Valid	.14	3	5.9	5.9	5.9
	.19	1	2.0	2.0	7.8
	.20	1	2.0	2.0	9.8
	.21	3	5.9	5.9	15.7
	.22	1	2.0	2.0	17.6
	.31	2	3.9	3.9	21.6
	.33	1	2.0	2.0	23.5
	.35	1	2.0	2.0	25.5
	.36	3	5.9	5.9	31.4
	.38	3	5.9	5.9	37.3
	.39	7	13.7	13.7	51.0
	.55	2	3.9	3.9	54.9
	.59	8	15.7	15.7	70.6
	.59	1	2.0	2.0	72.5
	.60	2	3.9	3.9	76.5
	.61	2	3.9	3.9	80.4
	.62	1	2.0	2.0	82.4

Figure 39 ***(cont.)***

	Resource Dependency			
	Frequency	Percent	Valid Percent	Cumulative Percent
.63	2	3.9	3.9	86.3
.76	2	3.9	3.9	90.2
1.00	1	2.0	2.0	92.2
1.01	1	2.0	2.0	94.1
1.03	1	2.0	2.0	96.1
1.03	1	2.0	2.0	98.0
1.82	1	2.0	2.0	100.0
Total	51	100.0	100.0	

For those cases in which security community = 0 and the dependent variable = 3, however, the descriptive statistics change dramatically:

Figure 40 Descriptive statistics of the resource dependency variable in MNLM III, when the outcome is unbounded intervention

	Descriptive Statistics				
	N	Minimum	Maximum	Mean	Std. Deviation
Resource Dependency	6	.14	.60	.4652	.17938
Valid N (listwise)	6				

		Resource Dependency			
		Frequency	Percent	Valid Percent	Cumulative Percent
Valid	.14	1	16.7	16.7	16.7
	.36	1	16.7	16.7	33.3
	.55	2	33.3	33.3	66.7
	.59	1	16.7	16.7	83.3
	.60	1	16.7	16.7	100.0
	Total	6	100.0	100.0	

Appendix D: Descriptive Statistics of Dataset Variables: Frequencies

Figure 41 Descriptive statistics of dataset variables: frequencies

Statistics									
		Intervention Type	Security Community	Relative Military Power	Resource Dependency	Nationalism	Pro-Globalization Sentiment	Economic Competitiveness	Inward Foreign Direct Investment
N	Valid	209	209	209	209	209	209	209	203
	Missing	0	0	0	0	0	0	0	6
Mean		.66	.76	7.45	.62	.49	5.89	4.88	77.77
Std. Deviation		.98	.43	22.96	.35	.19	1.01	.87	53.24
Variance		.96	.19	527.15	.12	.04	1.02	.75	2834.11
Minimum		.00	.00	.00	.10	.20	2.54	2.91	−25.03
Maximum		3.00	1.00	158.86	1.83	.76	7.97	6.94	164.53
Percentiles	25	.00	1.00	.08	.38	.37	5.28	4.17	31.96
	50	.00	1.00	.47	.59	.47	6.25	5.01	70.69
	75	1.00	1.00	4.78	.72	.71	6.58	5.52	99.44

Appendix E: Bivariate Correlations of Dataset Variables

Figure 42 Bivariate correlations of dataset variables

	Statistics								
		Security Community	Relative Military Power	Resource Dependency	Nationalism	Pro-Globalization Sentiment	Economic Competitiveness	Inward Foreign Direct Investment	Interest Group Position
Security Community	Pearson Correlation	1	.104	.182**	−.002	−.117	.126	−.043	.024
	Sig. (2-tailed)		.135	.008	.973	.092	.070	.544	.732
	N	209	209	209	209	209	209	203	209
Relative Military Power	Pearson Correlation	.104	1	.370**	−.285**	.084	.125	−.244**	.086
	Sig. (2-tailed)	.135		.000	.000	.226	.071	.000	.214
	N	209	209	209	209	209	209	203	209
Resource Dependency	Pearson Correlation	.182**	.370**	1	−.529**	−.058	−.153*	−.374**	−.039
	Sig. (2-tailed)	.008	.000		.000	.401	.027	.000	.574
	N	209	209	209	209	209	209	203	209
Nationalism	Pearson Correlation	−.002	−.285**	−.529**	1	.364**	.486**	.389**	.329**
	Sig. (2-tailed)	.973	.000	.000		.000	.000	.000	.000
	N	209	209	209	209	209	209	203	209
Pro-Globalization Sentiment	Pearson Correlation	−.117	.084	−.058	.364**	1	.625**	.369**	.801**
	Sig. (2-tailed)	.092	.226	.401	.000		.000	.000	.000
	N	209	209	209	209	209	209	203	209
Economic Competitiveness	Pearson Correlation	.126	.125	−.153*	.486**	.625**	1	.065	.670**
	Sig. (2-tailed)	.070	.071	.027	.000	.000		.357	.000
	N	209	209	209	209	209	209	203	209
Inward Foreign Direct Investment	Pearson Correlation	−.043	−.244**	−.374**	.389**	.369**	.065	1	.385**
	Sig. (2-tailed)	.544	.000	.000	.000	.000	.357		.000
	N	203	203	203	203	203	203	203	203
Interest Group Position	Pearson Correlation	.024	.086	−.039	.329**	.801**	.670**	.385**	1
	Sig. (2-tailed)	.732	.214	.574	.000	.000	.000	.000	
	N	209	209	209	209	209	209	203	209

** *Correlation is significant at the 0.01 level (2-tailed).*
* *Correlation is significant at the 0.05 level (2-tailed).*

Appendix F: Negative Case Selection

In Chapter 6, four negative cases were chosen for study on the basis of insights from Mahoney and Goertz's "Possibility Principle" (see Mahoney & Goertz 2004; Skocpol 1984). These scholars' approaches needed to be slightly adapted, because of the probabilistic nature of this study's hypotheses and the use of continuous independent variables.

First, Mahoney and Goertz's Possibility Principle offers some "ideal" guidelines for case selection, but these are not always practical or practicable for all forms of inquiry. The Possibility Principle posits that "only cases where the outcome of interest is possible should be included in the set of negative cases; cases where the outcome is impossible should be relegated to a set of uninformative and hence irrelevant observations" (Mahoney & Goertz 2004, 653). Yet, this methodology is most useful for those using typological theory or Boolean algebra, rather than the type of probabilistic theory employed in this study (Mahoney & Goertz 2004, 654).

Furthermore, their approach is ideal for research that primarily employs dichotomous variables, which this work does not – and their method for selecting "relevant cases" on the basis of continuous variables is problematic. They argue that "the analyst" should examine the range of each independent variable from the minimum to the maximum, and for each variable "must [then] decide and justify the exact threshold or cutoff point at which the outcome is considered possible" (Mahoney & Goertz 2004, 659). "In practice," they claim,

> one often sets this threshold at a fairly high level (e.g., >.50 [assuming a variable that is continuous from 0 to 1]) to ensure that at least one variable is clearly present in all cases. Under some circumstances, however, the analyst may be better served by intentionally setting the threshold at a lower level. This is especially true if the analyst has good reason to believe that the higher threshold will exclude too many cases as irrelevant (Mahoney & Goertz 2004, 659)

In other words, the application of the principle to continuous variables requires that the author make a subjective choice about the level at which each variable can be considered to have reached a threshold beyond which the hypothesized outcome will be affected. Such subjective choices are always open to counterargument, and are even more difficult to make when more than one outcome must be taken into consideration. This author set the threshold first at the median value of each independent variable (because the variables used in this dataset do not all have a 0–1 range, this was considered the closest approximation to the ">.50" advised level), and then again at the average value of each. Each threshold is high, but still only a negligible number of cases could be dismissed as "irrelevant" in this manner. This is likely because the population of cases has already been well defined by sector and size. Setting the threshold any higher would unnecessarily exclude cases as "irrelevant" that might not be.

Furthermore, Mahoney and Goertz argue that irrelevant cases should be extracted from the sample of cases studied, primarily because their inclusion increases the potential that the true significance of the relationship between the variables will be hidden, or deflated (Mahoney & Goertz 2004, 654). Yet, if the relationship still shines through with a certain degree of clarity, this is not necessarily as great a problem as if the relationship were inflated. In other words, "irrelevant" cases might make the researcher's job harder, but this certainly doesn't detract from any significant relationships between the dependent and independent variables that are found. It only implies that those relationships might be even stronger than they appear. Finally, by asking the researcher to make subjective decisions that affect the "relevant"/"irrelevant" divide within a case universe, Mahoney and Goertz's approach may actually hide some vital and interesting observations that can be drawn from a population of "negative" cases. Populations that haven't been parsed in such a manner may offer valuable insights both for a particular hypothesis, and for the building of the greater theory surrounding it.

What is important, however, is the basic argument on the part of Mahoney and Goertz that negative cases should be selected on the basis that they exhibit similar values on the independent variables to "positive cases," and that the positive outcome was therefore "possible" in these cases (see Mahoney & Goertz 2004, 653–4). Thus, having excluded the "irrelevant" using possibility principle, the key is to make a determination concerning which cases within the population are most relevant. As the approach taken within this study is a probabilistic one, the threshold values set earlier can be used in conjunction with qualitative data on the variables to show which cases were most likely to have had a positive outcome (i.e., which had the highest presence of economic nationalism and/or geopolitical competition concerns). A random sample of four was chosen from among these cases. In summary, then, each of the four cases discussed in Chapter 6 could have resulted in a positive outcome (i.e., bounded or unbounded intervention), because of the presence of a high level of economic nationalism and/or geopolitical competition, but did not, and can therefore be considered "relevant" for the purposes of hypothesis testing according to the Possibility Principle.

References

ABASAL. 2015. *Report of the Task Force on Foreign Investment Review*. American Bar Association Section of Antitrust Law, September 28. www.americanbar.org/content/dam/aba/administrative/antitrust_law/20150928_foreign_investment.authcheckdam.pdf.

Abdelsamad, O. 2006. Middle East: Ports and Politics; Sinking US-UAE Relations. *Harvard International Review* 28 (July): 12–13.

Adler, E. and M. Barnett, eds. 1998. *Security Communities*. Cambridge: Cambridge University Press.

AFP. 2005a. Asia-Pacific Economic News Summary. *Agence France Presse*, June 7.

2005b. Unocal Accepts Sweetened Chevron Bid, Snubs China's CNOOC. *Agence France Presse*, July 20.

2006a. Alcatel-Lucent Merger Said Imminent; Thales Deal Up In Air. *Agence France Presse*, March 31.

2006b. Bush Worried about Impact of Dubai Ports Withdrawal. *Agence France Presse*, March 10.

2006c. EU Clears Alcatel-Lucent Merger. *Agence France Presse*, July 24.

2006d. Labour Rights, Investments Dominate US-UAE Trade Talks. *Agence France Presse*, May 10.

AFX. 2005a. Bid for Unocal Marks China's Foray into Global Oil. *AFX International Focus*, June 23.

2005b. Bid for Unocal Marks China's Foray into Global Oil – Update 2. *AFX International Focus*, June 23.

2005c. House Panel Denounces CNOOC, Unocal Merger. *AFX International Focus*, July 13.

2005d. Florida Official Seeks Scrutiny of CNOOC/Unocal Bid. *AFX International Focus*, July 18.

2006a. Alcatel, Lucent Agree to Merge – Update. *AFX International Focus*, April 2.

2006b. Alcatel, Lucent Merger Opposed by Key US Lawmaker on Security Grounds. *AFX International Focus*, April 30.

2006c. Blair Rules Out "Back Door Protectionism" on Foreign Takeovers of UK. *AFX Asia*, February 23.

2006d. DP World Seeks Second Review of Ports Deal Amid Security Worries. *AFX Asia*, February 27.

2006e. Forex–Dollar Gets Fillip From Strong US Labor Market Data. *AFX Asia*, March 10.

2006f. Italy Gas Supplies from Russia Down 24 pct, 6 pct of Total – Eni CEO. *AFX News Limited*, January 2.

2007. China Agency Proposes Panel to Review M&As by Foreign Firms – Report. *AFX Asia*, February 4.

Ahearn, R. J. 2006. Europe: Rising Economic Nationalism? (CRS Report No. RS22468). Washington, DC: Congressional Research Service (July 6).

Aitoro, J. R. 2005. Should You Stick with IBM's PC Division? *VARBusiness*, February 21.

Al-Bawaba News. 2006. US Opposition to UAE Port Takeover Could Harm Trade Negotiations. *Al-Bawaba News*, March 7.

Alcatel. 2006a. Form 6-K: Report of Foreign Private Issuer for the Month of November 2006. Filed November 20. www.secinfo.com/d18TY3.v3Zk.htm.

2006b. Galileo Sends First Signals to Earth Based on Alcatel Alenia Space's Technology. Alcatel, press release, January 17. www.spaceref.com/news/viewpr.html?pid=18781.

Alcatel-Lucent. 2008. Bell Labs Top 10 Innovations. www.al-enterprise.com/en.

Alden, E. and S. Kirchgaessner. 2005. CNOOC Critics Received Chevron Donations. *Financial Times*, June 29.

S. Kirchgaessner, and A. Ward. 2006a. Calmer Voices Drowned Out by Rhetoric on Security Threat. *Financial Times*, February 22.

S. Kirchgaessner, and A. Ward. 2006b. Calmer Voices Drowned Out by Rhetoric on Security Threat – Experts Say Fears Over Foreign Ownership Are Greatly Exaggerated. *Financial Times*, February 23.

S. Kirchgaessner, and D. Sevastopulo. 2006c. Dubai Cedes Control of US Ports. *Financial Times*, March 9.

Amaewhule, O. 2005. CNOOC Pushes for Quick Regulatory Review of Unocal Bid as Political Pressure Mounts. *Global Insight*, July 4. www.globalinsight.com.

Ambrogi, S. 2006. No Risk to US from Arab Port Takeover-Experts. *Reuters News*, February 22.

AMF. 2005. Communiqué de Presse: AMF Statement Regarding Rumours of a Takeover Bid for Danone 2005. Autorité des Marchés Financiers. www.amf-france.org.

Asia Times. 2005. CNOOC Withdraws Its Bid for Unocal. *The Asia Times Online*, August 4.

Aslund, A. 2006. Russia's WTO Accession: Testimony at the Hearing on EU Economic and Trade Relations with Russia. *Committee on International Trade, European Parliament*, Brussels: Peterson Institute for International Economics, November 21. http://iie.com/publications/papers/paper.cfm?ResearchID=686.

Atkins, R. and D. Weinland. 2016. ChemChina Clears Hurdle in $44bn Takeover of Syngenta. *Financial Times*, August 22.

Auchard, E. 2005a. Update 3 – IBM, Lenovo Pass US Security Review of PC Deal. *Reuters News*, March 9.

2005b. Update 4 – IBM, Lenovo Pass US Security Review of PC Deal. *Reuters News*, March 9.

Auger, J. 2006. Approval Given for Dubai Firm's Takeover of British Supplier to US Military. *Global Insight Daily Analysis*, May 8. www.globalinsight.com.

and A. Marashlian. 2006. DP World Bows to Fierce Pressure from US Congress Over Ports Control. *Global Insight Daily Analysis*, March 10. www.globalinsight.com.

Australia DFAT. 2007a. Australia–China Nuclear Material Transfer Agreement and Nuclear Cooperation Agreement – Frequently Asked Questions. Australia Department of Foreign Affairs and Trade. www.dfat.gov.au/geo/china/treaties/faq.html.

2007b. People's Republic of China Country Brief – December 2007; Overview of Australia–China Relations. Australia Department of Foreign Affairs and Trade. www.dfat.gov.au.

2008. Asia–Pacific Economic Cooperation (APEC) and Australia. Australia Department of Foreign Affairs and Trade. www.dfat.gov.au/apec/.

Australian Government. 2016a. Foreign Investment Reforms Factsheet: Foreign Investment in Australia. Foreign Investment Review Board, Australian Government. http://firb.gov.au/resources/faq/.

2016b. Foreign Investment Reforms Factsheet: Legislative overview. Foreign Investment Review Board, Australian Government. http://firb.gov.au/resources/faq/.

Australian Treasurer. 2001. Foreign Investment Proposal – Shell Australia Investments Limited's (Shell) Acquisition of Woodside Petroleum Limited (Woodside). Statement by Peter Costello, Treasurer of Australia, media release, April 23.

2013. Foreign Investment Application: Archer Daniels Midland Company's Proposed Acquisition of GrainCorp Limited. Statement by the Honorable Joe Hockey, Treasurer of Australia, media release, November 29.

2015. Statement on Decision to Prevent Sale of S. Kidman & Co. Limited. Statement by the Honorable Scott Morrison MP, Treasurer of Australia, media release, November 19.

2016. Australia's Foreign Investment Policy. Treasurer of the Commonwealth of Australia, July 1. https://firb.gov.au/files/2015/09/Australias-Foreign-Investment-Policy-2016-2017.pdf.

Aviation Week. 2006. The European Commission. *Aviation Week & Space Technology* 166 (April 9): 18.

Baker, L. B., K. G. Qing, and J. Zhu. 2016. Chinese Government Money Backs Buyout Firm's Deal for U.S. Chip Maker. *Reuters*, November 28.

Barker, A. 2011. Brussels Sues Germany over VW "Golden Share." *Financial Times*, November 24.

Barnett, M. N. 1996. Identity and Alliances in the Middle East. In *The Culture of National Security; Norms and Identity in World Politics*, ed. Peter J. Katzenstein. New York: Cornell University Press.

Barton, J. and R. M. Hall. 2005. Letter to President George W. Bush Regarding the Proposed Acquisition of Unocal by CNOOC.

June 27. http://votesmart.org/public-statement/116423/barton-hall-urge-opposition-to-chinese-bid-for-unocal#.WIYd6LaLT-Z.

BBC. 2006. Ukraine "Stealing Europe's Gas." *BBC Online*, January 2. http://news.bbc.co.uk/1/hi/world/europe/4574630.stm.

Beattie, A. 2006. Request for US Ports Access Underlines Sensitivity of WTO Services Reforms. *Financial Times*, March 6.

Bennhold, K. 2006a. France Tones Down Cries of "Economic Patriotism." *International Herald Tribune*, January 6.

2006b. Suez Deal Poses Quandary for French Labor. *International Herald Tribune.*

Benoit, B. 2008. Berlin Cancels Auction of State Printing Plant. *Financial Times*, July 17.

Bergsten, C. F., B. Gill, N. R. Lardy, and D. J. Mitchell. 2006. *China: The Balance Sheet.* Center for Strategic and International Studies and the Institute for International Economics. Cambridge: Perseus Books.

Berman, J. 2006. Takeover of Port Terminal Operator Will Have Little Effect on Security. *Logistics Management*, March 1.

Betts, P. 2005. Economic Patriotism. *Financial Times*, October 3.

2009. Acciona and Enel Negotiate a Friendly Spanish Divorce. *Financial Times*, January 12.

2010. Paris Unusually Quiet in Lagardère Battle. *Financial Times*, April 26.

2011. Italian Industry Must Look Beyond Protectionism. *Financial Times*, March 24.

Bilefsky, D. 2006. EU Tells Spain to Drop Endesa Sale Conditions. *International Herald Tribune*, December 20.

Bilodeau, O. 2005. IBM Offers Concessions on Lenovo Sale to Ease Concern – Update 5. *Bloomberg*, February 24.

and S. Kennedy. 2005. IBM PC Unit Sale to Lenovo Faces Hurdle, People Say – Update 8. *Bloomberg*, January 24.

Blair, T. 2006. Remarks by Tony Blair, British Prime Minister, in an Address to Business Leaders in Dubai, Discussing Relations Between the UK and the UAE, the Middle East Peace Process, and the Fight Against Extremism. 10 Downing Street, London: Federal News Service.

Blitz, J. and S. Wagstyl. 2006. Gazprom Block over Centrica Ruled Out. *Financial Times*, April 26.

Blitzer, W., E. Henry, A. Tatton, et al. 2006a. Tour of DP World; New Moves Aimed at Keeping Ports Safe; Dubai's Economy is Booming; South Dakota Passes Strict Ban on Abortion; Advisor to Crown Prince of UAE Reacts to Ports Deal. CNN: The Situation Room. USA: Voxant, March 6.

E. Henry, J. Roberts, et al. 2006b. Searching for a Compromise in the Ports Controversy; Remembering Dana Reeve and Her Fight for Stem Cell Research; Interview with Chairman of DP World. CNN: The Situation Room. USA: Voxant, March 7.

E. Henry, D. Bash, et al. 2006c. Storm Over Ports; What is CSI?; New Terror Tape. CNN: The Situation Room. USA: Voxant, March 6.

Block, R. 2006. Chertoff Says US Ports Takeover Would Tighten Grip on Security. *The Wall Street Journal*, March 7.

Bloomberg. 2006. Beijing Dials a Wrong Number in Hong Kong. *Bloomberg*, November 30.

Blustein, P. 2005. National Security Panel Will Evaluate IBM Deal. *Newsbyte News Network, January 29.*

and M. Musgrove. 2005. US May Scrutinize IBM's China Deal. *Newsbytes News Network*, January 25.

Bodini, S. 2013. Germany Wins EU Court Battle over VW Law, Escapes Fines. *Bloomberg*, October 22.

Bohan, C. and S. Cornwell. 2006. Amid Dispute, Bush Stands by Dubai Ports Deal. *Reuters News*, February 28.

Borrus, M. and J. Zysman. 1991. *Industrial Competitiveness and American National Security*. Berkeley Roundtable on the International Economy. Berkeley, CA: University of California. http://repositories.cdlib.org/brie/BRIEWP39.

Bortolotti, B., V. Fotak, W. Megginson, and W. Maracky. (2009) Sovereign Wealth Fund Investment Patterns and Performance. Working Paper No. 22, Fondazione Eni Enrico Mattei (FEEM), 6 April.

Boston Herald. 2004. Editorial: What's in a (Brand) Name. *Boston Herald*, December 12.

Boys, P. 2005. Anticipated Acquisition by Finmeccanica Societa Per Azioni of BAE Systems PLC'S Avionics and Communications Business. A Report to the Secretary of State for Trade and Industry Pursuant to Article 4(2)–(5) of the Enterprise Act 2002 (Protection of Legitimate Interests) Order 2003, March 14. http://webarchive.nationalarchives.gov.uk/20090609003228/http://www.berr.gov.uk/files/file32731.pdf.

Brawley, M. R. 2004. The Political Economy of Balance of Power Theory. In *Balance of Power; Theory and Practice in the 21st Century*, eds. T.V. Paul, J. J. Wirtz, and M. Fortmann. Stanford, CA: Stanford University Press.

Bream, R. 2008. BHP Plan in Balance after Chinalco Strikes. *Financial Times*, February 3.

and P. Smith. 2008. Chinese Intervention Throws BHP Takeover Strategy into Disarray. *Financial Times*, February 2.

K. Burgess, L. Saigol, and G. Dyer. 2008. Dawn Raid for Rio Tinto Stuns BHP. *Financial Times*, February 1.

Brennan, L. 2006. State Loses Bid to Probe Port Deal. *New Jersey Law Journal*, March 6.

Bridis, T. 2006. Email Says Arab Firm's Subsidiary Has No Plans to Sell Florida Operation. *Associated Press Newswire*, March 13.

Brockmeier, J. 2006. Check Point Withdraws from Sourcefire Acquisition. *Linux .com*, March 24.

Brooks, S. G. and W. C. Wolforth. 2005. Hard Times for Soft Balancing. *International Security* 30 (1): 72–108.

Brothers, C. and M. Robbins. 2005. Pepsi-Danone Talk Stirs French Nationalism; PM Promises to Help Deter Any Hostile Bid From US Food Giant. *The Globe and Mail*, July 21.

Brown, J. and D. Robinson. 2016. Philips Lighting Unit Sale to Chinese Group Collapses on US Concern. *Financial Times*, January 22.

Browne, A. and J. Dean. 2010. The Big Read: Multinational Companies Sour on their Dealings with China. *The Wall Street Journal*, March 18.

Brown-Waite, Rep. V. 2006. Safe and Secure Borders Include America's Ports. February 24.

Buchanan, S. 2006. Coffee, Sugar Importers Ready for Arab-Run Port Co. *Dow Jones Commodities Service*, March 1.

Buck, T. 2006. Madrid Facing Fresh Eon Blow. *Financial Times*, November 29.

P. Hollinger, and T. Barber. 2006a. Brussels Backs GdF Golden Share Plan. *Financial Times*, September 7.

P. Hollinger, and T. Braithwaite. 2006b. Brussels Threat to Challenge French Law. *Financial Times*, January 4.

Buckley, N. and I. Gorst. 2011. Pipeline Gives Moscow the Edge in Gas Supply Balance of Power. *Financial Times*, September 6.

Bullock, T. and K. Xiao. 2005a. Bush Administration Says Review of Chinese Unocal Bid Premature. *America.gov*, July 19.

and K. Xiao. 2005b. Congress Cites Security Concerns over Chinese Bid for Unocal. *America.gov*, July 19.

Bundesdruckerei. 2009. Germany's Federal Government Buys Back Bundesdruckerei. Press Release by the German Bundesdruckerei, March 6.

Burns, R. N. 2004. NATO Remains Our Essential Alliance. *US Foreign Policy Agenda* 9 (2): 5–8.

Bush, President G. H. W. 1990. Message to the Congress on the China National Aero-Technology Import and Export Corporation Divestiture of MAMCO Manufacturing, Incorporated. White House, press release, February 2.

Business Daily. 2005. Don't Politicize Business. *Business Daily Update*, January 31.

Busvine, D. 2006. Troika Is Considering Strategic Alliances, IPO. *St. Petersburg Times/Reuters*, December 12.

Butler, G. and M. Michelson. 2006. Update 2 – Alcatel-Lucent Merger Talks Fan Thales Speculation. *Reuters News*, March 24.

Cai, J. 2016. China Issues Several Implementing Rules to Reform its Foreign Investment Administrative System. *Lexology*, Duane Morris LLP, October 14. www.lexology.com/library/detail.aspx?g=6ab9ea0b-2fd8-419f-83ab-9c0f52ccb573.

Cafritz, E. 2014. French Decree Extends List of Foreign Investments Requiring Government Approval in Strategic Business Sectors. Fried Frank Memorandum, June 11. Fried, Frank, Harris, Shriver & Jacobson LLP: London. www.friedfrank.com/index.cfm?pageID=25&itemID=6940.

Canadian Press. 2005. Biz-China-Unocal-CNOOC. Broadcast News. *The Canadian Press*, July 13.

Carlson, J., G. Goodale, M. Grant, et al. 2014. National Security Law. *The Year in Review*, 48: 471–87. American Bar Association Section of International Law. www.americanbar.org/content/dam/aba/uncategorized/international_law/nationalsecurity.authcheckdam.pdf.

Carnegy, H., M. Stothard, and E. Rigby. 2014. French "Nuclear Weapon" Against Foreign Takeovers Sparks UK Blast. *Financial Times*, May 15.

Castle, S. 2011. European Union Seeks to Remove Market Obstacles. *New York Times*, April 13.

CBS. 2006. Dubai Firm Outlines Port Sales Plan; Expects To Sell All US Port Operations To US Buyer Within Six Months. *CBS News*, March 15. www.cbsnews.com/stories/2006/03/15/politics/main1405723.shtml.

CECC. 2012. China Revises Foreign Investment Guidance Catalogue. Congressional-Executive Commission on China, April 10. www.cecc.gov/publications/commission-analysis/china-revises-foreign-investment-guidance-catalogue.

Chan, B., Z. Zhou, and B. Huang. 2015a. China Unveils Draft New Foreign Investment Law. Linklaters LLP, January 22. www.linklaters.com/Insights/AsiaNews/LinkstoChina/Pages/China-Unveils-Draft-New-Foreign-Investment-Law.aspx.

Z. Zhou, and D. Fong. 2015b. National Security Review of Foreign Investment Further Developed in China's Free Trade Zones. Linklaters, July 1. www.linklaters.com/Insights/AsiaNews/LinkstoChina/Pages/National-Security-Review-Foreign-Investment-Further-Developed-Free-Trade-Zones.aspx.

Chan, C. and J. Fellman. 2006. PCCW Bidders Thwarted by Group of Hong Kong Investors – Update 5. *Bloomberg*, July 10.

Chanda, N. 2006. US Ports in a Storm. *The Statesman*, February 28.

Chassany, A. 2006. EDF Throws Hat Into Deal Ring. *The Wall Street Journal*, February 24.

Chazan, G. and S. Wagstyl. 2016. Berlin Pushes for EU-Wide Rules to Block Chinese Takeovers. *Financial Times*, October 28.

Check Point. 2005. Check Point Software Technologies to Acquire Sourcefire. Check Point Software Technologies Ltd., press release, October 6. www.checkpoint.com/press/2005/sf100605.html.

2006a. Check Point Software Provides Update on Sourcefire Acquisition. Check Point Software Technologies Ltd., press release, February 13. www.checkpoint.com/press/2006/sourcefire021306.html.

2006b. Check Point and Sourcefire to Explore Alternative Business Relationship. Check Point Software Technologies Ltd., press release, March 23. www.checkpoint.com/press/2006/sourcefire032306.html.

Chen, S. J. 2005. CNOOC Approaches Unocal. *The Deal.Com*, January 10.

Cheng, W. G. and L. Ng. 2005. Fu Fighter From Way Back. *The Australian*, July 20.

Chickowski, E. 2006. Check Point: Delays, Political Climate to Blame for Cancelled Merger. *SC Magazine*, March 24.

Chikwanha, J. 2010. China Probes Big Three Iron Ore Firms. *The Star (South Africa)*, April 16.

Chon, G. 2014. Chinese Group Wins CFIUS Legal Case. *Financial Times*, July 16.

Christensen, T. and J. Snyder. 1990. Chain Gangs and Passed Bucks: Predicting Alliance Patterns in Multipolarity. *International Organization* 44 (2).

Chung, J. 2007a. Opaque Investors Poised to Take Reins. *Financial Times*, October 4.

2007b. A Quartet of Global Interests That Are Reshaping Trends in the Finance World. *Financial Times*, October 4.

CIA. 2005. *The World Factbook*. The Central Intelligence Agency of the United States. www.cia.gov/library/publications/the-world-factbook/.

2007. *The World Factbook*. The Central Intelligence Agency of the United States. https://www.cia.gov/library/publications/the-world-factbook/.

2008. *The World Factbook*. The Central Intelligence Agency of the United States. https://www.cia.gov/library/publications/the-world-factbook/.

Cincinnati Post. 2005. Chinese Oil Firm Makes Unocal Bid. *The Cincinnati Post*, June 23.

CMP TechWorld. 2005. Feds OK IBM-Lenovo Deal. *CMP TechWeb*, March 9.

CNOOC. 2005. CNOOC Limited to Withdraw Unocal Bid. The Chinese National Offshore Oil Company, press release, August 2. www.cnoocltd.com/en/news_info.aspx?newsid=20070620163702296.

Cohn, M. 2006. Fate of Contracts Still to be Fleshed Out. *The Baltimore Sun*, March 10.

ComputerWire. 2005. IBM–Lenovo Deal Opponents Highlight Security Concerns. *ComputerWire News*, January 25.

Condie, B. 2006. Dubai Hits Back at US Ports Bid critics. *The Evening Standard*, March 6.

Corcoran, T. 2005. L'état, ce n'est pas Pepsi, c'est la Chine. *Financial Post*, July 26.

Cornwell, S. 2006. Move to Calm Ports Storm. *New Zealand Herald*, March 11.

and J. Crawley. 2006. Dubai Flap Threatens Other Investment in US. *Reuters News*, March 2.

Cox, J. B. 2004. IBM Says Planned Sale of Computer Division Won't Affect Raleigh, NC-Area Jobs. *The News & Observer* (KRTBN), December 8.

Cox, M. 2012. Power Shifts, Economic Change and the Decline of the West? Kenneth N. Waltz Lecture. *International Relations* 26 (4): 374–5.

Crea, J. 2006. Full Disclosure; Influence; Influence. *Legal Times*, March 13.

Cronin, J. 2005. Antonio Fazio: Italy's Embattled Banker. *BBC News*, October 11. http://news.bbc.co.uk/2/hi/business/4319090.stm.

Crooks, E. 2012. Obama Blocks Chinese Wind Farm Plan. *Financial Times*, September 28.

Dagoni, R. 2006. Analysts: Check Point – Sourcefire Deal was Doomed. *Israel Business Arena*, March 27.

Daily Express. 2006. Why Do All Our Brands Fall Into Foreign Hands? *The Daily Express*, July 14.

Daily Mail. 2006a. Americans Delay a Second Dubai Deal. *The Daily Mail*, March 21.

2006b. British? Forget It! *The Daily Mail*, April 13.

Daily Star. 2006. Rice Assures UAE on Ports Deal. *Daily Star*, February 25.

Dairy Reporter. 2006. EU Warned Over Economic Nationalism. *The Dairy Reporter*, March 7. www.dairyreporter.com/news/ng.asp?id=66249-danone-takeover-eu.

Dasgupta, S. 2006. Mulling over Mittal – Is This India's Achievement or the Achievement of an Indian? *The Telegraph*, June 30.

Datamonitor. 2005. IBM–Lenovo Deal Gets Both Approval and Disapproval. *Datamonitor News and Comment*, January 28.

Davidson, A. 2005. How CNOOC prepared for its Bid for Unocal. *NPR: All Things Considered*, June 29.

Davis, T. 2006. NJ Resolute in Opposing Ports Deal. *The Record*, February 27.

and H. Jackson. 2006. Dubai Company Pulling Out of Port Deal. *The Record*, March 10.

de Beaupuy, F. 2005. France's Breton Says Limits on Takeovers Comply with EU Laws. *Bloomberg*, September 25.

and E. Vandore. 2005. Chirac Says Possible Danone Takeover Prompts "Vigilance." *Bloomberg*, July 21.

Dempsey, J. and K. Bennhold. 2007. GDF-Suez Merger Deals a Blow to EU Ambition to Open Energy Sector. *International Herald Tribune*, September 3.

Deshpande, S. 2006. Dubai Port's UK Deal May Have Indian Fallout. *The Times of India*, April 18.

Dickie, M. 2006. China Halts Foreign Investment in TV Firms. *Financial Times*, December 7.

Dietch, C. 2008. Société Générale and the Puzzle of French Protectionism. *Newsletter of the European Union Center of Excellence at Indiana University* 2 (2).

Dinmore, G., R. Sanderson, and P. Hollinger. 2011. French-Italian Takeover Tensions Rise. *Financial Times*, April 2.

DMA. 2005. Miscellany; UK Defense Mergers & Acquisitions, (April) 17. www.infobasepub.com.

Dobbs, L., E. Henry, L. Sylvester, et al. 2006a. Coast Guard Warned White House of Security Risks in Port Deal. *CNN: Lou Dobbs Tonight: Voxant*, February 27.

E. Henry, L. Sylvester, et al. 2006b. New Security Fears Over Ports Deal; UAE Strong Opponent of Many US Policies; US Coast Guard: Stretched Too Thin? *CNN: Lou Dobbs Tonight: Voxant*, March 1.

E. Henry, D. Bash, et al. 2006c. Republicans Deeply Split Over Dubai Ports Deal; Suing for Security; Senator Collins Interview; Zogby Says Ports Deal Shows Anti-Arab Racism. *CNN: Lou Dobbs Tonight: Voxant*, February 28.

L. Sylvester, B. Tucker, et al. 2006d. Senators Today Blasted Government Officials Who Tried to Win Support for the Administration's Port Deal; A Look at Whether or Not Terminal Operators Are Involved in Security at US Ports. *CNN: Lou Dobbs Tonight: Voxant*, February 23.

Dombrowski, P. 2005. *Guns and Butter: The Political Economy of International Security*. Boulder, CO: Lynne Reinner Publishers.

Done, K. 2006. Open Skies Treaty Stalled by US Objections – Civil Aviation. *Financial Times*, May 3.

Dow Jones. 2005a. Beijing Wants China, US to Gain in CNOOC-Unocal Takeover. *OsterDowJones Commodity Wire*, June 30.

2005b. Energy Highlights: US Working Gas in Storage. *Dow Jones International News*, June 23.

2005c. House Panel Sets Hearing on Possible CNOOC-Unocal Bid. *Dow Jones International News*, July 8.

2005d. US Officials Review of CNOOC-Unocal Bid Would Be Routine. *Dow Jones International News*, July 5.

2006a. Congress Should've Gotten Better Notice on Ports. *Dow Jones Commodities Service*, February 28.

2006b. The Morning Brief: Port Deal Widens the Divide. *Dow Jones New Service (WSJ.Com)*, March 9.

2006c. The Skeptic: Alcatel Attempts to Square Off Thales. *Dow Jones International News*, March 28.

2006d. Thales Buys Alcatel Security Ops for EUR 1.74B. *Dow Jones International News*, April 5.

2006e. TSY Official: US Security Review of Alcatel-Lucent Rigorous. *Dow Jones International News*, November 14.

2006f. TSY Official: US Security Review of Alcatel-Lucent Rigorous. *Dow Jones International News*, November 20.

2006g. US Intelligence Didn't See "Red Flags" in Ports Deal. *Dow Jones Commodities Service*, February 28.

2006h. White House: Congress Will Come Around on Ports. *Dow Jones Business News*, February 22.

DPW. 2006a. Press Release: DP World's Acquisition of the Peninsular and Oriental Steam Navigation Company. *Dubai Ports World*, March 9.

2006b. Press Statement: Untitled. *Dubai Ports World*, March 9.

DSS. 2008. Foreign Ownership, Control, or Influence; Comparison – Special Security Agreement & Proxy Agreement. Defense Security Service, Industrial Security, April 30. www.dss.mil/GW/ShowBinary/DSS/isp/foci/compar_spec_sec_prox.html.

2016a. FOCI Mitigation Instruments. Defense Security Service, US Department of Defense. www.dss.mil/isp/foci/foci_mitigation.html#sec_con_agree.

2016b. Foreign Ownership, Control or Influence (FOCI). Defense Security Service, US Department of Defense. www.dss.mil/isp/foci/foci_info.html.

Dyer, G., S. Tucker, and T. Mitchell. 2006. Foreign Deals in China hit New Resistance. *Financial Times*, August 7.

Eckert, Paul. 2005. US Critics See Security Threat in China Oil Bid. *Reuters News*, July 13.

Economist. 2006a. Japan's Basic Industries under Pressure. *The Economist*, September 7.

2006b. Patriot Games: French Business. *The Economist*, July 1.

EIA. 2008a. Crude Oil and Total Petroleum Imports Top 15 Countries. The Energy Information Administration of the United States, January 15. www.eia.doe.gov/pub/oil_gas/.petroleum/data_publications/company_level_imports/current/import.html.

2008b. Russia – Natural Gas. Country Analysis Briefs. The Energy Information Administration of the United States, May. www.eia.doe.gov/emeu/cabs/Russia/NaturalGas.html.

2008c. US Crude Oil and Petroleum Products Imports from All Countries. The Energy Information Administration of the United States. www.eia.doe.gov/pub/oil_gas/petroleum/data_publications/company_level_imports/current/import.html.

2008d. US Imports by Country of Origin. The Energy Information Administration of the United States. http://tonto.eia.doe.gov/dnav/pet/pet_move_impcus_a2_nus_ep00_im0_mbbl_m.htm.

EIRO. 2006. New Legislation Aimed at Regulating Takeover Bids. European Industrial Relations Observatory On-Line. www.fr.eurofound.eu.int/eiro/2006/04/articles/fr0604039i.htm.

EIU. 2003. Country Commerce Report: Russia. New York: Economist Intelligence Unit.

2005. Business China. New York: Economist Intelligence Unit, August 29.

2006. USA Politics: Honours Uneven. Economist Intelligence Unit, ViewsWire, March 10.

Elman, C. and M. F. Elman. 2003. *Progress in International Relations Theory: Appraising the Field.* Cambridge, MA: The MIT Press.

E-Mining Jrn. 2010. Regulators Thwart Rio Tinto/BHP Billiton Plans for JV. *Engineering and Mining Journal* 211 (9): 5–6.

Encyclopedia of Earth. 2007. Energy Profile of France. *The Encyclopedia of Earth.* www.eoearth.org.

Enel. 2006. Press Release. Enel, press release, February 25. www.enel.it/azienda_en/sala_stampa/comunicati/ss_comunicatiarticolo.asp?IdDoc=1457711.

Enix-Ross, D. 2006. Report to the House of Delegates. American Bar Association, Section of International Law.

Euractiv. 2006. Kroes: Nationalism Has No Place in Cross-Border Mergers. *Euractiv*, March 16. www.euractiv.com/en/financial-services/kroes-nationalism-place-cross-border-mergers/article-153438.

2009. Commission Warns Against "Economic Nationalism." *Euractiv*, February 26. www.euractiv.com/transport/commission-warns-economic-nationalism/article-179761.

European Commission. 2006a. Case No. Comp/M.4214 – Alcatel/Lucent Technologies; Regulation (EC) No139/2004 Merger Procedure, Article 6(1)(b) Non-Opposition. Commission of the European Communities, Office for Official Publications of the European Communities L-2985 Luxembourg, July 24. http://ec.europa.eu/comm/competition/mergers/cases/decisions/m4214_20060724_20310_en.pdf.

2006b. Mergers: Commission approves merger of Gaz de France and Suez, subject to conditions. European Commission, press release. Brussels (Document Reference No. IP/06/1558), November 14. http://europa.eu/rapid/pressReleasesAction.do?reference=IP/06/1558.

2012. Competition: Energy Overview. Brussels: European Commission. http://ec.europa.eu/competition/sectors/energy/overview_en.html.

European Parliament. 2004. Directive 2004/25/EC of the European Parliament and of the Council of 21 April 2004 on Takeover Bids. EurLex

(Official Journal L 142, 30/04/2004). http://eur-lex.europa.eu/LexUriServ/LexUriServ.do?uri=CELEX:32004L0025:EN:HTML.

European Union. 2016. Consolidated Versions of the Treaty on European Union and the Treaty on the Functioning of the European Union (2016/C 202/01). *Official Journal of the European Union* 59 (7): 1–366.

FAS. 2015. *About the FAS Russia: 25th Anniversary of the Russian Competition Regulation*. Moscow: Federal Antimonopoly Service. http://en.fas.gov.ru/about/what-we-do/.

FD. 2005. CNOOC Limited Proposes Merger with Unocal. *FD (Fair Disclosure) Wire*, June 22.

2006. Event Brief of Q4 2005 Check Point Software Technologies Earnings Conference Call – Final. *FD (Fair Disclosure) Wire*, January 30.

Feaver, P. and E. Lorber. 2015. Diminishing Returns? The Future of Economic Coercion. Economic Statecraft Series. Center for a New American Security, November.

Federal News Service. 2006. Highlights of US Broadcast News Coverage of the Middle East from March 9, 2006. *Federal News Service*, March 10.

Federal Register. 2005. Granting of Request for Early Termination of the Waiting Period Under the Premerger Notification Rules. *Federal Register*, November 2.

Feeney, T. and J. S. Orr. 2006. Dockworkers Unload on UAE Port Deal – Hundreds Rally at Port Newark. *The Star-Ledger*, February 28.

and J. P. Martin. 2006. Judge Orders Bush to Answer Suit Filed by New Jersey Over Port Deal. *The Star-Ledger*, February 25.

Fellman, J. 2006. PCCW to Resume Trading After Rejecting Macquarie, TPG-Newbridge. *Bloomberg*, July 26.

and J. Ong. 2006. China Network May Block PCCW's Sale of Phone and Media Assets. *Bloomberg*, June 22.

Financial Express. 2004. China Muscling its Way into the Global Race. *Financial Express (Financial Times Limited)*, December 17.

Financial Times. 2005a. China to Increase Tariffs on Textile Exports. *Financial Times*, May 20.

2005b. The Jurisdiction Tug of War Over Takeovers. *Financial Times*, November 17.

2005c. Volkswagen. *Financial Times*, December 3.

2006a. Big Bang in Defence Europe Needs to Consolidate Arms Demand More Than Supply. *Financial Times*, April 7.

2006b. Chilling Effect on Bids Wall Street Wakes up to French Practices on Capitol Hill. *Financial Times*, March 31.

2009. Hungary's PM Opposed to Takeover of MOL. *Financial Times*, April 19.

Finfacts. 2005. European Commission Warns France on Industrial Protectionism. *Finfacts*, September 5. www.finfacts.com/irelandbusinessnews/publish/article_10003131.shtml.

FINRA. 2008. Glossary of the Financial Industry Regulatory Authority: Institutional Investor. Financial Industry Regulatory Authority. www.finra.org/Glossary/P011041.

Grundman, S. and J. J. Roncka. 2006. National Security Considerations Related to Foreign Direct Investment in the US Aerospace and Defense Industry. *CRA International*, May.

Guardian. 2006. Sale to End Row Over Arab Ownership of US Ports. *The Guardian*, December 11.

Guerrera, F. and J. Polti. 2005. Proxy Firm Backs Chevron Bid for Unocal. *Financial Times*, August 2.

Gutierrez, C. M. 2006. Remarks to US-Russia Business Council. October 11. www.commerce.gov/opa/speeches/Secretary_Gutierrez/2006/Oct./11_US_Russia_Business_Council_NY.htm.

Ha, H. and G. O'Brien. 2008. Competition Guide: China's Anti-Monopoly Law – A Great Leap forward? *Asialaw*, March.

Hachman, M. 2004. IBM PC Retreat Would Shift Market Balance to Asia. *eWeek*, December 3.

Hall, J. 2008. Global M&A Falls in 2008, Ends 5 Years of Growth. *Reuters*, December 22.

Han, K. 2006. Protectionist Moves "Could Shackle S-E Asian Trade with US." *Straits Times*, May 29.

Handelman, S. 2006. Canada's Dubai Problem. *Time (Canada Edition)*, March 13.

Harman, J. 2006. *Introductory Statement on Joint Resolution. Extensions of Remarks. Congressional Record* 152 (23), February 28: E214.

Harmsen, P. 2009. China Raises Nationalist Banner with Coke Veto: Analysts. *Agence France Presse*, March 19.

Harrison, M. 2005. Porsche Purrs, VW Circles the Wagons, but Germany's National Solution Isn't the Answer. *The Independent*, September 27.

Harrison, S. 2006. Port Operator Continues to Fight. *The Miami Herald*, March 3.

Hawksworth, J. and D. Chan. 2015. The World in 2050 Will the Shift in Global Economic Power Continue? *PWC Economics*, February. www.pwc.com/gx/en/issues/the-economy/assets/world-in-2050-february-2015.pdf.

Helleiner, E. and A. Pickel. 2005. *Economic Nationalism in a Globalizing World.* Ithaca, NY: Cornell University Press.

Hensel, B. 2006a. Ill Effects of Port Deal Remain in Middle East. *Houston Chronicle*, June 29.

2006b. A Whole World Works at Port. *Houston Chronicle*, February 26.

Hepher, T. 2014. How France Expanded Takeover Controls from Gaming to Energy. *Reuters*, May 15.

Hindustan Times. 2006. Sens. Schumer, Snowe Demand Answers from Homeland Security Department over Coast Guard's Dubious Assessment of Dubai Ports Deal. *Hindustan Times*, February 28.

Hirschman, A. O. 1945. *National Power and the Structure of Foreign Trade.* Berkeley, CA: University of California Press.

Hitt, G. and S. Ellison. 2006a. Abandon Ship: Dubai Firm Bows to Public Outcry – Media Sparked Firestorm as Bush Got Snagged in Bipartisan Criticism – Frist Takes an Early Stand. *The Wall Street Journal*, March 10.

2006b. Lobbyist, Media Fanned Port Flames. *The Wall Street Journal*, March 10.

and N. King Jr. 2006. Small Florida Firm Sowed Seed of Port Dispute – Eller's Suits and Lob Lie Behind Dubai Furor; Approval Delayed in UK. *The Wall Street Journal*, February 28.

and J. Singer. 2006. Bush's Effort to Calm Storm Falters. *The Globe and Mail*, March 3.

Huang, D. and D. Richardson. 2005. China's Proposed Antimonopoly Law. Dorsey & Whitney LLP. www.dorsey.com/Resources/Detail.aspx?pub=bdd82a88-75ab-4aa3-bca8-5e4a5c0e4978.

Hull Daily Mail. 2006. Bush Vows to Veto Congress Efforts to Block Port Takeover. *Hull Daily Mail*, February 23.

Hume, N. 2016. Iron Ore's Surprise Rally Looks on Borrowed Time. *Financial Times*, April 25.

Hunter, G., L. Dobbs, J. Roberts, et al. 2006. CNN: Paula Zahn Now: Voxant.

ICEM. 2006. Unions Win Important Legal Battle in GDF-Suez Merger Saga. ICEM News In Brief. International Federation of Chemical, Energy, Mine, and General Workers' Unions. www.icem.org/en/78-ICEM-InBrief/2047-Unions-Win-Important-Legal-Battle-in-GDF-Suez-Merger-Saga.

IEA. 2006. Energy Balances of OECD Countries. The International Energy Agency.

IFLR. 2002. Russia: Mergers and Acquisitions. *International Financial Law Review*, July 5. www.iflr.com/IssueArticle/2027127/Supplements/Mergers-and-Acquisitions.html?supplementListId=69194.

IGR. 2005. CNOOC/Unocal Bid Rocks US Boat. *International Gas Report*, July 1.

2008. Hungary Modifies MOL Law for EC. *International Gas Report*, October 20.

Ikenberry, G. J. 2001. *After Victory; Institutions, Strategic Restraint, and the Rebuilding of Order after Major Wars*. Princeton, NJ: Princeton University Press.

IMD. 2007a. IMD All Criteria List. Switzerland: The IMD World Competitiveness Center. www.imd.ch/research/publications/wcy/index.cfm.

2007b. World Competitiveness Yearbook Database: Years 2001–2007. Switzerland: The IMD World Competitiveness Center. www.imd.org/wcc.

2016. Methodology and Principles of Analysis. Switzerland: The IMD World Competitiveness Center. www.imd.org/uupload/imd.website/wcc/methodology.pdf.

Inside US Trade. 2006a. Blunt to Introduce CFIUS Reform Bill Before Memorial Day Recess. *Inside US Trade* 24 (18), May 5.

2006b. Hunter Probes CFIUS Review of Alcatel-Lucent Merger. *Inside US Trade* 24 (46), November 17.

2006c. Text: Business Letter on CFIUS. *Inside US Trade* 24 (49), December 8.

International Herald Tribune. 2006a. PCCW Shares Surge on Report of Sale. *The International Herald Tribune*, June 20.

2006b. Rome, in Frosty Response, Calls Off Meeting. *International Herald Tribune*, February 26.

2008. French Court Puts Brakes on Merger of Gaz de France and Suez. *International Herald Tribune*, January 22.

International Oil Daily. 2005a. CNOOC Bid Faces Security, Antitrust Reviews in Washington. *The International Oil Daily*, June 24.

2005b. Key US Republican Threatens to Block Any CNOOC-Unocal Deal. *The International Oil Daily*, July 14.

2005c. US Congressmen Rail Against Chinese Bid. *The International Oil Daily*, June 29.

Interview. 2006. Interview with Equity Research Analyst, December 6.

2007. Interview with Members of the Legal Community, January 11.

2008a. Interview with Member of the Energy Industry, September 22.

2008b. Interview with Member of the Financial Industry, July 1.

2008c. Interview with Equity Research Analyst, November 13.

2008d. Interview with Hedge Fund Analyst, November 28.

Investor Words. 2007. Online Investor Glossary. *InvestorWords.com*, January 6. www.investorwords.com.

2008. Hostile Takeover. *InvestorWords.com*, www.investorwords.com/2344/hostile_takeover.html.

Iosco County Republicans. 1999. Long Beach Naval Station. *Iosco County Republicans Website*, January. www.ioscorepublicans.org/arclbns.htm.

ISC. 2013. Foreign Involvement in the Critical National Infrastructure: The Implications for National Security. Intelligence and Security Committee, UK Parliament (Cm 8629). London: TSO (June). www.gov.uk/government/uploads/system/uploads/attachment_data/file/205680/ISC-Report-Foreign-Investment-in-the-Critical-National-Infrastructure.pdf.

ISED. 2016. *Annual Report: Investment Canada Act 2015–16*. Ottowa: Innovation, Science and Economic Development Canada, Government of Canada. www.ic.gc.ca/eic/site/ica-lic.nsf/eng/h_lk81126.html.

ISSP. 2003. National Identity II. International Social Survey Programme. www.issp.org/.

Ivanovich, David. 2005. Energy Debate Flares. *Houston Chronicle*, July 13.

Jackson, J. K. 2007. Exon-Florio Foreign Investment Provision: Overview of H.R. 556. (CRS Report No. RL33856). Washington, DC: Congressional Research Service (March 21).

2010. The Committee on Foreign Investments in the United States (CRS Report No. RL33388). Washington, DC: Congressional Research Service (February 4).

2011a. The Committee on Foreign Investment in the United States (CRS Report No. RL33388). Washington, DC: Congressional Research Service (March 30).

2011b. Foreign Investment, CFIUS, and Homeland Security: An Overview (CRS Report No. RS22863). Washington, DC: Congressional Research Service (March 30).

2013. Foreign Investment and National Security: Economic Considerations (CRS Report No. RL34561). Washington, DC: Congressional Research Service (April 4).

2016a. The Committee on Foreign Investment in the United States (CRS Report No. RL33388). Washington, DC: Congressional Research Service (February 19).

2016b. The Committee on Foreign Investment in the United States (CRS Report No. RL33388) Washington, DC: Congressional Research Service (August 12).

Jalinous, F., N. Nègre-Eveillard, T. Heinrich, et al. 2016. National Security Reviews: A Global Perspective. New York: White & Case LLP (November). www.whitecase.com/sites/whitecase/files/files/download/publications/national-security-reviews.pdf.

Jane's Defence Weekly. 2006. Alcatel/Lucent Merger Raises US Fears Over National Security. *Jane's Defence Weekly*, April 19.

Jervis, R. 1976. *Perception and Misperception in International Politics*. Princeton, NJ: Princeton University Press.

Jian, F. and G. Yu. 2014. Public Mergers and Acquisitions in China: Overview. Linklaters LLP, Practical Law, Thomson Reuters (October 1). uk.practicallaw.com/6-422-4423.

Johnson, G. 2006. Law and Regulation Briefly Noted. *TheDeal.Com*, June 9.

Jones, Ambassador Richard H. 2006. AMCHAM New Year's Reception Remarks. The Embassy of the United States in Tel Aviv, Israel.

Joseph, A. 2006. Dubai Ports Makes a Quiet Exit from Gwadar Venture. *The Economic Times*, November 30.

Kagan, D., E. A. Cohen, C. F. Doran, and M. Mandelbaum. 1999. Is Major War Obsolete? An Exchange. *Survival* 41 (2): 139–52.

Kang, C. S. E. 1997. US Politics and Greater Regulation of Inward Foreign Direct Investment. *International Organization* 51 (2): 301–33.

Kanter, J. 2006. France Delays Proposal to Privatize Gaz de France. *International Herald Tribune*, June 20.

Katzenstein, P. J. ed. 1996. *The Culture of National Security; Norms and Identity in World Politics*. New York: Cornell University Press.

Kazin, M. 2016. Trump and American Populism. *Foreign Affairs* 95 (6): 17–24.

Keeler, T. 2010. The United States Blocks on National Security Grounds a Chinese Investment in a US Telecommunications and Solar Technology Firm. *Mondaq Business Briefing*, July 8.

Kekic, L. and K. P. Sauvant, eds. 2006. *World Investment Prospects to 2010; Boom or Backlash?* London and New York: The Economist Intelligence Unit and the Columbia Program on International Investment.

Keller, M. 2005. Congressmen Scrutinize IBM, Lenovo Deal; Chinese Firm to Buy IBM PC Unit. *USA Today*, January 28.

Keohane, R. O., 1986. *Neorealism and its Critics*. New York: Columbia University Press.

and J. S. Nye. 1989. *Power and Interdependence*. New York: Pearson Publishing.

and J. S. Nye. 2001. *Power and Interdependence*. New York: Pearson Publishing.

Kessler, M. 2005. Congressmen Scrutinize IBM, Lenovo Deal. *USA Today*, January 27.

Khalaf, R. 2006. UAE Denies Political Motive in Foreign Exchange Shift to Euros – FT Interview Sultan Bin Nasser Al-Suwaidi. *Financial Times*, July 14.

Kirchgaessner, S. 2005. "Congressional Angst" Scuppers Chinese Bid – Defeat By Backlash. *Financial Times*, August 3.

2010. White House Scuppers Emcore Deal Over National Security Fear. *Financial Times*, June 30.

and D. Sevastopulo. 2006. DP World to Divest US Port Holdings. *Financial Times*, March 9.

and P. Taylor. 2013. US Raise Flag over Softbank's Sprint Bid. *Financial Times*, May 24.

R. McGregor, and D. Roberts. 2005. A New Asian Invasion: China's Champions Bid High for American Brands and Resources. *Financial Times*, June 24.

Knight Ridder. 2006. Congress Expected to Seek Veto Over Foreign Takeovers of Some Firms. *Knight Ridder Washington Bureau*, March 3.

Koty, A. C. and Z. Qian. 2017. China's 2017 Foreign Investment Catalogue Opens Access to New Industries. *China Briefing, Dezan Shira Associates*, July 11.

Kroes, N. 2008. Structural Reforms to the Energy Market European Affairs Platform. Brussels: European Affairs Platform, 27 February (SPEECH/08/106). europa.eu/rapid/pressReleasesAction.do?reference=SPEECH/08/106&format=HTML&aged=0&language=EN&guiLanguage=en.

Krupa, P. 2015. President signed the act protecting Polish companies. Ministry of Treasury, Republic of Poland, press release, August 8.

Kudlow. 2005. Interview: Jerry Taylor of CATO Inst. and Frank Gaffney of Center for Security Policy Discusses CNOOC's Bid for Unocal. *CNBC: Kudlow & Company*, July 14.

Kuhnhenn, J. 2006. Ports Deal Crumbles as Dubai Firm Promises to Sell US Assets. *Knight Ridder Washington Bureau*, March 10.

and W. Douglas. 2006. Port Flap Likely to Spur New Rules, Lawmakers Say; Some Want Power to Reject Foreign Deals. *The Record*, March 3.

Kupchan, C. A. 2002. *The End of the American Era: US Foreign Policy and the Geopolitics of the Twenty-first Century*. New York: Vintage Books.

2006. How to Keep NATO Relevant. *International Herald Tribune*, October 5.

Kwong, V. 2006. Macquarie, Newbridge May Drop PCCW Bid if Opposed, Paper Says. *Bloomberg*, June 27.

La Fondation Charles de Gaulle. 2008. De Gaulle and NATO. www.charles-de-gaulle.org.

Laitner, S. and G. Parker. 2005. France Warned over Protectionism. European Commission.

Larson, A. P. and D. M. Marchick. 2006. *Foreign Investment and National Security; Getting the Balance Right*. New York: Council on Foreign Relations Press.

LA Times. 2005. Chinese Firm Presses Its Offer for Unocal. *LA Times*, June 28, 2005.

Lau, J. 2006. Murdoch Says Macquarie May Lose PCCW Bid. *Financial Times*, June 29.

and T. Mitchell. 2006a. Companies International: Beijing Casts Shadow Over PCCW Battle. *Financial Times*, June 23.

and T. Mitchell. 2006b. Macquarie Proposal Favors China Netcom. *Financial Times*, June 23.

and T. Mitchell. 2006c. US Warned About Hardline Ports Stance. *Financial Times*, April 18.

Lau, L. and J. Stiglitz. 2005. China's Alternative to Revaluation. *Financial Times*, April 24.

Layne, C. 2004. The War on Terrorism and the Balance of Power: The Paradoxes of American Hegemony. In *Balance of Power; Theory and Practice in the 21st Century*, eds. T.V. Paul, J. J. Wirtz, and M. Fortmann. Stanford, CT: Stanford University Press.

Legal Memorandum. 2009. Re: Committee on Foreign Investment in the United States. Davis Graham & Stubbs LLP and Reed Smith LLP, December 14. http://graphics8.nytimes.com/packages/images/nytint/docs/memo-regarding-the-sale-of-firstgold-corp/original.pdf.

Lemos, R. 2006. Check Point Calls Off Sourcefire Buy. *Security Focus*, March 24. www.securityfocus.com/print/news/11382.

Lenihan, A. T. 2014. Sovereign Wealth Funds and the Acquisition of Power. *New Political Economy* 19 (2): 227–57.

Lentner, H. H. 2004. *Power and Politics in Globalization; the Indispensable State*. New York: Routledge.

Les Echoes. 2006. Shareholders to Vote on Alcatel-Lucent Merger on September 7 (La Fusion Alcatel-Lucent Recoit le Soutien du Cabinet ISS). *Les Echos*, August 25.

Levans, M. A. 2006. A Containerload of Misinformation. *Logistics Management*, March 1.

Lex. 2005a. CNOOC/Unocal. *Financial Times*, January 6.

2005b. CNOOC/Unocal. *Financial Times*, June 7.

2005c. CNOOC/Unocal. *Financial Times*, June 22.

Lexology. 2016. Frequently Asked Questions Concerning the Investment Canada Act. *Lexology*, June 27. www.lexology.com/library/detail.aspx?g=dbdfe3b6-9642-4be5-8c00-1336e822ff4c.

Lieber, R. J. 2005. *The American Era: Power and Strategy for the 21st Century*. New York: Cambridge University Press.

Linebaugh, K., M. Pottinger, and G. Hitt. 2005. Learning Curve: After Earlier Fumbles, CNOOC Uses Wall Street Tactics in UNOCAL Bid. *The Wall Street Journal*, June 27.

Linklaters. 2015. Guide to Foreign Investment in the PRC. Linklaters LLP (October). www.linklaters.com/Insights/AsiaNews/LinkstoChina/Pages/Guide-Foreign-Investment-PRC.aspx.

Litterick, D. 2006. Wall Street Warns of Protectionism. *(London) Telegraph*, March 30.

Livdahl, D., J. Sheng, and A. Liu. 2016. China Simplifies its Legal Administration of Foreign Direct Investments. *Lexology*, Pillsbury Winthrop Shaw Pittman LLP, October 20. www.lexology.com/library/detail.aspx?g=64dd7fae-6bac-4bab-bcad-879c4b54f1da.

Lloyd's. 2006. DP World Divests US Interests. *Lloyd's Shipping Economist*, April 1.

Lobell, S., N. Ripsman, and J. Taliaferro, eds. 2009. *Neoclassical Realism, the State, and Foreign Policy*. Cambridge: Cambridge University Press.

Lohr, S. 2005. Unocal Bid Opens Up New Issues of Security. *The New York Times*, July 13.

Lucent. 2006. Form 8-K Current Report. Filed April 2. www.secinfo.com/drDX9.v7j.8.htm.

Lyons, J. 2006. Workers Have Nothing to Fear From Foreign Takeovers. *Press Association National Newswire*, February 23.

MacMillan, R. 2006. Alcatel, Lucent Merger Faces Obstacles. *Reuters News*, March 24.

Mahoney, J. and G. Goertz. 2004. The Possibility Principle and Case Selection: Choosing Negative Cases in Comparative Analysis. *American Political Science Review*, 98 (November): 653–70.

Mallaby, S. 2015. The World Economy in 2016: Watch China. Council on Foreign Relations, December 23. www.cfr.org.

Managing Intellectual Property. 2007. China: China Adopts Anti-Monopoly Law: Managing Intellectual Property. www.managingip.com/Article/1684921/China-adopts-anti-monopoly-law.html.

Mandelbaum, M. 1998/99. Is Major War Obsolete? *Survival* 40 (4): 20–38.

Manoj, P. 2007. We Will Invest Another $500 mn in Near Future. *Live Mint*, November 16.

Marciano, J., K. Martin, and A. Rosenberg. 2015. Wind Developer Ralls Corp. vs. US Government: Case Settled. *North American Windpower*, December 10. http://nawindpower.com/wind-developer-ralls-corp-vs-us-government-case-settled.

Market News Publishing. 2004. IBM Corp – Lenovo to Acquire IBM Personal Computing Division. *Market News Publishing*, December 7.

Marsh, V. 2001. Down Under: The Weakness of Australia's Currency and a Spate of Foreign Takeovers Have Provoked Fears That the Country Will Become an Isolated Loser in the Process of Globalisation. *Financial Times*, May 4.

Martin, K. 2006. US Officials Investigate Sourcefire Purchase. *Security Focus*, March 2. www.securityfocus.com/brief/153.

Matheny, R. 2013. CFIUS Invokes National Security in Ordering Indian Company to Divest Equity in US Company. Client Alert, Goodwin Proctor LLP, September 27.

Mathews, C. 2006. Hardball for March 9, 2006. *MSNBC: Hardball: Voxant Inc.*

Matlack, C. 2006. Concerns Weigh Over Alcatel-Lucent Merger; Critics on Both Sides Don't Like the Price. But the Union of the French and US Telco Giants Looks Likely to be OK'd by Shareholders. *BusinessWeek Online*, September 1.

Matthews, S. 2005. Danone ADRs Rise on Report of Possible PepsiCo Bid – Update 1. *Bloomberg*.

May, T. 2016. We Can Make Britain a Country that Works for Everyone. Speech, July 11. http://press.conservatives.com/post/147947450370/we-can-make-britain-a-country-that-works-for.

McAuliff, M. 2006. New Port Probe OK'd. But Deal Stays on Track. *New York Daily News*, February 27.

McDermott, J. P. 2006. Ports in a Storm. *The Post and Courier*, February 26.

McDonald, J. 2005. China CNOOC Unocal. *Associated Press*, June 30.

McGregor, R. 2005. Chevron Mends Fences in China. *Financial Times*, September 28.

McKay, M. 2006a. All Industry Eyes Watch Possible Merger Between Lucent, French Rival Alcatel. *Knight Ridder Tribune Business News (KRTBN)*, March 28.

2006b. Lucent, Alcatel Merger Delayed; French Firm Seeks to Sell Satellite Arm. *The Record (New Jersey)*, April 1.

2006c. Mixed Emotions: Reaction to Alcatel-Lucent Merger. *Knight Ridder Tribune Business News (KRTBN)*, April 4.

McLaughlin, K. 2006. Check Point, Sourcefire Call Off Merger. *Computer Reseller News*, April 3.

McLean, C. 2006. Telco Giant is Born as Alcatel Buys Lucent for $13.4 Billion. *The Globe and Mail*, April 3.

McMillan, R. 2005. IBM, Lenovo Executives Outline Plans. *Computerworld*, March 7.

Mearsheimer, J. J. 2001. *The Tragedy of Great Power Politics*. New York: W.W. Norton.

and S. M. Walt. 2007. *The Israel Lobby and US Foreign Policy*. New York: Farrar, Straus and Giroux.

MEJ. 2006. Chronology: United Arab Emirates (UAE). *Middle East Journal*, July 1.

Mercer, C. 2005. Danone Chair Supports Takeover Transparency Law. September 22. www.foodanddrinkeurope.com/news/ng.asp?id=62711-danone-pepsico-acquisition.

Merger Market. 2006. France's "Danone Amendment" Will Impose UK-Style "Put Up or Shut Up" Deadline. *Merger Market*, March 17. www.mergermarket.com/public/default.asp?pagename=editorial_detail&docid=853.

Messmer, E. 2006. Check Point to Acquire Sourcefire. *Network World*, June 10.

Meunier, S. 2012. *Political Impact of Chinese Foreign Direct Investment in the European Union on Transatlantic Relations*. Brussels: European Parliament.

Migdalovitz, C. 2007. Israel: Background and Relations with the United States (CRS Report No. RL33476). Washington, DC: Congressional Research Service (July 6).

Mist News. 2006. Arab Investment in US at Risk. *Mist News*, May 3.

Mitchell, T. 2006. PCCW Deal Raises Political Concerns. *Financial Times*, June 25.

MOFCOM. 2011. NO. 53 Announcement of 2011 of the Ministry of Commerce Concerning the Provisions of the Ministry of Commerce for the Implementation the Security Review System for Merger and Acquisition of Domestic Enterprises by Foreign Investors. Ministry of Commerce of the People's Republic of China. (August 25). www.fdi.gov.cn/pub/FDI_EN/Laws/law_en_info.jsp?docid=138085.

Molchanov, P. 2005. US Revives Japan Inc Fears Over China's Buying Spree. *National Business Review*, August 12.

Moody, E. 2005. IBM Says US Clears PC Unit Sale to China's Lenovo – Update 1. *Bloomberg*, March 9.

Moore, The Hon. J. 2013. Archived Statement by the Honourable James Moore on the Proposed Acquisition of the Allstream Division of Manitoba Telecom Services Inc. by Accelero Capital Holdings. Canadian Minister of Industry, October 7. http://news.gc.ca/web/article-en.do?nid=778709&_ga=1.186604842.227257422.1473615953.

Moran, T. H. 1990. The Globalization of America's Defense Industries; Managing the Threat of Foreign Dependence. *International Security* 15 (1): 57–99.

1993. *American Economic Policy and National Security*. New York: Council on Foreign Relations Press.

Morgan, B. 2006. Economic Nationalism Rises in China Five Years after WTO Entry. *Ottowa Citizen*, December 12.

Morse, J. 2006. Alcatel-Lucent Talks May Spur Competitors to Partner. *RCR Wireless News*, 27 March.

Mosk, M. 2006. Ehrlich Leans Toward Accepting Port Takeover by Arab Company. *Washington Post*, February 24.

Moteff, J. and P. Parfomak. 2004. Critical Infrastructure and Key Assets: Definition and Identification (CRS Report No. RL32631). Washington, DC: Congressional Research Service (October 1).

Mouwad, J. and D. Barboza. 2005. In Seeking Unocal, Chevron Ruffles an Asian Partner. *The New York Times*, July 5.

MPR. 2005. Committee on Foreign Investment in the United States May Block Sale of IBM's Computer Business to China's Lenovo. *Minnesota Public Radio: Marketplace*, January 24.

Mudde, C. 2016. Europe's Populist Surge. *Foreign Affairs* 95 (6): 25–30.

Mueller, J. 1988. The Essential Irrelevance of Nuclear Weapons: Stability in the Postwar World. *International Security* 13 (2): 55–79.

Mulligan, M. 2009. Case Study: Acciona Plans for a Sustainable Future. *Financial Times*, June 9.

and G. Dinmore. 2009. Enel Agrees €11bn deal for Endesa Control. *Financial Times*, February 21.

Murphy, K. and B. Norington. 2006. Police Pass on US-Arab Port Row. *The Australian*, February 23.

Murray, A. 2005. Washington a Threat to CNOOC's Bid to Buy Unocal. *The Asian Wall Street Journal*, June 28.

NATO. 1949. The North Atlantic Treaty. www.nato.int/docu/basictxt/treaty.htm.

Natural Gas Intelligence. 2005. Rumors Surface that CNOOC May Find US Partner to Handle Unocal's Domestic Assets. *Natural Gas Intelligence*, August 1.

Neveling, N. 2006. Takeover Panel Refuses to Block Foreign Buyers. *Accountancy Age*, April 13.

Ng, D. 2006. Suez-GDF Deal Raises Question of Government Intervention. *Forbes.com*, March 1. www.forbes.com/2006/03/01/suez-gdf-0301markets16.html.

Ng, E. and N. Gough. 2005. Bloodied CNOOC Remains Undeterred. *South China Morning Post*, July 29.

NIC. 2004. *Mapping the Global Future; Report of the National Intelligence Council's 2020 Project.* Washington, DC: National Intelligence Council.

2008. Global Trends 2025: A Transformed World. Washington, DC: National Intelligence Council (November). https://fas.org/irp/nic/2025.pdf.

2010. Global Governance 2025: At a Critical Juncture. Washington, DC: National Intelligence Council (September). http://permanent.access.gpo.gov/gpo12194/2025_Global_Governance.pdf.

2012. Global Trends 2030: Alternative Worlds. Washington, DC: National Intelligence Council (December). www.dni.gov/nic/globaltrends.

Nichol, J., S. Woehrel, and B. Gelb. 2006. Russia's Cutoff of Natural Gas to Ukraine: Context and Implications (CRS Report No. RS22378). Washington, DC: Congressional Research Service (February 15).

Nikiforov, D. and A. Maximenko. 2014. Amendments to Regulation of Foreign Investments in Strategic Companies. Client Update, Debevoise & Plimpton, November 18.

Nikkei. 2004. Lenovo-IBM Deal Attests to China's Leadership in the PC Market. *Nikkei Report*, December 20.

NPR. 2006. The Marketplace Report: Bids for London Exchange. *NPR: Day to Day*, March 13.

Nussbaum, A. 2006. Workers Slam Port Deal; Politicians Join Them at Noisy Dockside Demonstration. *The Record*, February 28.

Nye, J. S. 2002. *The Paradox of American Power: Why the World's Only Superpower Can't Go It Alone.* New York: Oxford University Press.

2011. *The Future of Power.* New York: Perseus Books.

2017. "Will the Liberal Order Survive." *Foreign Affairs* 96 (1): 10–16.

Obama, President B. H. 2012. Order Signed by the President regarding the Acquisition of Four US Wind Farm Project Companies by Ralls Corporation. White House, press release, September 28.

2016. Presidential Order Regarding the Proposed Acquisition of a Controlling Interest in Aixtron SE by Grand Chip Investment GMBH. White House, press release, December 2.

O'Driscoll, M. 2005. Energy Policy; CNOOC Amendment Added to Conference Report. *Greenwire*, July 26.

OECD. 2006a. *Freedom of Investment, National Security and "Strategic Industries"; Summary of Discussions Prepared by the Secretariat.* Paris: OECD.

2006b. *Preventing Investment Protectionism.* Paris: OECD. www.oecd.org/document/7/0,2340,en_2649_34529562_37363207_1_1_1_34529562,00.html.

2007. *International Investment Perspectives: Freedom of Investment in a Changing World, 2007 Edition.* Paris: OECD.

2008. *OECD Benchmark Definition of Foreign Direct Investment*, 4th Edition. Paris: OECD.

2009. *Guidelines for Recipient Country Investment Policies Relating to National Security: Recommendation Adopted by the OECD Council.* Paris: OECD Investment Division. www.oecd.org/daf/inv/investment-policy/43384486.pdf.

Oil Daily. 2005a. Energy Bill Amendment Aims to Delay US Review of CNOOC Bid. *The Oil Daily*, July 15.

2005b. States Voice CNOOC Concerns. *The Oil Daily*, July 8.

Optical Networks Daily. 2006. Alcatel-Lucent Establishes LGD Subsidiary to Address US Government Sector. *Optical Networks Daily*, December 4.

Orol, R. 2005a. IBM-Lenovo Merger Under Scrutiny. *The Deal.com*, January 25.

2005b. IBM-Lenovo Probe Nears End. *The Deal.com*, February 23.

2005c. Lawmakers Assail CNOOC-Unocal Deal. *The Deal.com*, July 14.

2005d. A Move to Block CNOOC's Bid. *The Deal.com*, June 29.

2005e. Pols Attack IBM-Lenovo Deal. *The Deal.com*, January 27.

and C. K. Lindell. 2005. Congress Frets Over CNOOC Bid. *The Deal.com*, June 24.

Orr, J. S. 2006a. Dubai Firm Scraps Plan for US Ports. *The Star-Ledger*, March 10.

2006b. President Holds Firm on Port Deal – Panel that Cleared Sale Will Probe Security Issues, Raising Concerns. *The Star-Ledger*, March 1.

Osborn, A. 2006. Russia Threatens to Cut Off Gas to Belarus. *The Independent*, December 29.

O'Shaughnessy, M. 2007. Smartmatic Announces Sale of Sequoia Voting Systems. Office of Representative Carolyn B. Malone, US House of Representatives, press release, November 8. http://maloney.house.gov/index.php?option=com_content&task=view&id=1491&Itemid=61.

Osler, D. 2006. Israeli Boycott May Be Problematic for Arab-Owned Dubai Ports World. *Lloyd's List*, March 6.

Pacific Shipper. 2006. Political Volume Stays High on Ports Deal. *Pacific Shipper*, March 2.

Pagnamenta, R. 2006. Dubai Hires Presidential Candidate. *The Express on Sunday*, March 5.

Paleit, A. 2006. How the DP World Deal Unravelled. *Financial Times*, March 10.

Palmer, D. 2006. Update 5 – US Accepts 45-Day Review of Dubai Ports Deal. *Reuters News*, February 26.

Pape, R. A. 2005. Soft Balancing Against the United States. *International Security* 30 (1): 7–45.

Parameswaran, P. 2005. US Technology-Transfer Fears Behind Review of IBM Lenovo Deal. *Xinhua Financial Network*, January 26.

Parker, G. 2017. Theresa May Steps Back from Tough Stance on Foreign Investment. *Financial Times*, January 20.

and C. Smyth. 2006. Mandelson Warns against EU Protectionism. *Financial Times*, March 8.

and J. Thornhill. 2005. France Reminded of Takeover Laws. *Financial Times*, August 30.

Paul, T. V. 2005. Soft Balancing in the Age of Us Primacy. *International Security* 30 (1): 46–71.

J. J. Wirtz, and M. Fortmann, eds. 2004. *Balance of Power; Theory and Practice in the 21st Century*. Stanford, CT: Stanford University Press.

Pavliva, H. 2007. Deripaska Ready to "Give Up" Rusal to Russian State, FT Says. *Bloomberg*, July 13.

Perri, C. and M. Deen. 2005. Danone Drops as Regulator Says PepsiCo Won't Make Bid – Update 6. *Bloomberg*, July 25.

Pew Global Attitudes Project. 2003. *Trouble Behind, Trouble Ahead? A Year of Contention at Home and Abroad; 2003 Year-End Report*. Washington, DC: The Pew Research Center for the People and the Press. http://pewglobal.org/.

Pickard, D., N. Daly, and U. Neelakantan. 2013. CFIUS Forces Chinese Government-Backed Firm to Divest Interest in Canadian Mining Company With US Operations. WileyRein LLP, June 25. www.wileyrein.com/newsroom-articles-2752.html.

Pierce, E. and T. Newmeyer. 2005. A War Over Oil. *Roll Call*, June 29.

Pine, A. 2006. From the K Street Corridor; Issues & Ideas: Port Protection Looks Overseas. *National Journal*, March 11.

PINR. 2005. Economic Brief: French Protectionism. *Power and Interest News Report*, September 15. www.pinr.com/report.php?ac=view_printable&report_id=367&language_id=1.

Platts. 2005. CNOOC Board Meets Late Thursday, Likely to Raise Unocal Bid. *Platts Commodity News*, July 28.

2008. Oil & Gas News; Hungary: Takeover Law to be Amended. *Platts Energy in East Europe* 150, October 24.

Plotkin, M., D. Fagan, and D. Chambers. 2009. A Question of National Security. *Legal Week*, January 29.

PNG Post Courier. 2006. Concern Over Port Deal. *PNG Post Courier*, March 1.

Powell, B. 2005. A Chinese Oil Company is Thinking of Bidding for a US One. Does That Make Sense? *TIMEasia Magazine*, May 23.

PR Newswire. 2005. Xinhua Far East Places the AAA Domestic Currency Issuer Rating of CNOOC Ltd. on Review for Possible Downgrade. *PR Newswire*, June 23.

Preeg, E. H. 2002. Exchange Rate Manipulation to Gain an Unfair Competitive Advantage: The Case Against Japan and China. In *Dollar Overvaluation and the World Economy*, ed. C. F. Bergsten and J. Williamson. Washington, DC: Institute for International Economics, pp. 267–85.

Prince, T. and J. Baer. 2006. JPMorgan Held Talks to Buy Troika Dialog, People Say – Update 2. *Bloomberg*, August 28.

Puljak, N. 2008. France Announces Sovereign Wealth Fund to Protect Champions. *Agence France Presse*, October 23.

Putnam, R. D. 1988. Diplomacy and Domestic Politics: the Logic of Two-Level Games. *International Organization* 42 (Summer): 427–60.

PZMN. 2005. China Business Strategy: US May Block IBM Lenovo Deal Over Security Issues. *PrimeZone Media Network*, January 27.

Qian, Z. 2016. Anatomy of a Takeover: Conducting a Company Acquisition in China. *China Briefing, Dezan Shira Associates* 166 (June and July): 6–10. www.asiabriefing.com/store/book/understanding-mergers-acquisitions-in-china-5978.html.

Radio Free Europe. 2006. Gazprom Gains Control of Sakhalin Project. *Radio Free Europe, Radio Liberty Online*, December 21.

Raice, S. and A. Dowell. 2011. Huawei Drops US Deal Amid Opposition. *Wall Street Journal*, February 21.

Ramstad, E. 2004. The Technological Rise of China Was Speedy. *Dow Jones Chinese Financial Newswire*, December 21.

Rash, W. 2005. Suppose IBM Lenovo Deal Doesn't Happen. *eWeek*, January 24.

Record. 2006. Homeland Security Balked at Ports Deal. *The Record*, February 26.

Reguly, E. 2005. China's Oil Sands Play: Is US Seeing Red? *The Globe and Mail*, June 23.

Reuters. 2005a. Fitch Says CNOOC's Unocal Offer Could Impact Rating. *Reuters News*, June 22.

2005b. IBM–Lenovo Deal Faces US Security Challenge Report. *Reuters News*, January 23.

2006a. Bush Approves Alcatel Lucent Merger. *Reuters News*, November 18.

2006b. Chronology – Major Acquisitions by Gulf Arab Investors. *Reuters News*, October 6.

2006c. Euronext OK with Dubai Minority Stake, Not Majority. *Reuters News*, May 2.

2006d. UAE Points to Its Anti-Terror Role in US Port Row. *Reuters News*, February 17.

2006e. US–UAE Trade at Risk from Ports Deal – Business Group. *Reuters News*, March 8.

2009. US May Block China Mine Investment Near Navy Site. *Reuters News*, December 18.

Reynolds, J. B. 2004. Foreign Direct Investment in US Critical Infrastructure. *Wiley Rein LLP*, March 12. www.wileyrein.com.

Rhodes, C. 2016. Industrial Strategy. House of Commons Library Briefing Paper, No. 07682, October 14. http://researchbriefings.parliament.uk/ResearchBriefing/Summary/CBP-7682#fullreport.

Rice, C. 2005. Secretary of State Condoleezza Rice Press Conference in China. Beijing.

Ripsman, N. M. 2005. False Dichotomies: Why Economics Is High Politics. In *Guns and Butter; the Political Economy of International Security*, ed. Dombrowski, P. Boulder, CO: Lynne Reinner Publishers, pp. 15–34.

Roberts, P. 2006. Collapse of Check Point/Sourcefire Deal Raises Questions; Government Reviews Could Present Obstacles for Future Mergers. *InfoWorld*, April 3.

Robin, B. 2006. Concerns Over Planned Gaz de France–Suez Merger. *France: Institute for Economic and Social Research (IRES)*, September 25. www.eurofound.europa.eu/eiro/2006/03/articles/fr0603039i.htm.

Roden, D. 2006. Suez–Gaz de France. European Research; European Merger Report. New York: Lehman Brothers, June 12.
2007. Suez–Gaz de France. European Research; European Merger Report. New York: Lehman Brothers, September 3.
2008. Suez–Gaz de France. European Research; European Merger Report. New York: Lehman Brothers, January 22.
Rose, G. 1998. Neoclassical Realism and Theories of Foreign Policy. *World Politics* 51 (1): 144–72.
Rothman, M. 2006. Xenophobia's Bad for the Security Business. *Network World*, April 10.
Roumeliotis, G. 2016. Lawmakers Ask US to Block Chinese Takeover of Lattice Semiconductor. *Reuters*, December 5.
Rowe, S. 2006. P&O Takeover Clears Final Legal Hurdle. *Estates Gazette Interactive*, March 7.
Rutenberg, J. and A. E. Kramer. 2006. As Tensions Rise, US and Moscow Falter on Trade. *New York Times*, July 16.
Sage, A. 2006. Merger Meets with Approval in Paris. *The Times*, March 25.
Salidjanova, N. 2011. Going Out: An Overview of China's Outward Foreign Direct Investment. USCC Staff Research Report, US–China Economic & Security Review Commission, March 30.
Sanderson, R., P. Betts, and S. Pignal. 2011. Italy Seeks to Staunch Foreign Takeovers. *Financial Times*, March 22.
Sanger, D. E. 2005. US Punishes 8 Chinese Firms for Aiding Iran. *The New York Times*, January 18.
Scheiffer, B., J. Axelrod, G. Borger, et al. 2006. Weight of Public Opinion, Partisan Politics Sinks Ports Deal. *CBS News: Evening News*, March 9.
Schuman, J. 2005. The Morning Brief Nomination May Not Prompt Fight. *Dow Jones News Service (WSJ.com)*, July 20.
Schwankert, S. 2006. PCCW Assets Sought by Macquarie, Tenbridge. *NetworkWorld*, June 22.
Schweller, R. 1998. *Deadly Imbalances: Tripolarity and Hitler's Strategy of World Conquest*. New York: Columbia University Press.
2004. Unanswered Threats: A Neoclassical Realist Theory of Underbalancing. *International Security* 29 (2).
Scott, M. 2008. An Uncertain Future for Europe's Utilities. *Business Week*, February 25.
Seawright, J. 2002. Testing for Necessary and/or Sufficient Causation: Which Cases Are Relevant? *Political Analysis* 10 (Spring): 178–93.
SEC. 2008. Accredited Investors. US Securities and Exchange Commission. www.sec.gov/answers/accred.htm.
Seely, A. 2016. Mergers & Takeovers: The Public Interest Test. House of Commons Library Briefing Paper, No. 05374, September, 1. http://researchbriefings.parliament.uk/ResearchBriefing/Summary/SN05374.
Sevastopulo, D. and S. Kirchgaessner. 2006. US to Investigate Security Issue of Ports Takeover. *Financial Times*, March 3.
Shah, S. 2006. Dubai Ports Group Sails into Political Storm in India. *The Independent*, March 20.

Shambaugh, G. E. 1999. *States, Firms, and Power; Successful Sanctions in United States Foreign Policy*. Albany, NY: State University of New York Press.

Sharif, A. 2006. Gulf News: UAE Companies Will Continue to Face Discrimination Like DP World. *Financial Times*, May 29.

Shinkle, K. 2006. US Needs Foreign Investment but Congress is Growing Wary. *Investor's Business Daily*, April 3.

Shumpeter. 2014. Blocking Foreign Takeovers: France Fights Back. *The Economist*, May 15.

Silva, J. 2006a. Alcatel Continues to Defend Acquisition of Lucent Against Security Concerns. *RCR Wireless News*, May 8.

2006b. White House Approves Lucent–Alcatel Merger. *RCR Wireless News*, November 27.

Simon, B. 2008. Canada Shields Space Unit from Attack. *Financial Times*, April 16.

2009. Canada Cools to Foreign Investors in Nortel. *Financial Times*, August 6.

H. Thomas, and W. MacNamara. 2010. Canada Rejects BHP Bid for Potash. *Financial Times*, November 4.

Singer, J. 2006. UK Judge Delays Formal OK of P&O Takeover by DPW. *Dow Jones International News*, February 28.

Sinocast. 2005a. IBM Lenovo Deal Sees Changes. *Sinocast China IT Watch*, February 3.

2005b. Probe of IBM–Lenovo Deal Prolonged to 45 Days. *Sinocast China IT Watch*, February 2.

SIPRI. 2004. *Membership of Multilateral Military Related Export Control Regimes*. Stockholm: Stockholm International Peace Research Institute.

2006. *SIPRI Military Expenditure Database*. Stockholm: Stockholm International Peace Research Institute.

Skocpol, T. 1984. Emerging Agendas and Recurrent Strategies in Historical Sociology. In *Vision and Method in Historical Sociology*, ed. T. Skocpol. Cambridge: Cambridge University Press.

Smartmatic. 2007. Smartmatic Announces the Sale of its Subsidiary Sequoia Voting Systems. Smartmatic, press release, November 8. www.smartmatic.com/pressroom/article/article/smartmatic-announces-the-sale-of-its-subsidiary-sequoia-voting-systems/.

Smith, P. 2011. Australia Confirms Rejection of SGX–ASX Deal. *Financial Times*, April 8.

Smith, R. 2006. *President Bush Reserves Power to Withdraw Approvals of Foreign Investment in the US on National Security Grounds*. Washington, DC: Willkie Farr & Ghallagher.

Spooner, J. G. 2005a. IBM–Lenovo Deal Clears Potential Block. *CNET News.com*, January 10.

2005b. IBM–Lenovo Faces Security Investigation. *ZDNet UK*, January 25.

States News Service. 2005a. Congress Cites Security Concerns Over Chinese Bid for Unocal. *The States News Service*, July 19.

2005b. Senators Urge Executive Branch Study of Implications from Possible CNOOC-Unocal Deal. *The States News Service*, July 22.

Stephens, P. 2006. A Perilous Collision Between Nationalism and Globalization. *Financial Times*, March 3.

Stewart, D. T. and J. Wasserstrom. 2016. The Global Populist Surge Is More than Just a Western Story – Just Look at Asia. *The Diplomat*, December 10.

Stoljarskij, A. 2011. Foreign Investments in Strategic Sectors in Russia. *Beiten Burkhardt* (March). www.beiten-burkhardt.com/de/component/attachments/download/1839.

2012. Industry Specific Aspects of Investing in Russia: Update on Foreign Investments in Strategic Sectors in Russia. *Beiten Burkhardt*. www.beiten-burkhardt.com/de/component/attachments/download/2383.

Stratford, T. and Y. Luo. 2015. *China Law & Practice: National Security Review Creates FDI Hurdle*. Beijing: Covington & Burling (July 13). www.cov.com/~/media/files/corporate/publications/2015/07/national_security_review_creates_fdi_hurdle.pdf.

Subramanian, A. 2016. The Inevitable Superpower. *Foreign Affairs*, February 22.

Sullivan, C. 2004. The End of an Era; In a Remarkable Move, IBM has Sold its Personal Computing Division to a Chinese Company. Where Does the Industry Go from Here? *Newsweek Web Exclusive*, December 4.

Sun. 2006. Bush Port Deal Fury. *The Sun*, March 11.

Syedain, H. 2007. Leadership Lessons: Russia's Global Banker. Interview with Ruben Vardanian, President, Troika Dialog. *Management Today*, April 1.

Syrbe, T., I. Pavlovich, and S. Nogovitsyna. 2014. A Legal Overview of Foreign Investment in Russia's Strategic Sectors. Briefing Note, Moscow: Clifford Chance (May 23). www.cliffordchance.com/briefings/2014/05/a_legal_overviewofforeigninvestmenti.html.

Tait, N., R. Wright, and S. Kirchgaessner. 2006. London Court Urged to Block Port Takeover. *Financial Times*, February 28.

Tardy, T. 2003–04. France and the US; The Inevitable Clash? *International Journal* (Winter): 1–22.

Taylor, G. 2005. Chevron Gains Upper Hand in Bid for Unocal; Unocal Warns Shareholder Suit May Delay Vote. *Platts Oilgram Price Report* 83 (142), July 26.

2013. Softbank Clears Big Hurdle Over Sprint. *Financial Times*, May 29.

Teather, D. 2006. Washington Digs in Against Invaders. *The Guardian*, April 4.

TelecomWeb. 2006a. Alcatel–Lucent Merger Talks Go Into Orbit. *TelecomWeb News Digest*, April 3.

2006b. Lucatel: It's a Good Thing. *TelecomWeb News Digest*, April 3.

2006c. Lucatel Satellite Deal Keeps Everyone in the Dark. *TelecomWeb News Digest*, April 5.

Terada, S. 2008. Japan Blocks TCI from Upping J-Power Stake. *Japan Times*, April 17.

Theil, S. 2005. Close the Door; Voices Arguing for a Return to Protectionism are Getting Louder Across the Region. *Newsweek*, November 7.

Thiruvengadam, M. 2006. Ports Transaction has Texas Implications. *San Antonio Express-News*, March 3.

Thomas, G. and S. Lilly. 2016. *Australia's New Foreign Investment Regime*. Perth: Norton Rose Fullbright (June).

Thompson, J. 2011. EDF Unveils Edison Takeover Details. *Financial Times*, December 27.

Thornhill, J. and A. Jones. 2005. French PM Firm on "Patriotism." *Financial Times*, September 23.

Thornton, P. 2006a. Arab Central Banks Move Assets Out of Dollar. *The Independent*, March 14.

2006b. French Gas Merger Raises Fresh Fears of Fortress Europe. *The Independent*, February 27.

Times. 2006. France Faces EU Fight Over "National Champions." *The Times Online*, March 2. www.timesonline.co.uk/tol/sport/football/european_football/article736561.ece.

Times of India. 2006. French Resistance: Mittal's Bid Hostile. *Times of India Online*, February 21.

Timmons, H. 2005. China Oil Giant Expected to Vote Today in Unocal Bid. *The New York Times*, June 22.

Tiron, R. 2006. Dubai Threat to Hit Back. *The Hill*, March 9.

Traffic World. 2006. DP World: We'll Be Back. *Traffic World*, May 29.

TR Daily. 2006. Alcatel–Lucent Merger Gets CFIUS Clearance. *TR Daily*, November 20.

Trump, President D. J. 2017. Order Regarding the Proposed Acquisition of Lattice Semiconductor Corporation by China Venture Capital Fund Corporation Limited. White House, press release, September 13.

Tsuruoka, D. 2005. IBM PC Division Sale to Lenovo Expected to Get Regulator's OK; Big Blue is Big Lobbyist, PCs are not High Tech, So Most Experts Content. *Investor's Business Daily*, February 9.

Tucker, S. 2006. Macquarie Refocuses on PCCW. *Financial Times*, August 21.

and T. Mitchell. 2006. PCCW Spurns Two $7bn Offers. *Financial Times*, July 25.

Tyson, L. D. 1992. *Who's Bashing Whom? Trade Conflict in High-Technology Industries*. Washington, DC: Institute for International Economics.

UK BEIS. 2016. Government Confirms Hinkley Point C Project Following New Agreement in Principle with EDF. Department for Business, Energy, and Industrial Strategy, press release, September 15. www.gov.uk/government/news/government-confirms-hinkley-point-c-project-following-new-agreement-in-principle-with-edf.

UNCTAD. 2006. World Investment Report 2006 – FDI from Developing and Transition Economies: Implications for Development. Geneva: United Nations.

2010a. The Iron Ore Market 2009–2011 Abstract. Geneva: United Nations Conference on Trade and Development.

2010b. Review of Maritime Transport 2010; Report by the UNCTAD secretariat. Geneva: United Nations Conference on Trade and Development.

2011. World Investment Report 2011 – Non-Equity Modes of International Production and Development. New York: United Nations Conference on Trade and Development.

2016a. Demand for Iron Ore Leveled Off in 2015, Reflecting Weak Growth in World Steel Production. Geneva: UNCTAD News Online (February 17).

2016b. World Investment Report 2016 – Investor Nationality: Policy Challenges. Geneva: United Nations.

Unocal. 2005. Form 10-Q for the Period Ending March 31. Filed May 5. www.getfilings.com/o0000716039-05-000062.html.

Urquhart, D. 2006. US Outcry Reeks of Hypocrisy. *The Business Times Singapore*, February 27.

US Bureau of the Census. 2008. Trade in Goods (Imports, Exports and Trade Balance) with China. Prepared by the Data Dissemination Branch, United States Bureau of the Census, January 11. www.census.gov/foreign-trade/balance/c5700.html#2005.

US–China ESRC. 2005. C. Richard D'Amato Holds Hearing on China and the World Trade Organization Committee Hearing. US–China Economic and Security Review Commission (Political Transcripts by Federal Document Clearing House), February 4.

2007. Testimony of Barry Naughton: "China's State Sector, Industrial Policies and the 11th Five Year Plan" at the Hearing on the "Extent of the Government's Control of China's Economy, and Implications for the United States." US–China Economic and Security Review Commission.

US DOD. 2005. *Annual Report to Congress; the Military Power of the People's Republic of China 2005*. Washington, DC: Office of the Secretary of Defense, The Department of Defense of the United States of America.

US DOS. 2009. France: 2009 Investment Climate Statement. Washington, DC: Department of State.

2014a. Australia: 2014 Investment Climate Statement. Washington, DC: Department of State.

2014b. Germany: 2014 Investment Climate Statement. Washington, DC: Department of State.

2015. Russia: 2015 Investment Climate Statement. Washington, DC: Department of State.

2016a. China: 2016 Investment Climate Statement. Washington, DC: Department of State.

2016b. Russia: 2016 Investment Climate Statement. Washington, DC: Department of State.

2017. China: 2017 Investment Climate Statement. Washington, DC: Department of State.

US DOT. 2007. Committee on Foreign Investment in the United States; Exon Florio. US Department of the Treasury – Office of International Affairs, December 18. www.treas.gov/offices/International-affairs/exon-florio/.

2008. Committee on Foreign Investment in the United States; Annual Report to Congress (CY 2007). US Department of the Treasury, December.

2009. Committee on Foreign Investment in the United States; Annual Report to Congress (CY 2008). US Department of the Treasury, November.

2010. Committee on Foreign Investment in the United States; Annual Report to Congress (CY 2009). US Department of the Treasury, November.

2011. Committee on Foreign Investment in the United States; Annual Report to Congress (CY 2010). US Department of the Treasury, December.

2012. Committee on Foreign Investment in the United States; Annual Report to Congress (CY 2011). US Department of the Treasury, December.

2013. Committee on Foreign Investment in the United States; Annual Report to Congress (CY 2012). US Department of the Treasury, December.

2015. Committee on Foreign Investment in the United States; Annual Report to Congress (CY 2013). US Department of the Treasury, February.

2016a. Committee on Foreign Investment in the United States; Annual Report to Congress (CY 2014). US Department of the Treasury, February.

2016b. Statement on the President's Decision Regarding the US Business of Aixtron SE. Press Center, press release, US Department of the Treasury, December 2.

2017. Statement On The President's Decision Regarding Lattice Semiconductor Corporation. Press Center, press release, US Department of the Treasury, September 13.

US Fed News. 2006a. Oliver North's Common Sense Commentary: Misunderestimated Disconfirmation. *US Fed News*, February 26.

2006b. Sen. Sarbanes Issues Statement on "Continued Examination of Implementation of the Exon-Florio Amendment: Focus on Dubai Ports World's Acquisition of P&O." *US Fed News*, March 2.

2006c. Sens. Schumer, Snowe Demand Answers from Homeland Security Department Over Coast Guard's Dubious Assessment of Dubai Ports Deal. *US Fed News*, February 28.

US GAO. 1996. Foreign Investment; Foreign Laws and Policies Addressing National Security Concerns. (GAO/NSIAD-96-61). Washington, DC: US Government Accountability Office (April).

2008. Foreign Investment; Laws and Policies Regulating Foreign Investment in 10 Countries. (GAO-08-320). Washington, DC: US Government Accountability Office (February).

US House. 1998. National Defense Authorization Act for Fiscal Year 1999. H.R. 3616 EAS. 105th Congress.

2004. Overview of US Policy Toward Taiwan by James A. Kelly. House International Relations Committee, April 21. www.state.gov/p/eap/rls/rm/2004/31649.htm.

2005a. To Ensure Jobs for Our Future with Secure, Affordable, and Reliable Energy (The Energy Policy Act of 2005). H.R. 6. 109th Congress.

2005b. Making Appropriations for the Departments of Transportation, Treasury, and Housing and Urban Development, the Judiciary, District of Columbia, and Independent Agencies for the Fiscal Year Ending September 30, 2006, and for other purposes. H.R. 3058. 109th Congress.

2005c. Whereas Oil and Natural Gas Resources are Strategic Assets Critical to National Security and the Nation's Economic Prosperity (Engrossed as Agreed to or Passed by House). H. RES. 344 EH. 109th Congress.

2006a. Disapproving the Results of the Review Conducted by the Committee on Foreign Investment in the United States (CFIUS) into the Purchase of Peninsular and Oriental Steam Navigation (P&O) by Dubai Ports World

(DP World). H.J. Res. 79. 109th Congress (Sponsored by Representative Jane Harman).

2006b. Making Emergency Supplemental Appropriations for the Fiscal Year Ending September 30, 2006, and for Other Purposes. H.R. 4939. 109th Congress (Sponsored by Representative Jerry Lewis).

2006c. To Promote the National Defense by Establishing Requirements for the Ownership, Management, and Operation of Critical Infrastructure in the United States, and for Other Purposes. H.R. 4881. (Sponsored by Representative Duncan Hunter).

2006d. To Require an Investigation under the Defense Production Act of 1950 of the Acquisition by Dubai Ports World of the Peninsular and Oriental Steam Navigation Company, and for Other Purposes. H.R. 4807. 109th Congress (Sponsored by Representative Peter T. King).

2012. Investigative Report on the US National Security Issues Posed by Chinese Telecommunications Companies Huawei and ZTE by Mike Rogers and Dutch Ruppersberger. House Permanent Select Committee on Intelligence, October 8. https://intelligence.house.gov/sites/intelligence.house.gov/files/documents/Huawei-ZTE%20Investigative%20Report%20(FINAL).pdf.

US NCIX. 2006. Annual Report to Congress on Foreign Economic Collection and Industrial Espionage: 2005. US National Counterintelligence Executive and Office of the Director of National Intelligence, August, Homeland Security Digital Library. www.hsdl.org/?abstract&did=469063.

US Senate. 2005. To Prohibit the Merger, Acquisition, or Takeover of Unocal Corporation by CNOOC Ltd. of China. 109th Congress – 1st Session. S. 1412 I.S. 109th Congress.

2006a. A Bill to Prohibit the Merger, Acquisition, or Takeover of Peninsular and Oriental Steam Navigation Company by Dubai Ports World. S. 2341. 109th Congress. (Sponsored by Senator Byron L. Dorgan.)

2006b. A Bill to Require an Investigation under the Defense Production Act of 1950 of the Acquisition by Dubai Ports World of the Peninsular and Oriental Steam Navigation Company, and for Other Purposes. S. 2333. 109th Congress. (Sponsored by Senator Charles Schumer.)

2006c. A Joint Resolution Disapproving the Results of the Review Conducted by the Committee on Foreign Investment in the United States (CFIUS) into the Purchase of Peninsular and Oriental Steam Navigation (P&O) by Dubai Ports World (DP World). S.J. Res. 32. 109th Congress. (Sponsored by Senator Susan M. Collins.)

Vaas, L. 2005. Check Point Snaps Up Sourcefire. *eWEEK*, October 6.

Vandore, E. 2005a. France's Breton Counsels Calm on Danone Bid Rumors – Update 2. *Bloomberg*, July 21.

2005b. France's Chirac, De Villepin Seek Curbs on Takeovers – Update 1. *Bloomberg*, July 27.

Vasquez, J. A. 2003. The New Debate on Balancing Power: A Reply to My Critics. In *Realism and the Balancing of Power; A New Debate*, eds. J. A. Vasquez and C. Elman. New Jersey, NJ: Prentice Hall, pp. 87–113.

and C. Elman, eds. 2003. *Realism and the Balancing of Power; A New Debate*. New Jersey, NJ: Prentice Hall.

Veritas. 2006. Schedule 14A: Proxy Statement. Filed December 1. http://google.brand.edgar-online.com.

Verjee, Z., J. Clancy, S. Bindra, et al. 2006. Bush, Singh Seal Landmark Nuclear Energy Pact; Pakistan Explosion; Deepening Political Divide in Iraq. *CNN: Your World Today: Voxant*.

Voice of America. 2005. CNOOC/Unocal Deal. Voice of America Press Release and Documents, July 14.

Wallace, K. N. and R. Armon. 2005. Washington Weekly. New York: Lehman Brothers.

Wallis, W. 2006. Ports Backlash Makes Arab Investors Wary. *Financial Times*, March 2.

Walt, S. M. 1987. *The Origins of Alliances*. Ithaca, NY: Cornell University Press.

2005. *Taming American Power*. New York: W. W. Norton & Company.

Walton, A. 2008. The Town the Navy Left Behind; Long Beach Reinvents Itself as Tourist, Shipping Port of Call. *CNN.com*.

Waltz, K. N. 1979. *Theory of International Politics*. New York: McGraw Hill.

1993. The Emerging Structure of International Politics. *International Security* 18 (2): 44–79.

1999. Globalization and Governance. *PS: Political Science and Politics* 32 (4): 693–700.

Wang, X. and A. Emch. 2013. Five Years of Implementation of China's Anti-Monopoly Law – Achievements and Challenges. *Journal of Antitrust Enforcement* 1 (2): 247–71.

Wang, Z. 2016. The New Nationalism: "Make My Country Great Again." *The Diplomat*, May 10.

Ward, A. 2006. Transport Chiefs Warn on Ports Takeover Opposition; Protectionism. *Financial Times*, March 8.

Watson, A. 2006. Sky High Dubai. *Daily Express*, March 15.

2006. Jumbo Sale. *Property Week*, March 17.

WDI. 2008. World Development Indicators. The World Bank Group. http://databank.worldbank.org/data/home.aspx.

2016. World Development Indicators. The World Bank Group. http://databank.worldbank.org/data/home.aspx.

Wehrlé, F. and J. Pohl. 2016. Investment Policies Related to National Security: A Survey of Country Practices. OECD Working Papers on International Investment (2016/02). Paris: OECD Publishing (June 14). http://dx.doi.org/10.1787/5jlwrrf038nx-en.

Weisman, J. 2006a. Port Deal To Have Broader Review; Dubai Firm Sought US Security Probe. *Washington Post*, February 27.

2006b. Coast Guard Saw "Intelligence Gaps" on Ports. *Washington Post*, February 28.

and S. Schmidt. 2006. US Reviewing 2nd Dubai Firm; Israeli Deal Also Faces Security Check. *Washington Post*, March 2.

Wendlandt, A. 2006. Alcatel-Lucent's Russo Says No Iran Business for Her. *Reuters News*, December 1.

White, B. 2005. Chinese Drop Bid to Buy US Oil Firm. *Washington Post*, August 3.

White, G. 2012. China to Examine Iron Ore Market. *The Telegraph*, February 20.

Whitfield, F., A. Raman, M. Chinoy, et al. 2006. Los Angeles Port Already Run by Foreign Owned Company. *CNN: Live From: Voxant.*

Wickham, R. 2006. Parlez-Vouse Alcatel/Lucent? Considerations Make it Too Close to Call. If the Two Companies Agree to Merge, Who Knows if it Will Pass the Competitive Litmus Test. *Wireless Week* 12 (8): 6.

Williams, C. 2006. Feds Nix Check Point's Sourcefire Bid. *The Register*, March 24.

Wilson, M. 2006. Vancouver OK with DP World – P&O Port Deal. *Canadian Sailings*, March 6.

Wilson, D. and R. Purushothaman. 2003. Dreaming With BRICs: The Path to 2050. Global Economics Paper (No. 99), Goldman Sachs, 1 October. www.goldmansachs.com/our-thinking/archive/archive-pdfs/brics-dream.pdf.

Witte, G. 2004. IBM Reassures Workers After Milestone China Deal. *Washington Post*, December 9.

Wohlforth, W. 1993. *The Elusive Balance: Power and Perceptions during the Cold War.* Ithaca, NY: Cornell University Press.

Wolffe, R. and H. Bailey. 2006. No Safe Harbor Here: How a Routine Sale Became a Political Gale – And What's Next for Bush in the Ports Storm. *Newsweek*, March 6.

World Bank. 2009. Globalization. World Bank.org, archived June 5. www.worldbank.org/en/webarchives/.

WPO. 2006. 20 Nation Poll Finds Strong Global Consensus: Support for Free Market System, But also More Regulation of Large Companies. *World Public Opinion.org*, January 11. www.worldpublicopinion.org/pipa/articles/btglobalizationtradera/154.php?nid=&id=&pnt=154.

Wright, B. 2005. CNOOC Aiming for Last Laugh. *Upstream*, July 1.

Wright, R. and S. Kirchgaessner. 2006. DP World Sells Us Ports to AIG. *Financial Times*, December 11.

WSA. 2007. Steel Industry Calls for Review. World Steel Association, Press Release (November 19).

WSJ. 2005a. Nonprofit France. *The Wall Street Journal Europe*, September 23.

2005b. Sell PCs to Beijing, Not Weapons. *The Asian Wall Street Journal*, January 27.

WVS. 2001–04. World Values Survey: Third Wave. www.worldvaluessurvey.org.

XFN. 2006a. China at Risk of Moving Backwards on Market Access Reforms – US Official. *Xinhua Financial Network (XFN) News*, July 31.

2006b. New Rules on China Investment Prompt Fears of Economic Nationalism. *Xinhua Financial Network (XFN) News*, August 14.

Yan, D. 2006. Foreign Takeover Controversial. *China Daily*, March 11.

Ye, W. 2016. What a Negative List! *Lexology*, King & Wood Mallesons, October 11. www.lexology.com/library/detail.aspx?g=1c758c21-f0d5-4348-bb07-59ec3ec7dfb3.

Yeager, H. 2006. Ports Sale Unrest Deepens Bush Political Woes. *Financial Times*, March 9.

Ylagan, A. H. C. 2006. Corporate Watch: Torn Between Two Lovers. *Business World*, March 20, S1–S5.

Zakaria, F. 2016. Populism on the March. *Foreign Affairs* 95 (6): 9–15.

Zeng, T. 2007. China: To Retain Control Over 7 Sectors Of Econ – State TV. *Dow Jones International News*, December 18.

Zephyr. 2005a. Complete Record; Deal No. 224968. Zephyr M&A Database. Bureau Van Dijk Electronic Publishing (BVDEP). www.bvdep.com/en/ZEPHYR.html.

2005b. Complete Record; Deal No. 323950. Zephyr M&A Database. BVDEP.

2005c. Complete Record; Deal No. 356064. Zephyr M&A Database. BVDEP.

2005d. Complete Record; Deal No. 364945. Zephyr M&A Database. BVDEP.

2005e. Zephyr M&A Database. BVDEP.

2006a. Complete Record; Deal No. 390555. Zephyr M&A Database. BVDEP.

2006b. Complete Record; Deal No. 430518. Zephyr M&A Database. BVDEP.

2006c. Complete Record; Deal No. 453929. Zephyr M&A Database. BVDEP.

2006d. Zephyr M&A Database. BVDEP.

2007a. Complete Record; Deal No. 299966. Zephyr M&A Database. BVDEP.

2007b. Complete Record; Deal No. 356064. Zephyr M&A Database. BVDEP.

2007c. Complete Record; Deal No. 390555. Zephyr M&A Database. BVDEP.

2007d. Complete Record; Deal No. 414862. Zephyr M&A Database. BVDEP.

2007e. Complete Record; Deal No. 47128. Zephyr M&A Database. BVDEP.

Index